MONTHLY GIRLS' NOZAKI-KUN

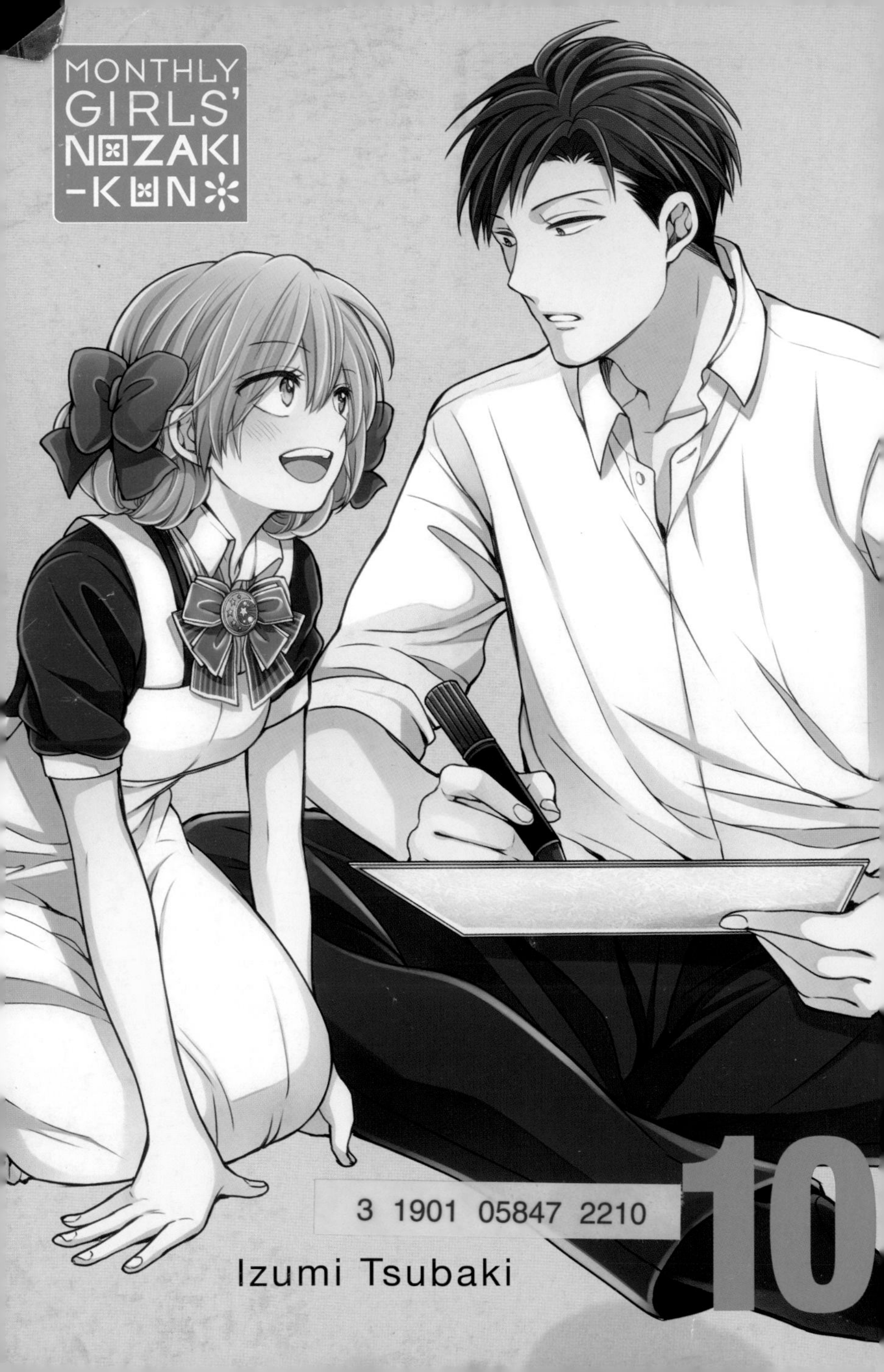

10

Izumi Tsubaki

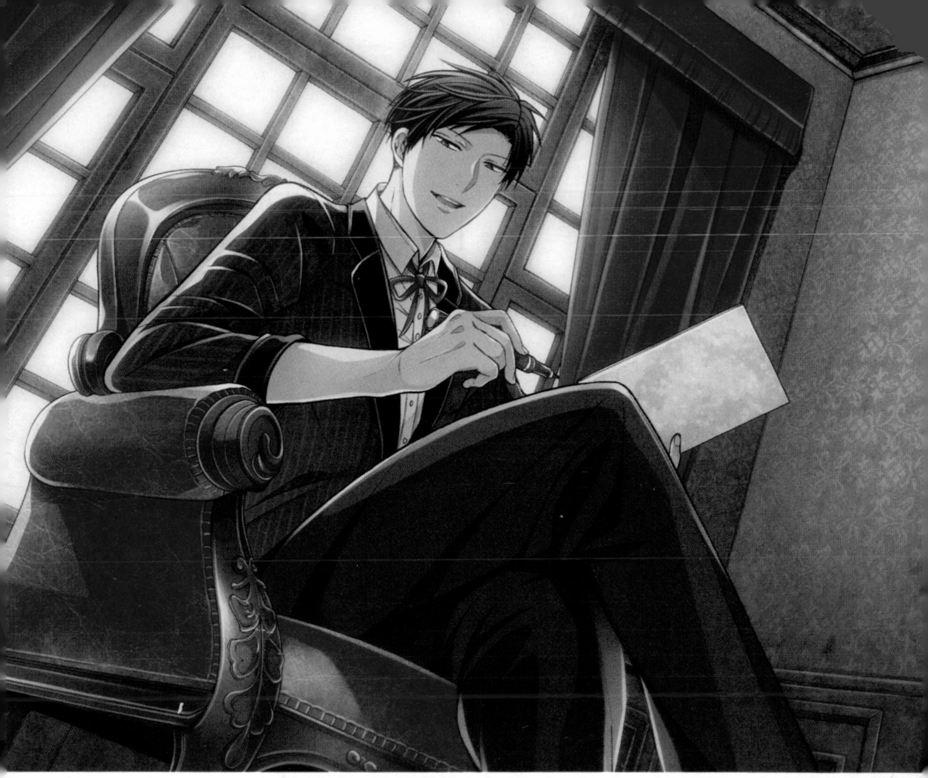

MONTHLY GIRLS' NOZAKI-KUN 10

contents

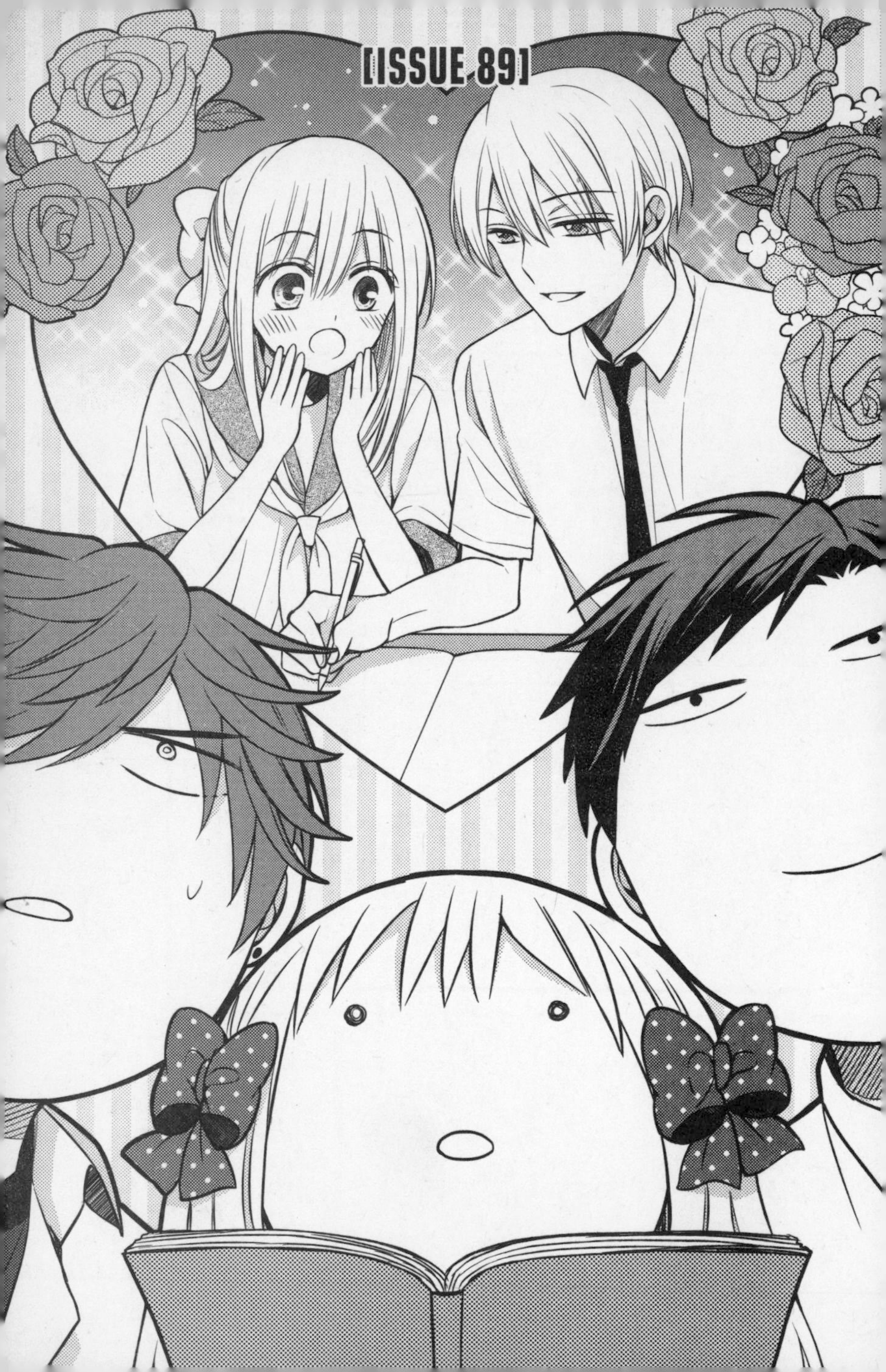
[ISSUE 89]

THE EXCITEMENT YOU'RE LOOKING FOR♡

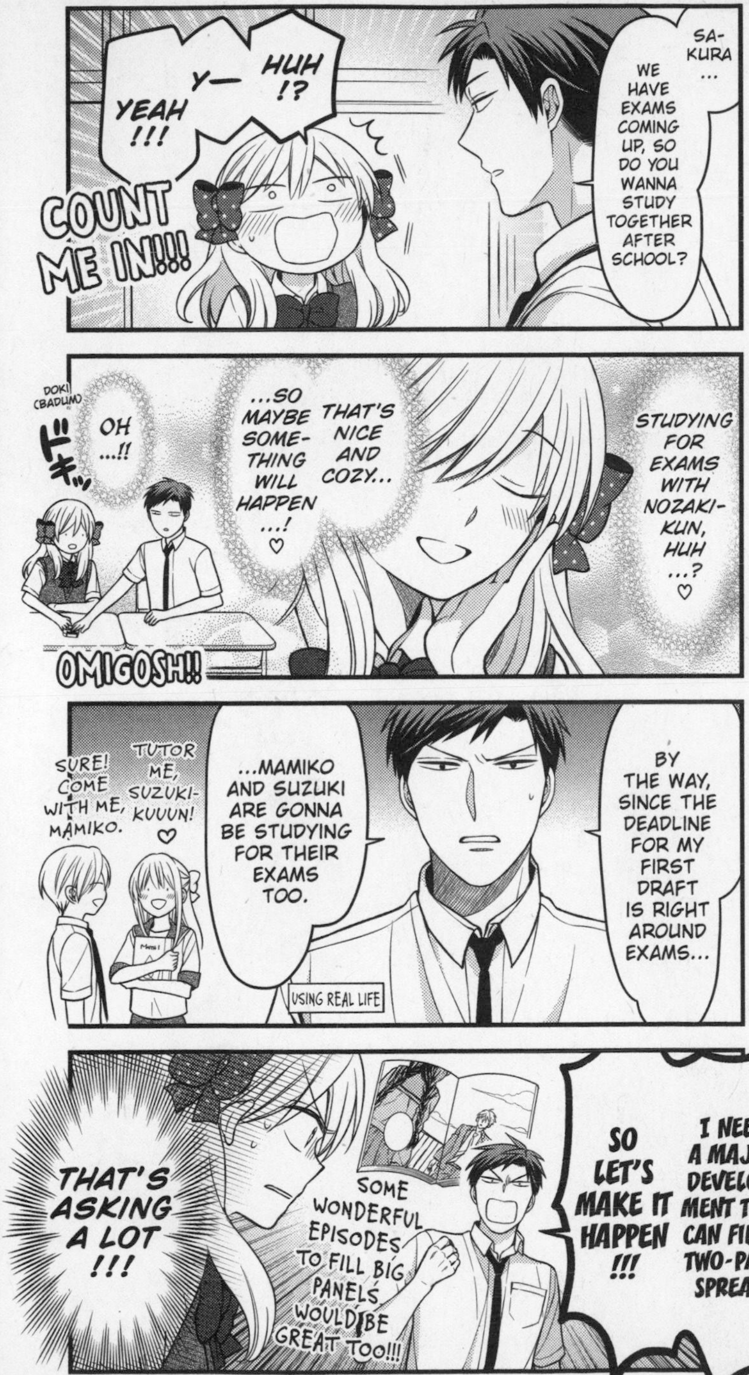

SAKURA... WE HAVE EXAMS COMING UP, SO DO YOU WANNA STUDY TOGETHER AFTER SCHOOL?
HUH!? Y— YEAH!!!
COUNT ME IN!!!
STUDYING FOR EXAMS WITH NOZAKI-KUN, HUH...? ♡
THAT'S NICE AND COZY...
...SO MAYBE SOMETHING WILL HAPPEN...! ♡
OH...!!
DOKI (BADUM)
ドキッ
OMIGOSH!!
BY THE WAY, SINCE THE DEADLINE FOR MY FIRST DRAFT IS RIGHT AROUND EXAMS...
...MAMIKO AND SUZUKI ARE GONNA BE STUDYING FOR THEIR EXAMS TOO.
TUTOR ME, SUZUKI-KUUUN! ♡
SURE! COME WITH ME, MAMIKO.
USING REAL LIFE
I NEED A MAJOR DEVELOPMENT THAT CAN FILL A TWO-PAGE SPREAD!
SO LET'S MAKE IT HAPPEN!!!
SOME WONDERFUL EPISODES TO FILL BIG PANELS WOULD BE GREAT TOO!!!
THAT'S ASKING A LOT!!!

MORE THAN USUAL

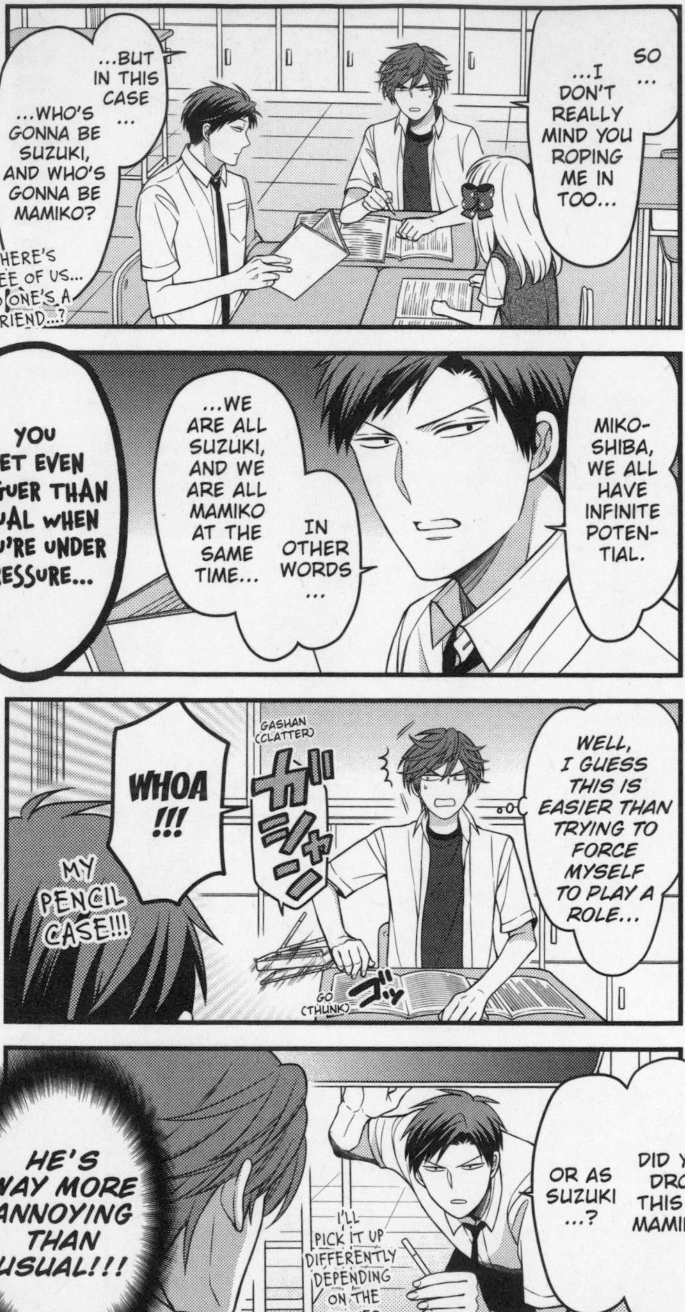

SO ... ...I DON'T REALLY MIND YOU ROPING ME IN TOO...
...BUT IN THIS CASE ... ...WHO'S GONNA BE SUZUKI, AND WHO'S GONNA BE MAMIKO?
THERE'S THREE OF US... SO ONE'S A FRIEND...?
MIKO-SHIBA, WE ALL HAVE INFINITE POTEN-TIAL.
IN OTHER WORDS ...
...WE ARE ALL SUZUKI, AND WE ARE ALL MAMIKO AT THE SAME TIME...
YOU GET EVEN VAGUER THAN USUAL WHEN YOU'RE UNDER PRESSURE...
WELL, I GUESS THIS IS EASIER THAN TRYING TO FORCE MYSELF TO PLAY A ROLE...
GASHAN (CLATTER)
ガシャーン
GO (THUNK)
ゴッ
WHOA !!!
MY PENCIL CASE!!!
DID YOU DROP THIS AS MAMIKO?
OR AS SUZUKI ...?
I'LL PICK IT UP DIFFERENTLY DEPENDING ON THE ANSWER.
HE'S WAY MORE ANNOYING THAN USUAL!!!

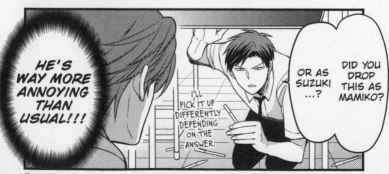

REFERENCE NOTES

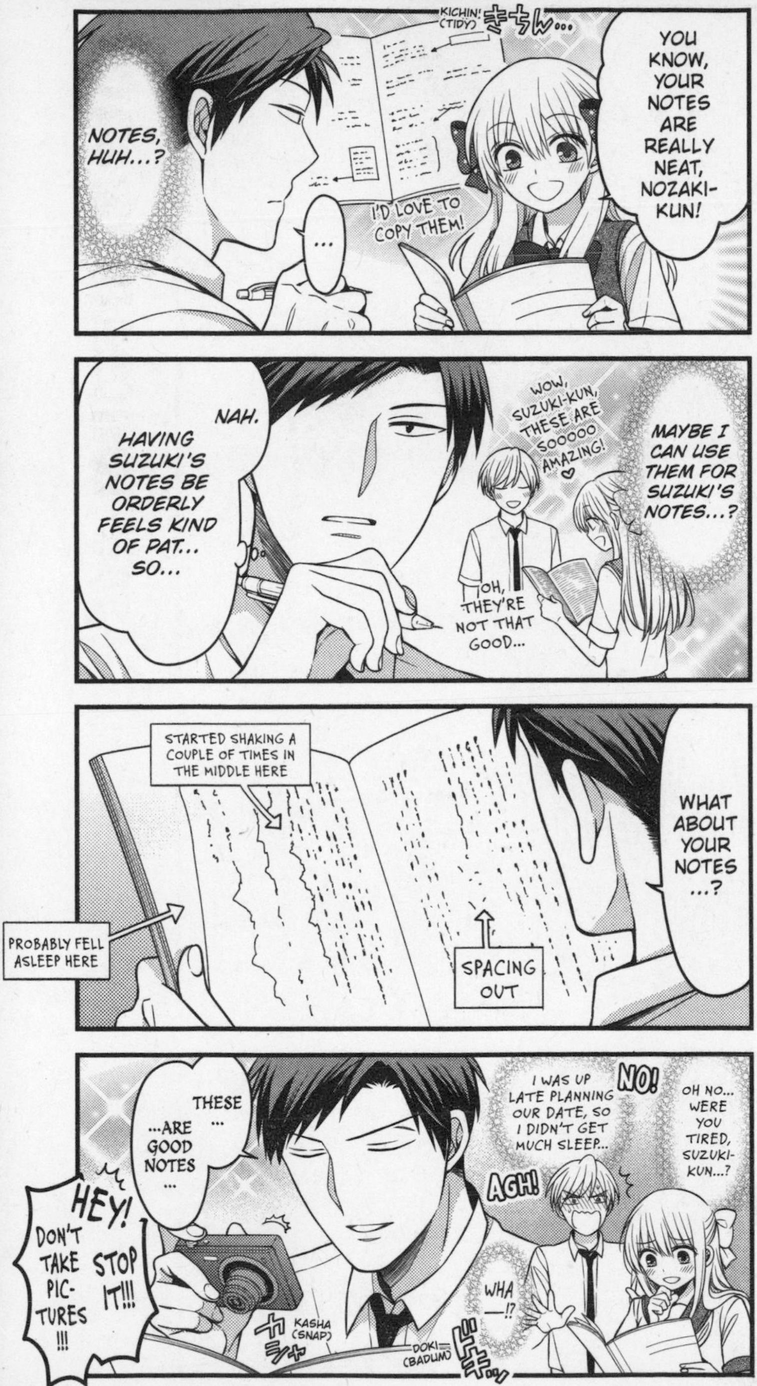
YOU KNOW, YOUR NOTES ARE REALLY NEAT, NOZAKI-KUN!
KICHIN! (TIDY) きちん…
I'D LOVE TO COPY THEM!
NOTES, HUH…?
…
MAYBE I CAN USE THEM FOR SUZUKI'S NOTES…?
WOW, SUZUKI-KUN, THESE ARE SOOOOO AMAZING! ♥
OH, THEY'RE NOT THAT GOOD…
NAH. HAVING SUZUKI'S NOTES BE ORDERLY FEELS KIND OF PAT… SO…
WHAT ABOUT YOUR NOTES …?
STARTED SHAKING A COUPLE OF TIMES IN THE MIDDLE HERE
SPACING OUT
PROBABLY FELL ASLEEP HERE
OH NO… WERE YOU TIRED, SUZUKI-KUN…?
NO!
I WAS UP LATE PLANNING OUR DATE, SO I DIDN'T GET MUCH SLEEP…
AGH!
THESE … …ARE GOOD NOTES …
WHA—!?
DOKI (BADUMP) ドキッ
KASHA (SNAP) カシャ
STOP IT!!!
HEY! DON'T TAKE PIC-TURES !!!

FOLLOW YOUR DESIRES

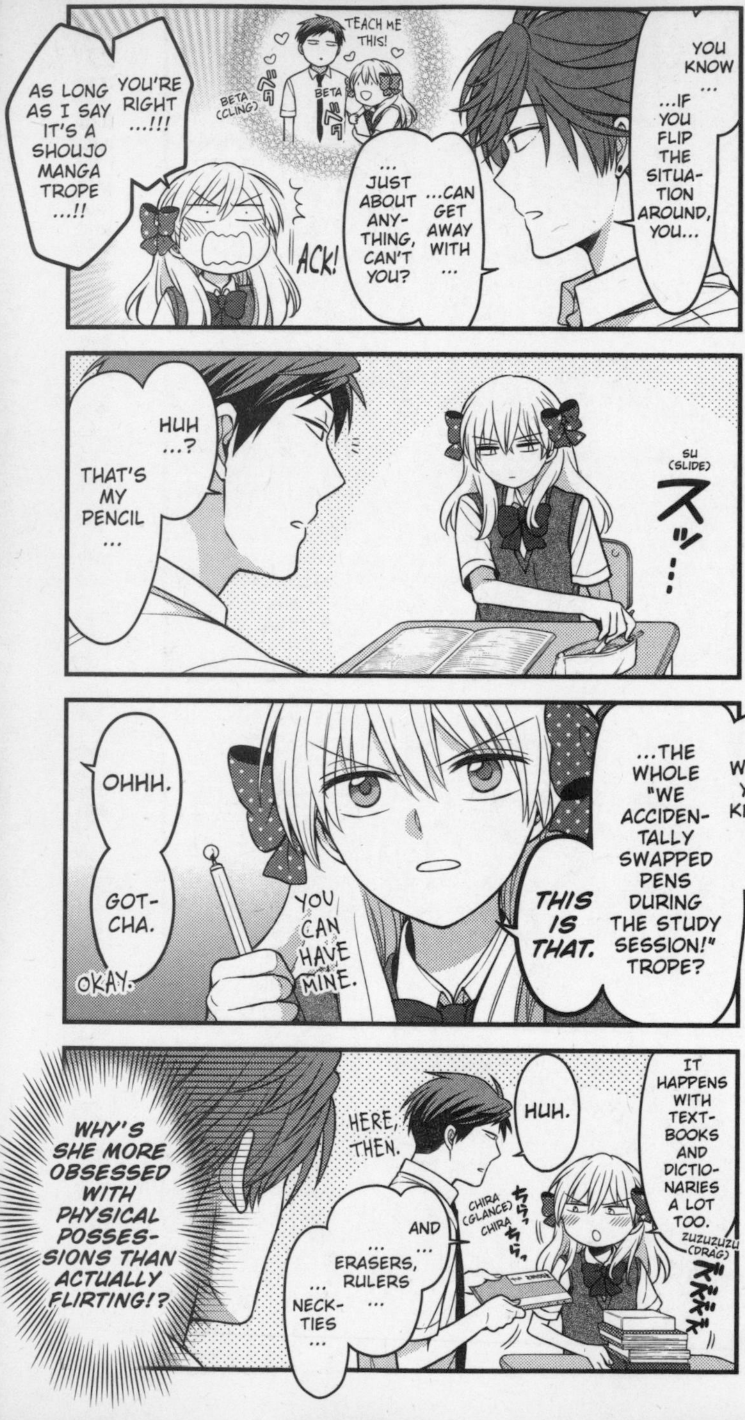
YOU KNOW ... ...IF YOU FLIP THE SITUATION AROUND, YOU...
...CAN GET AWAY WITH ...
... JUST ABOUT ANYTHING, CAN'T YOU?
TEACH ME THIS!
BETA
BETA (CLING)
ACK!
YOU'RE RIGHT ...!!!
AS LONG AS I SAY IT'S A SHOUJO MANGA TROPE ...!!
SU (SLIDE)
HUH ...?
THAT'S MY PENCIL ...
WELL, YOU KNOW ...
...THE WHOLE "WE ACCIDENTALLY SWAPPED PENS DURING THE STUDY SESSION!" TROPE?
THIS IS THAT.
YOU CAN HAVE MINE.
OHHH.
GOT-CHA.
OKAY.
IT HAPPENS WITH TEXTBOOKS AND DICTIONARIES A LOT TOO.
ZUZUZUZU (DRAG)
HUH.
HERE, THEN.
CHIRA (GLANCE) CHIRA
AND ...
... ERASERS, RULERS ...
... NECKTIES ...
WHY'S SHE MORE OBSESSED WITH PHYSICAL POSSESSIONS THAN ACTUALLY FLIRTING!?

(TEMPORARY) SUZUKI AND SUPPORTING CAST

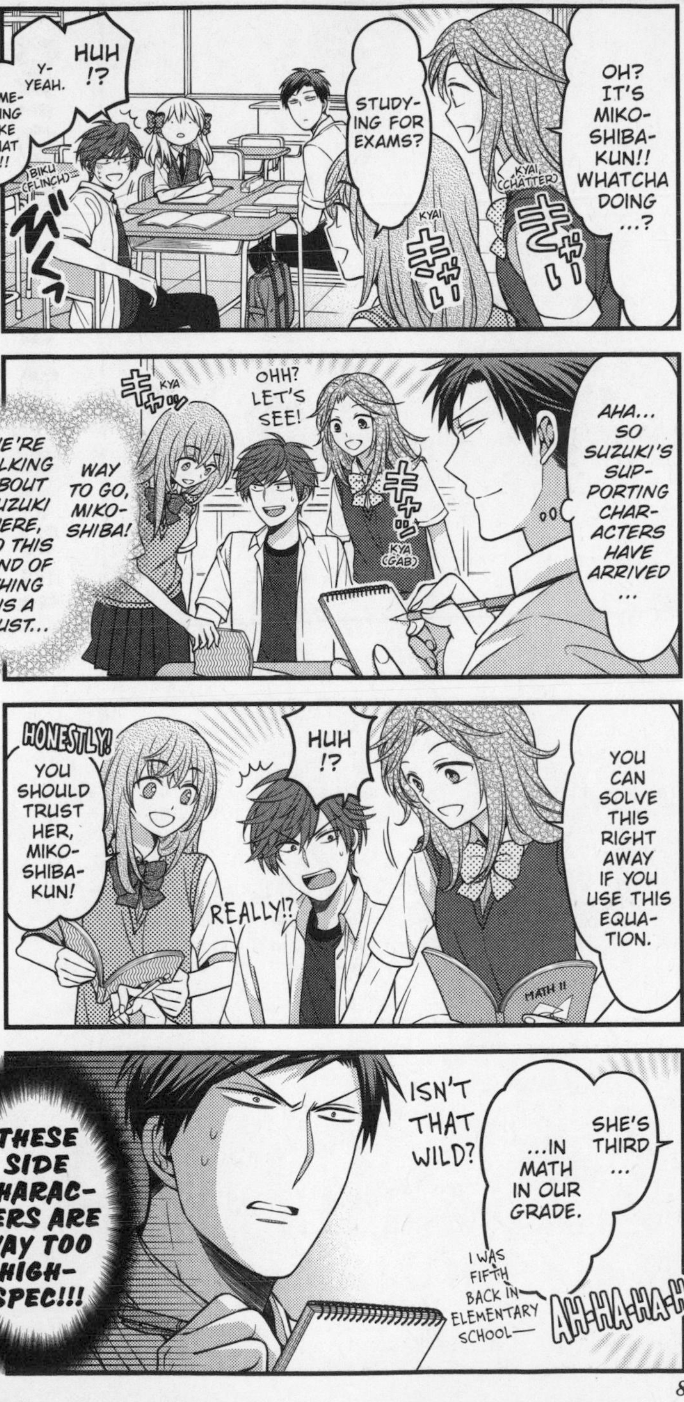
OH? IT'S MIKO-SHIBA-KUN!! WHATCHA DOING ...?
KYAI (CHATTER)
KYAI
STUDYING FOR EXAMS?
HUH !?
Y-YEAH. SOMETHING LIKE THAT !!!
BIKU (FLINCH)
AHA... SO SUZUKI'S SUPPORTING CHARACTERS HAVE ARRIVED ...
KYA (GAB)
OHH? LET'S SEE!
KYA
WAY TO GO, MIKO-SHIBA!
WE'RE TALKING ABOUT SUZUKI HERE, SO THIS KIND OF THING IS A MUST...
YOU CAN SOLVE THIS RIGHT AWAY IF YOU USE THIS EQUATION.
MATH II
HUH !?
REALLY!?
HONESTLY!
YOU SHOULD TRUST HER, MIKO-SHIBA-KUN!
SHE'S THIRD ...
...IN MATH IN OUR GRADE.
ISN'T THAT WILD?
AH-HA-HA-HA!
I WAS FIFTH BACK IN ELEMENTARY SCHOOL—
THESE SIDE CHARACTERS ARE WAY TOO HIGH-SPEC!!!

THEIR GOOD SUBJECTS

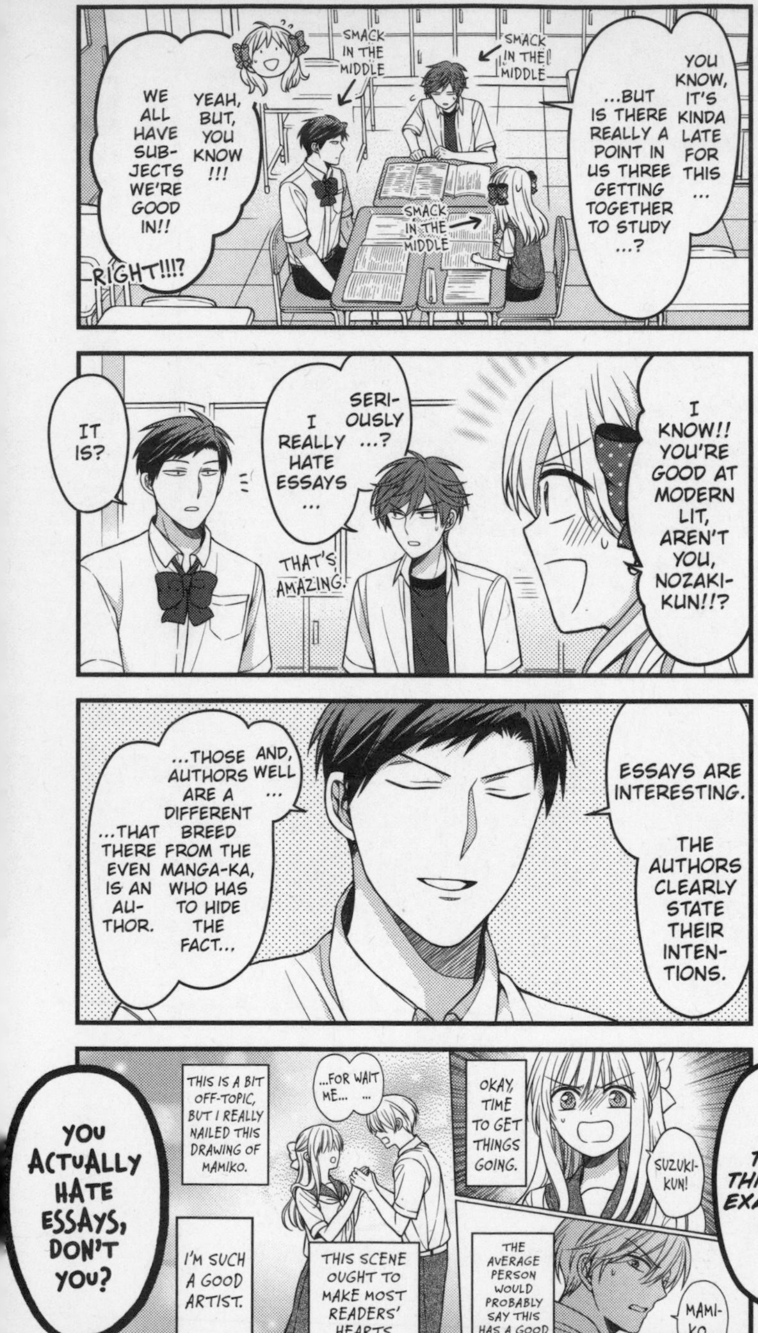
YOU KNOW, IT'S KINDA LATE FOR THIS ...
...BUT IS THERE REALLY A POINT IN US THREE GETTING TOGETHER TO STUDY ...?
SMACK IN THE MIDDLE
SMACK IN THE MIDDLE
SMACK IN THE MIDDLE
YEAH, BUT, YOU KNOW !!!
WE ALL HAVE SUBJECTS WE'RE GOOD IN!!
RIGHT!!!?
I KNOW!! YOU'RE GOOD AT MODERN LIT, AREN'T YOU, NOZAKI-KUN!!?
SERIOUSLY ...?
I REALLY HATE ESSAYS ...
THAT'S AMAZING.
IT IS?
ESSAYS ARE INTERESTING.
THE AUTHORS CLEARLY STATE THEIR INTENTIONS.
AND, WELL ...
...THOSE AUTHORS ARE A DIFFERENT BREED FROM THE MANGA-KA, WHO HAS TO HIDE THE FACT...
...THAT THERE EVEN IS AN AUTHOR.
TAKE THIS FOR EXAMPLE.
SUZUKI-KUN!
OKAY, TIME TO GET THINGS GOING.
MAMI-KO...
THE AVERAGE PERSON WOULD PROBABLY SAY THIS HAS A GOOD FLOW.
WAIT ...
...FOR ME...
THIS IS A BIT OFF-TOPIC, BUT I REALLY NAILED THIS DRAWING OF MAMIKO.
THIS SCENE OUGHT TO MAKE MOST READERS' HEARTS SKIP A BEAT.
I'M SUCH A GOOD ARTIST.
YOU ACTUALLY HATE ESSAYS, DON'T YOU?

SHOUJO MANGA BRAIN

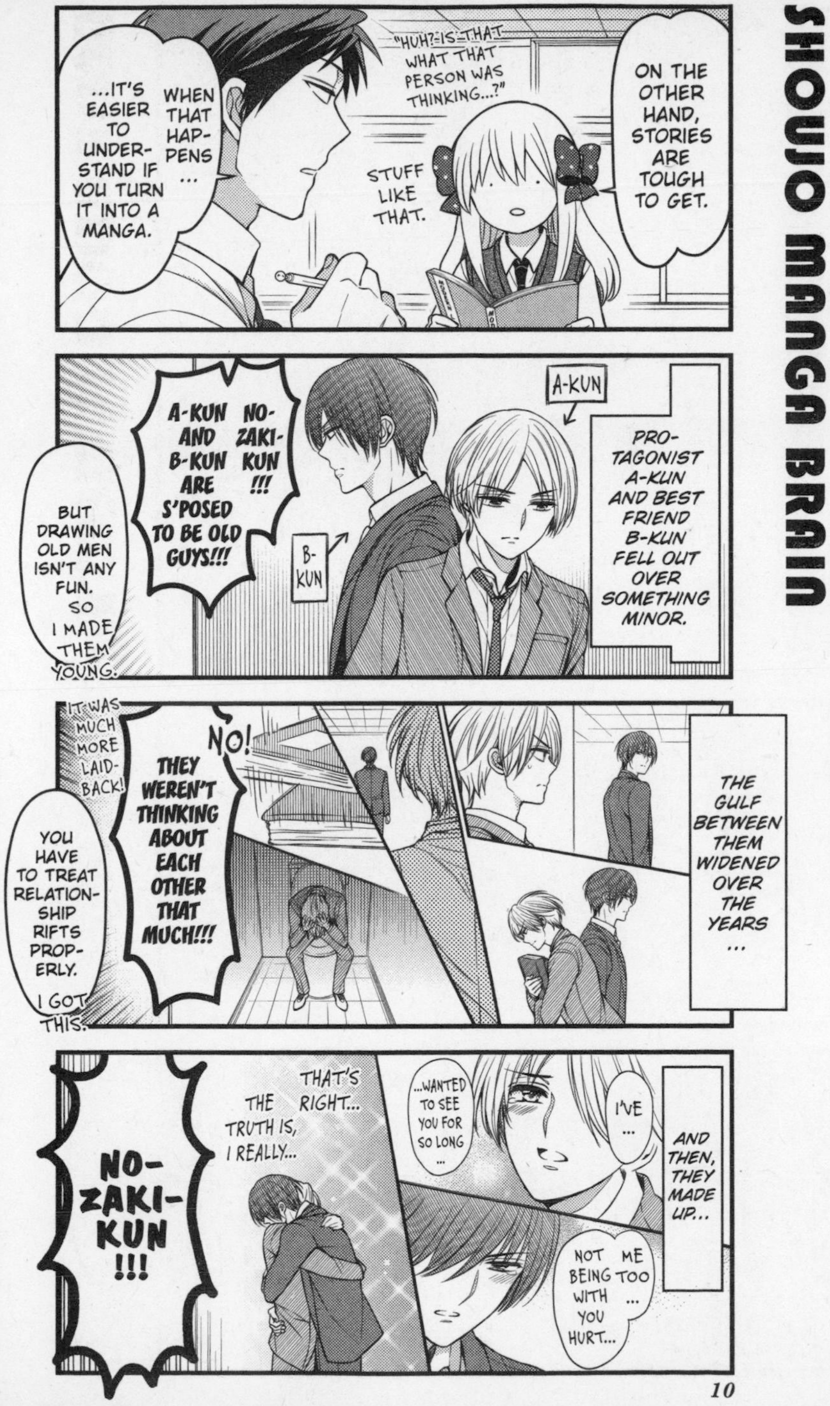
ON THE OTHER HAND, STORIES ARE TOUGH TO GET.
"HUH?-IS THAT WHAT THAT PERSON WAS THINKING...?"
STUFF LIKE THAT.
WHEN THAT HAPPENS...
...IT'S EASIER TO UNDERSTAND IF YOU TURN IT INTO A MANGA.
PROTAGONIST A-KUN AND BEST FRIEND B-KUN FELL OUT OVER SOMETHING MINOR.
A-KUN
B-KUN
NOZAKI-KUN!!!
A-KUN AND B-KUN ARE S'POSED TO BE OLD GUYS!!!
BUT DRAWING OLD MEN ISN'T ANY FUN. SO I MADE THEM YOUNG.
THE GULF BETWEEN THEM WIDENED OVER THE YEARS...
NO!
THEY WEREN'T THINKING ABOUT EACH OTHER THAT MUCH!!!
IT WAS MUCH MORE LAID-BACK!
YOU HAVE TO TREAT RELATIONSHIP RIFTS PROPERLY.
I GOT THIS.
AND THEN, THEY MADE UP...
I'VE...
...WANTED TO SEE YOU FOR SO LONG...
NOT BEING WITH YOU HURT... ME TOO...
THAT'S RIGHT...
THE TRUTH IS, I REALLY...
NOZAKI-KUN!!!

AND THEN, THE VICTIMS MULTIPLIED

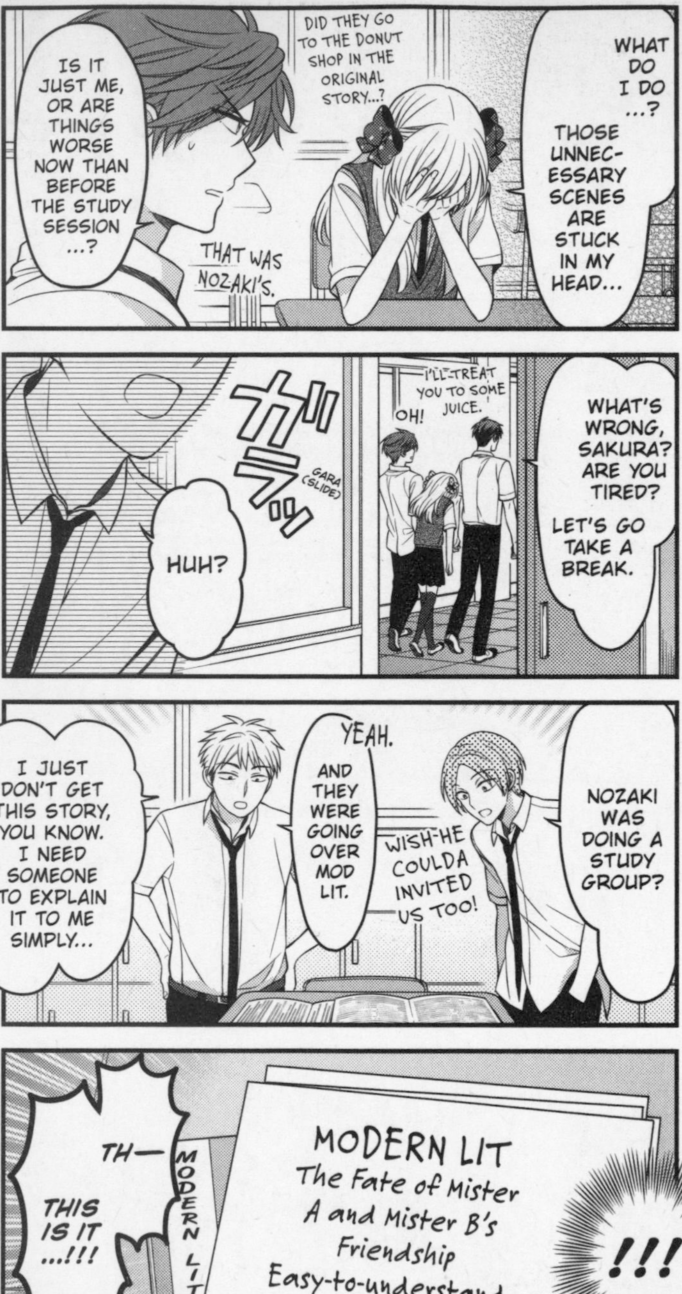
WHAT DO I DO ...?
THOSE UNNECESSARY SCENES ARE STUCK IN MY HEAD...
DID THEY GO TO THE DONUT SHOP IN THE ORIGINAL STORY...?
IS IT JUST ME, OR ARE THINGS WORSE NOW THAN BEFORE THE STUDY SESSION ...?
THAT WAS NOZAKI'S.
WHAT'S WRONG, SAKURA? ARE YOU TIRED?
LET'S GO TAKE A BREAK.
I'LL TREAT YOU TO SOME JUICE.
OH!
GARA (SLIDE)
HUH?
NOZAKI WAS DOING A STUDY GROUP?
WISH HE COULDA INVITED US TOO!
YEAH.
AND THEY WERE GOING OVER MOD LIT.
I JUST DON'T GET THIS STORY, YOU KNOW. I NEED SOMEONE TO EXPLAIN IT TO ME SIMPLY...
!!!
MODERN LIT
The Fate of Mister A and Mister B's Friendship
Easy-to-understand, explanatory manga
MODERN LIT
TH—
THIS IS IT ...!!!

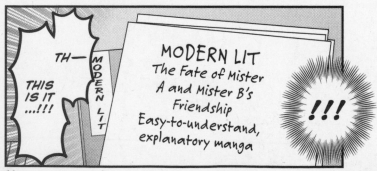

REFERENCE BLOG

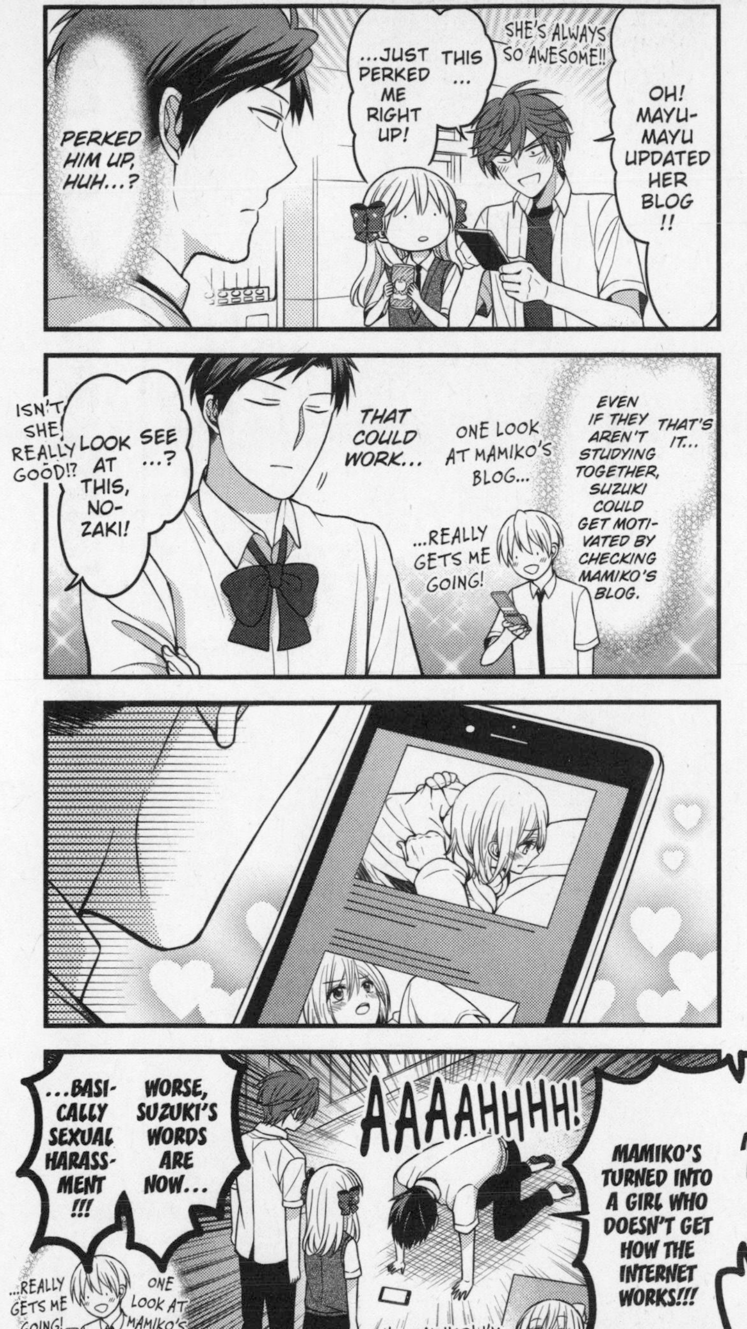
OH! MAYU-MAYU UPDATED HER BLOG!!
SHE'S ALWAYS SO AWESOME!!
THIS...
...JUST PERKED ME RIGHT UP!
PERKED HIM UP, HUH...?
THAT'S IT...
EVEN IF THEY AREN'T STUDYING TOGETHER, SUZUKI COULD GET MOTIVATED BY CHECKING MAMIKO'S BLOG.
ONE LOOK AT MAMIKO'S BLOG...
...REALLY GETS ME GOING!
THAT COULD WORK...
SEE...?
LOOK AT THIS, NOZAKI!
ISN'T SHE REALLY GOOD!?
MAMIKOOO...!!!
MAMIKO'S TURNED INTO A GIRL WHO DOESN'T GET HOW THE INTERNET WORKS!!!
AAAAHHHH!
I'M MAMIKO! I'M PUTTING MY PICS ON THE WEB!♡
WORSE, SUZUKI'S WORDS ARE NOW...
...BASICALLY SEXUAL HARASSMENT!!!
ONE LOOK AT MAMIKO'S BLOG...
...REALLY GETS ME GOING!

A GUY'S TRUE FEELINGS

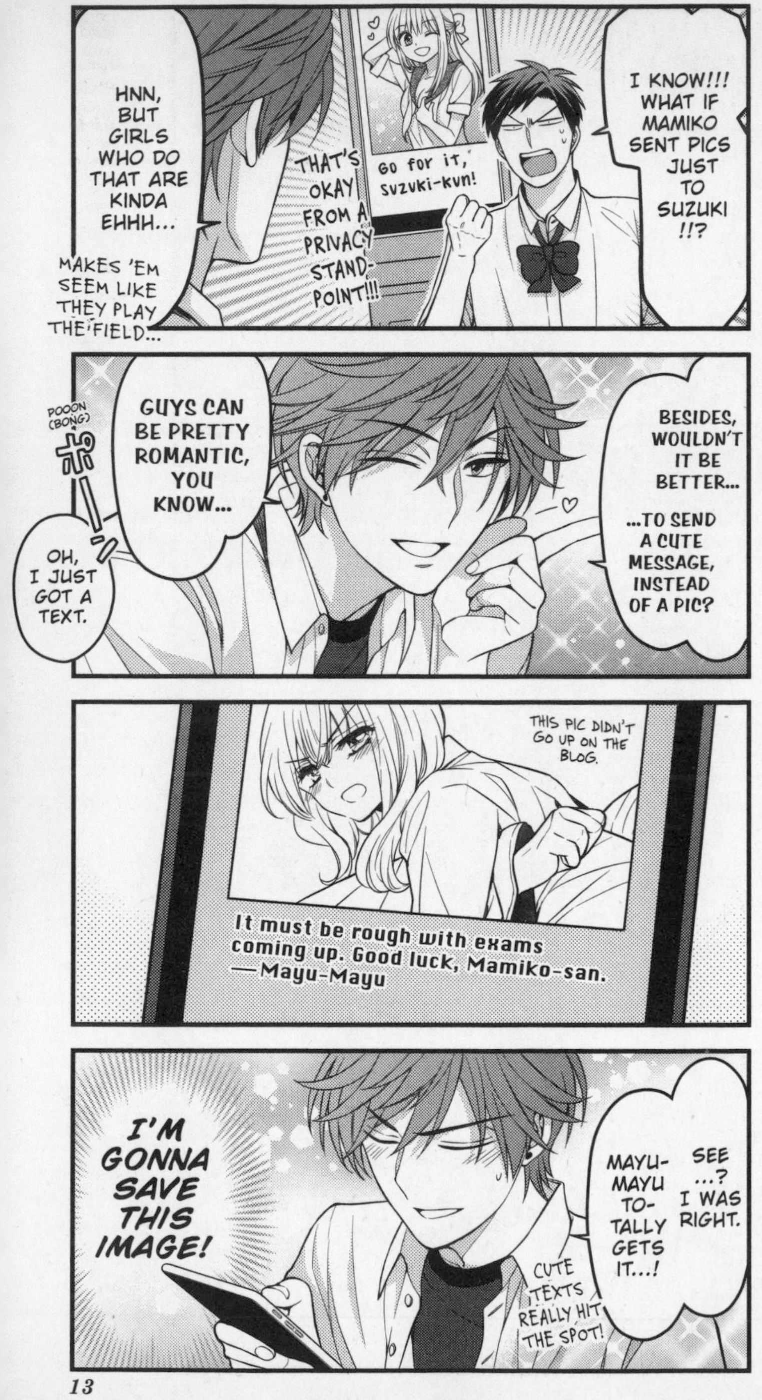
I KNOW!!! WHAT IF MAMIKO SENT PICS JUST TO SUZUKI!!?
Go for it, Suzuki-kun!
THAT'S OKAY FROM A PRIVACY STANDPOINT!!!
HNN, BUT GIRLS WHO DO THAT ARE KINDA EHHH...
MAKES 'EM SEEM LIKE THEY PLAY THE FIELD...
BESIDES, WOULDN'T IT BE BETTER...
...TO SEND A CUTE MESSAGE, INSTEAD OF A PIC?
GUYS CAN BE PRETTY ROMANTIC, YOU KNOW...
POOON (BONG)
OH, I JUST GOT A TEXT.
THIS PIC DIDN'T GO UP ON THE BLOG.
It must be rough with exams coming up. Good luck, Mamiko-san. —Mayu-Mayu
SEE...? I WAS RIGHT.
MAYU-MAYU TOTALLY GETS IT...!
CUTE TEXTS REALLY HIT THE SPOT!
I'M GONNA SAVE THIS IMAGE!

A KINDA NICE STORY

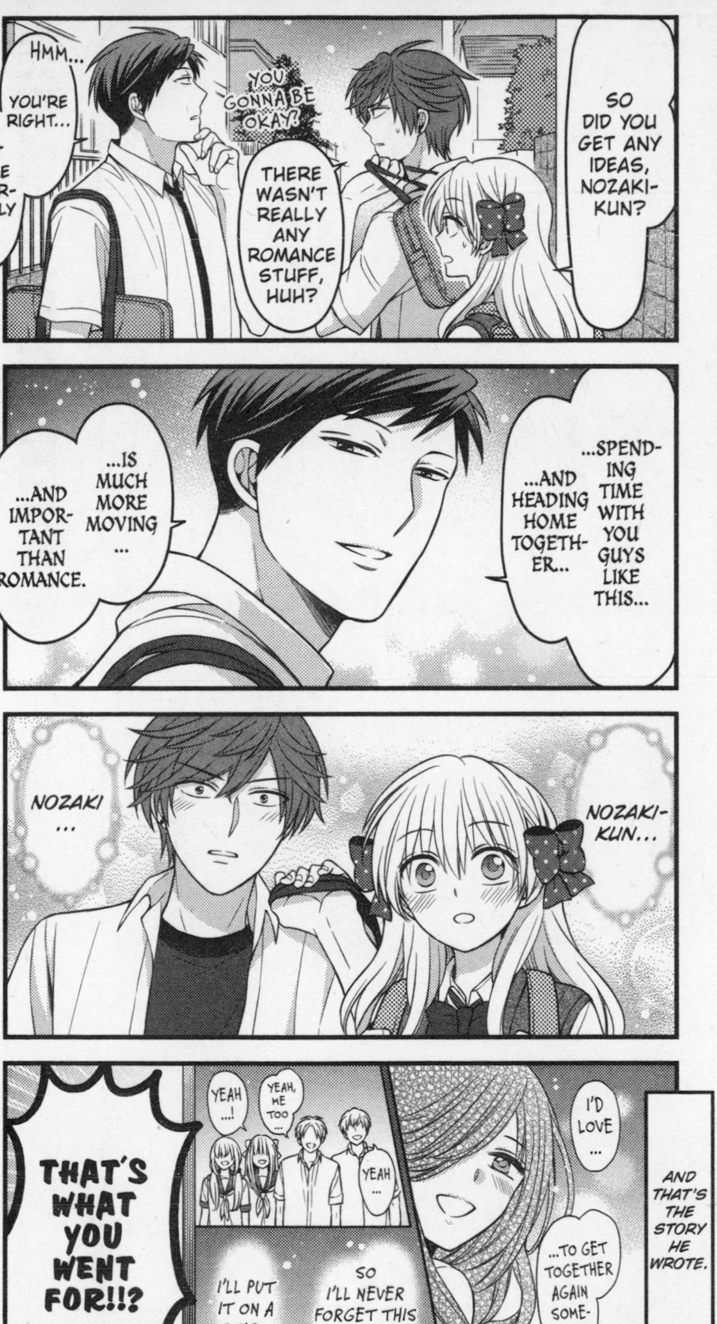
SO DID YOU GET ANY IDEAS, NOZAKI-KUN?
YOU GONNA BE OKAY?
THERE WASN'T REALLY ANY ROMANCE STUFF, HUH?
HMM... YOU'RE RIGHT...
BUT MORE IMPORTANTLY...
...SPENDING TIME WITH YOU GUYS LIKE THIS...
...AND HEADING HOME TOGETHER...
...IS MUCH MORE MOVING...
...AND IMPORTANT THAN ROMANCE.
NOZAKI-KUN...
NOZAKI...
AND THAT'S THE STORY HE WROTE.
I'D LOVE...
...TO GET TOGETHER AGAIN SOMETIME.
YEAH, ME TOO...
YEAH...!
YEAH...
SO I'LL NEVER FORGET THIS MOMENT...
I'LL PUT IT ON A STAR...
THAT'S WHAT YOU WENT FOR!!?
DAMMIT!!

THE VICTIMS' ANSWERS

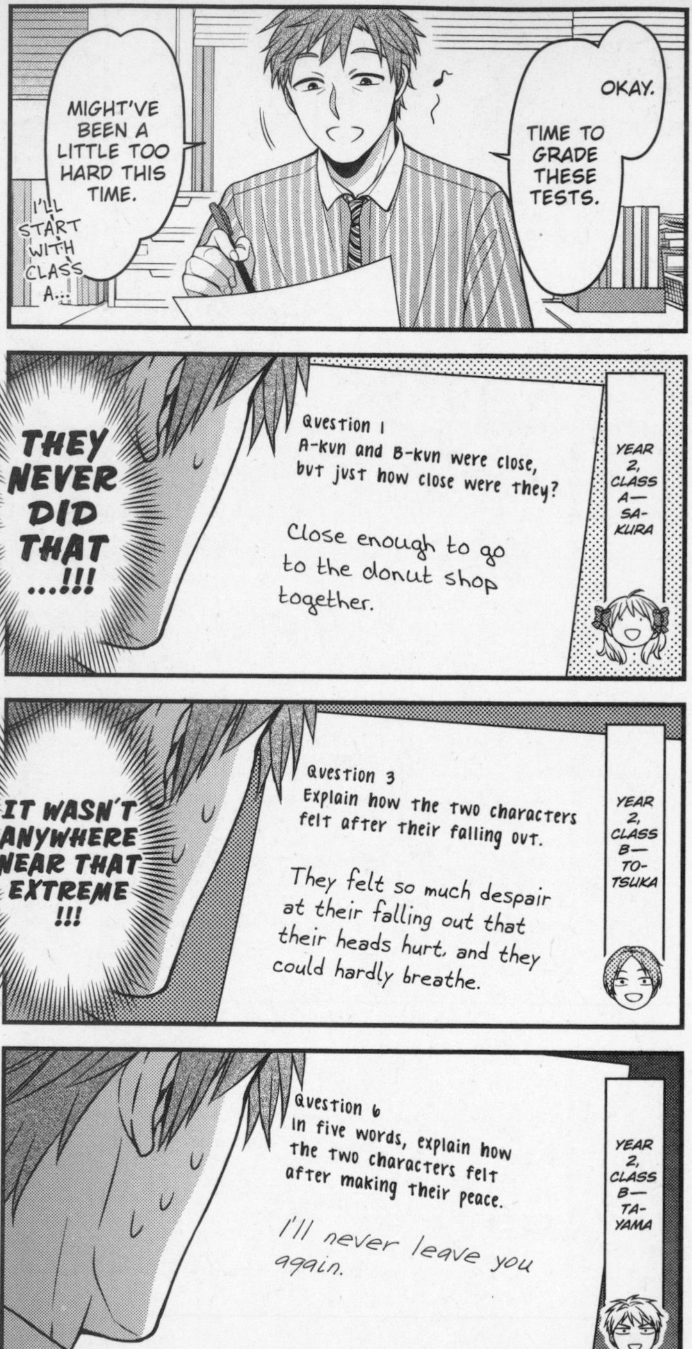

OKAY.
TIME TO GRADE THESE TESTS.
MIGHT'VE BEEN A LITTLE TOO HARD THIS TIME.
I'LL START WITH CLASS A...
YEAR 2, CLASS A—SAKURA
Question 1
A-kun and B-kun were close, but just how close were they?
Close enough to go to the donut shop together.
THEY NEVER DID THAT...!!!
YEAR 2, CLASS B—TOTSUKA
Question 3
Explain how the two characters felt after their falling out.
They felt so much despair at their falling out that their heads hurt, and they could hardly breathe.
IT WASN'T ANYWHERE NEAR THAT EXTREME!!!
YEAR 2, CLASS B—TAYAMA
Question 6
In five words, explain how the two characters felt after making their peace.
I'll never leave you again.

HER HAUL

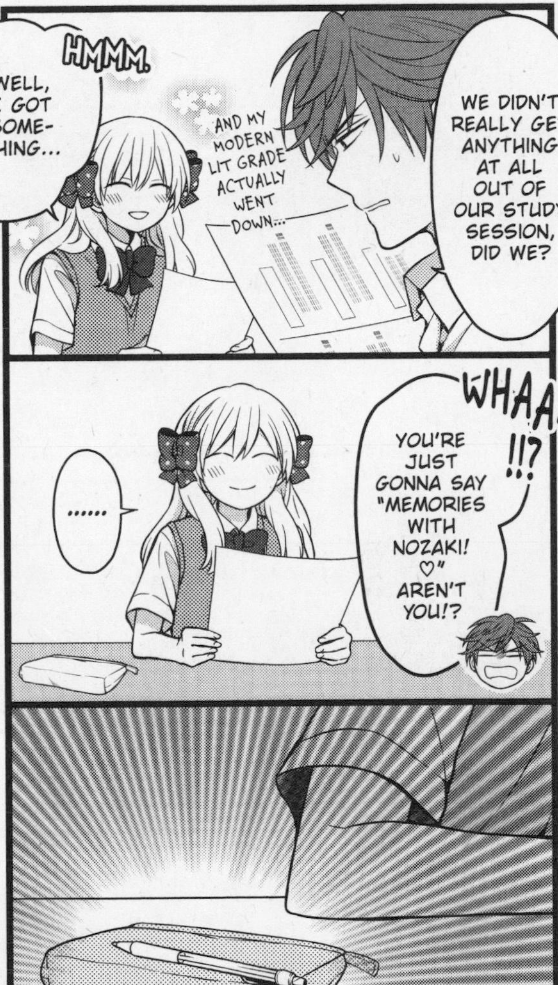
WE DIDN'T REALLY GET ANYTHING AT ALL OUT OF OUR STUDY SESSION, DID WE?
HMMM.
WELL, I GOT SOME-THING...
AND MY MODERN LIT GRADE ACTUALLY WENT DOWN...
WHAAAT!!?
YOU'RE JUST GONNA SAY "MEMORIES WITH NOZAKI! ♡" AREN'T YOU!?
......
NOZAKI'S MECHANICAL PENCIL

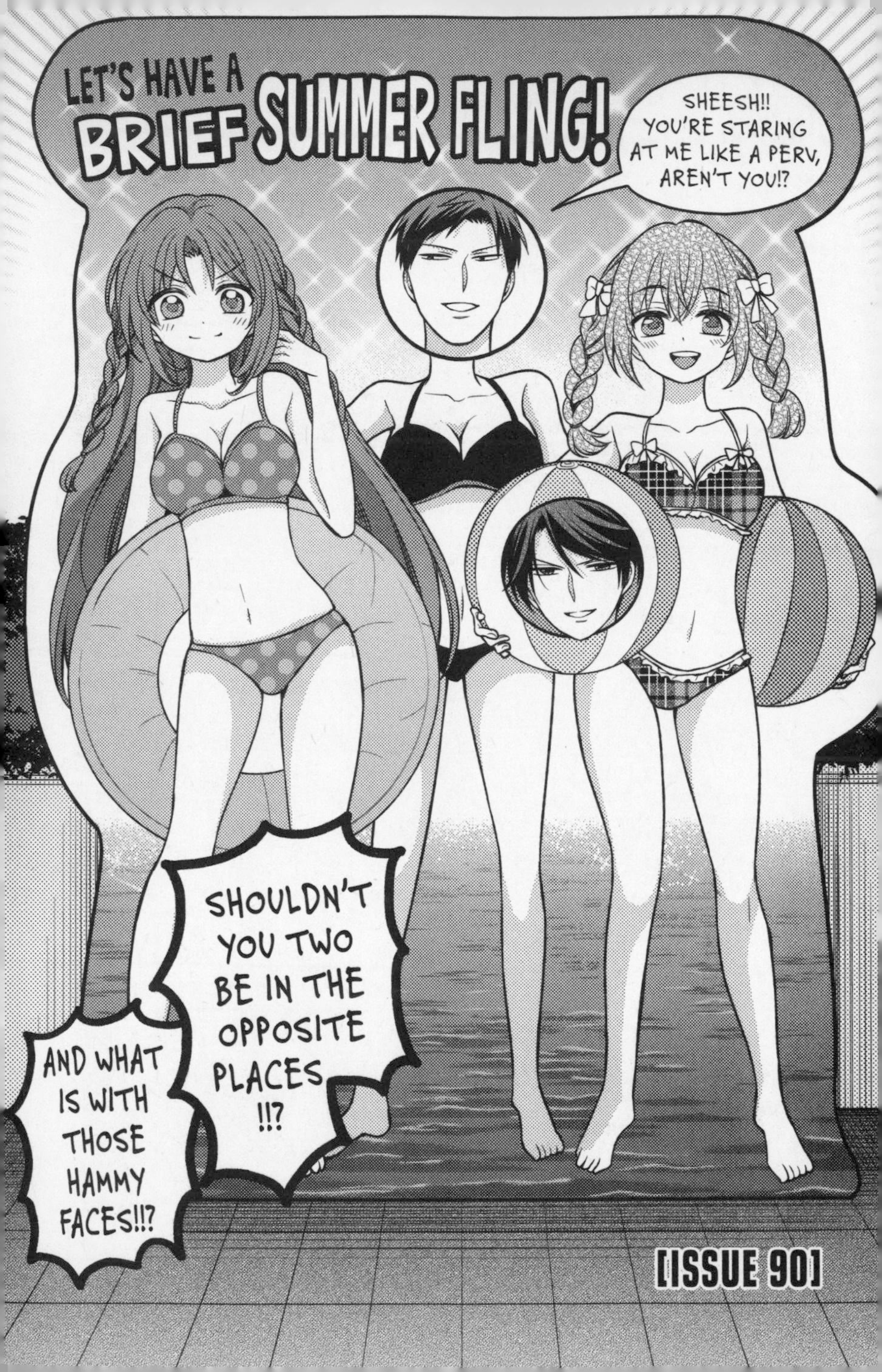
LET'S HAVE A BRIEF SUMMER FLING!
SHEESH!! YOU'RE STARING AT ME LIKE A PERV, AREN'T YOU!?
SHOULDN'T YOU TWO BE IN THE OPPOSITE PLACES !!?
AND WHAT IS WITH THOSE HAMMY FACES!!?
[ISSUE 90]

SEEING HIS IDEAL PERSON FACE-TO-FACE

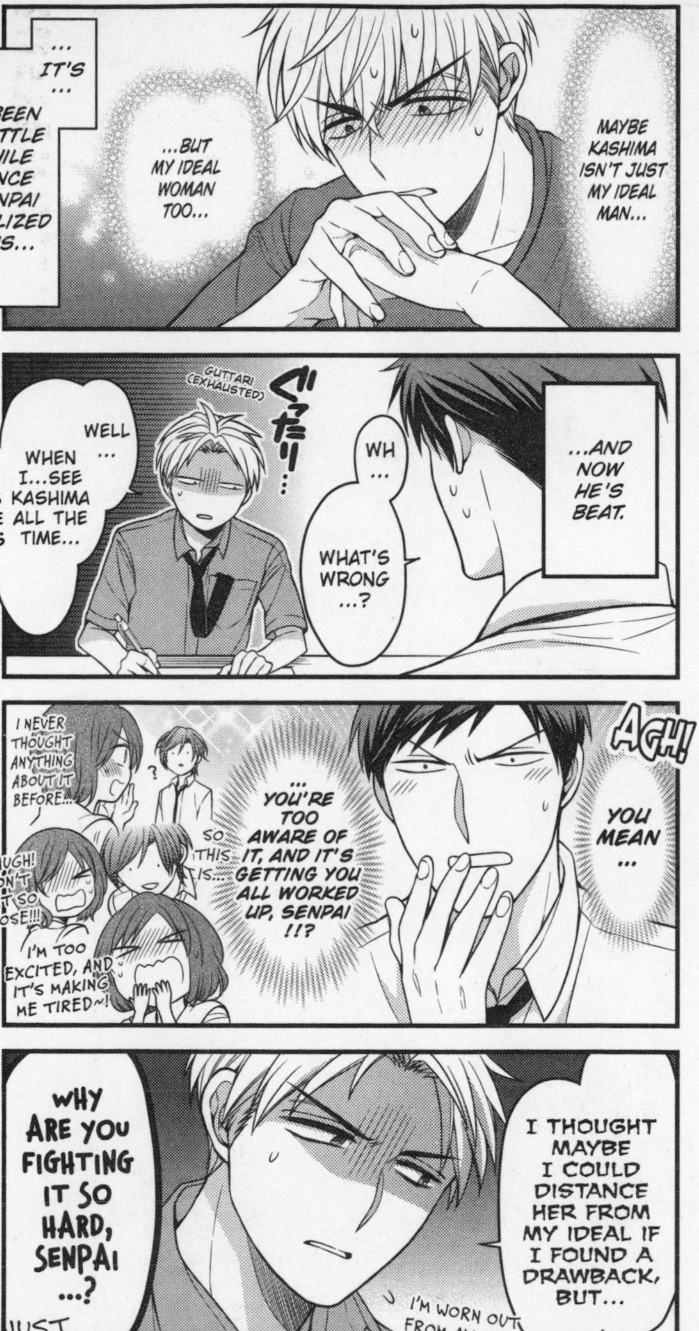
MAYBE KASHIMA ISN'T JUST MY IDEAL MAN...
...BUT MY IDEAL WOMAN TOO...
...IT'S... ...BEEN A LITTLE WHILE SINCE SENPAI REALIZED THIS...
...AND NOW HE'S BEAT.
GUTTARI (EXHAUSTED)
WH... WHAT'S WRONG...?
WELL... WHEN I...SEE KASHIMA ALL THE TIME... ...IT'S LIKE THIS...
AGH!
YOU MEAN...
...YOU'RE TOO AWARE OF IT, AND IT'S GETTING YOU ALL WORKED UP, SENPAI!!?
SO THIS IS...
I NEVER THOUGHT ANYTHING ABOUT IT BEFORE...!
AAAUGH! DON'T GET SO CLOSE!!!
I'M TOO EXCITED, AND IT'S MAKING ME TIRED~!
I THOUGHT MAYBE I COULD DISTANCE HER FROM MY IDEAL IF I FOUND A DRAWBACK, BUT...
I'M WORN OUT FROM ALL THE SEARCHING...
WHY ARE YOU FIGHTING IT SO HARD, SENPAI...?
JUST GIVE UP.

INSTEAD...

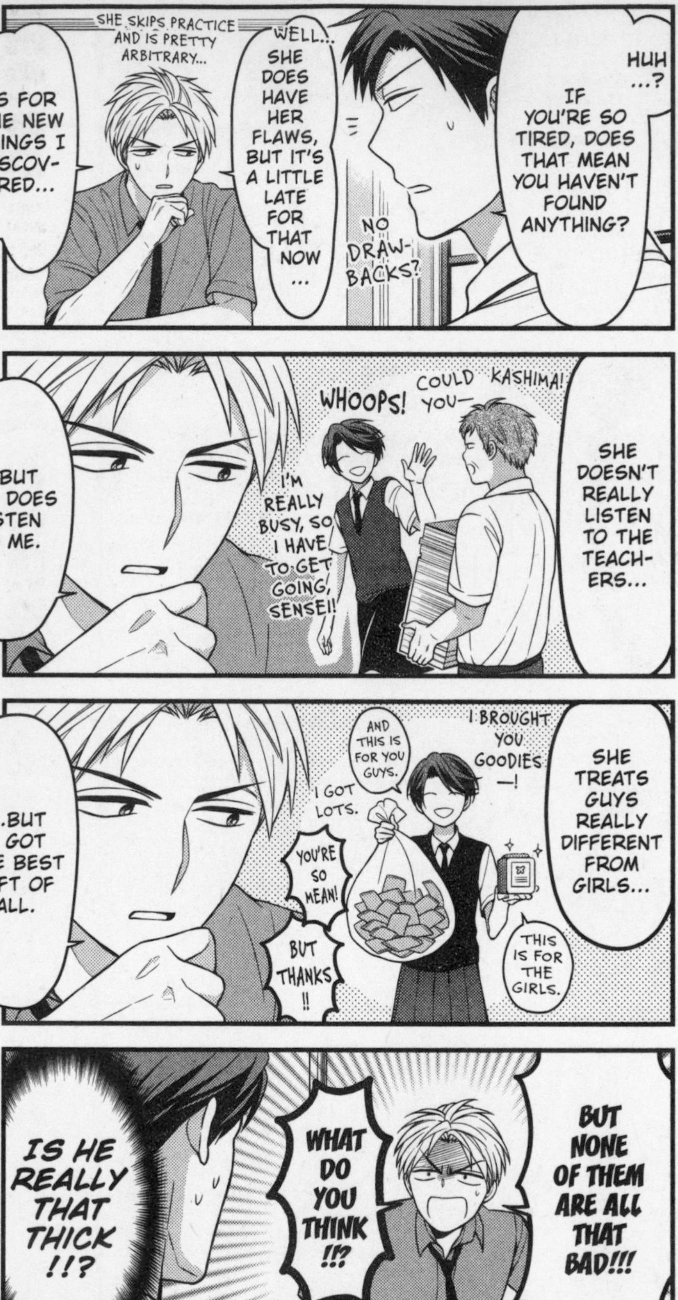
HUH ...?
IF YOU'RE SO TIRED, DOES THAT MEAN YOU HAVEN'T FOUND ANYTHING?
NO DRAW-BACKS?
WELL... SHE DOES HAVE HER FLAWS, BUT IT'S A LITTLE LATE FOR THAT NOW ...
SHE SKIPS PRACTICE AND IS PRETTY ARBITRARY...
AS FOR THE NEW THINGS I DISCOVERED...
SHE DOESN'T REALLY LISTEN TO THE TEACHERS...
KASHIMA! COULD YOU—
WHOOPS!
I'M REALLY BUSY, SO I HAVE TO GET GOING, SENSEI!
...BUT SHE DOES LISTEN TO ME.
SHE TREATS GUYS REALLY DIFFERENT FROM GIRLS...
I BROUGHT YOU GOODIES—!
THIS IS FOR THE GIRLS.
AND THIS IS FOR YOU GUYS.
I GOT LOTS.
YOU'RE SO MEAN!
BUT THANKS!!
...BUT I GOT THE BEST GIFT OF ALL.
BUT NONE OF THEM ARE ALL THAT BAD!!!
WHAT DO YOU THINK!!?
IS HE REALLY THAT THICK!!?

SEEING HER AS A WOMAN

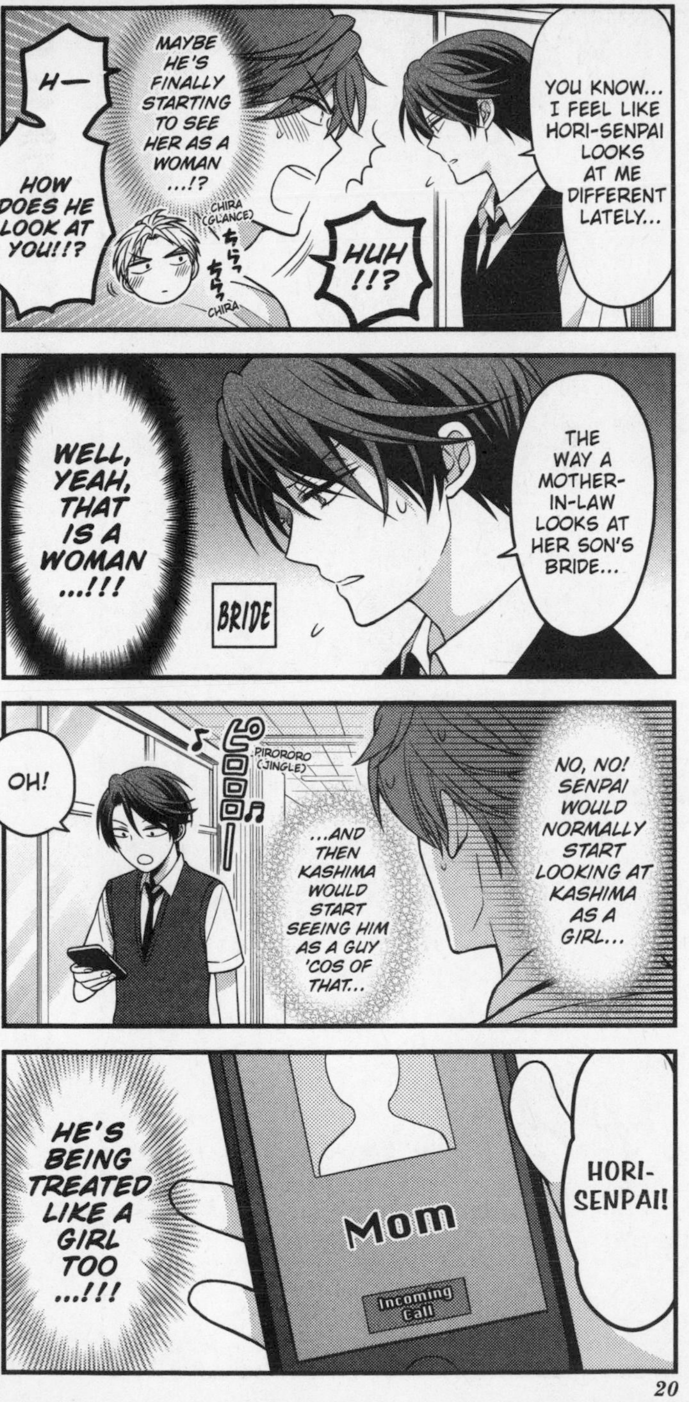
YOU KNOW... I FEEL LIKE HORI-SENPAI LOOKS AT ME DIFFERENT LATELY...
HUH!!?
CHIRA (GLANCE)
ちらっ ちらっ
CHIRA
MAYBE HE'S FINALLY STARTING TO SEE HER AS A WOMAN ...!?
H— HOW DOES HE LOOK AT YOU!!?
THE WAY A MOTHER-IN-LAW LOOKS AT HER SON'S BRIDE...
BRIDE
WELL, YEAH, THAT IS A WOMAN ...!!!
NO, NO! SENPAI WOULD NORMALLY START LOOKING AT KASHIMA AS A GIRL...
...AND THEN KASHIMA WOULD START SEEING HIM AS A GUY 'COS OF THAT...
ピロロロー
PIRORORO (JINGLE)
OH!
HORI-SENPAI!
Mom
Incoming Call
HE'S BEING TREATED LIKE A GIRL TOO ...!!!

IT'S NOT GOING WELL ON THIS END EITHER

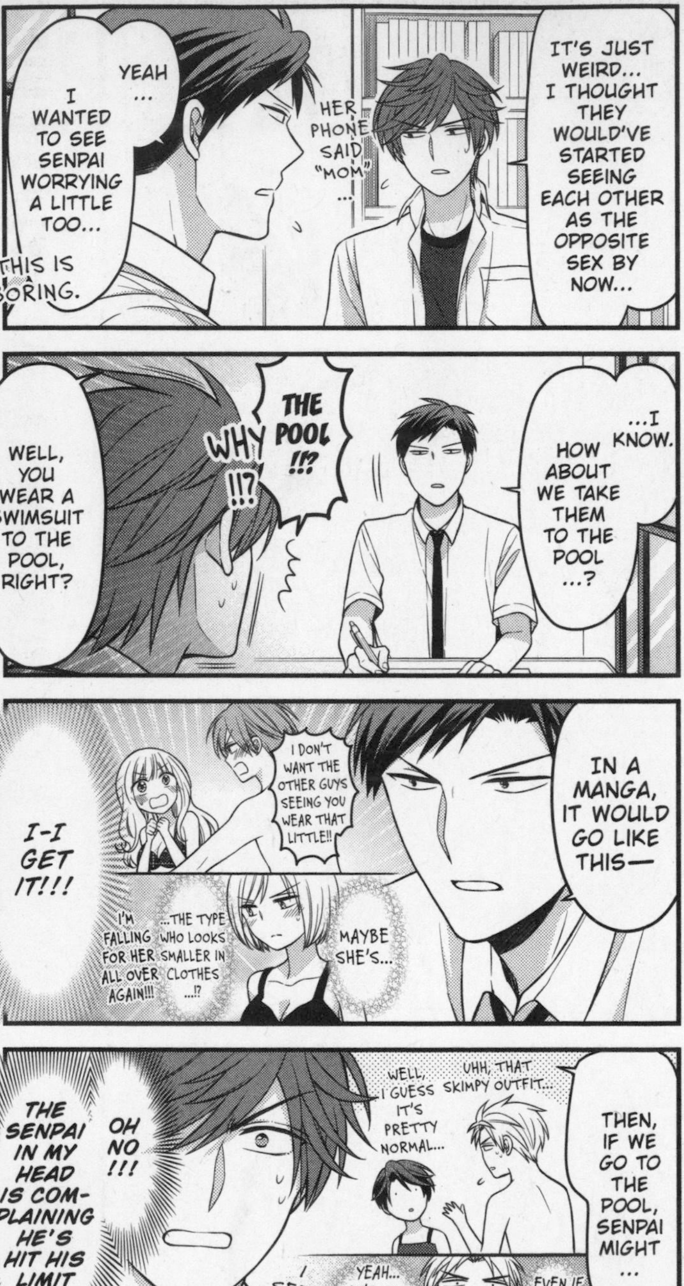
IT'S JUST WEIRD... I THOUGHT THEY WOULD'VE STARTED SEEING EACH OTHER AS THE OPPOSITE SEX BY NOW...
HER PHONE SAID "MOM" ...
YEAH ...
I WANTED TO SEE SENPAI WORRYING A LITTLE TOO...
THIS IS BORING.
...I KNOW. HOW ABOUT WE TAKE THEM TO THE POOL ...?
THE POOL !!?
WHY !!?
WELL, YOU WEAR A SWIMSUIT TO THE POOL, RIGHT?
IN A MANGA, IT WOULD GO LIKE THIS—
I DON'T WANT THE OTHER GUYS SEEING YOU WEAR THAT LITTLE!!
I-I GET IT!!!
MAYBE SHE'S...
...THE TYPE WHO LOOKS SMALLER IN CLOTHES ...!?
I'M FALLING FOR HER ALL OVER AGAIN!!!
THEN, IF WE GO TO THE POOL, SENPAI MIGHT ...
UHH, THAT SKIMPY OUTFIT...
WELL, I GUESS IT'S PRETTY NORMAL...
EVEN IF YOU TAKE OFF YOUR CLOTHES...
YEAH... IT'S NOT REALLY ALL THAT... YEAH...
I SEE...
OH NO !!!
THE SENPAI IN MY HEAD IS COMPLAINING HE'S HIT HIS LIMIT ...!!!

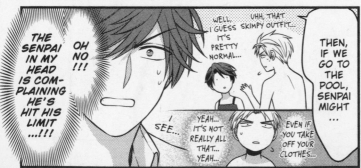

THE EFFECT THEY HOPED FOR

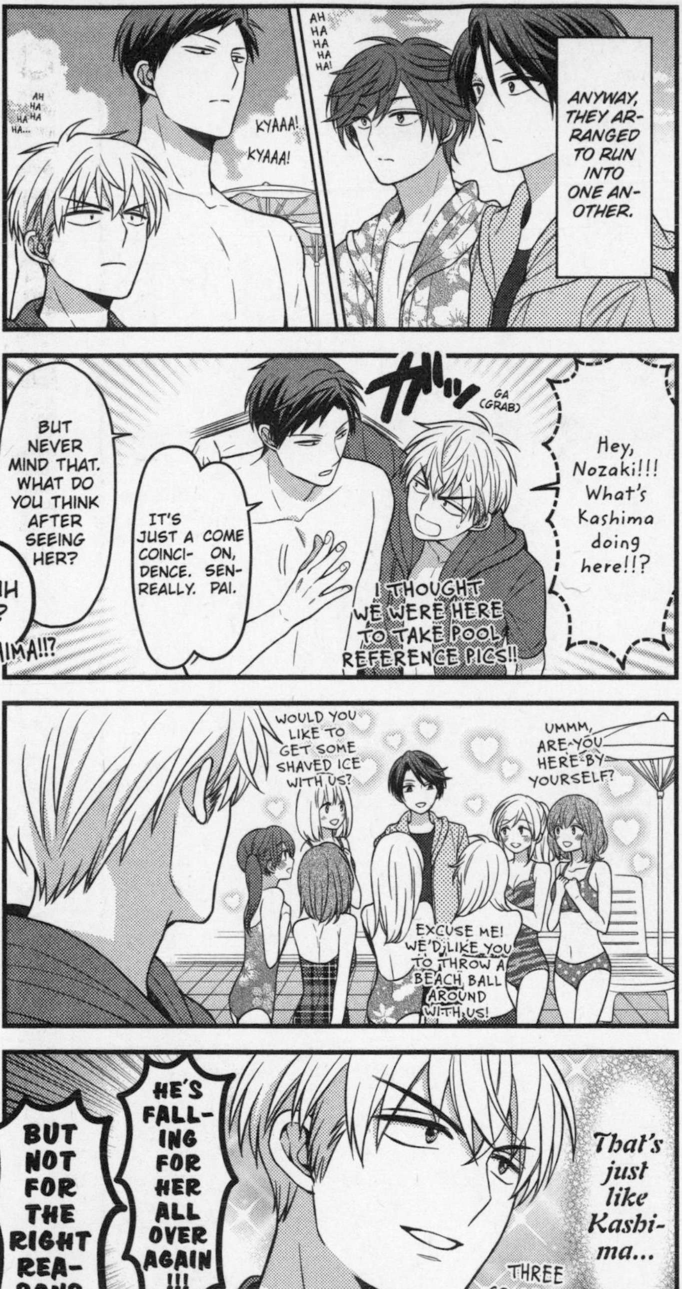
ANYWAY, THEY ARRANGED TO RUN INTO ONE ANOTHER.
AH HA HA HA HA!
KYAAA!
KYAAA!
AH HA HA HA...
Hey, Nozaki!!! What's Kashima doing here!!?
GA (GRAB)
I THOUGHT WE WERE HERE TO TAKE POOL REFERENCE PICS!!
COME ON, SEN-PAI.
IT'S JUST A COINCI-DENCE. REALLY.
BUT NEVER MIND THAT. WHAT DO YOU THINK AFTER SEEING HER?
HUH!?
KASHIMA!!?
UMMM, ARE YOU HERE BY YOURSELF?
WOULD YOU LIKE TO GET SOME SHAVED ICE WITH US?
EXCUSE ME! WE'D LIKE YOU TO THROW A BEACH BALL AROUND WITH US!
That's just like Kashi-ma...
THREE GROUPS AT ONCE...
HE'S FALL-ING FOR HER ALL OVER AGAIN!!!
BUT NOT FOR THE RIGHT REA-SONS!!!

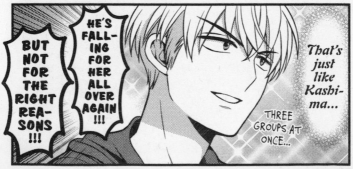

HORI-SENPAI'S PANIC

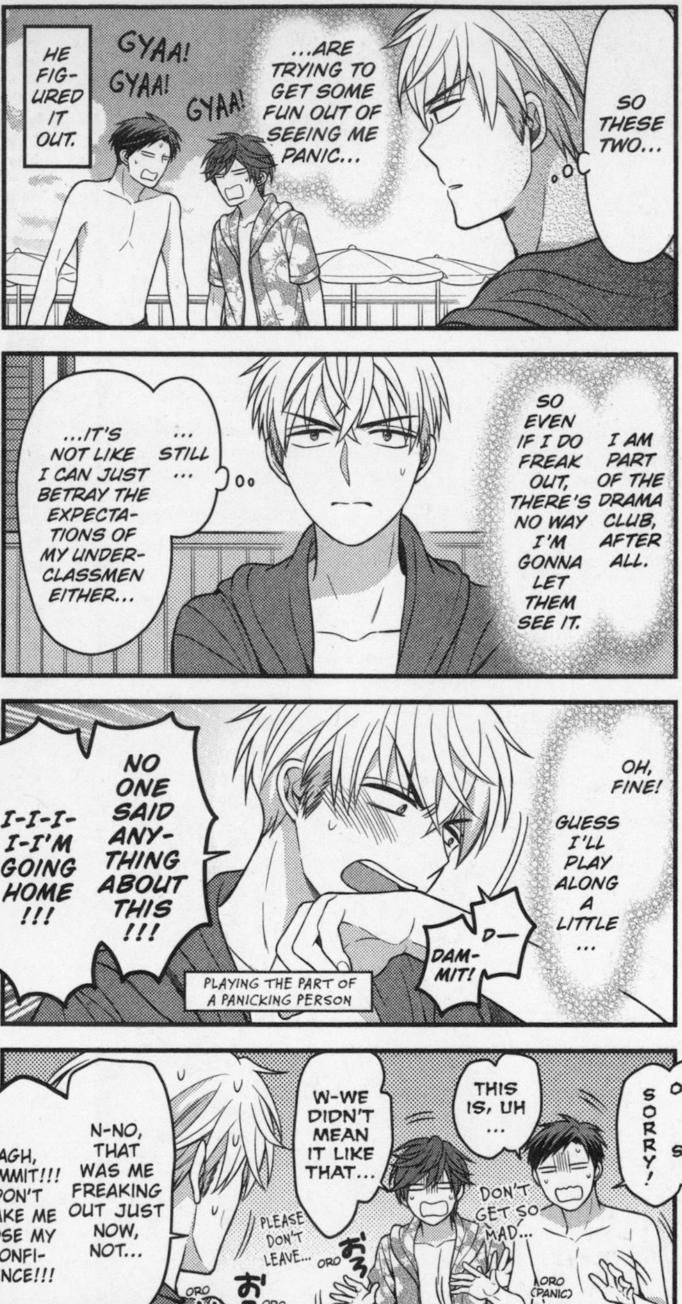
SO THESE TWO...
...ARE TRYING TO GET SOME FUN OUT OF SEEING ME PANIC...
GYAA! GYAA!
GYAA!
HE FIGURED IT OUT.
I AM PART OF THE DRAMA CLUB, AFTER ALL.
SO EVEN IF I DO FREAK OUT, THERE'S NO WAY I'M GONNA LET THEM SEE IT.
...STILL...
...IT'S NOT LIKE I CAN JUST BETRAY THE EXPECTATIONS OF MY UNDERCLASSMEN EITHER...
OH, FINE!
GUESS I'LL PLAY ALONG A LITTLE...
D— DAMMIT!
NO ONE SAID ANYTHING ABOUT THIS!!!
I-I-I-I-I'M GOING HOME!!!
PLAYING THE PART OF A PANICKING PERSON
OH! S— SORRY!
THIS IS, UH...
DON'T GET SO MAD...
ORO (PANIC) おろ
W-WE DIDN'T MEAN IT LIKE THAT...
PLEASE DON'T LEAVE...
ORO おろ
ORO おろ
N-NO, THAT WAS ME FREAKING OUT JUST NOW, NOT...
AGH, DAMMIT!!! DON'T MAKE ME LOSE MY CONFIDENCE!!!

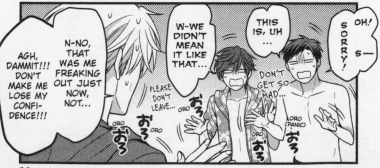

WHOLEHEARTED SPOILING

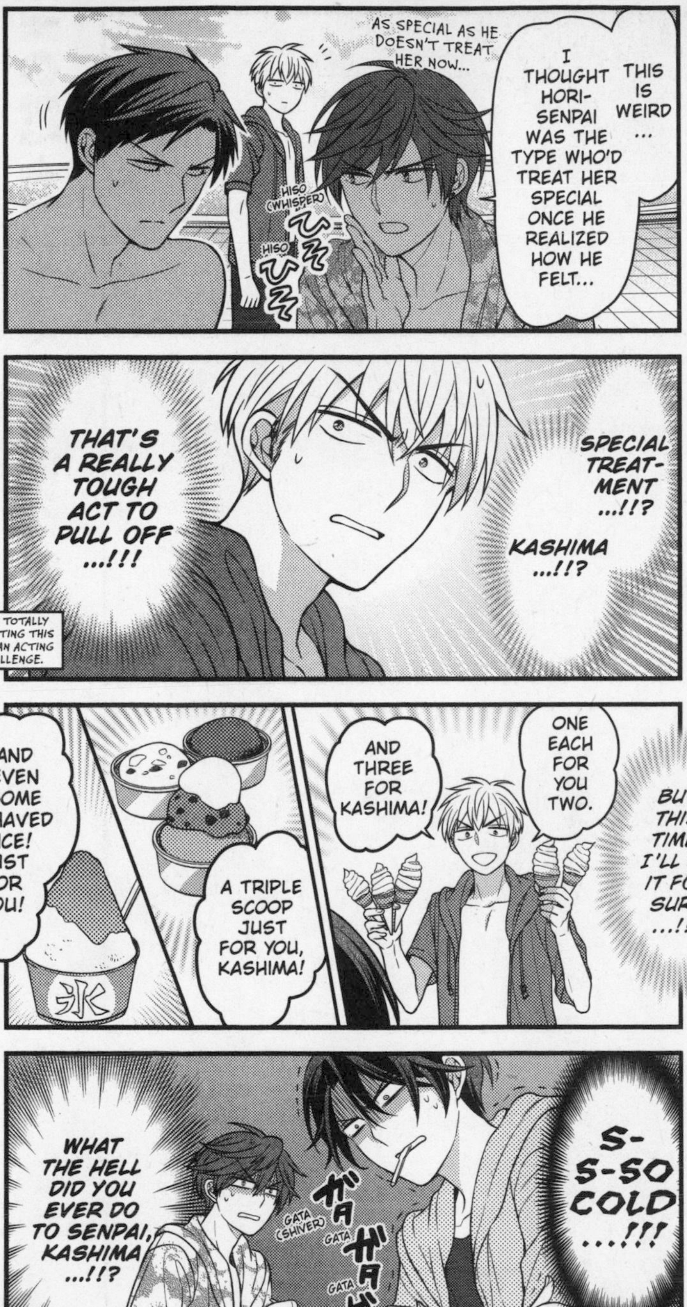
THIS IS WEIRD... I THOUGHT HORI-SENPAI WAS THE TYPE WHO'D TREAT HER SPECIAL ONCE HE REALIZED HOW HE FELT...
AS SPECIAL AS HE DOESN'T TREAT HER NOW...
HISO (WHISPER)
HISO
SPECIAL TREATMENT...!!?
KASHIMA...!!?
THAT'S A REALLY TOUGH ACT TO PULL OFF...!!!
HE'S TOTALLY TREATING THIS LIKE AN ACTING CHALLENGE.
BUT THIS TIME, I'LL DO IT FOR SURE...!!!
ONE EACH FOR YOU TWO.
AND THREE FOR KASHIMA!
A TRIPLE SCOOP JUST FOR YOU, KASHIMA!
AND EVEN SOME SHAVED ICE! JUST FOR YOU!
S-S-SO COLD...!!!
GATA (SHIVER)
GATA
GATA
WHAT THE HELL DID YOU EVER DO TO SENPAI, KASHIMA...!!?

I GET IT

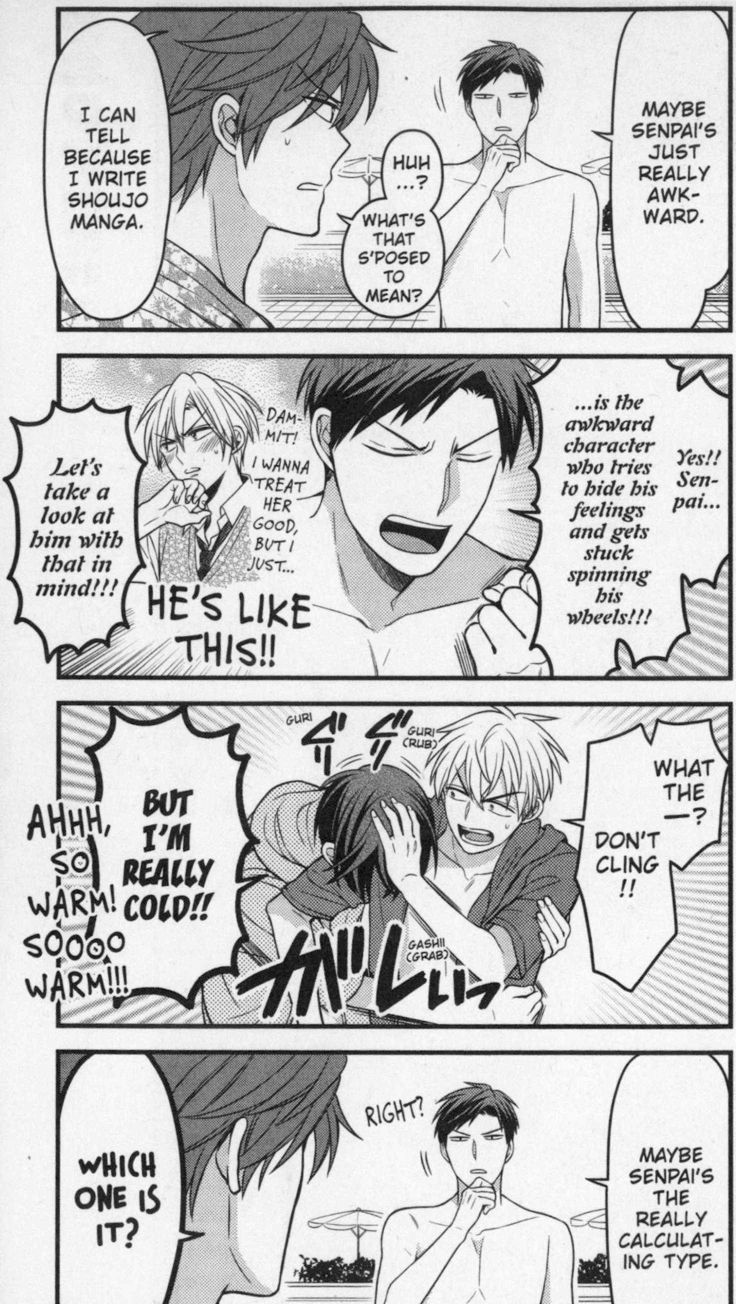
MAYBE SENPAI'S JUST REALLY AWK-WARD.
HUH...?
WHAT'S THAT S'POSED TO MEAN?
I CAN TELL BECAUSE I WRITE SHOUJO MANGA.
Yes!! Sen-pai...
...is the awkward character who tries to hide his feelings and gets stuck spinning his wheels!!!
DAM-MIT! I WANNA TREAT HER GOOD, BUT I JUST...
HE'S LIKE THIS!!
Let's take a look at him with that in mind!!!
WHAT THE—?
DON'T CLING!!
GURI
GURI (RUB)
GASHI! (GRAB)
BUT I'M REALLY COLD!!
AHHH, SO WARM! SOOOO WARM!!!
MAYBE SENPAI'S THE REALLY CALCULAT-ING TYPE.
RIGHT?
WHICH ONE IS IT?

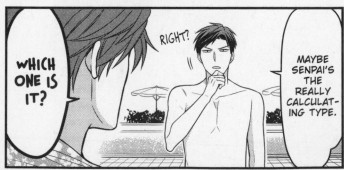

I CAN TELL ①

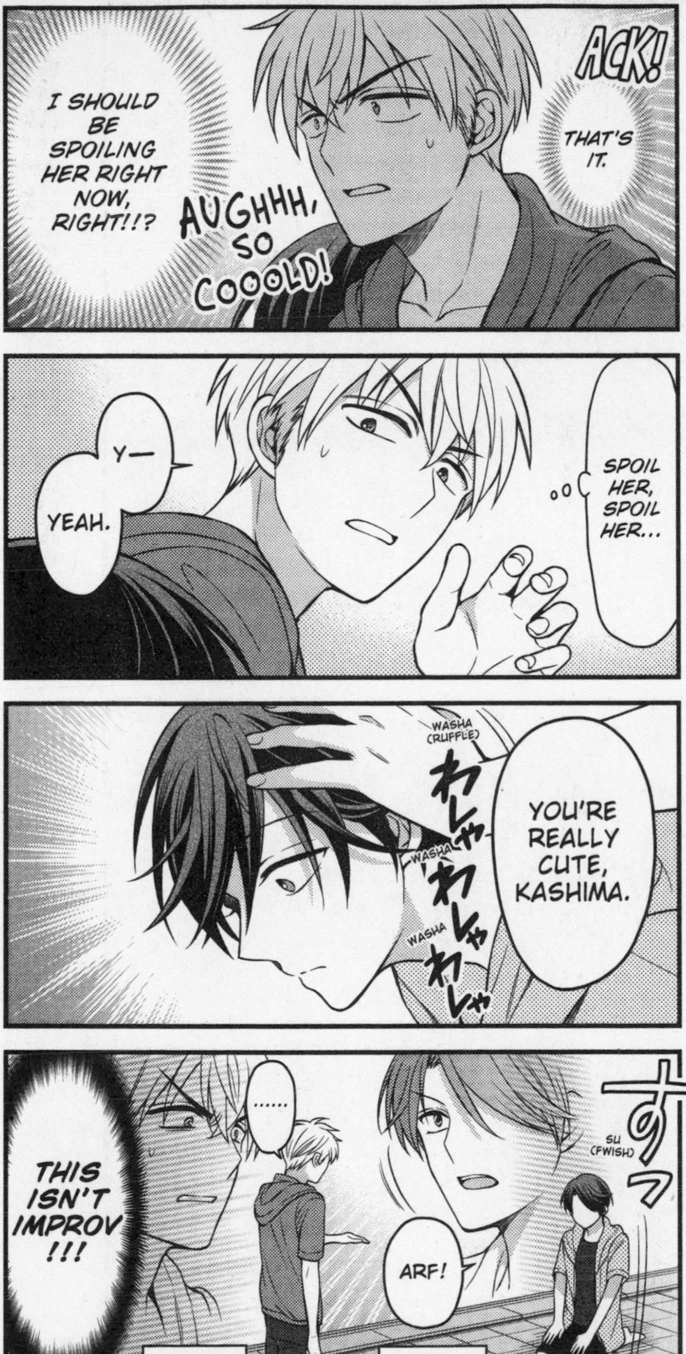
ACK!
THAT'S IT.
I SHOULD BE SPOILING HER RIGHT NOW, RIGHT!!?
AUGHHH, SO COOOLD!
SPOIL HER, SPOIL HER...
Y— YEAH.
YOU'RE REALLY CUTE, KASHIMA.
WASHA (RUFFLE)
わしゃ
WASHA
わしゃ
WASHA
わしゃ
すっ
SU (FWISH)
ARF!
....
THIS ISN'T IMPROV!!!
PET DOG
OWNER

A WELL-TRAINED TRAIT

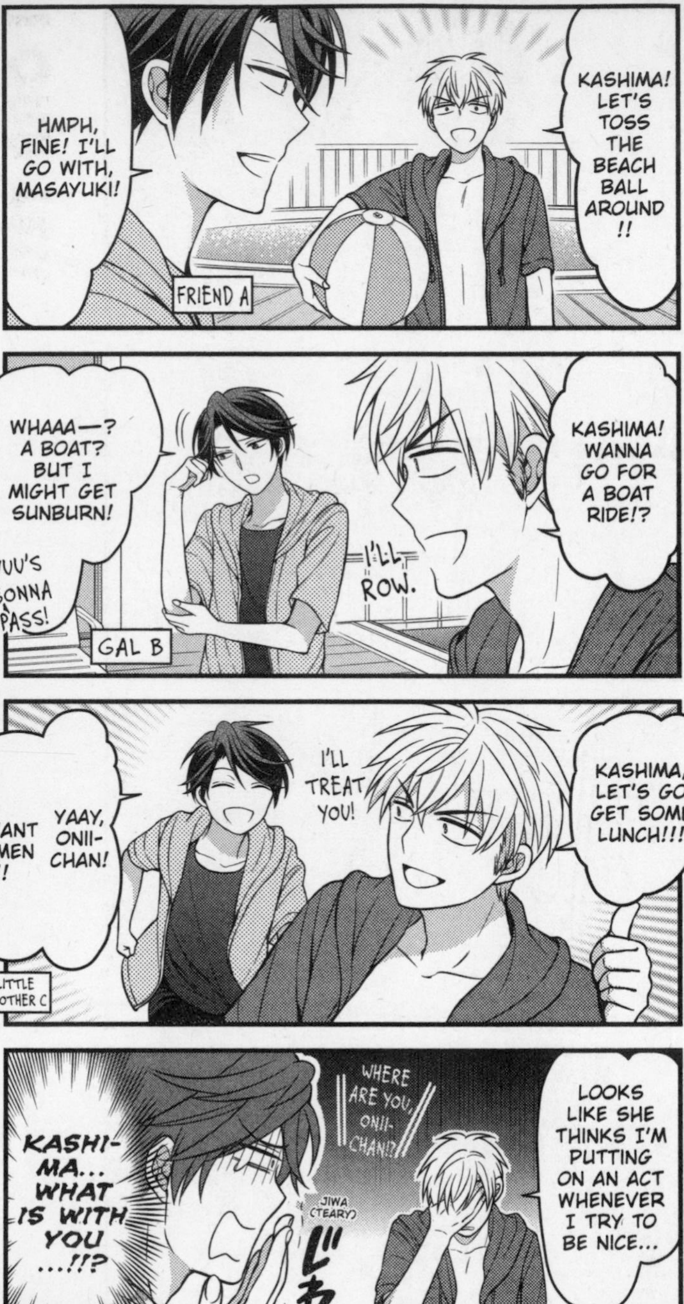

KASHIMA! LET'S TOSS THE BEACH BALL AROUND!!
HMPH, FINE! I'LL GO WITH, MASAYUKI!
FRIEND A
KASHIMA! WANNA GO FOR A BOAT RIDE!?
I'LL ROW.
WHAAA—? A BOAT? BUT I MIGHT GET SUNBURN!
YUU'S GONNA PASS!
GAL B
KASHIMA, LET'S GO GET SOME LUNCH!!!
I'LL TREAT YOU!
YAAY, ONII-CHAN!
I WANT RAMEN !!
LITTLE BROTHER C
LOOKS LIKE SHE THINKS I'M PUTTING ON AN ACT WHENEVER I TRY TO BE NICE...
WHERE ARE YOU, ONII-CHAN!?
JIWA (TEARY)
じわっ…
KASHIMA... WHAT IS WITH YOU ...!!?

I CAN TELL ②

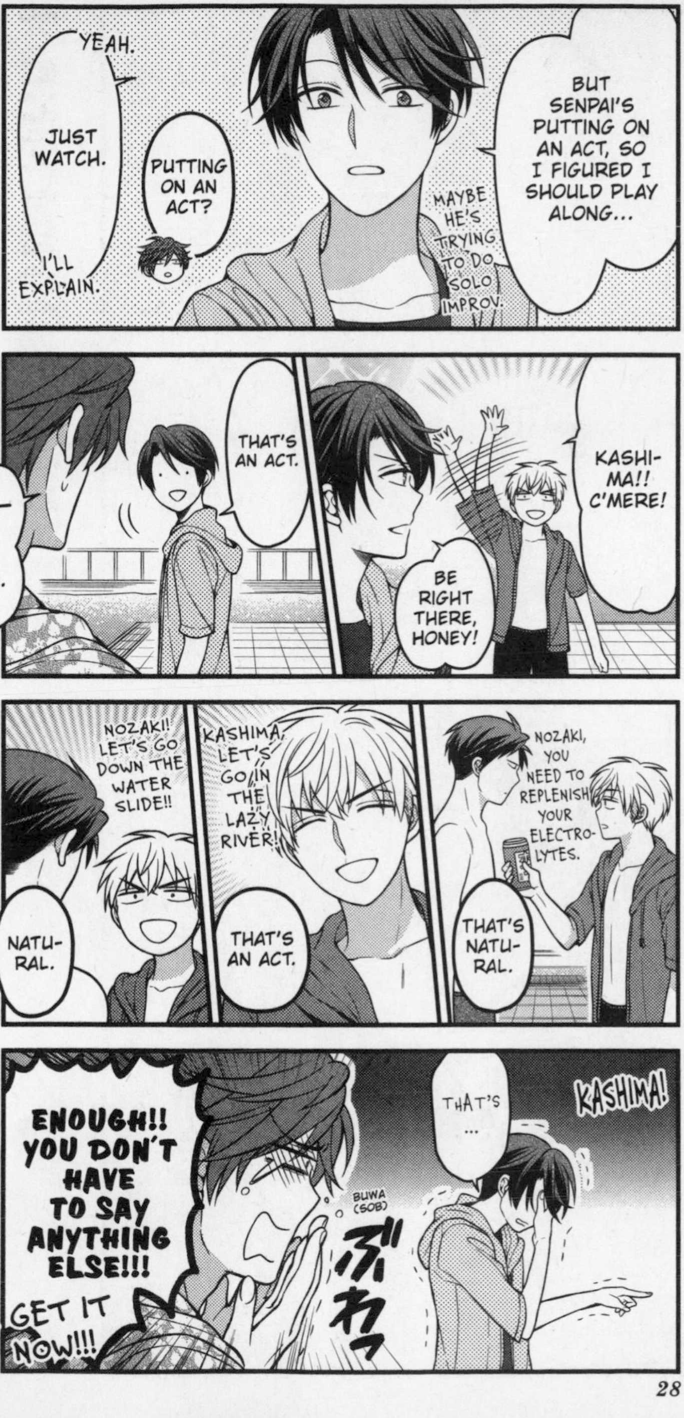
BUT SENPAI'S PUTTING ON AN ACT, SO I FIGURED I SHOULD PLAY ALONG...
MAYBE HE'S TRYING TO DO SOLO IMPROV.
PUTTING ON AN ACT?
YEAH.
JUST WATCH.
I'LL EXPLAIN.
KASHIMA!! C'MERE!
BE RIGHT THERE, HONEY!
THAT'S AN ACT.
O—
OH.
NOZAKI, YOU NEED TO REPLENISH YOUR ELECTROLYTES.
THAT'S NATURAL.
KASHIMA, LET'S GO IN THE LAZY RIVER!
THAT'S AN ACT.
NOZAKI! LET'S GO DOWN THE WATER SLIDE!!
NATURAL.
KASHIMA!
THAT'S ...
BUWA (SOB)
ENOUGH!! YOU DON'T HAVE TO SAY ANYTHING ELSE!!!
I GET IT NOW!!!

I CAN TELL ③

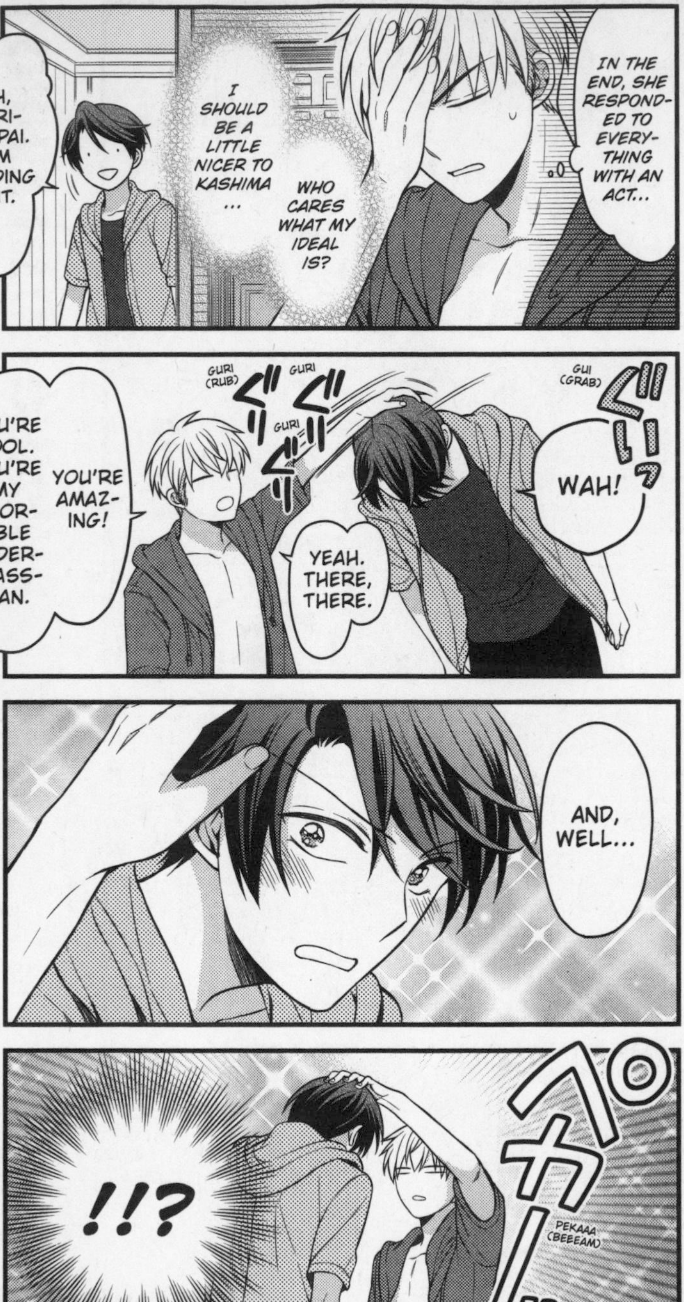
IN THE END, SHE RESPONDED TO EVERYTHING WITH AN ACT...
WHO CARES WHAT MY IDEAL IS?
I SHOULD BE A LITTLE NICER TO KASHIMA...
OH, HORI-SENPAI. I'M HEADING OUT.
ぐいっ
GUI (GRAB)
WAH!
ぐり
GURI (RUB)
ぐり
GURI
ぐり
GURI
YEAH. THERE, THERE.
YOU'RE AMAZING!
YOU'RE COOL. YOU'RE MY ADORABLE UNDERCLASSMAN.
AND, WELL...
ペカーッ
PEKAAA (BEEEAM)
!!?

SENPAI'S TIRED AGAIN

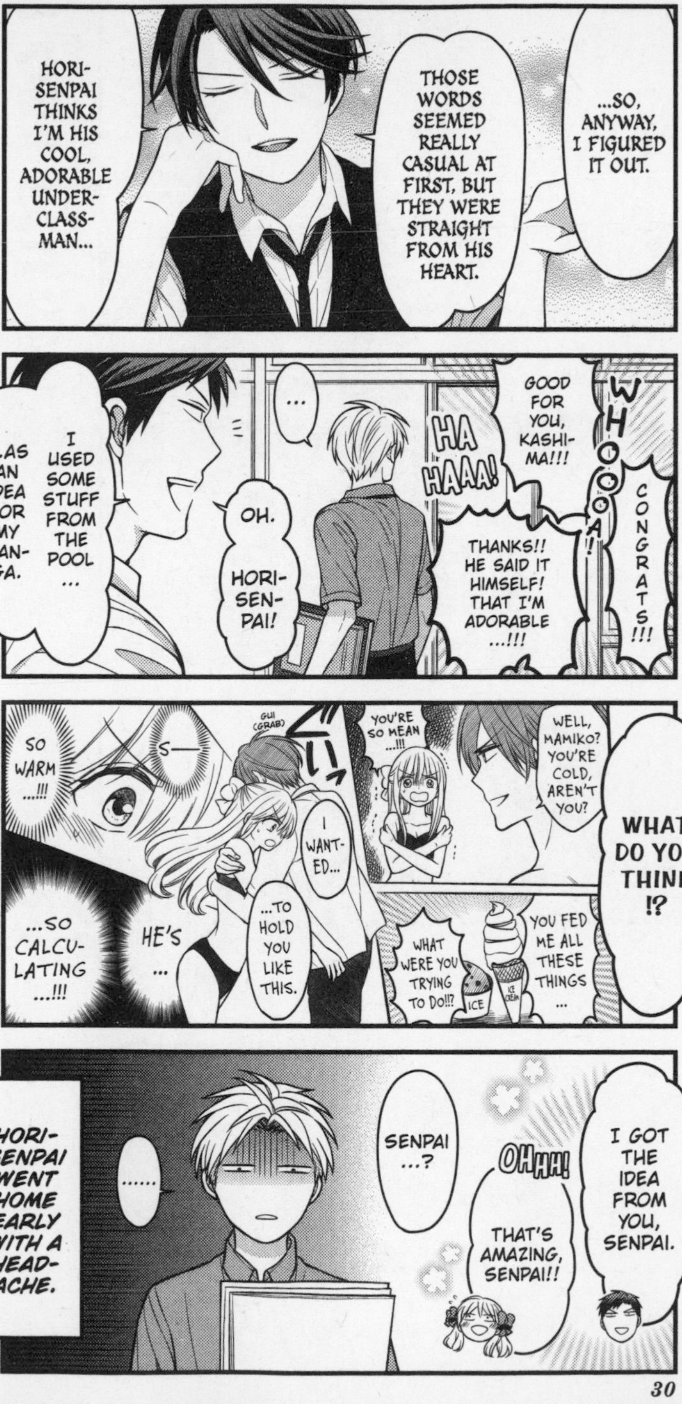
...SO, ANYWAY, I FIGURED IT OUT.
THOSE WORDS SEEMED REALLY CASUAL AT FIRST, BUT THEY WERE STRAIGHT FROM HIS HEART.
HORI-SENPAI THINKS I'M HIS COOL, ADORABLE UNDERCLASSMAN...
CONGRATS!!!
WHOOOOA!!
GOOD FOR YOU, KASHIMA!!!
HA HAAA!
THANKS!! HE SAID IT HIMSELF! THAT I'M ADORABLE ...!!!
...
OH.
HORI-SENPAI!
I USED SOME STUFF FROM THE POOL...
...AS AN IDEA FOR MY MANGA.
WHAT DO YOU THINK!?
WELL, MAMIKO? YOU'RE COLD, AREN'T YOU?
YOU FED ME ALL THESE THINGS...
YOU'RE SO MEAN...!!!
WHAT WERE YOU TRYING TO DO!!?
ICE CREAM
ICE
GUI (GRAB)
I WANTED...
...TO HOLD YOU LIKE THIS.
S—
SO WARM...!!!
HE'S...
...SO CALCULATING...!!!
I GOT THE IDEA FROM YOU, SENPAI.
OHHH!
THAT'S AMAZING, SENPAI!!
SENPAI...?
......
HORI-SENPAI WENT HOME EARLY WITH A HEADACHE.

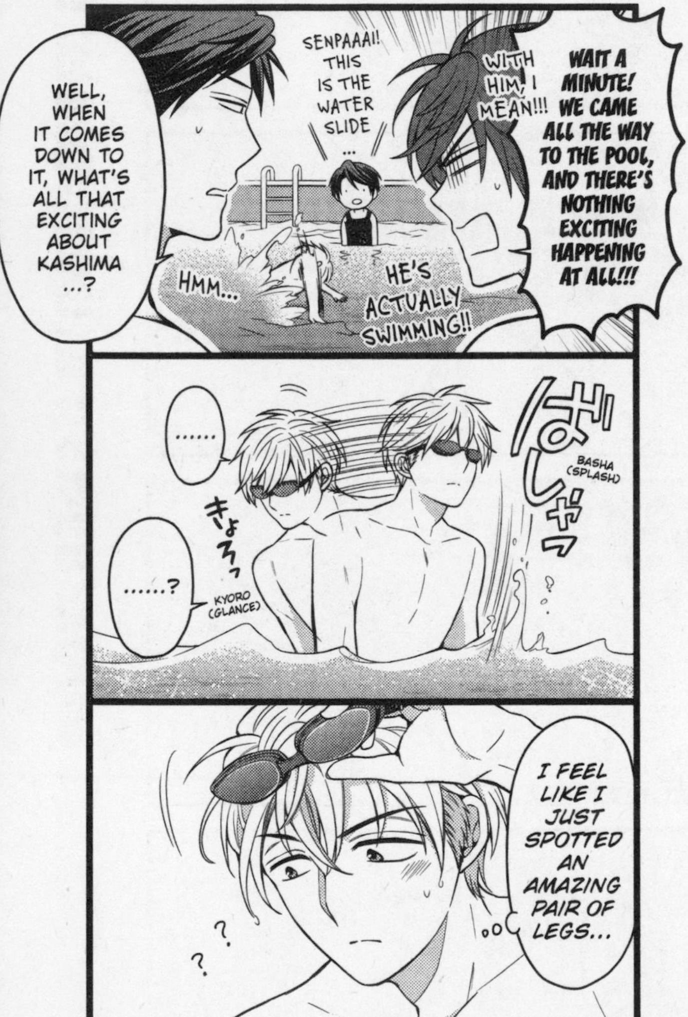
WAIT A MINUTE! WE CAME ALL THE WAY TO THE POOL, AND THERE'S NOTHING EXCITING HAPPENING AT ALL!!!
WITH HIM, I MEAN!!!
SENPAAAI! THIS IS THE WATER SLIDE ...
HE'S ACTUALLY SWIMMING!!
HMM...
WELL, WHEN IT COMES DOWN TO IT, WHAT'S ALL THAT EXCITING ABOUT KASHIMA ...?
ばしゃっ
BASHA (SPLASH)
......
きょろっ
KYORO (GLANCE)
......?
I FEEL LIKE I JUST SPOTTED AN AMAZING PAIR OF LEGS...

[Extra]

YOU GUYS WOULDN'T UNDERSTAND

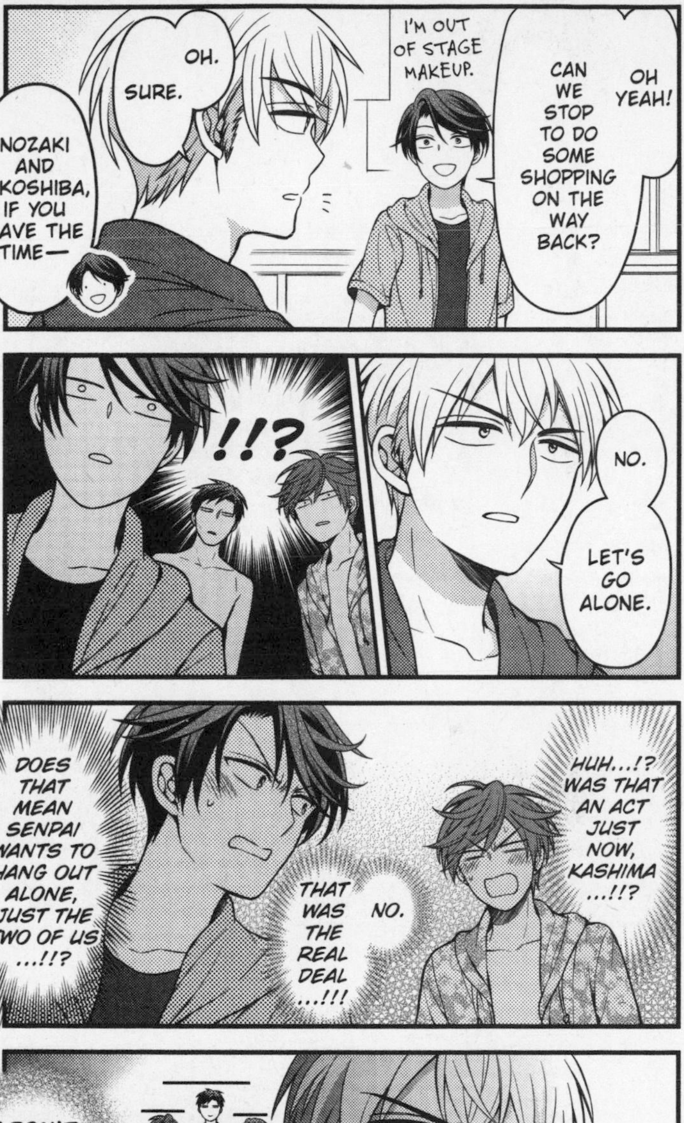
OH YEAH!
CAN WE STOP TO DO SOME SHOPPING ON THE WAY BACK?
I'M OUT OF STAGE MAKEUP.
OH.
SURE.
NOZAKI AND MIKOSHIBA, IF YOU HAVE THE TIME—
NO.
LET'S GO ALONE.
!!?
HUH...!? WAS THAT AN ACT JUST NOW, KASHIMA...!!?
NO.
THAT WAS THE REAL DEAL...!!!
DOES THAT MEAN SENPAI WANTS TO HANG OUT ALONE, JUST THE TWO OF US...!!?
I DON'T WANNA WALK AROUND SUR-ROUNDED BY A BUNCH OF GIANTS...

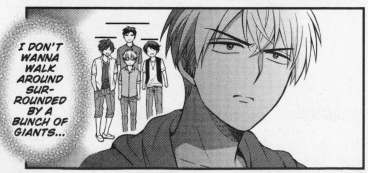

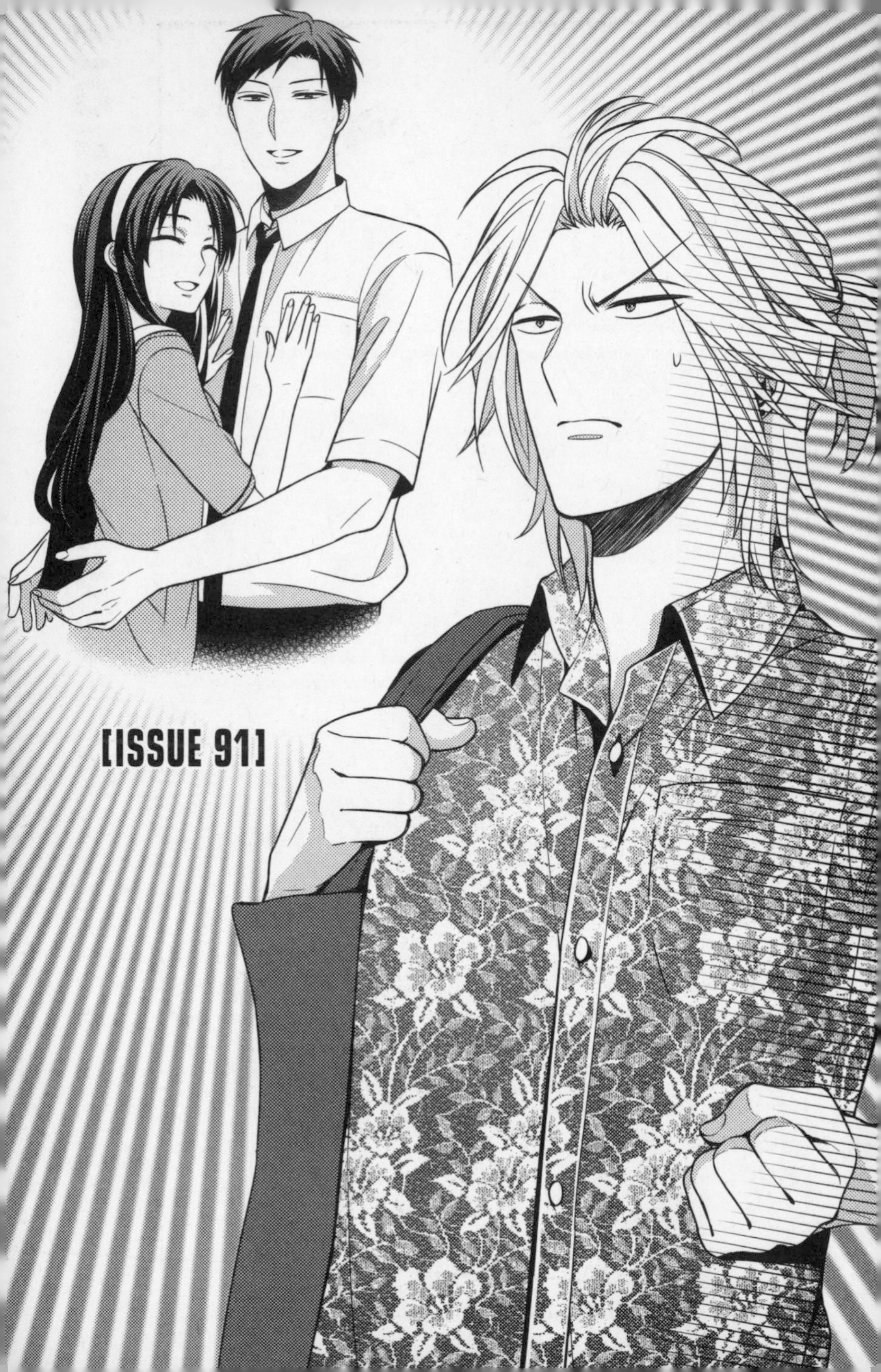
[ISSUE 91]

THE WORST SITUATION

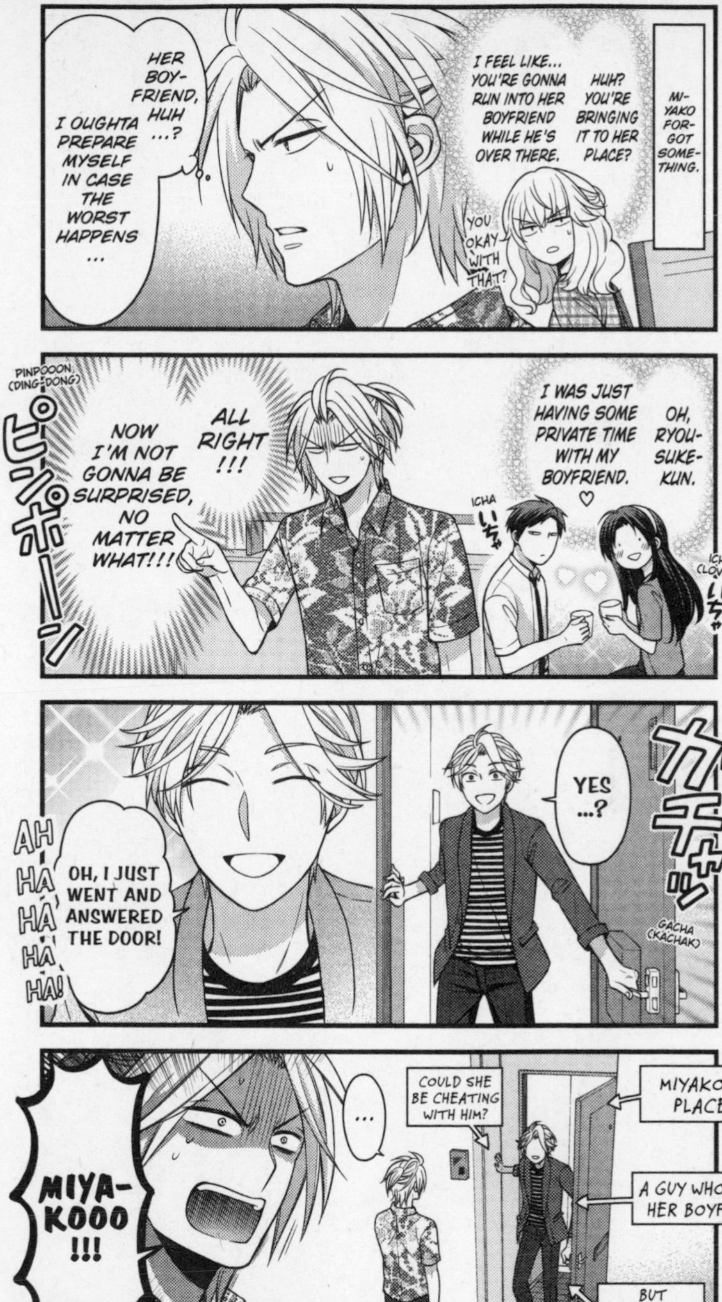

MIYAKO FORGOT SOMETHING.
HUH? YOU'RE BRINGING IT TO HER PLACE?
I FEEL LIKE... YOU'RE GONNA RUN INTO HER BOYFRIEND WHILE HE'S OVER THERE.
YOU OKAY WITH THAT?
HER BOYFRIEND, HUH ...?
I OUGHTA PREPARE MYSELF IN CASE THE WORST HAPPENS ...
OH, RYOUSUKE-KUN.
I WAS JUST HAVING SOME PRIVATE TIME WITH MY BOYFRIEND. ♡
いちゃ
ICHA (LOVEY)
いちゃ
ICHA
ALL RIGHT !!!
NOW I'M NOT GONNA BE SURPRISED, NO MATTER WHAT!!!
ピンポーン
PINPOOON (DING-DONG)
ガチャッ
GACHA (KACHAK)
YES ...?
OH, I JUST WENT AND ANSWERED THE DOOR!
AH HA HA HA HA!
MIYAKO'S PLACE
A GUY WHO'S NOT HER BOYFRIEND
BUT SEEMS LIKE A BOYFRIEND
COULD SHE BE CHEATING WITH HIM?
...
MIYA-KOOO !!!

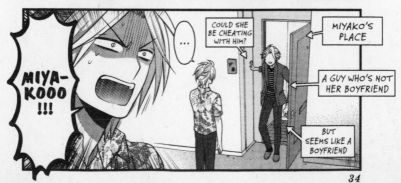

MAENO-SAN IS TALENTED

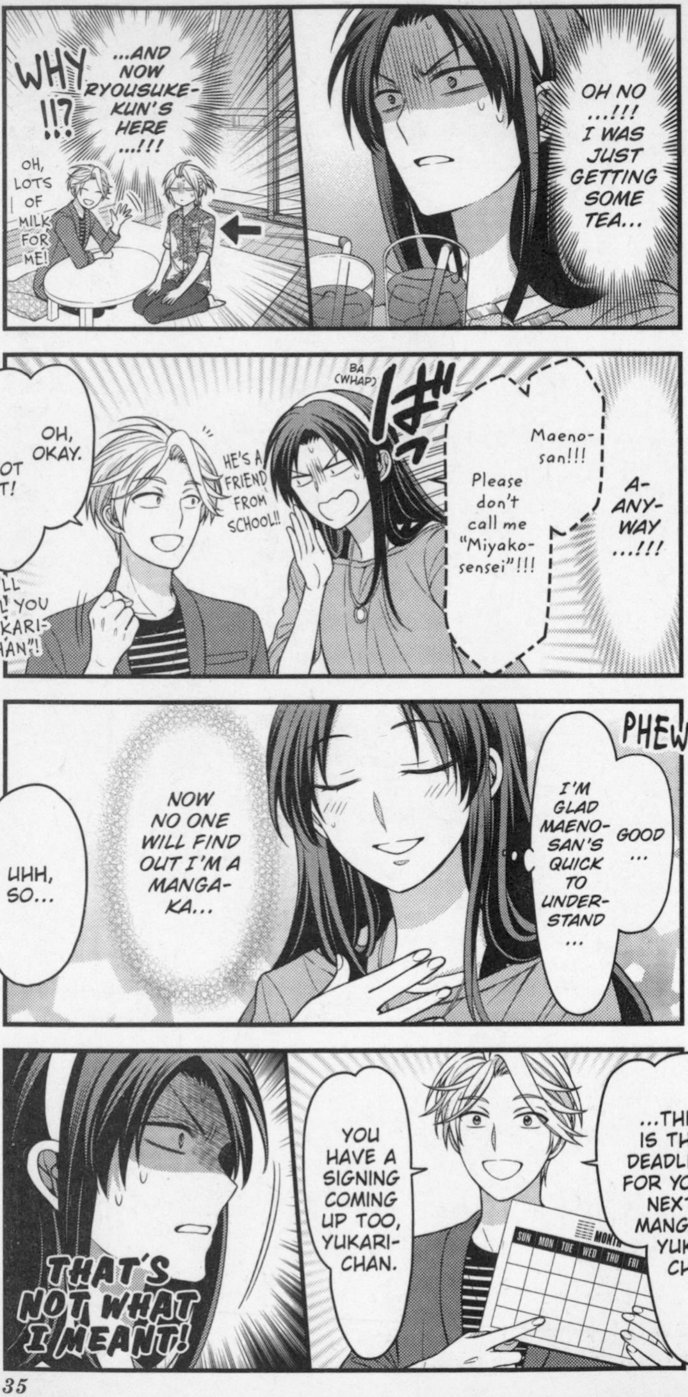
OH NO ...!!! I WAS JUST GETTING SOME TEA...
...AND NOW RYOUSUKE-KUN'S HERE ...!!!
WHY !!?
OH, LOTS OF MILK FOR ME!
A-ANYWAY ...!!!
Maeno-san!!! Please don't call me "Miyako-sensei"!!!
BA (WHAP)
HE'S A FRIEND FROM SCHOOL!!
OH, OKAY. GOT IT!
I'LL CALL YOU "YUKARI-CHAN"!
PHEW...
GOOD...
I'M GLAD MAENO-SAN'S QUICK TO UNDERSTAND...
NOW NO ONE WILL FIND OUT I'M A MANGAKA...
UHH, SO...
...THIS IS THE DEADLINE FOR YOUR NEXT MANGA, YUKARI-CHAN.
MONTH
SUN MON TUE WED THU FRI
YOU HAVE A SIGNING COMING UP TOO, YUKARI-CHAN.
THAT'S NOT WHAT I MEANT!

MANGA-KA AND CHEATER

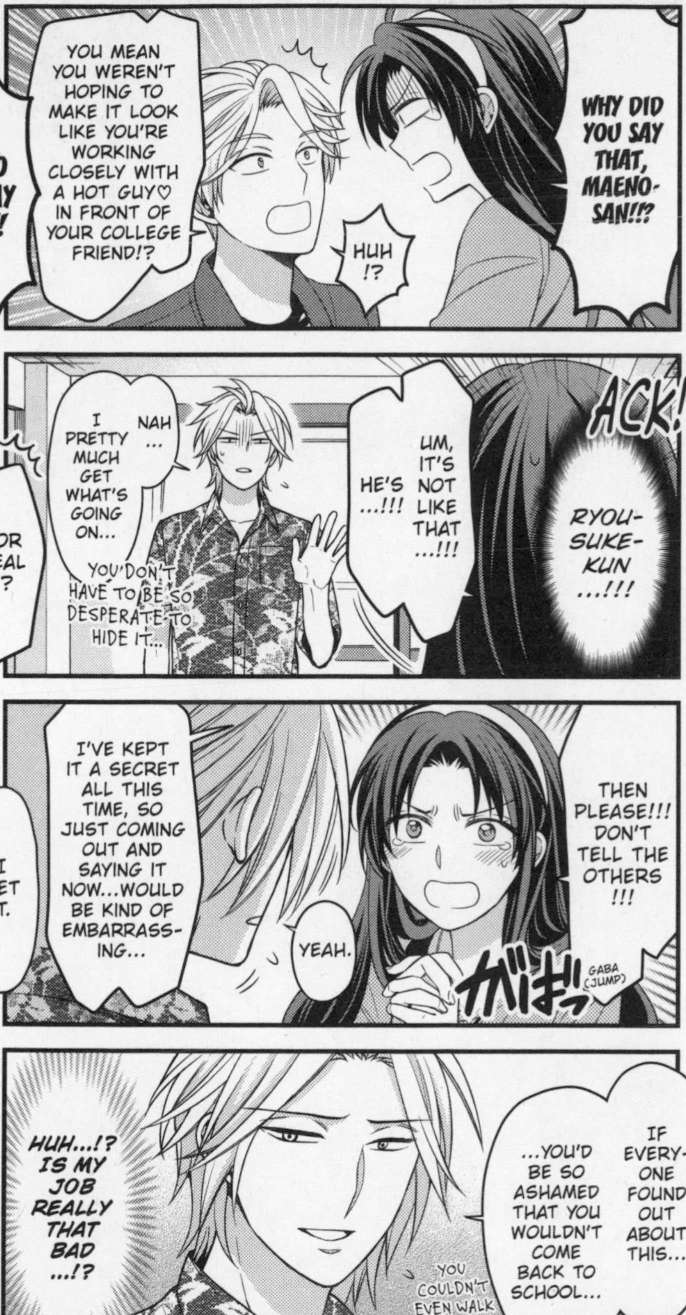

WHY DID YOU SAY THAT, MAENO-SAN!!?
HUH!?
YOU MEAN YOU WEREN'T HOPING TO MAKE IT LOOK LIKE YOU'RE WORKING CLOSELY WITH A HOT GUY♡ IN FRONT OF YOUR COLLEGE FRIEND!?
NO WAY!!!
ACK!
RYOU-SUKE-KUN...!!!
UM, IT'S NOT LIKE THAT...!!!
HE'S...!!!
NAH...
I PRETTY MUCH GET WHAT'S GOING ON...
YOU DON'T HAVE TO BE SO DESPERATE TO HIDE IT...
FOR REAL!?
THEN PLEASE!!! DON'T TELL THE OTHERS!!!
がばっ
GABA (JUMP)
YEAH.
I'VE KEPT IT A SECRET ALL THIS TIME, SO JUST COMING OUT AND SAYING IT NOW...WOULD BE KIND OF EMBARRASS-ING...
I GET IT.
IF EVERY-ONE FOUND OUT ABOUT THIS...
...YOU'D BE SO ASHAMED THAT YOU WOULDN'T COME BACK TO SCHOOL...
YOU COULDN'T EVEN WALK DOWN THE HALL.
HUH...!? IS MY JOB REALLY THAT BAD...!?

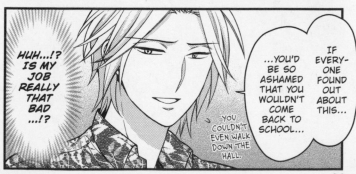

SOME RULE I DON'T KNOW

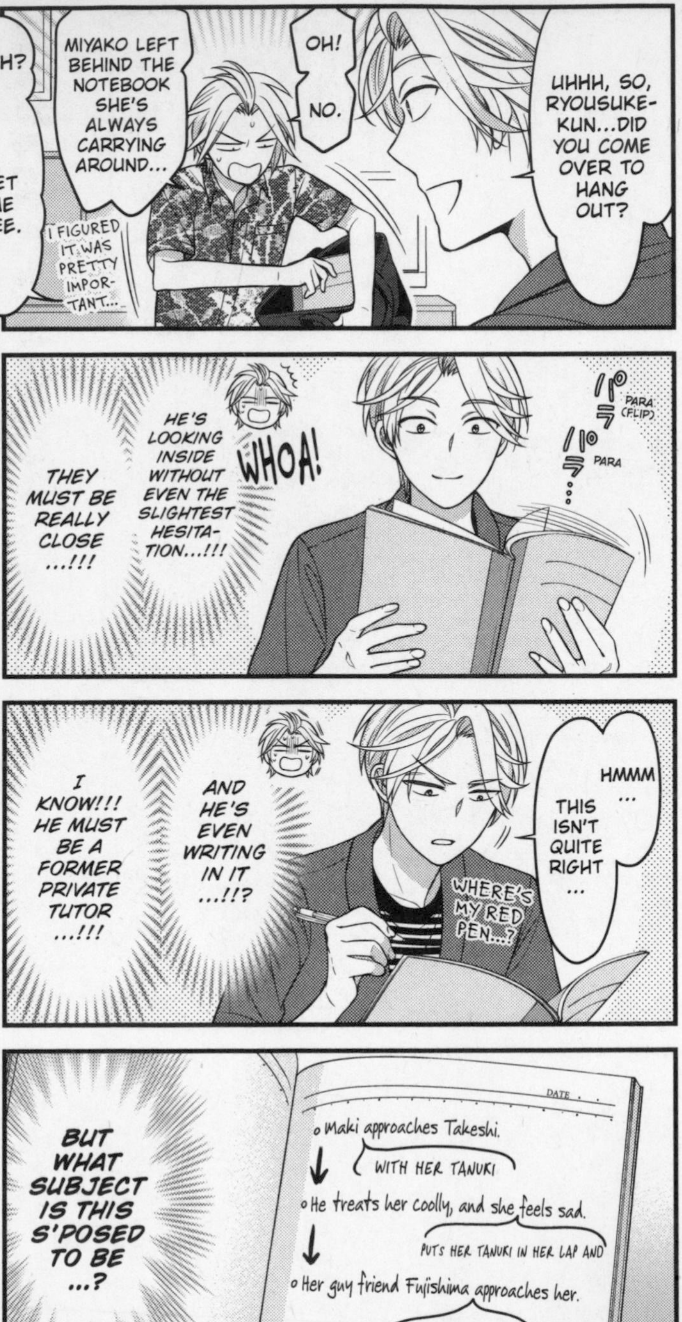
UHHH, SO, RYOUSUKE-KUN...DID YOU COME OVER TO HANG OUT?
OH!
NO.
MIYAKO LEFT BEHIND THE NOTEBOOK SHE'S ALWAYS CARRYING AROUND...
I FIGURED IT WAS PRETTY IMPORTANT...
OHH?
LET ME SEE.
パラ
PARA (FLIP)
パラ...
PARA
WHOA!
HE'S LOOKING INSIDE WITHOUT EVEN THE SLIGHTEST HESITATION...!!!
THEY MUST BE REALLY CLOSE...!!!
HMMM...
THIS ISN'T QUITE RIGHT...
WHERE'S MY RED PEN...?
AND HE'S EVEN WRITING IN IT...!!?
I KNOW!!! HE MUST BE A FORMER PRIVATE TUTOR...!!!
DATE
○Maki approaches Takeshi.
WITH HER TANUKI
○He treats her coolly, and she feels sad.
PUTS HER TANUKI IN HER LAP AND
○Her guy friend Fujishima approaches her.
WITH THREE TANUKI
BUT WHAT SUBJECT IS THIS S'POSED TO BE...?

WHAT'S GOING ON?

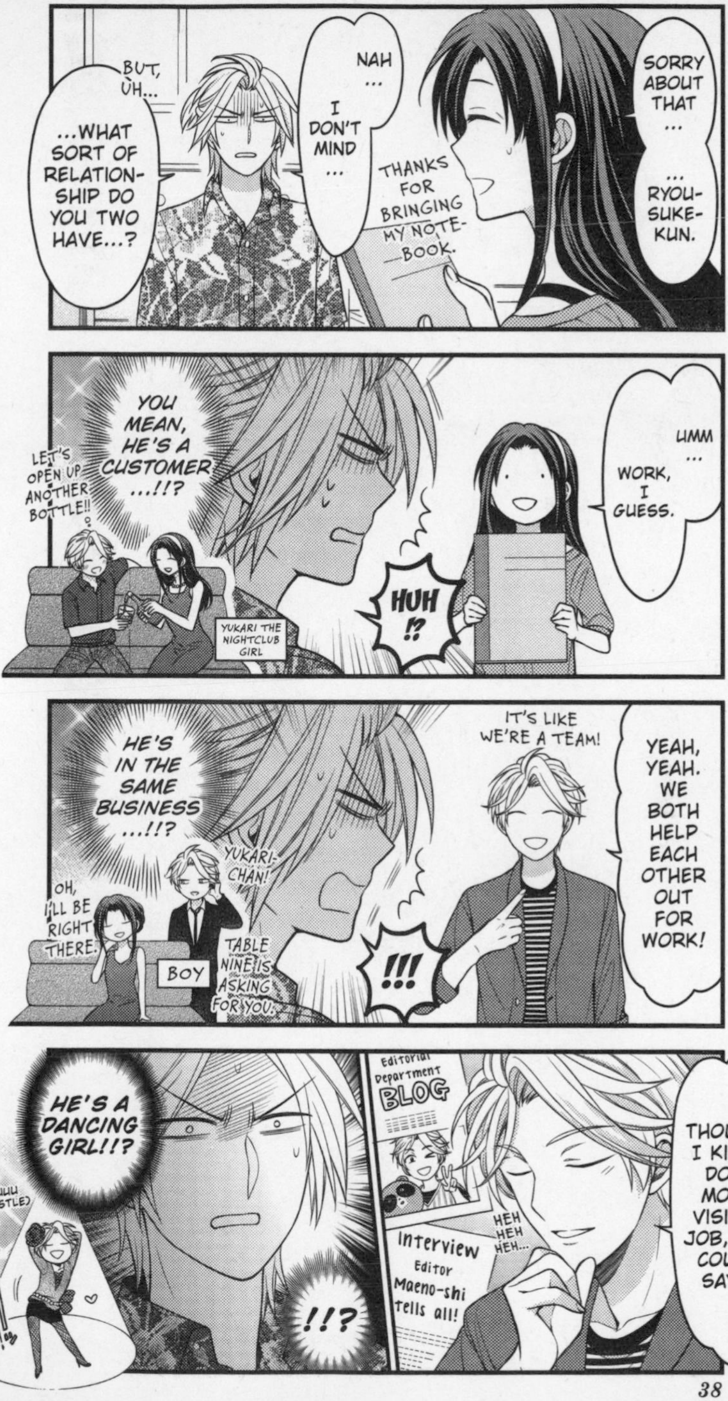
SORRY ABOUT THAT ... ... RYOUSUKE-KUN.
THANKS FOR BRINGING MY NOTEBOOK.
NAH ... I DON'T MIND ...
BUT, UH...
...WHAT SORT OF RELATIONSHIP DO YOU TWO HAVE...?
UMM ... WORK, I GUESS.
HUH!?
YOU MEAN, HE'S A CUSTOMER ...!!?
LET'S OPEN UP ANOTHER BOTTLE!!
YUKARI THE NIGHTCLUB GIRL
YEAH, YEAH. WE BOTH HELP EACH OTHER OUT FOR WORK!
IT'S LIKE WE'RE A TEAM!
!!!
HE'S IN THE SAME BUSINESS ...!!?
YUKARI-CHAN!
TABLE NINE IS ASKING FOR YOU.
OH, I'LL BE RIGHT THERE.
BOY
THOUGH, I KINDA DO A MORE VISIBLE JOB, YOU COULD SAY...
HEH HEH HEH...
Editorial Department BLOG
Interview Editor Maeno-shi tells all!
!!?
HE'S A DANCING GIRL!!?
PYUUU (WHISTLE)
HOO! HOO!

I'M THE ONLY ONE SEEING A FIGHT?

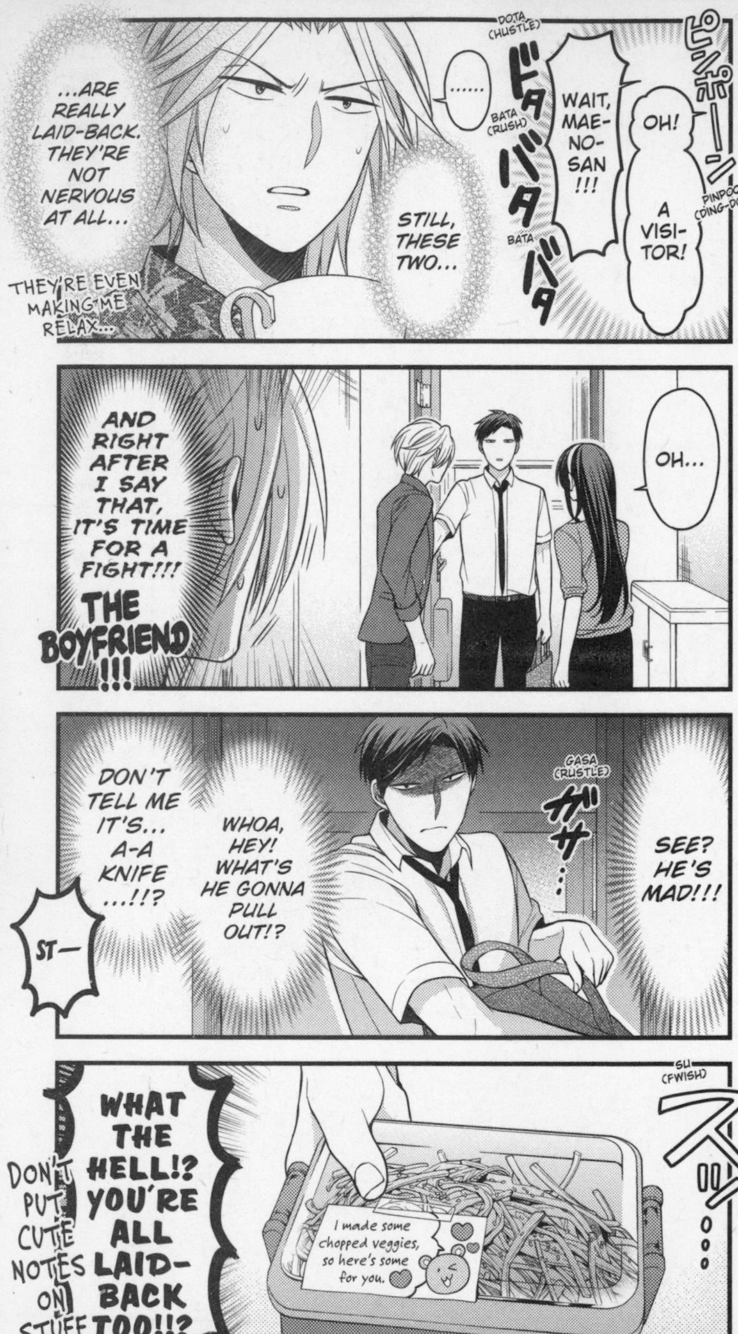
PINPOON (DING-DONG)
OH! A VISITOR!
WAIT, MAE-NO-SAN!!!
BATA (RUSH)
BATA
DOTA (HUSTLE)
......
STILL, THESE TWO...
...ARE REALLY LAID-BACK. THEY'RE NOT NERVOUS AT ALL...
THEY'RE EVEN MAKING ME RELAX...
OH...
AND RIGHT AFTER I SAY THAT, IT'S TIME FOR A FIGHT!!!
THE BOYFRIEND!!!
GASA (RUSTLE)
SEE? HE'S MAD!!!
WHOA, HEY! WHAT'S HE GONNA PULL OUT!?
DON'T TELL ME IT'S... A-A KNIFE ...!!?
ST—
SU (FWISH)
I made some chopped veggies, so here's some for you.
WHAT THE HELL!? YOU'RE ALL LAID-BACK TOO!!?
DON'T PUT CUTE NOTES ON STUFF!!!

A MIXED-UP RELATIONSHIP

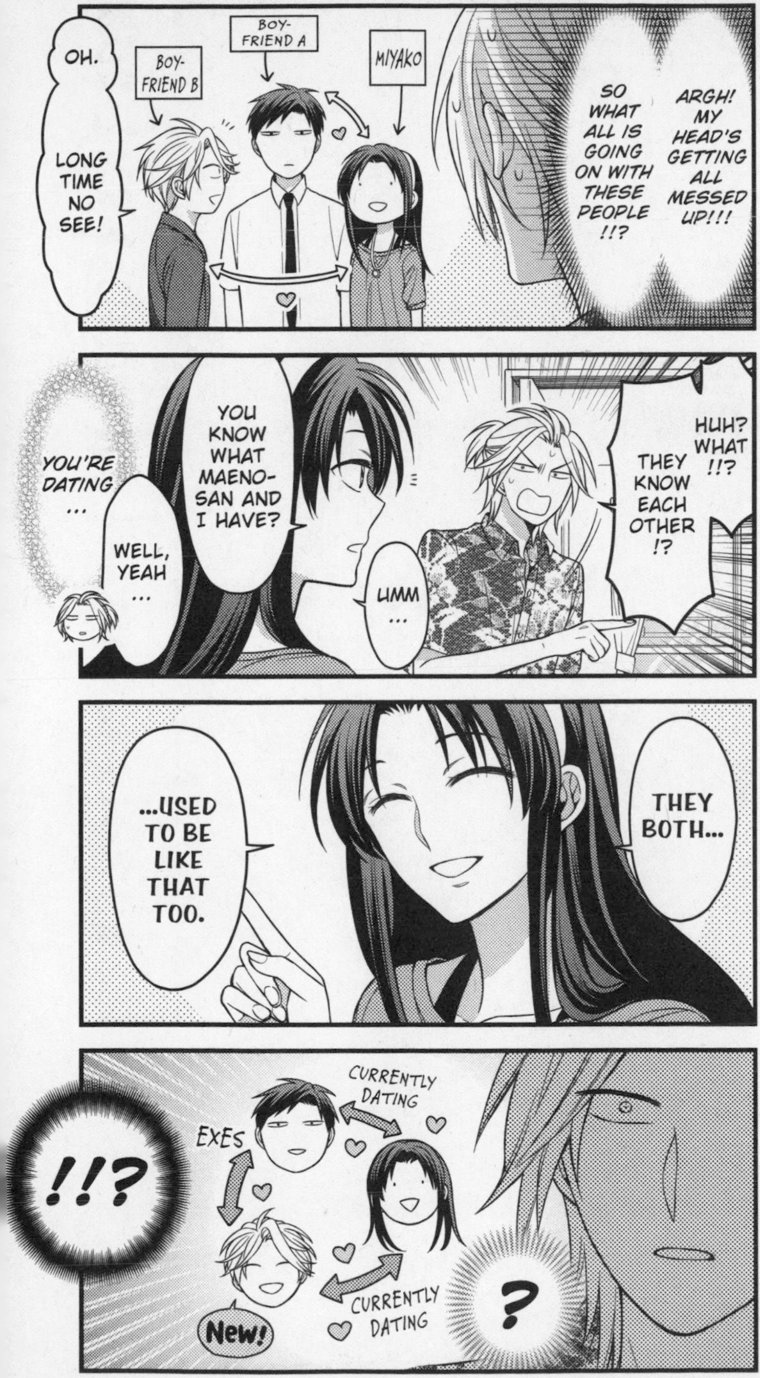
ARGH! MY HEAD'S GETTING ALL MESSED UP!!!
SO WHAT ALL IS GOING ON WITH THESE PEOPLE !!?
MIYAKO
BOY-FRIEND A
BOY-FRIEND B
OH. LONG TIME NO SEE!
HUH? WHAT !!?
THEY KNOW EACH OTHER !?
UMM ...
YOU KNOW WHAT MAENO-SAN AND I HAVE?
WELL, YEAH ...
YOU'RE DATING ...
THEY BOTH...
...USED TO BE LIKE THAT TOO.
?
CURRENTLY DATING
EXES
CURRENTLY DATING
New!
!!?

ANOTHER SHOCK

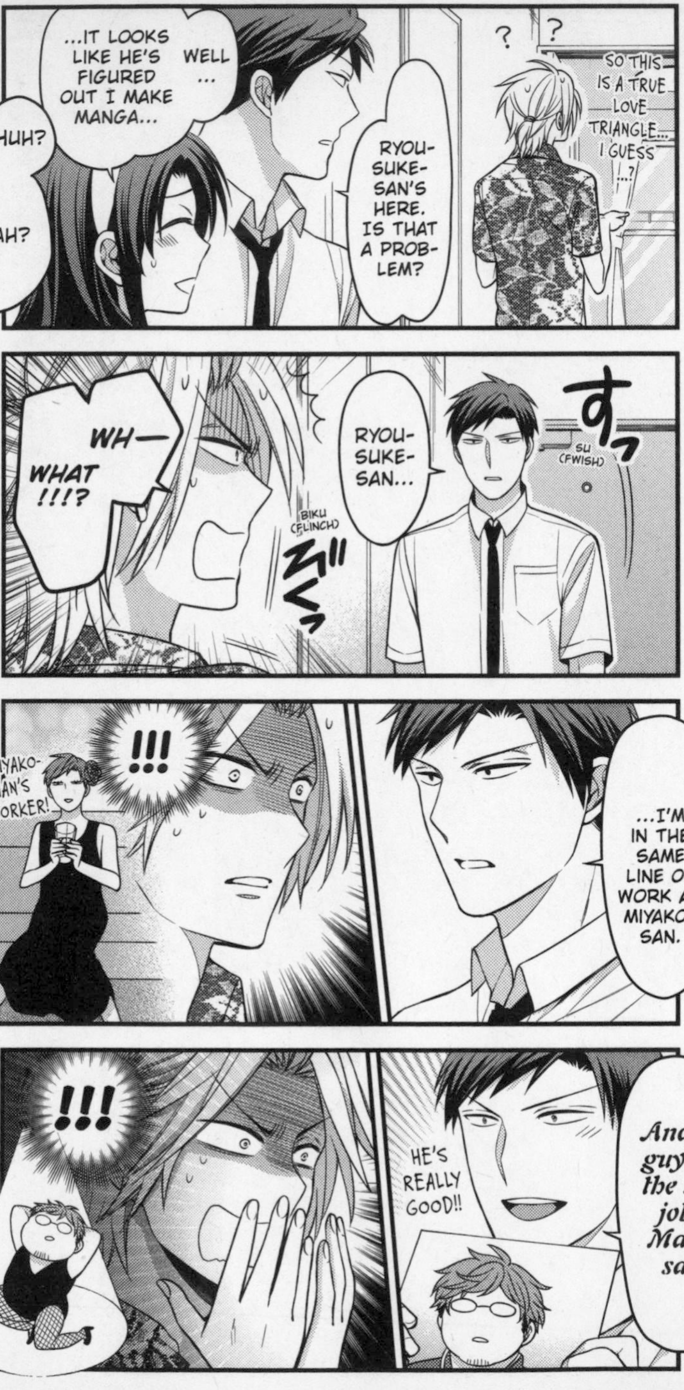
SO THIS IS A TRUE LOVE TRIANGLE... I GUESS ...?
RYOUSUKE-SAN'S HERE. IS THAT A PROBLEM?
WELL...
...IT LOOKS LIKE HE'S FIGURED OUT I MAKE MANGA...
HUH?
YEAH?
すっ
SU (FWISH)
RYOUSUKE-SAN...
BIKU (FLINCH)
WH— WHAT !!!?
THE TRUTH IS...
...I'M IN THE SAME LINE OF WORK AS MIYAKO-SAN.
!!!
I'M MIYAKO-CHAN'S COWORKER!
And this guy does the same job as Maeno-san!!
HE'S REALLY GOOD!!
!!!

HE'S VERY CONFUSED!

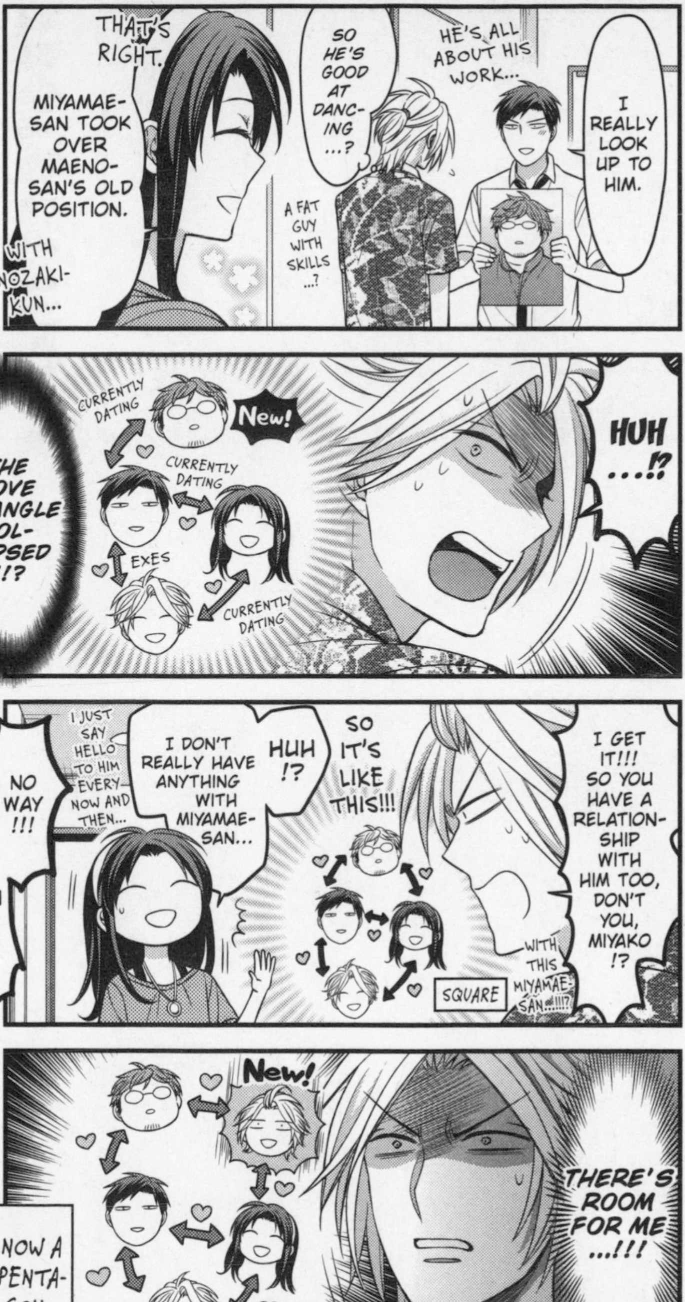
I REALLY LOOK UP TO HIM.
HE'S ALL ABOUT HIS WORK...
SO HE'S GOOD AT DANCING...?
A FAT GUY WITH SKILLS...?
THAT'S RIGHT.
MIYAMAE-SAN TOOK OVER MAENO-SAN'S OLD POSITION.
WITH NOZAKI-KUN...
HUH...!?
New!
CURRENTLY DATING
CURRENTLY DATING
EXES
CURRENTLY DATING
THE LOVE TRIANGLE COL-LAPSED!!?
I GET IT!!! SO YOU HAVE A RELATIONSHIP WITH HIM TOO, DON'T YOU, MIYAKO!?
WITH THIS MIYAMAE-SAN...!!!?
SO IT'S LIKE THIS!!!
SQUARE
HUH!?
I DON'T REALLY HAVE ANYTHING WITH MIYAMAE-SAN...
I JUST SAY HELLO TO HIM EVERY NOW AND THEN...
NO WAY!!!
THEN...!
THERE'S ROOM FOR ME...!!!
New!
NOW A PENTAGON...

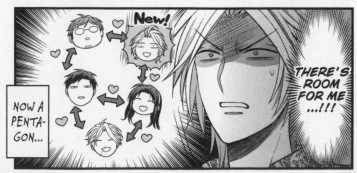

THE IMPORTANT MEN

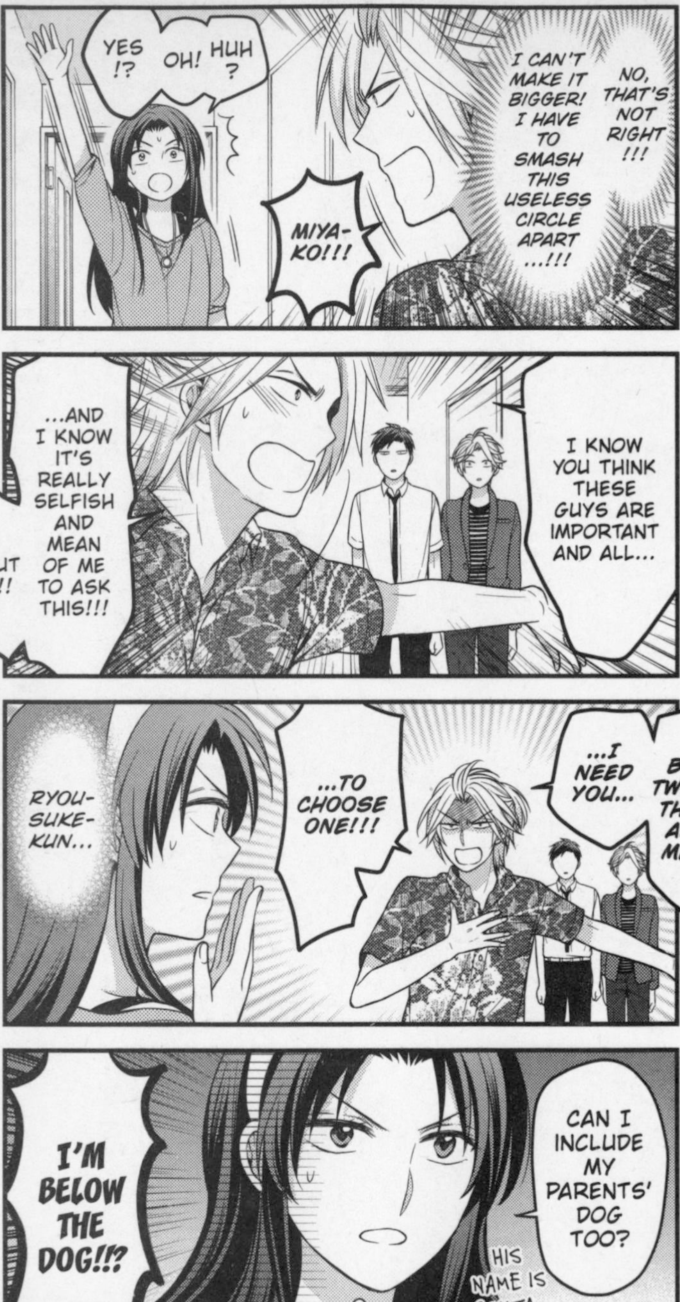
NO, THAT'S NOT RIGHT!!!
I CAN'T MAKE IT BIGGER! I HAVE TO SMASH THIS USELESS CIRCLE APART ...!!!
MIYA-KO!!!
HUH?
OH!
YES!?
I KNOW YOU THINK THESE GUYS ARE IMPORTANT AND ALL...
...AND I KNOW IT'S REALLY SELFISH AND MEAN OF ME TO ASK THIS!!!
BUT!!!
BE-TWEEN THEM AND ME...
...I NEED YOU...
...TO CHOOSE ONE!!!
RYOU-SUKE-KUN...
CAN I INCLUDE MY PARENTS' DOG TOO?
HIS NAME IS GONTA...
I'M BELOW THE DOG!!?

BUT YOU WERE SO LOVEY-DOVEY

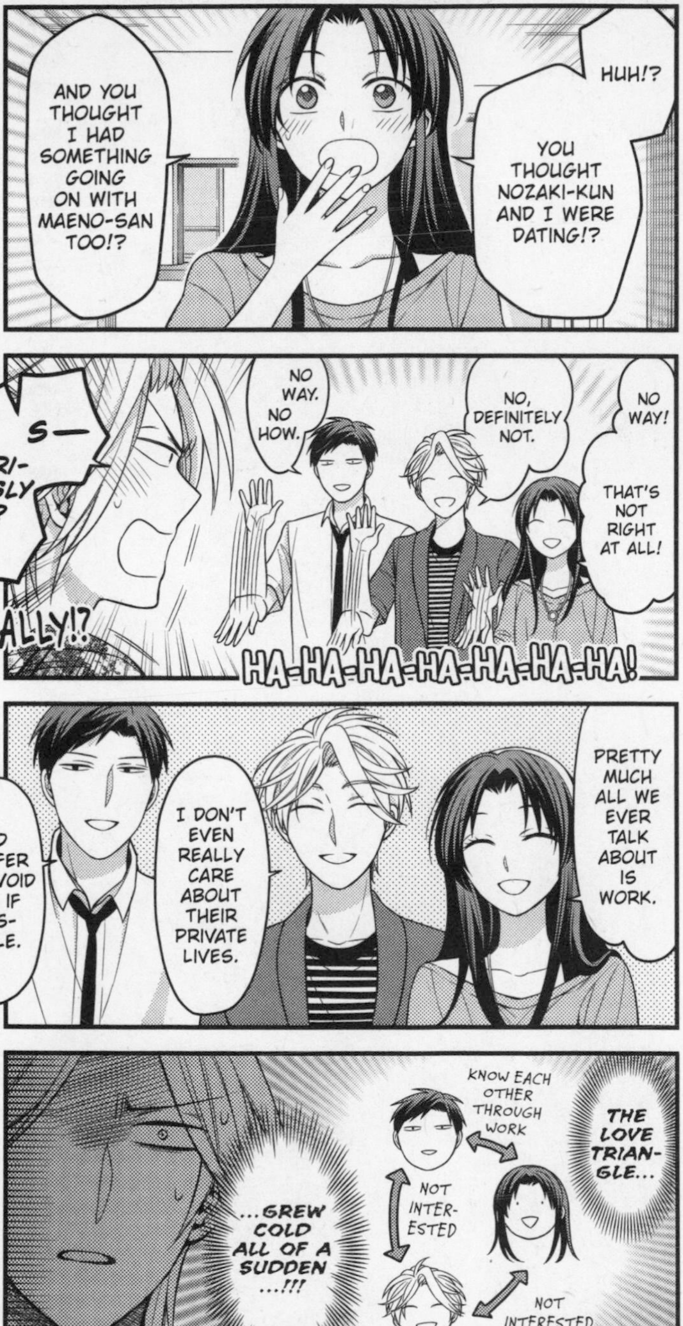
HUH!?
YOU THOUGHT NOZAKI-KUN AND I WERE DATING!?
AND YOU THOUGHT I HAD SOMETHING GOING ON WITH MAENO-SAN TOO!?
NO WAY!
THAT'S NOT RIGHT AT ALL!
NO, DEFINITELY NOT.
NO WAY. NO HOW.
S— SERI-OUSLY!?
REALLY!?
HA-HA-HA-HA-HA-HA-HA!
PRETTY MUCH ALL WE EVER TALK ABOUT IS WORK.
I DON'T EVEN REALLY CARE ABOUT THEIR PRIVATE LIVES.
I'D PREFER TO AVOID HIM IF POS-SIBLE.
THE LOVE TRIAN-GLE...
KNOW EACH OTHER THROUGH WORK
NOT INTER-ESTED
NOT INTERESTED
...GREW COLD ALL OF A SUDDEN ...!!!

THE UNCORRECTED MISUNDERSTANDING

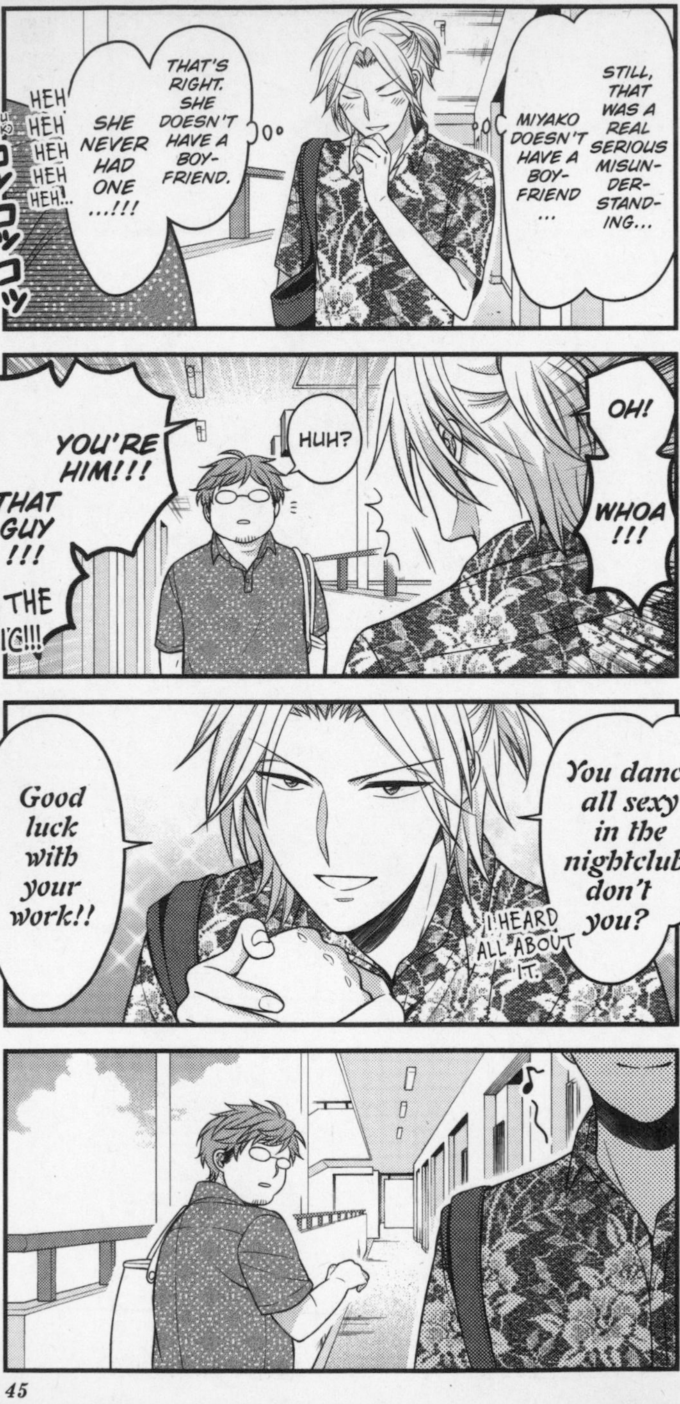
STILL, THAT WAS A REAL SERIOUS MISUNDER-STANDING...
MIYAKO DOESN'T HAVE A BOY-FRIEND...
THAT'S RIGHT. SHE DOESN'T HAVE A BOY-FRIEND.
SHE NEVER HAD ONE ...!!!
HEH HEH HEH HEH HEH!...
コッコッコッ
KOTSU (CLACK)
KOTSU
KOTSU
OH!
WHOA !!!
HUH?
YOU'RE HIM!!!
THAT GUY !!!
IN THE PIC!!!
You dance all sexy in the nightclub, don't you?
I HEARD ALL ABOUT IT.
Good luck with your work!!

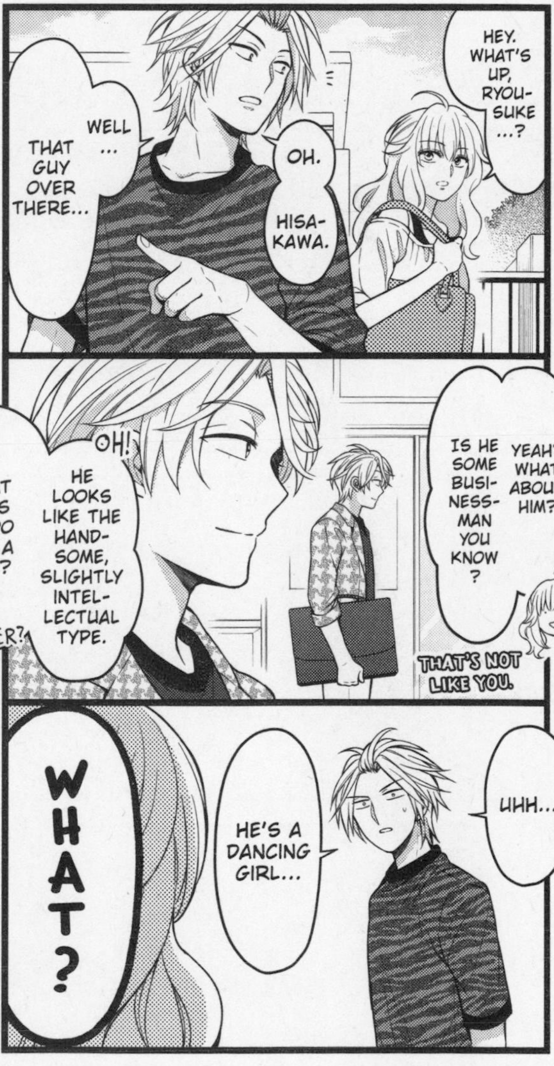
HEY. WHAT'S UP, RYOU-SUKE ...?
OH.
HISA-KAWA.
WELL ... THAT GUY OVER THERE...
YEAH? WHAT ABOUT HIM?
IS HE SOME BUSI-NESS-MAN YOU KNOW ?
THAT'S NOT LIKE YOU.
OH!
HE LOOKS LIKE THE HAND-SOME, SLIGHTLY INTEL-LECTUAL TYPE.
WHAT DOES HE DO FOR A JOB?
HE A DESIGNER?
UHH...
HE'S A DANCING GIRL...
WHAT?

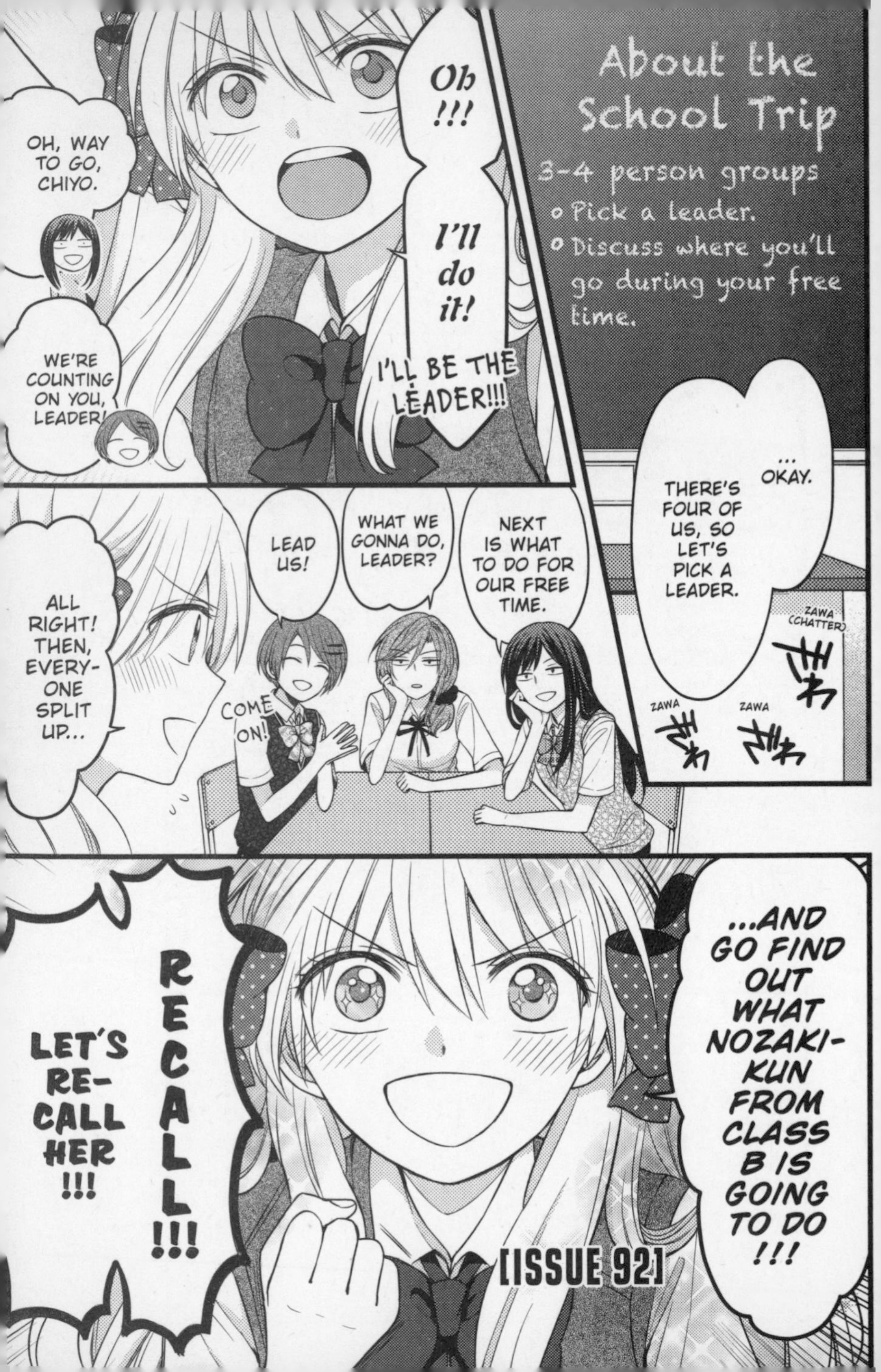
About the School Trip
3-4 person groups
o Pick a leader.
o Discuss where you'll go during your free time.
... OKAY.
THERE'S FOUR OF US, SO LET'S PICK A LEADER.
ZAWA (CHATTER)
ZAWA
ZAWA
Oh !!!
I'll do it!
I'LL BE THE LEADER!!!
OH, WAY TO GO, CHIYO.
WE'RE COUNTING ON YOU, LEADER!
NEXT IS WHAT TO DO FOR OUR FREE TIME.
WHAT WE GONNA DO, LEADER?
LEAD US!
COME ON!
ALL RIGHT! THEN, EVERY-ONE SPLIT UP...
...AND GO FIND OUT WHAT NOZAKI-KUN FROM CLASS B IS GOING TO DO !!!
[ISSUE 92]
RECALL!!!
LET'S RE-CALL HER !!!

MY LOVESTRUCK FRIEND

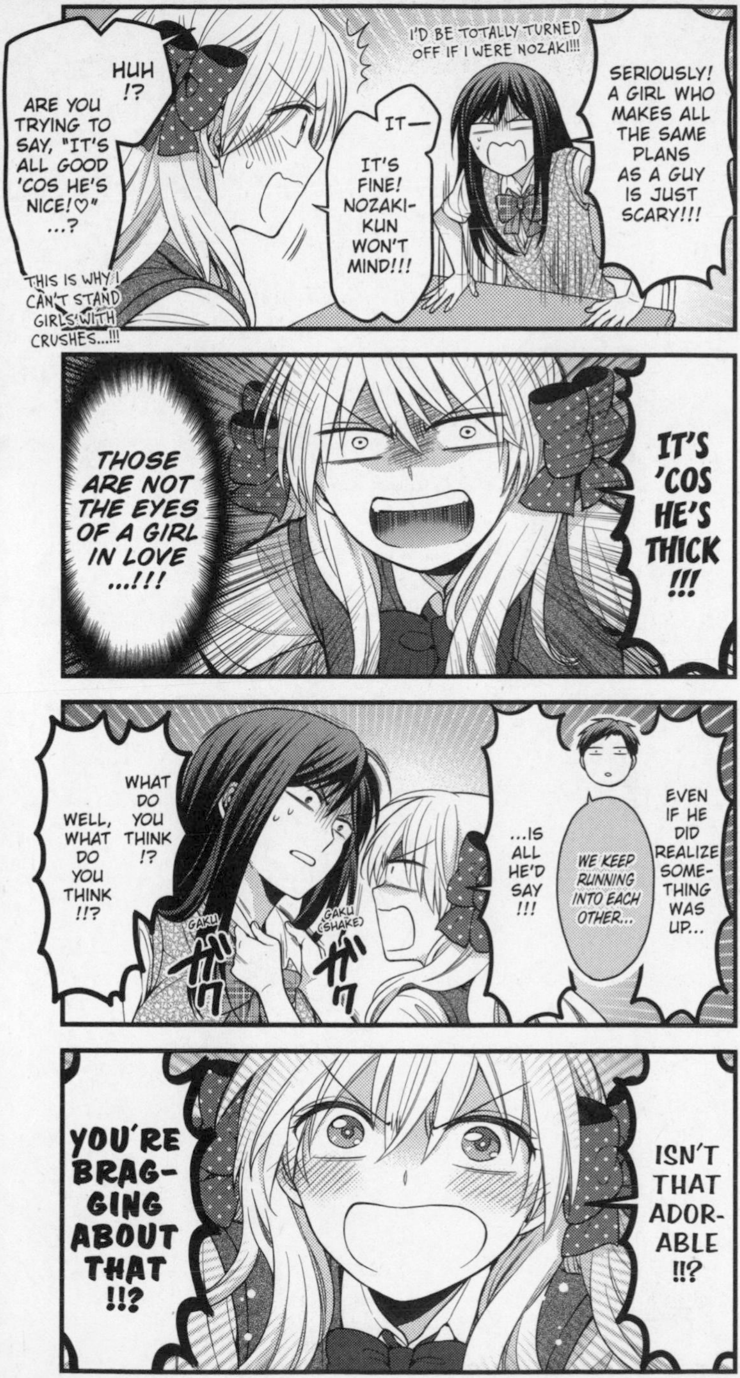

SERIOUSLY! A GIRL WHO MAKES ALL THE SAME PLANS AS A GUY IS JUST SCARY!!!
I'D BE TOTALLY TURNED OFF IF I WERE NOZAKI!!!
IT—
IT'S FINE! NOZAKI-KUN WON'T MIND!!!
HUH!?
ARE YOU TRYING TO SAY, "IT'S ALL GOOD 'COS HE'S NICE!♡" ...?
THIS IS WHY I CAN'T STAND GIRLS WITH CRUSHES...!!!
IT'S 'COS HE'S THICK!!!
THOSE ARE NOT THE EYES OF A GIRL IN LOVE ...!!!
EVEN IF HE DID REALIZE SOMETHING WAS UP...
WE KEEP RUNNING INTO EACH OTHER...
...IS ALL HE'D SAY!!!
GAKU (SHAKE)
ガク
WHAT DO YOU THINK!?
WELL, WHAT DO YOU THINK!!?
GAKU
ガク
ISN'T THAT ADORABLE!!?
YOU'RE BRAG-GING ABOUT THAT!!?

A GORGEOUS GROUP

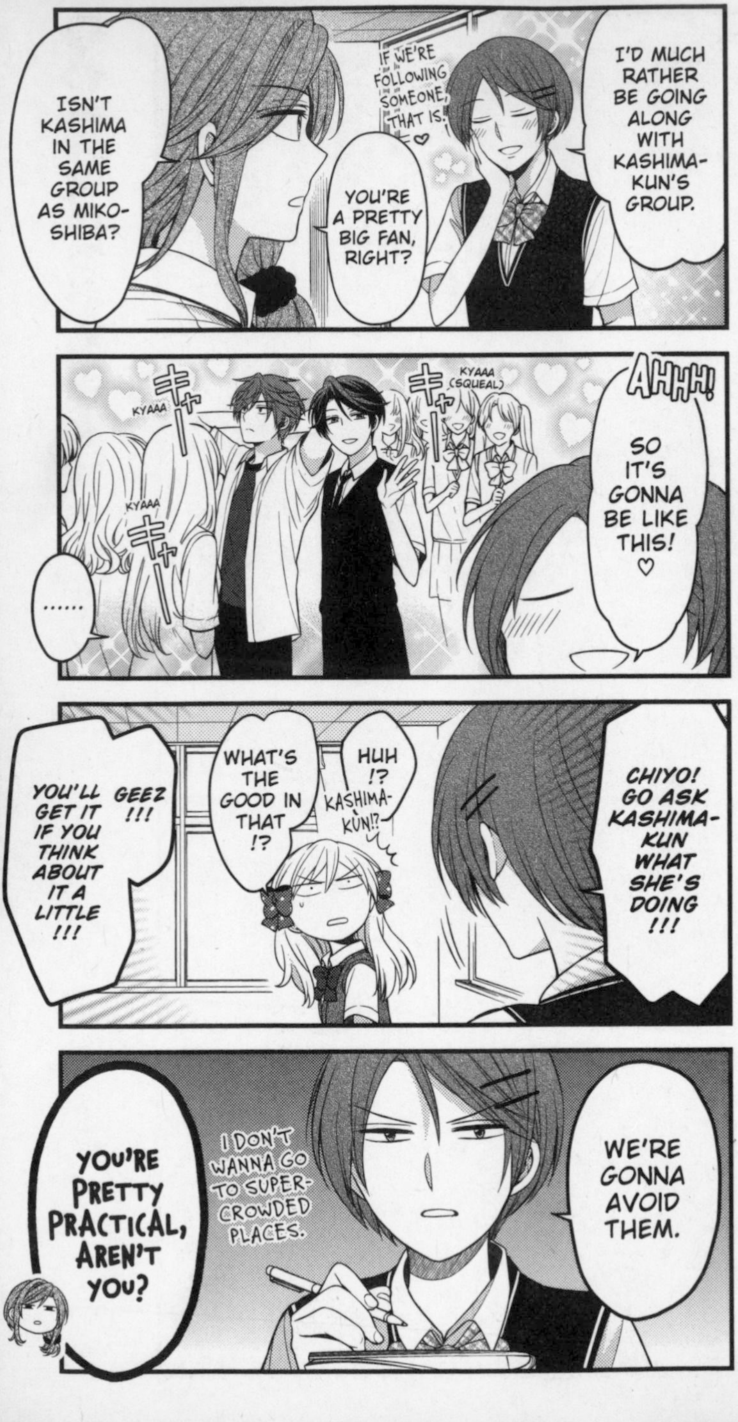
I'D MUCH RATHER BE GOING ALONG WITH KASHIMA-KUN'S GROUP.
IF WE'RE FOLLOWING SOMEONE, THAT IS. ♡
YOU'RE A PRETTY BIG FAN, RIGHT?
ISN'T KASHIMA IN THE SAME GROUP AS MIKO-SHIBA?
AHHH!
SO IT'S GONNA BE LIKE THIS! ♡
KYAAA (SQUEAL)
KYAAA
KYAAA
......
CHIYO! GO ASK KASHIMA-KUN WHAT SHE'S DOING!!!
HUH!? KASHIMA-KUN!?
WHAT'S THE GOOD IN THAT!?
GEEZ!!!
YOU'LL GET IT IF YOU THINK ABOUT IT A LITTLE!!!
WE'RE GONNA AVOID THEM.
I DON'T WANNA GO TO SUPER-CROWDED PLACES.
YOU'RE PRETTY PRACTICAL, AREN'T YOU?

DOES THAT WORK?

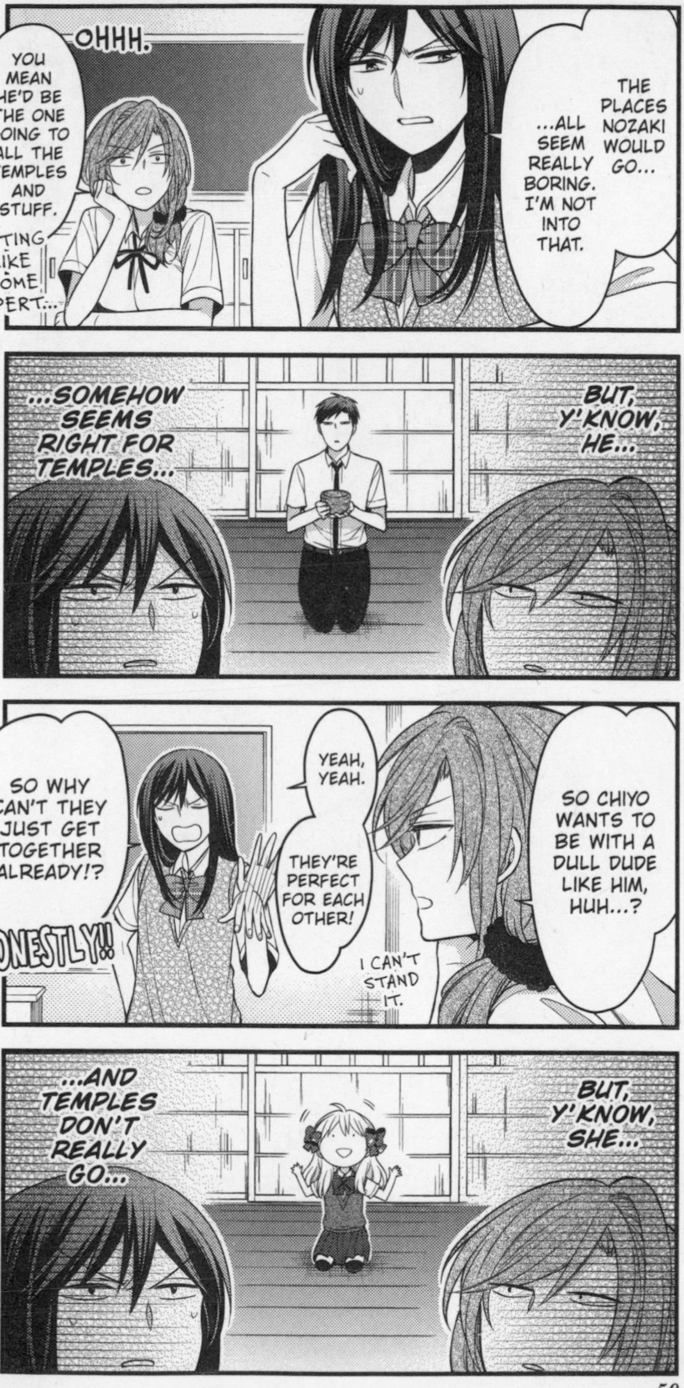
THE PLACES NOZAKI WOULD GO...
...ALL SEEM REALLY BORING. I'M NOT INTO THAT.
OHHH.
YOU MEAN HE'D BE THE ONE GOING TO ALL THE TEMPLES AND STUFF.
ACTING LIKE SOME EXPERT...
BUT, Y'KNOW, HE...
...SOMEHOW SEEMS RIGHT FOR TEMPLES...
SO CHIYO WANTS TO BE WITH A DULL DUDE LIKE HIM, HUH...?
YEAH, YEAH.
THEY'RE PERFECT FOR EACH OTHER!
I CAN'T STAND IT.
SO WHY CAN'T THEY JUST GET TOGETHER ALREADY!?
HONESTLY!!
BUT, Y'KNOW, SHE...
...AND TEMPLES DON'T REALLY GO...

THERE ARE THREE OF THEM, AFTER ALL

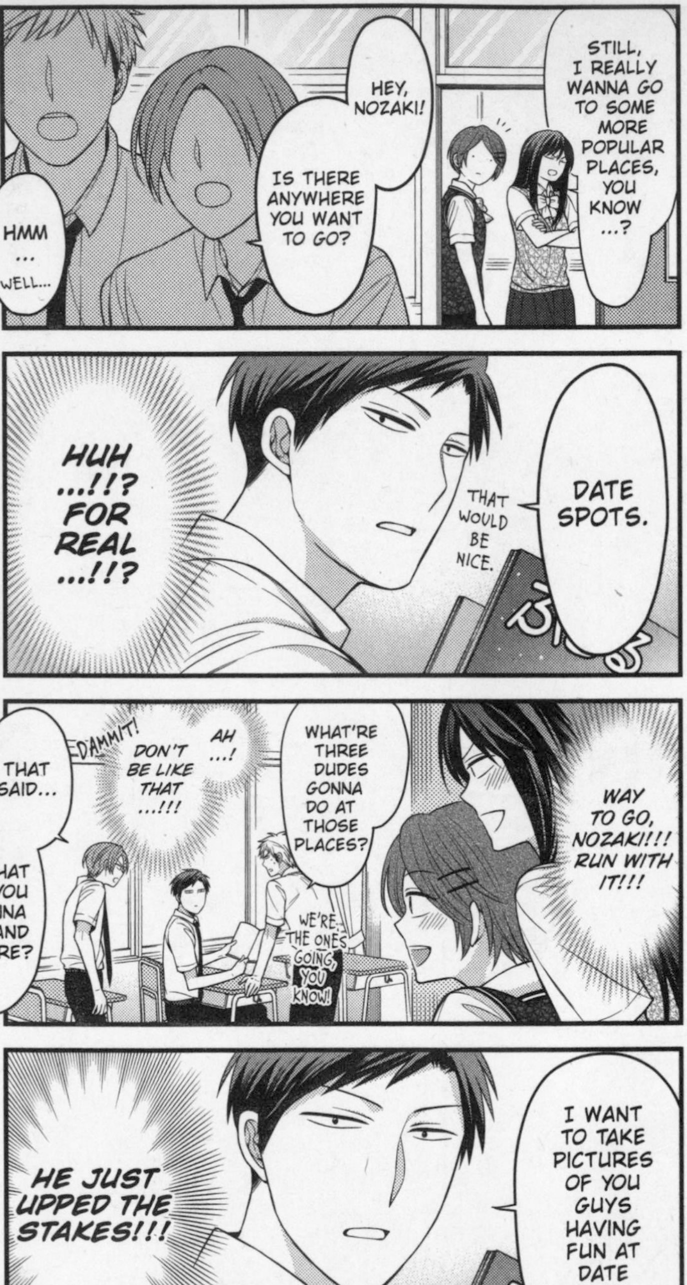
STILL, I REALLY WANNA GO TO SOME MORE POPULAR PLACES, YOU KNOW ...?
HEY, NOZAKI!
IS THERE ANYWHERE YOU WANT TO GO?
HMM ... WELL...
DATE SPOTS.
THAT WOULD BE NICE.
HUH ...!!? FOR REAL ...!!?
WAY TO GO, NOZAKI!!! RUN WITH IT!!!
WHAT'RE THREE DUDES GONNA DO AT THOSE PLACES?
WE'RE THE ONES GOING, YOU KNOW!
AH ...!
DON'T BE LIKE THAT ...!!!
DAMMIT!
THAT SAID...
...WHAT DO YOU WANNA DO AND WHERE?
I WANT TO TAKE PICTURES OF YOU GUYS HAVING FUN AT DATE SPOTS.
HE JUST UPPED THE STAKES!!!

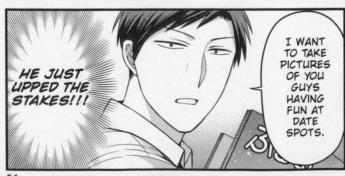

EXAGGERATED MISAPPROPRIATION

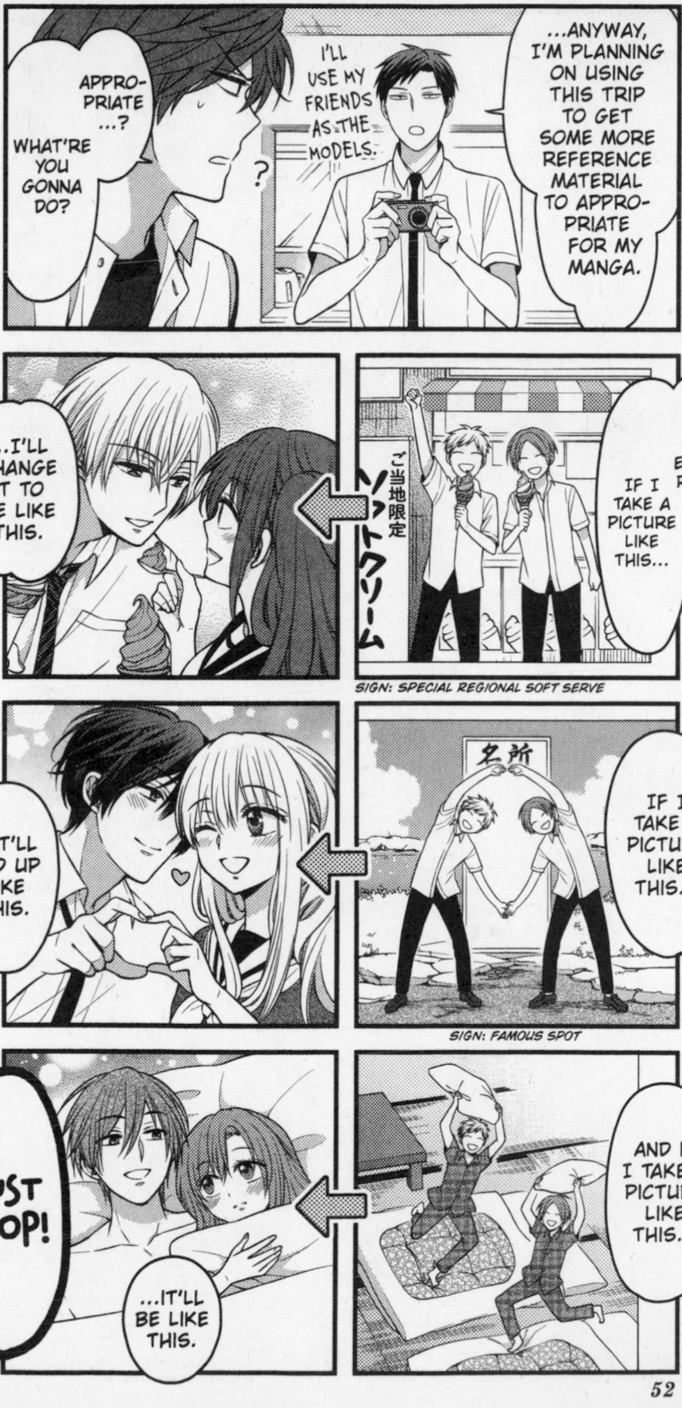

...ANYWAY, I'M PLANNING ON USING THIS TRIP TO GET SOME MORE REFERENCE MATERIAL TO APPROPRIATE FOR MY MANGA.
I'LL USE MY FRIENDS AS THE MODELS.
APPROPRIATE ...?
WHAT'RE YOU GONNA DO?
FOR EXAMPLE...
IF I TAKE A PICTURE LIKE THIS...
ご当地限定ソフトクリーム
...I'LL CHANGE IT TO BE LIKE THIS.
SIGN: SPECIAL REGIONAL SOFT SERVE
名所
IF I TAKE A PICTURE LIKE THIS...
...IT'LL END UP LIKE THIS.
SIGN: FAMOUS SPOT
AND IF I TAKE A PICTURE LIKE THIS...
...IT'LL BE LIKE THIS.
JUST STOP!

I WANT A PICTURE LIKE THIS♡

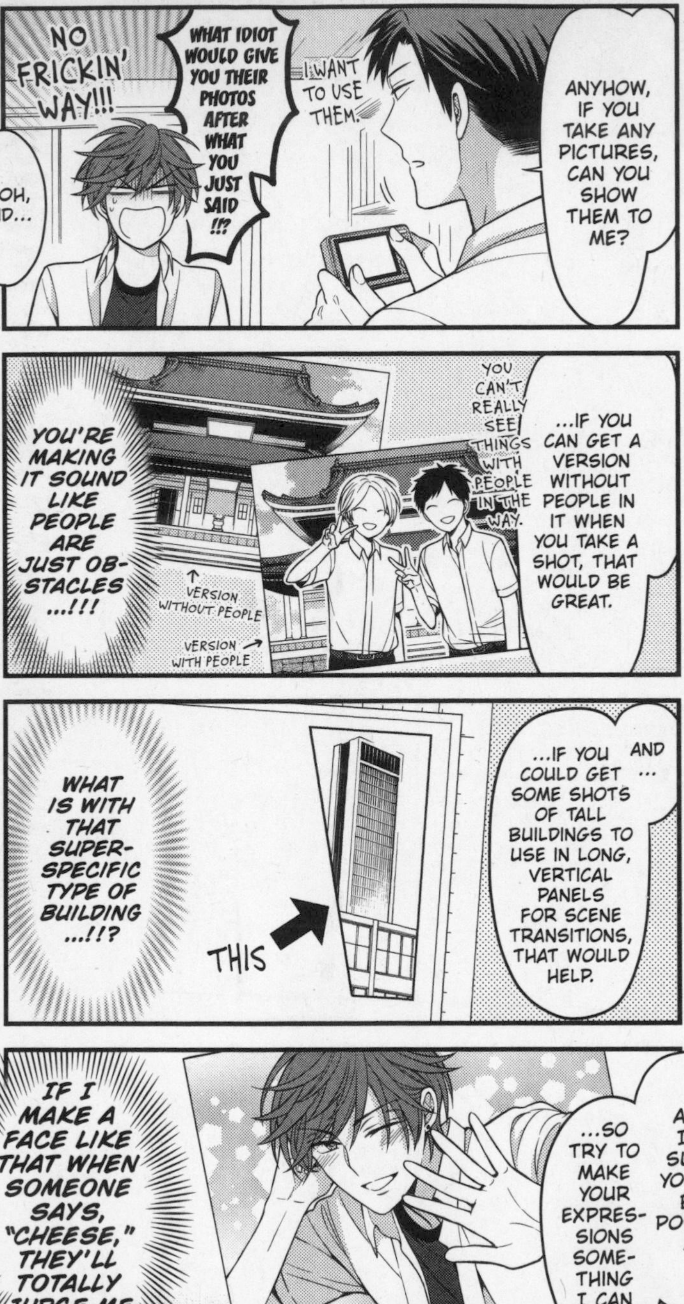

ANYHOW, IF YOU TAKE ANY PICTURES, CAN YOU SHOW THEM TO ME?
I WANT TO USE THEM.
WHAT IDIOT WOULD GIVE YOU THEIR PHOTOS AFTER WHAT YOU JUST SAID!!?
NO FRICKIN' WAY!!!
...OH, AND...
...IF YOU CAN GET A VERSION WITHOUT PEOPLE IN IT WHEN YOU TAKE A SHOT, THAT WOULD BE GREAT.
YOU CAN'T REALLY SEE THINGS WITH PEOPLE IN THE WAY.
↑ VERSION WITHOUT PEOPLE
VERSION WITH PEOPLE →
YOU'RE MAKING IT SOUND LIKE PEOPLE ARE JUST OB-STACLES...!!!
AND...
...IF YOU COULD GET SOME SHOTS OF TALL BUILDINGS TO USE IN LONG, VERTICAL PANELS FOR SCENE TRANSITIONS, THAT WOULD HELP.
THIS
WHAT IS WITH THAT SUPER-SPECIFIC TYPE OF BUILDING...!!?
AND I'M SURE YOU'LL BE POSING...
...SO TRY TO MAKE YOUR EXPRES-SIONS SOME-THING I CAN USE.
LIKE THIS.
IF I MAKE A FACE LIKE THAT WHEN SOMEONE SAYS, "CHEESE," THEY'LL TOTALLY JUDGE ME...!!!

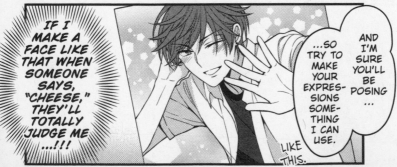

THE CHANGES I'M THINKING OF

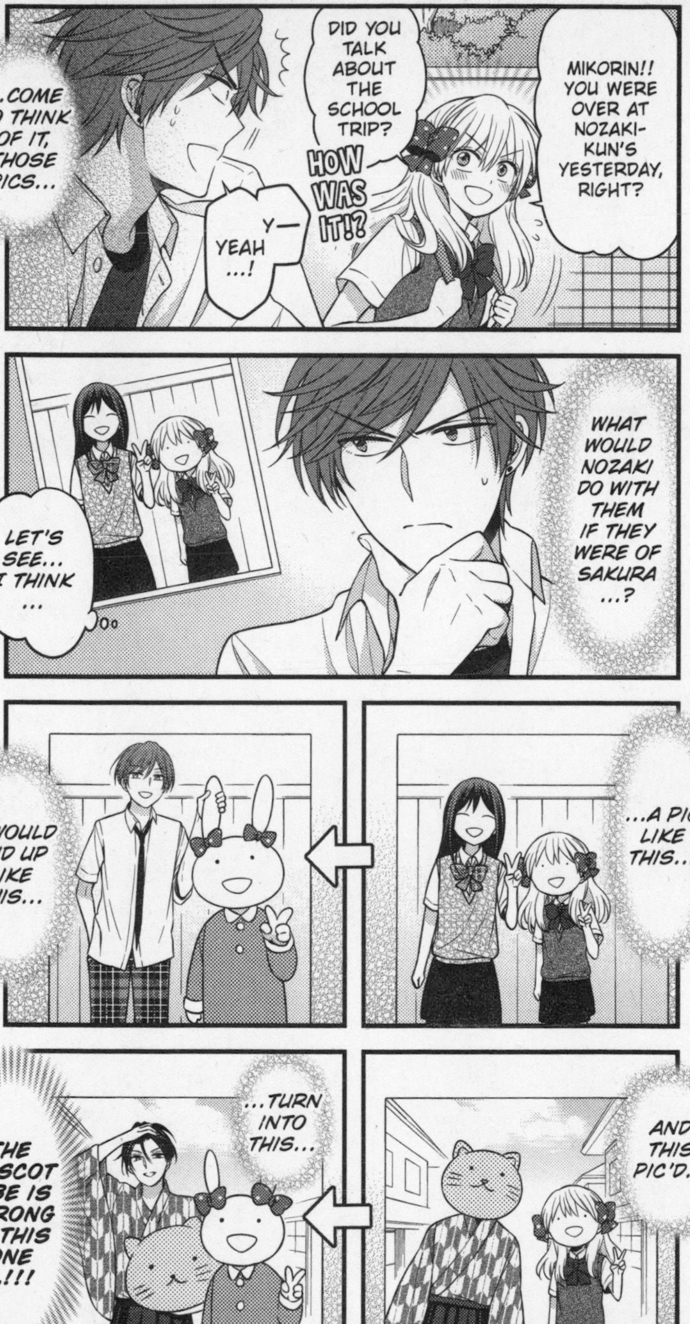
MIKORIN!! YOU WERE OVER AT NOZAKI-KUN'S YESTERDAY, RIGHT?
DID YOU TALK ABOUT THE SCHOOL TRIP?
HOW WAS IT!?
Y— YEAH ...!
...COME TO THINK OF IT, THOSE PICS...
WHAT WOULD NOZAKI DO WITH THEM IF THEY WERE OF SAKURA ...?
LET'S SEE... I THINK ...
...A PIC LIKE THIS...
...WOULD END UP LIKE THIS...
AND THIS PIC'D...
...TURN INTO THIS...
THE MASCOT VIBE IS STRONG IN THIS ONE ...!!!

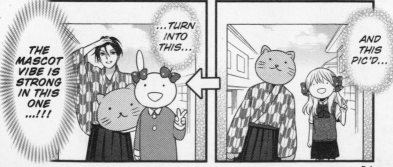

MY DEAR, DEAR UNDERCLASSMAN

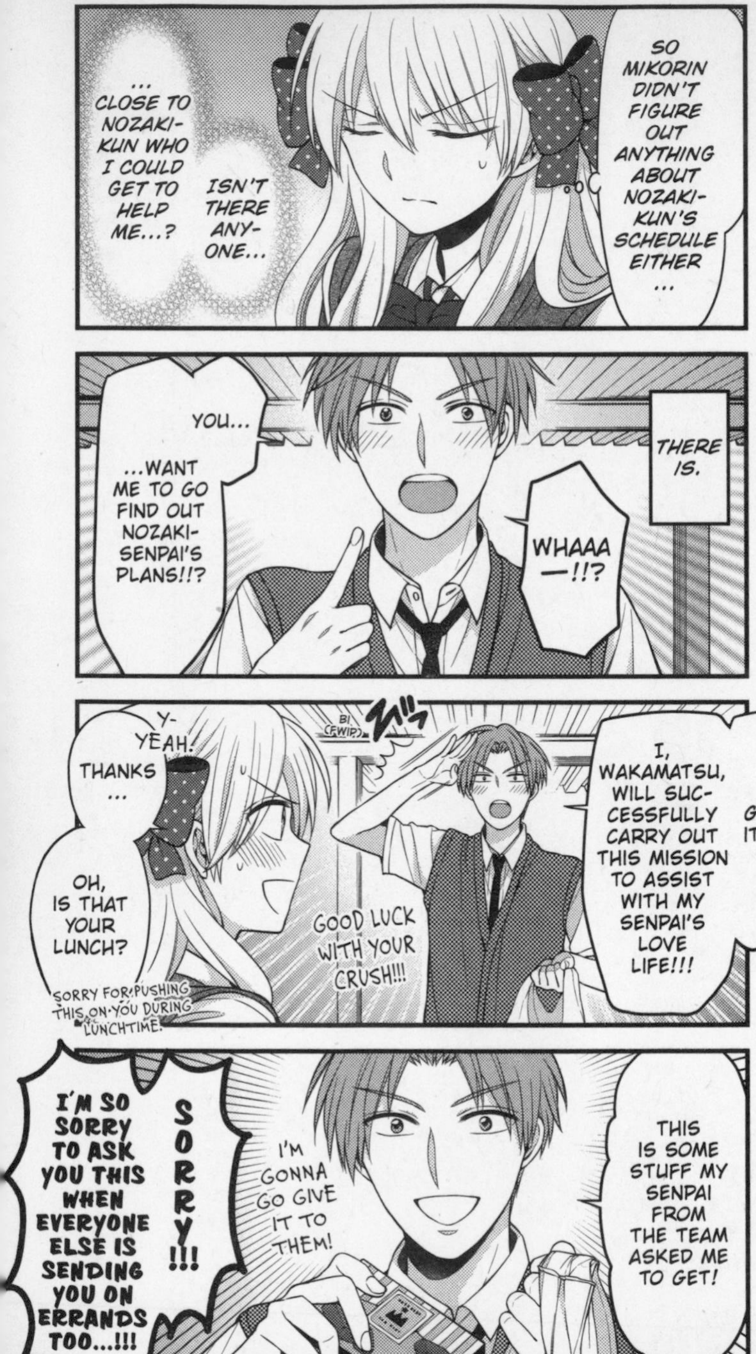
SO MIKORIN DIDN'T FIGURE OUT ANYTHING ABOUT NOZAKI-KUN'S SCHEDULE EITHER ...
ISN'T THERE ANYONE...
... CLOSE TO NOZAKI-KUN WHO I COULD GET TO HELP ME...?
THERE IS.
WHAAA—!!?
YOU...
...WANT ME TO GO FIND OUT NOZAKI-SENPAI'S PLANS!!?
GOT IT!!!
I, WAKAMATSU, WILL SUCCESSFULLY CARRY OUT THIS MISSION TO ASSIST WITH MY SENPAI'S LOVE LIFE!!!
BI (FWIP)
Y-YEAH! THANKS ...
GOOD LUCK WITH YOUR CRUSH!!!
OH, IS THAT YOUR LUNCH?
SORRY FOR PUSHING THIS ON YOU DURING LUNCHTIME.
THIS IS SOME STUFF MY SENPAI FROM THE TEAM ASKED ME TO GET!
I'M GONNA GO GIVE IT TO THEM!
SORRY!!!
I'M SO SORRY TO ASK YOU THIS WHEN EVERYONE ELSE IS SENDING YOU ON ERRANDS TOO...!!!

SEO-SENPAI!

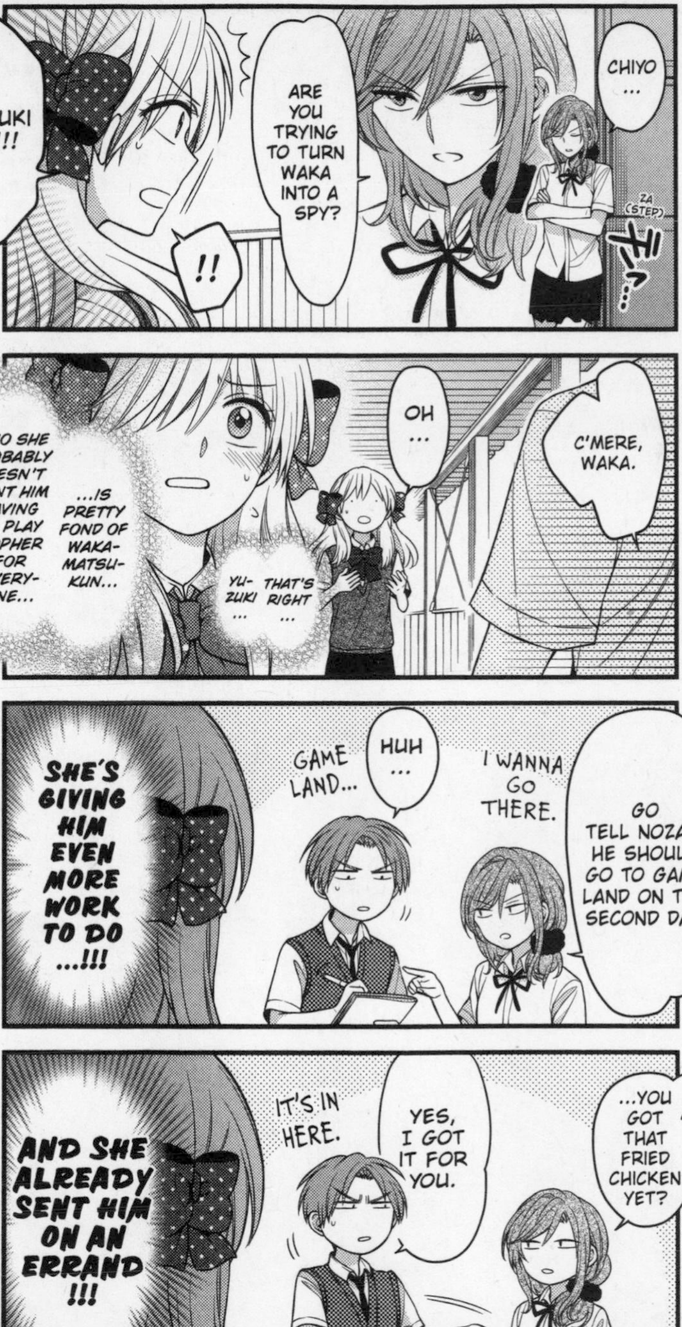

CHIYO ...
ZA (STEP)
ARE YOU TRYING TO TURN WAKA INTO A SPY?
!!
YUZUKI ...!!!
C'MERE, WAKA.
OH ...
THAT'S RIGHT ...
YU-ZUKI ...
...IS PRETTY FOND OF WAKA-MATSU-KUN...
...SO SHE PROBABLY DOESN'T WANT HIM HAVING TO PLAY GOPHER FOR EVERY-ONE...
LISTEN UP!
GO TELL NOZAKI HE SHOULD GO TO GAME LAND ON THE SECOND DAY.
I WANNA GO THERE.
HUH ...
GAME LAND...
SHE'S GIVING HIM EVEN MORE WORK TO DO ...!!!
AND ...
...YOU GOT THAT FRIED CHICKEN YET?
YES, I GOT IT FOR YOU.
IT'S IN HERE.
AND SHE ALREADY SENT HIM ON AN ERRAND !!!

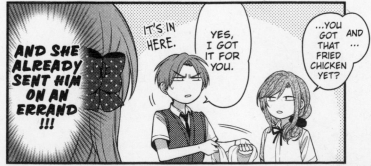

WITH YOU

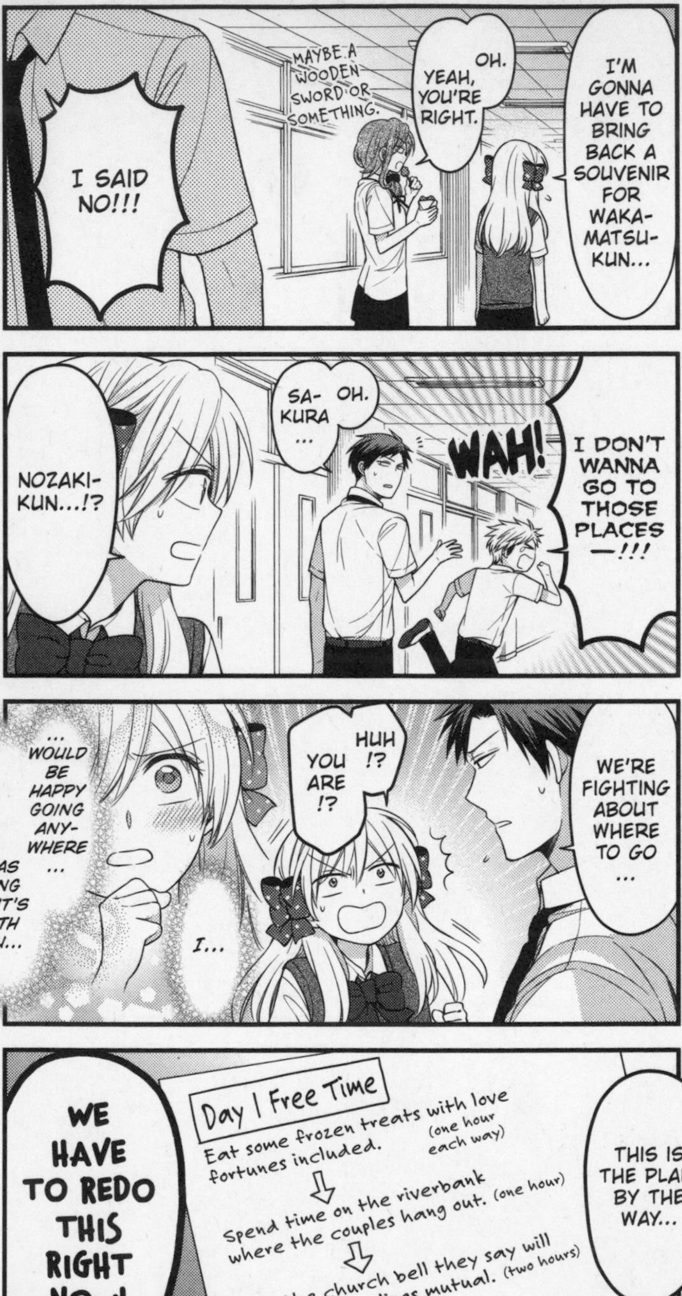
I'M GONNA HAVE TO BRING BACK A SOUVENIR FOR WAKA-MATSU-KUN...
OH. YEAH, YOU'RE RIGHT.
MAYBE A WOODEN SWORD OR SOMETHING.
I SAID NO!!!
I DON'T WANNA GO TO THOSE PLACES—!!!
WAH!
OH.
SA-KURA...
NOZAKI-KUN...!?
WE'RE FIGHTING ABOUT WHERE TO GO...
HUH!?
YOU ARE!?
I...
...WOULD BE HAPPY GOING ANYWHERE...
...AS LONG AS IT'S WITH YOU...
THIS IS THE PLAN, BY THE WAY...
Day 1 Free Time
Eat some frozen treats with love fortunes included. (one hour each way)
Spend time on the riverbank where the couples hang out. (one hour)
Ring the church bell they say will make your feelings mutual. (two hours)
nice dinner at a restaurant
pretty night view.
WE HAVE TO REDO THIS RIGHT NOW!

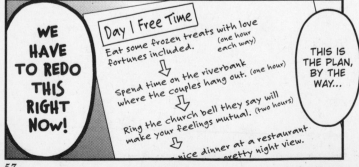

THAT'S NOT WHAT IT LOOKS LIKE

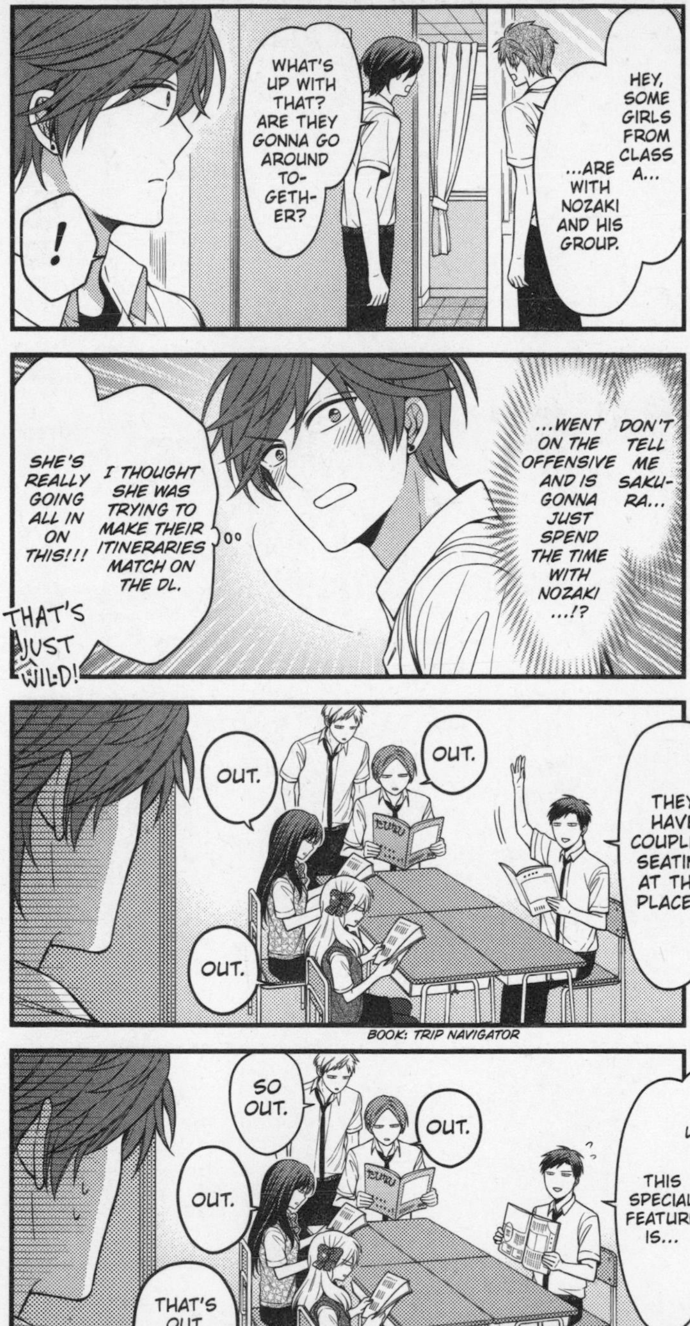
HEY, SOME GIRLS FROM CLASS A...
...ARE WITH NOZAKI AND HIS GROUP.
WHAT'S UP WITH THAT? ARE THEY GONNA GO AROUND TO-GETH-ER?
!
DON'T TELL ME SAKURA...
...WENT ON THE OFFENSIVE AND IS GONNA JUST SPEND THE TIME WITH NOZAKI...!?
I THOUGHT SHE WAS TRYING TO MAKE THEIR ITINERARIES MATCH ON THE DL.
SHE'S REALLY GOING ALL IN ON THIS!!!
THAT'S JUST WILD!
UH... THEY HAVE COUPLES' SEATING AT THIS PLACE...
OUT.
OUT.
OUT.
BOOK: TRIP NAVIGATOR
UH... THIS SPECIAL FEATURE IS...
OUT.
SO OUT.
OUT.
THAT'S OUT, NOZAKI-KUN.

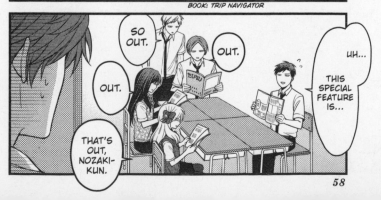

HE'S HEARD THAT SOMEWHERE

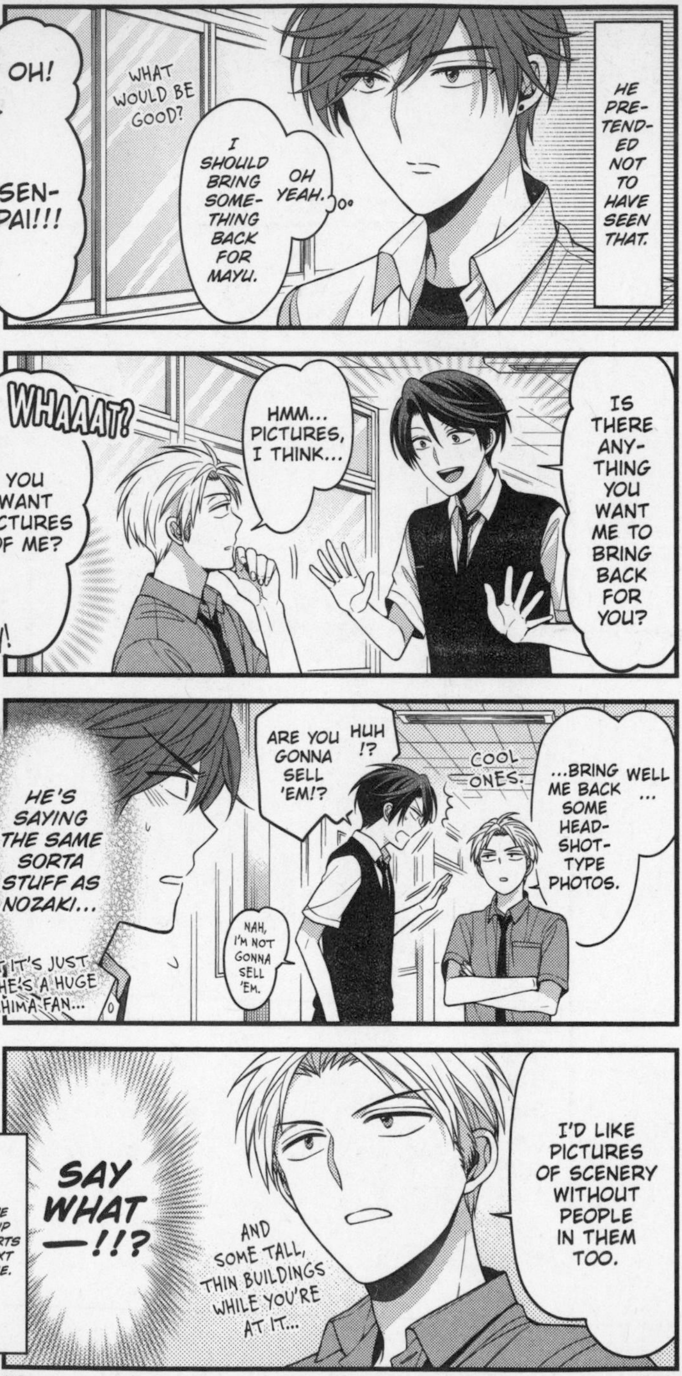
HE PRETENDED NOT TO HAVE SEEN THAT.
OH YEAH.
I SHOULD BRING SOMETHING BACK FOR MAYU.
WHAT WOULD BE GOOD?
OH! SENPAI!!!
IS THERE ANYTHING YOU WANT ME TO BRING BACK FOR YOU?
HMM... PICTURES, I THINK...
WHAAAT?
YOU WANT PICTURES OF ME?
NO WAY!
WELL...
...BRING ME BACK SOME HEAD-SHOT-TYPE PHOTOS.
COOL ONES.
HUH!?
ARE YOU GONNA SELL 'EM!?
NAH, I'M NOT GONNA SELL 'EM.
HE'S SAYING THE SAME SORTA STUFF AS NOZAKI...
I BET IT'S JUST 'COS HE'S A HUGE KASHIMA FAN...
I'D LIKE PICTURES OF SCENERY WITHOUT PEOPLE IN THEM TOO.
AND SOME TALL, THIN BUILDINGS WHILE YOU'RE AT IT...
SAY WHAT—!!?
THE TRIP STARTS NEXT TIME.

SAKURA-SENPAI'S ERRAND

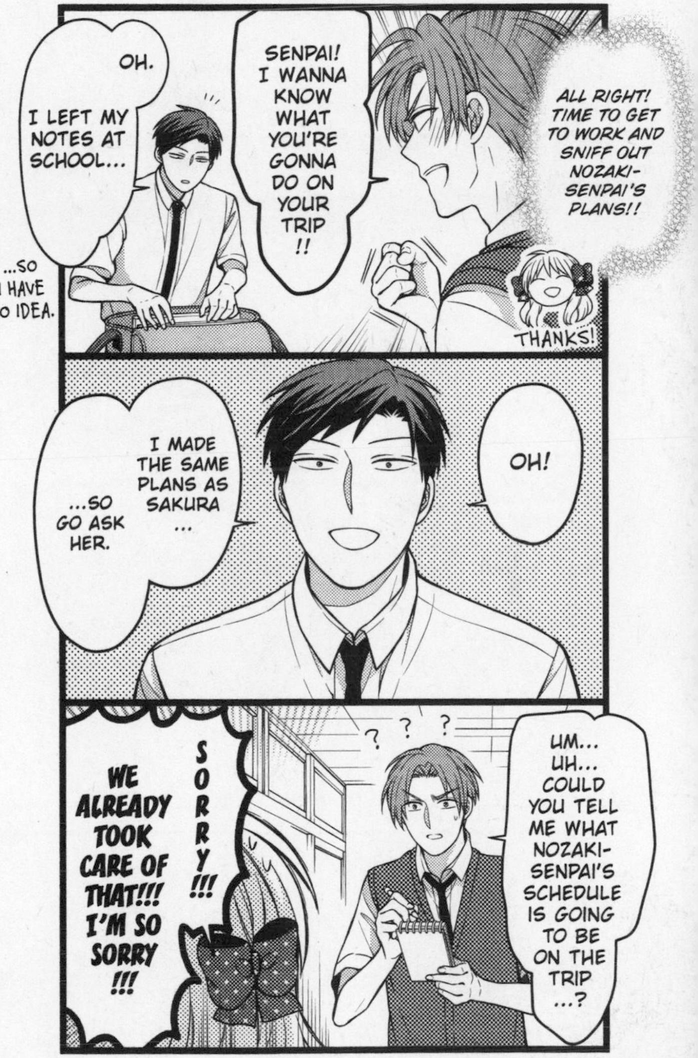
ALL RIGHT! TIME TO GET TO WORK AND SNIFF OUT NOZAKI-SENPAI'S PLANS!!
THANKS!
SENPAI! I WANNA KNOW WHAT YOU'RE GONNA DO ON YOUR TRIP !!
OH.
I LEFT MY NOTES AT SCHOOL...
...SO I HAVE NO IDEA.
OH!
I MADE THE SAME PLANS AS SAKURA ...
...SO GO ASK HER.
? ? ?
UM... UH... COULD YOU TELL ME WHAT NOZAKI-SENPAI'S SCHEDULE IS GOING TO BE ON THE TRIP ...?
SORRY!!!
WE ALREADY TOOK CARE OF THAT!!! I'M SO SORRY!!!

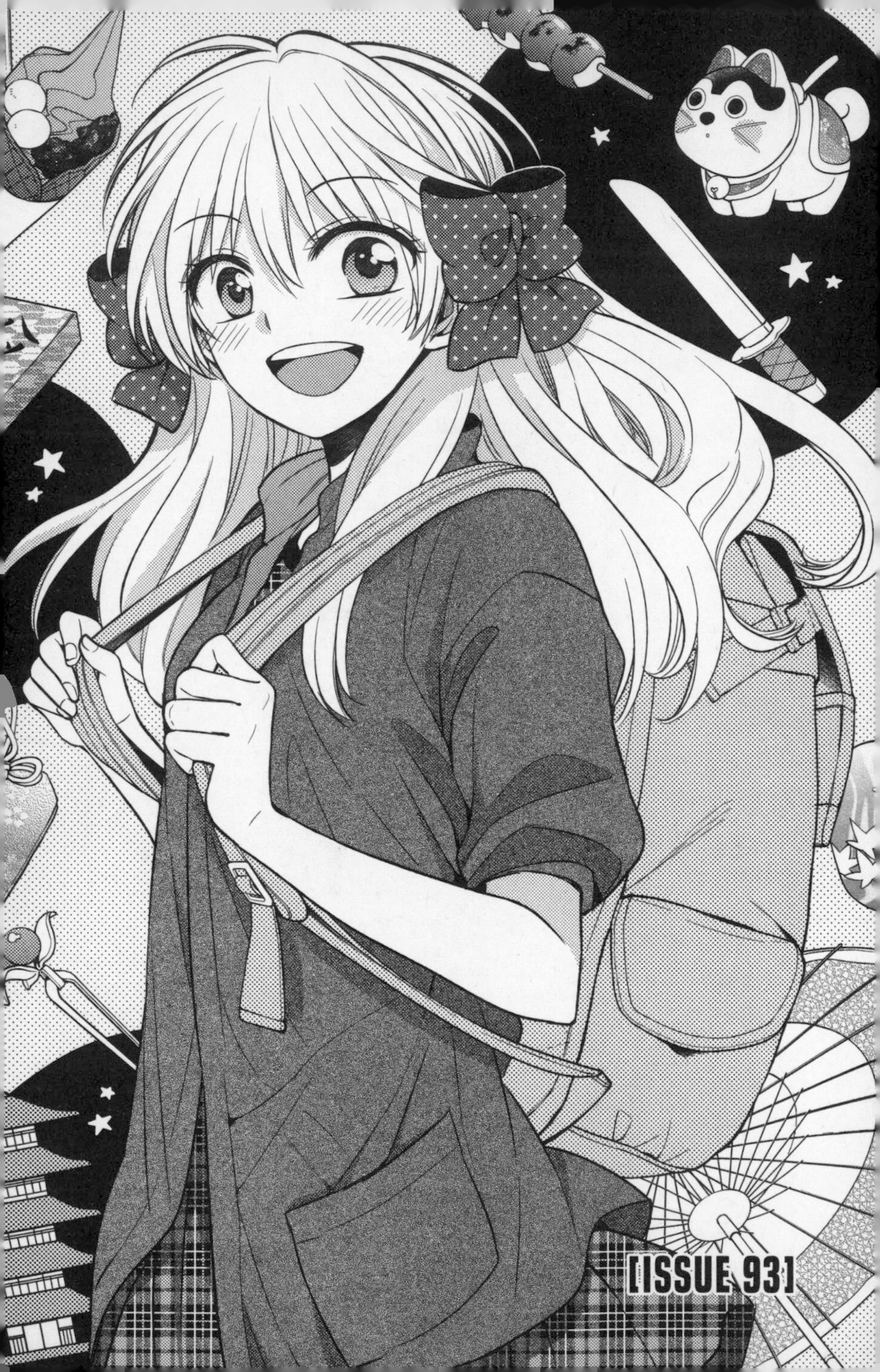
[ISSUE 93]

TRIP GOALS

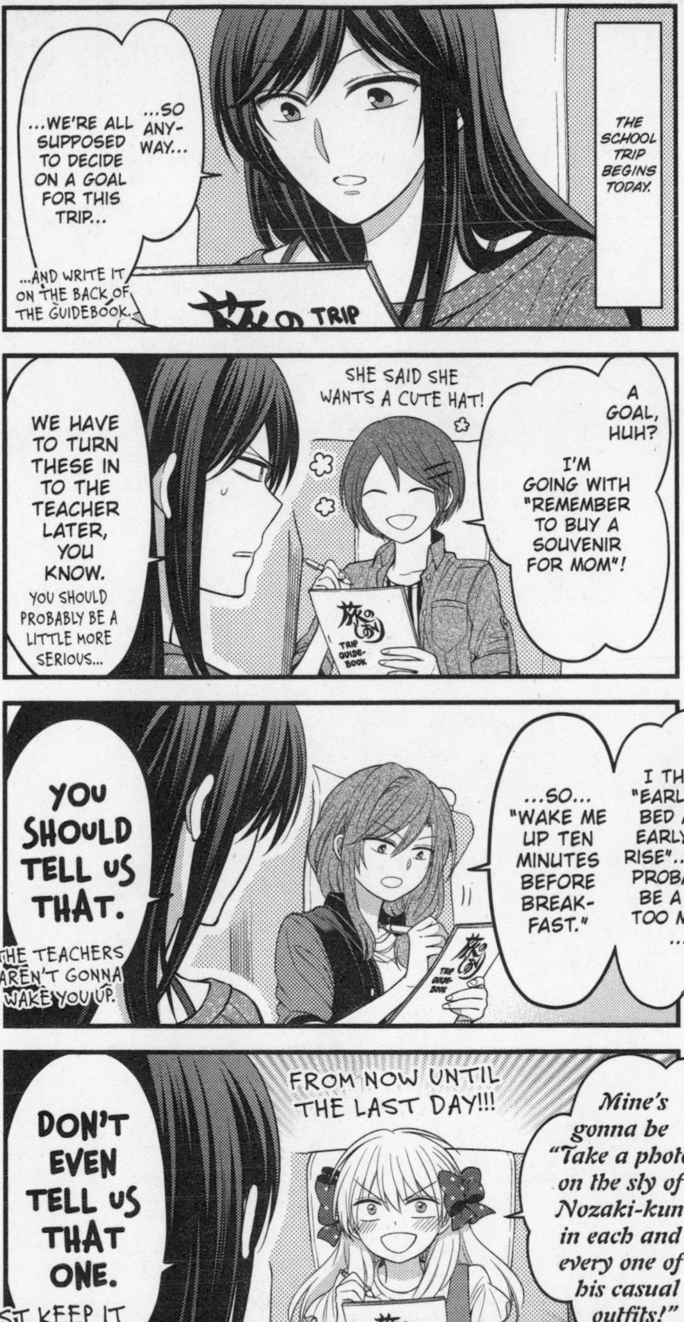

THE SCHOOL TRIP BEGINS TODAY.
...SO ANYWAY...
...WE'RE ALL SUPPOSED TO DECIDE ON A GOAL FOR THIS TRIP...
...AND WRITE IT ON THE BACK OF THE GUIDEBOOK.
旅の TRIP
A GOAL, HUH? I'M GOING WITH "REMEMBER TO BUY A SOUVENIR FOR MOM"!
SHE SAID SHE WANTS A CUTE HAT!
WE HAVE TO TURN THESE IN TO THE TEACHER LATER, YOU KNOW.
YOU SHOULD PROBABLY BE A LITTLE MORE SERIOUS...
旅のしおり TRIP GUIDE-BOOK
I THINK "EARLY TO BED AND EARLY TO RISE"...WILL PROBABLY BE A BIT TOO MUCH...
...SO... "WAKE ME UP TEN MINUTES BEFORE BREAK-FAST."
YOU SHOULD TELL US THAT.
THE TEACHERS AREN'T GONNA WAKE YOU UP.
旅のしおり TRIP GUIDE-BOOK
Mine's gonna be "Take a photo on the sly of Nozaki-kun in each and every one of his casual outfits!"
FROM NOW UNTIL THE LAST DAY!!!
DON'T EVEN TELL US THAT ONE.
JUST KEEP IT TO YOURSELF.

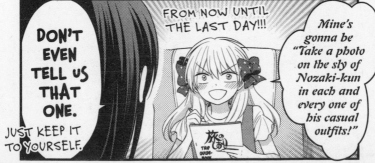

RARITY

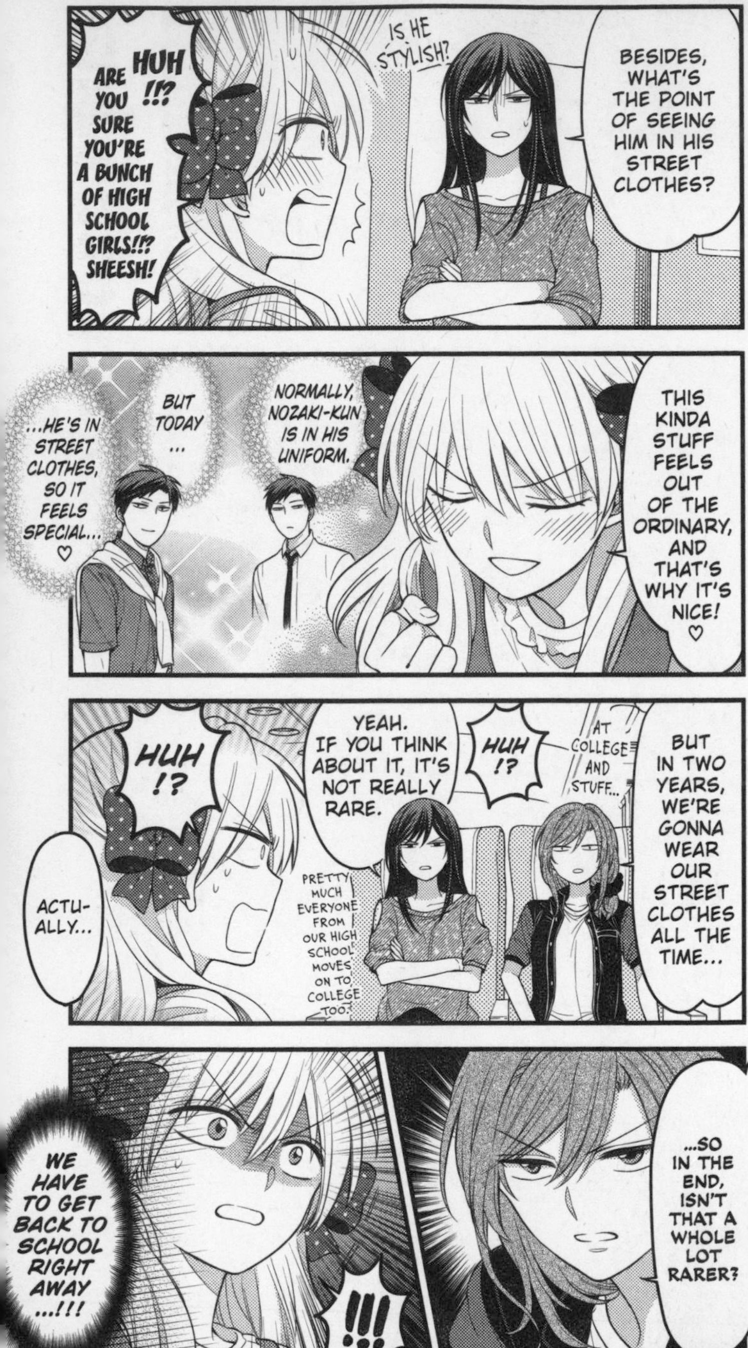
BESIDES, WHAT'S THE POINT OF SEEING HIM IN HIS STREET CLOTHES?
IS HE STYLISH?
HUH!!?
ARE YOU SURE YOU'RE A BUNCH OF HIGH SCHOOL GIRLS!!? SHEESH!
THIS KINDA STUFF FEELS OUT OF THE ORDINARY, AND THAT'S WHY IT'S NICE! ♡
NORMALLY, NOZAKI-KUN IS IN HIS UNIFORM.
BUT TODAY ...
...HE'S IN STREET CLOTHES, SO IT FEELS SPECIAL... ♡
BUT IN TWO YEARS, WE'RE GONNA WEAR OUR STREET CLOTHES ALL THE TIME...
AT COLLEGE AND STUFF...
HUH!?
YEAH. IF YOU THINK ABOUT IT, IT'S NOT REALLY RARE.
PRETTY MUCH EVERYONE FROM OUR HIGH SCHOOL MOVES ON TO COLLEGE TOO.
HUH!?
ACTU-ALLY...
...HE'S ONLY GONNA BE IN UNIFORM A LITTLE LONGER ...
...SO IN THE END, ISN'T THAT A WHOLE LOT RARER?
!!!
WE HAVE TO GET BACK TO SCHOOL RIGHT AWAY...!!!

SORRY ABOUT THAT

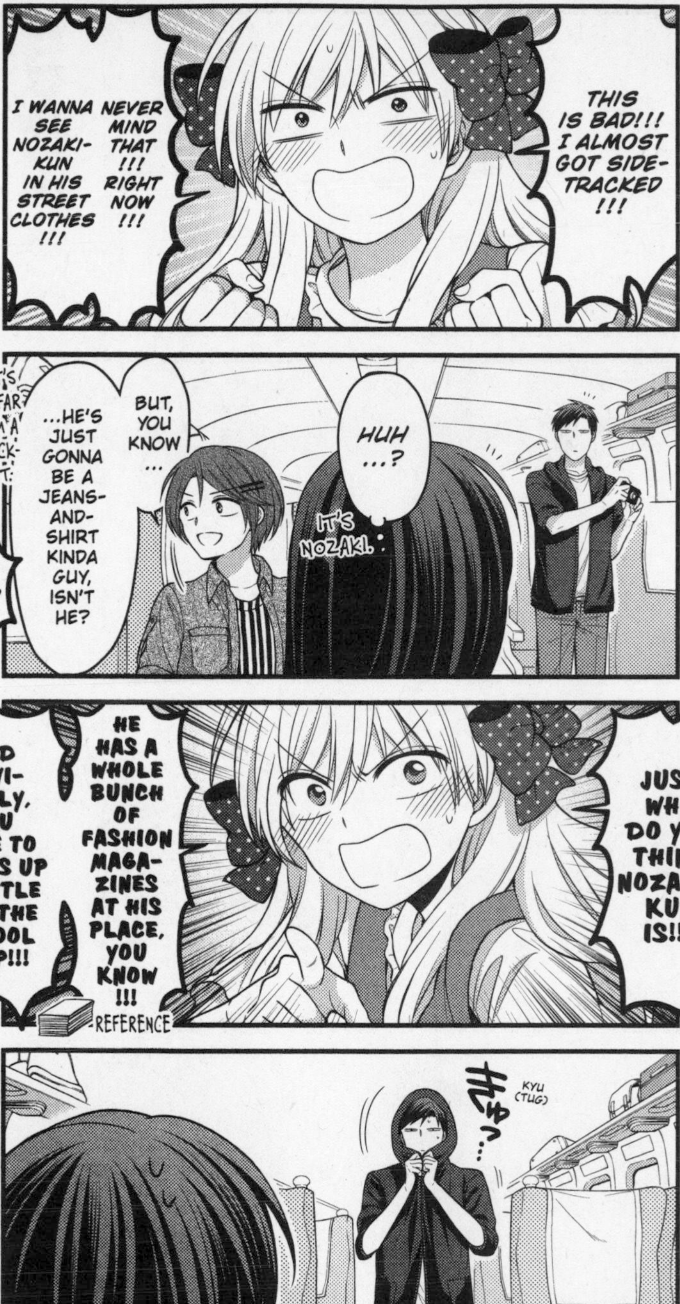

THIS IS BAD!!! I ALMOST GOT SIDE-TRACKED!!!
NEVER MIND THAT!!! RIGHT NOW!!!
I WANNA SEE NOZAKI-KUN IN HIS STREET CLOTHES!!!
HUH...?
IT'S NOZAKI.
BUT, YOU KNOW...
...HE'S JUST GONNA BE A JEANS-AND-SHIRT KINDA GUY, ISN'T HE?
THAT'S NOT FAR FROM A TRACKSUIT!
WHA—!?
JUST WHO DO YOU THINK NOZAKI-KUN IS!!!?
HE HAS A WHOLE BUNCH OF FASHION MAGAZINES AT HIS PLACE, YOU KNOW!!!
-REFERENCE
AND OBVIOUSLY, YOU HAVE TO DRESS UP A LITTLE FOR THE SCHOOL TRIP!!!
きゅっ…
KYU (TUG)

WE ARE INCREDIBLY FAR APART

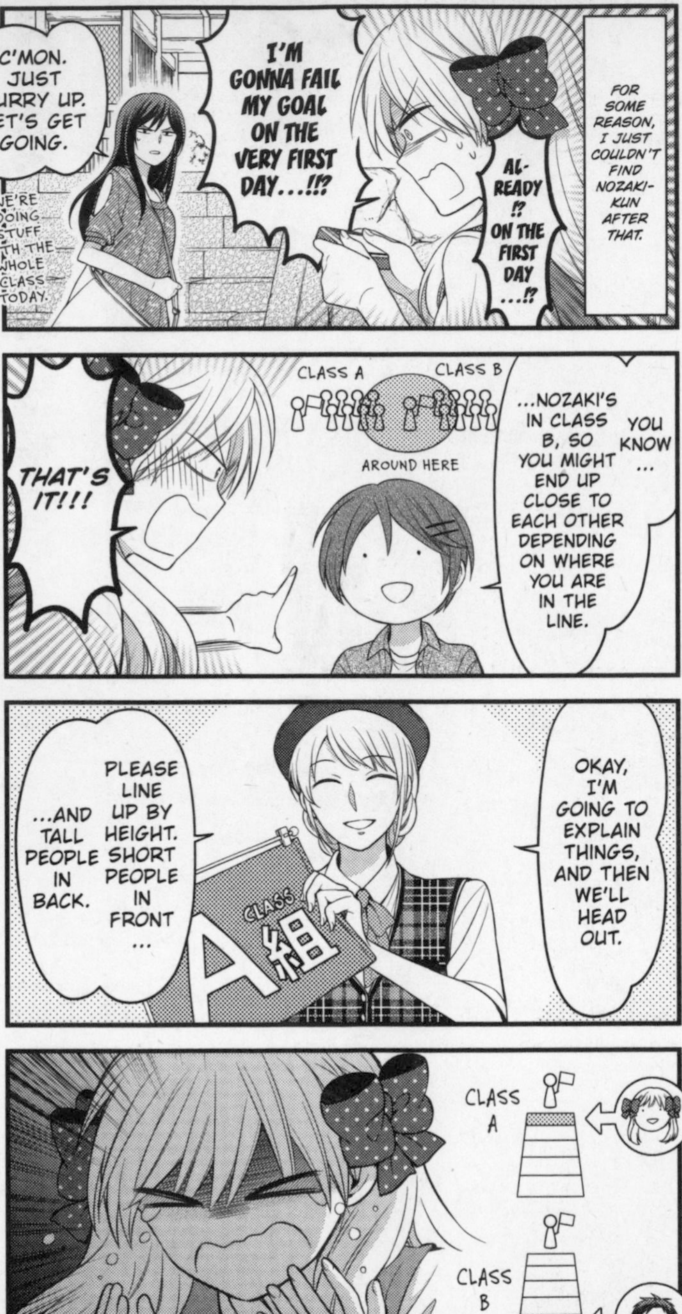
FOR SOME REASON, I JUST COULDN'T FIND NOZAKI-KUN AFTER THAT.
AL-READY!? ON THE FIRST DAY...!?
I'M GONNA FAIL MY GOAL ON THE VERY FIRST DAY...!!?
C'MON. JUST HURRY UP. LET'S GET GOING.
WE'RE DOING STUFF WITH THE WHOLE CLASS TODAY.
YOU KNOW...
...NOZAKI'S IN CLASS B, SO YOU MIGHT END UP CLOSE TO EACH OTHER DEPENDING ON WHERE YOU ARE IN THE LINE.
CLASS B
CLASS A
AROUND HERE
THAT'S IT!!!
OKAY, I'M GOING TO EXPLAIN THINGS, AND THEN WE'LL HEAD OUT.
CLASS A 組
PLEASE LINE UP BY HEIGHT. SHORT PEOPLE IN FRONT...
...AND TALL PEOPLE IN BACK.
CLASS A
CLASS B

RIGHT AWAY, PLEASE

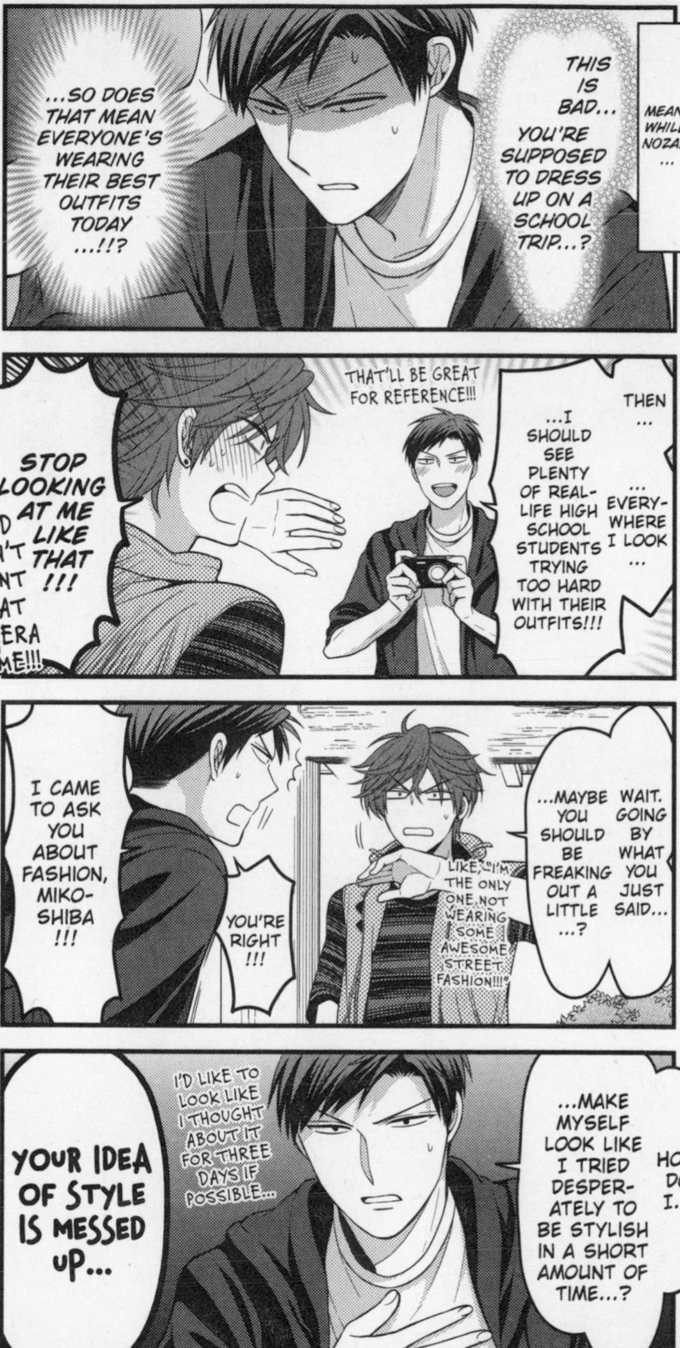
MEANWHILE, NOZAKI...
THIS IS BAD... YOU'RE SUPPOSED TO DRESS UP ON A SCHOOL TRIP...?
...SO DOES THAT MEAN EVERYONE'S WEARING THEIR BEST OUTFITS TODAY...!!?
THEN... ...EVERYWHERE I LOOK...
...I SHOULD SEE PLENTY OF REAL-LIFE HIGH SCHOOL STUDENTS TRYING TOO HARD WITH THEIR OUTFITS!!!
THAT'LL BE GREAT FOR REFERENCE!!!
STOP LOOKING AT ME LIKE THAT!!!
AND DON'T POINT THAT CAMERA AT ME!!!
WAIT. GOING BY WHAT YOU JUST SAID...
...MAYBE YOU SHOULD BE FREAKING OUT A LITTLE...?
LIKE, "I'M THE ONLY ONE NOT WEARING SOME AWESOME STREET FASHION!!!"
YOU'RE RIGHT!!!
I CAME TO ASK YOU ABOUT FASHION, MIKOSHIBA!!!
HOW DO I...
...MAKE MYSELF LOOK LIKE I TRIED DESPERATELY TO BE STYLISH IN A SHORT AMOUNT OF TIME...?
I'D LIKE TO LOOK LIKE I THOUGHT ABOUT IT FOR THREE DAYS IF POSSIBLE...
YOUR IDEA OF STYLE IS MESSED UP...

LOCAL

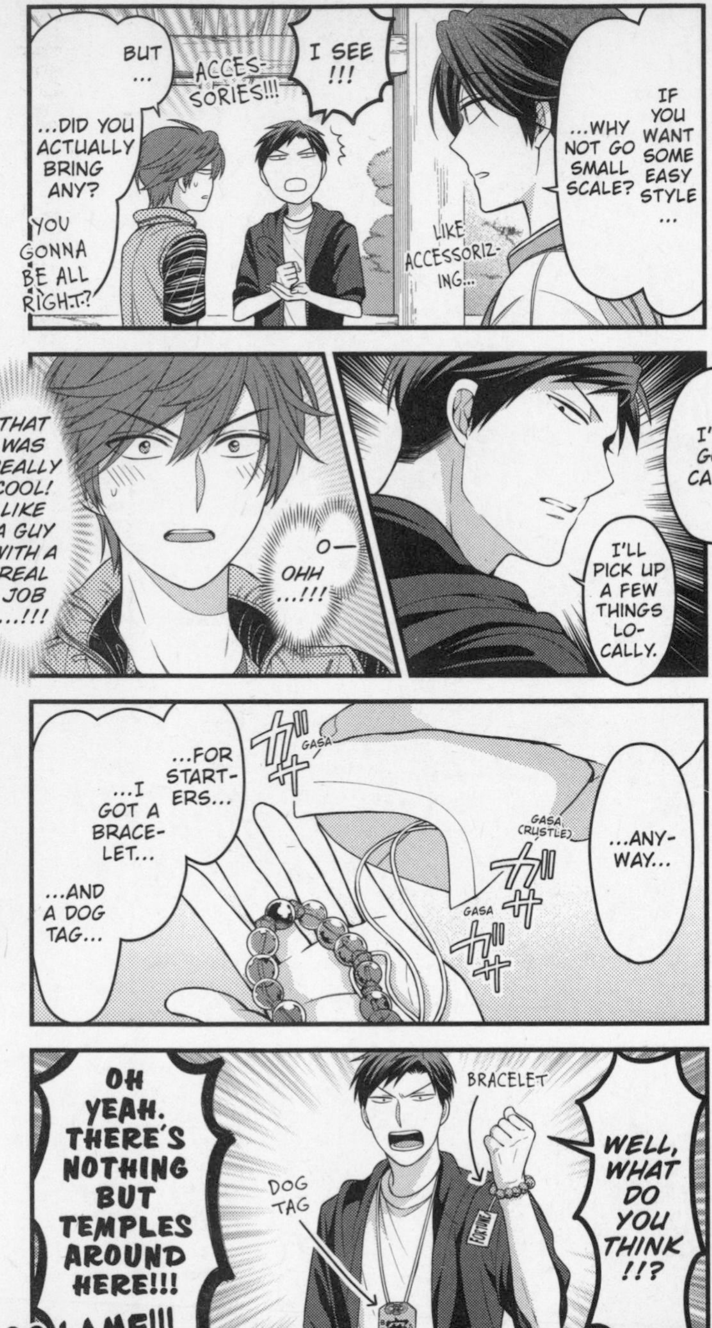
IF YOU WANT SOME EASY STYLE ...
...WHY NOT GO SMALL SCALE?
LIKE ACCESSORIZ-ING...
I SEE !!!
ACCES-SORIES!!!
BUT ...
...DID YOU ACTUALLY BRING ANY?
YOU GONNA BE ALL RIGHT?
I'VE GOT CASH.
I'LL PICK UP A FEW THINGS LO-CALLY.
O— OHH ...!!!
THAT WAS REALLY COOL! LIKE A GUY WITH A REAL JOB ...!!!
...ANY-WAY...
GASA (RUSTLE)
GASA
GASA
...FOR START-ERS...
...I GOT A BRACE-LET...
...AND A DOG TAG...
WELL, WHAT DO YOU THINK!!?
BRACELET
FORTUNE
DOG TAG
BIRTH SAFE
OH YEAH. THERE'S NOTHING BUT TEMPLES AROUND HERE!!!
SO LAME!!!

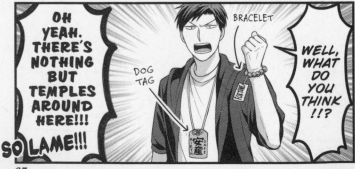

SO CLOSE BY

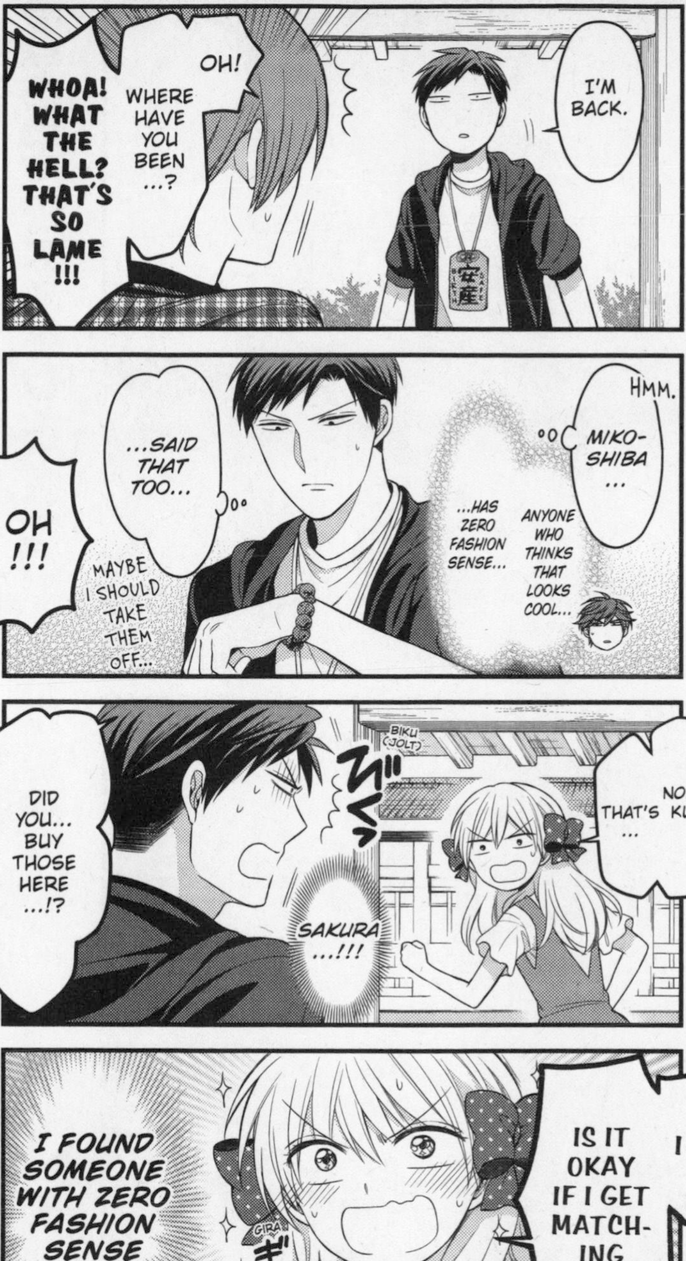

I'M BACK.
OH!
WHERE HAVE YOU BEEN ...?
WHOA! WHAT THE HELL? THAT'S SO LAME !!!
HMM.
MIKO-SHIBA ...
ANYONE WHO THINKS THAT LOOKS COOL...
...HAS ZERO FASHION SENSE...
...SAID THAT TOO...
MAYBE I SHOULD TAKE THEM OFF...
OH !!!
NOZAKI-KUN... THAT'S ...
BIKU (JOLT)
SAKURA ...!!!
DID YOU... BUY THOSE HERE ...!?
I—
IS IT OKAY IF I GET MATCH-ING ONES!!?
GIRA
ギラ
GIRA
ギラ
GIRA (GLINT)
ギラ
I FOUND SOMEONE WITH ZERO FASHION SENSE ...!!!

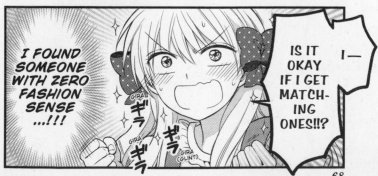

A SOUVENIR FOR THAT PERSON

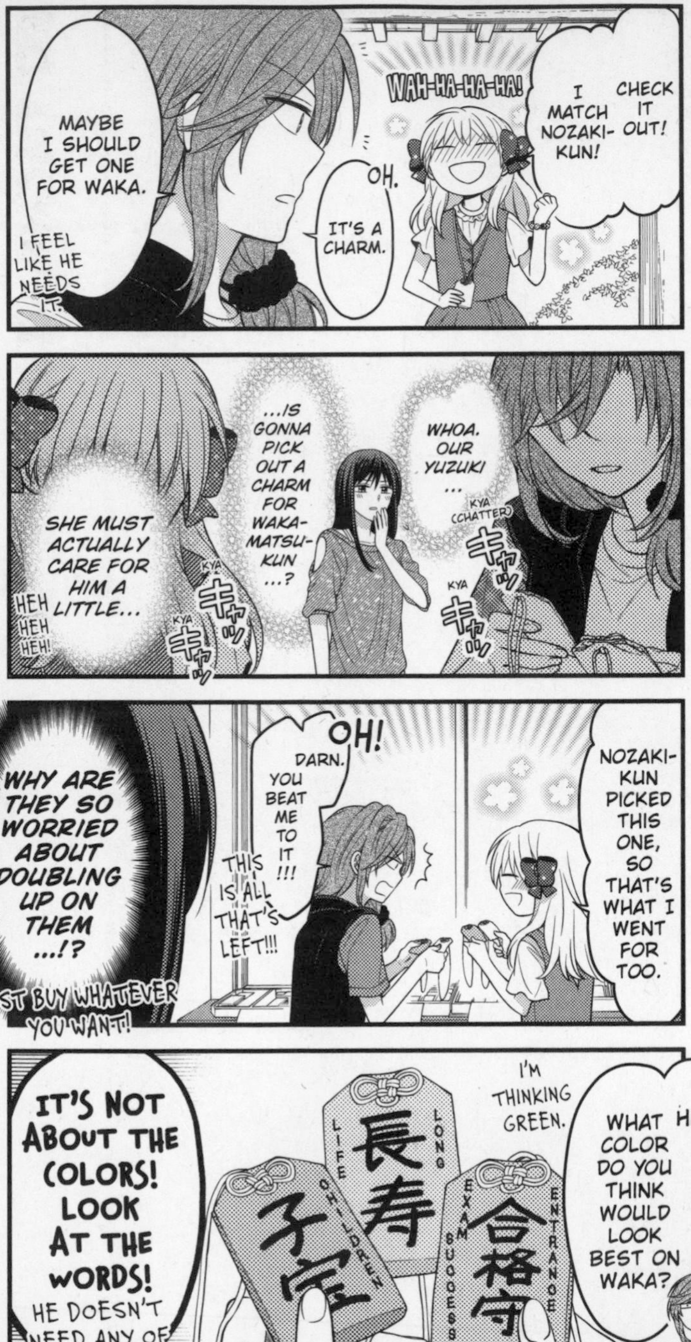
CHECK IT OUT! I MATCH NOZAKI-KUN!
WAH-HA-HA-HA!
OH.
IT'S A CHARM.
MAYBE I SHOULD GET ONE FOR WAKA.
I FEEL LIKE HE NEEDS IT.
WHOA. OUR YUZUKI...
KYA (CHATTER) キャッ
KYA キャッ
...IS GONNA PICK OUT A CHARM FOR WAKAMATSU-KUN...?
KYA キャッ
KYA キャッ
SHE MUST ACTUALLY CARE FOR HIM A LITTLE...
HEH HEH HEH!
NOZAKI-KUN PICKED THIS ONE, SO THAT'S WHAT I WENT FOR TOO.
OH!
DARN. YOU BEAT ME TO IT!!!
THIS IS ALL THAT'S LEFT!!!
WHY ARE THEY SO WORRIED ABOUT DOUBLING UP ON THEM...!?
JUST BUY WHATEVER YOU WANT!
HEY. WHAT COLOR DO YOU THINK WOULD LOOK BEST ON WAKA?
I'M THINKING GREEN.
合格守 ENTRANCE EXAM SUCCESS
長寿 LONG LIFE
子宝 CHILDREN
IT'S NOT ABOUT THE COLORS! LOOK AT THE WORDS!
HE DOESN'T NEED ANY OF THOSE!!!

IMITATING HER FRIENDS

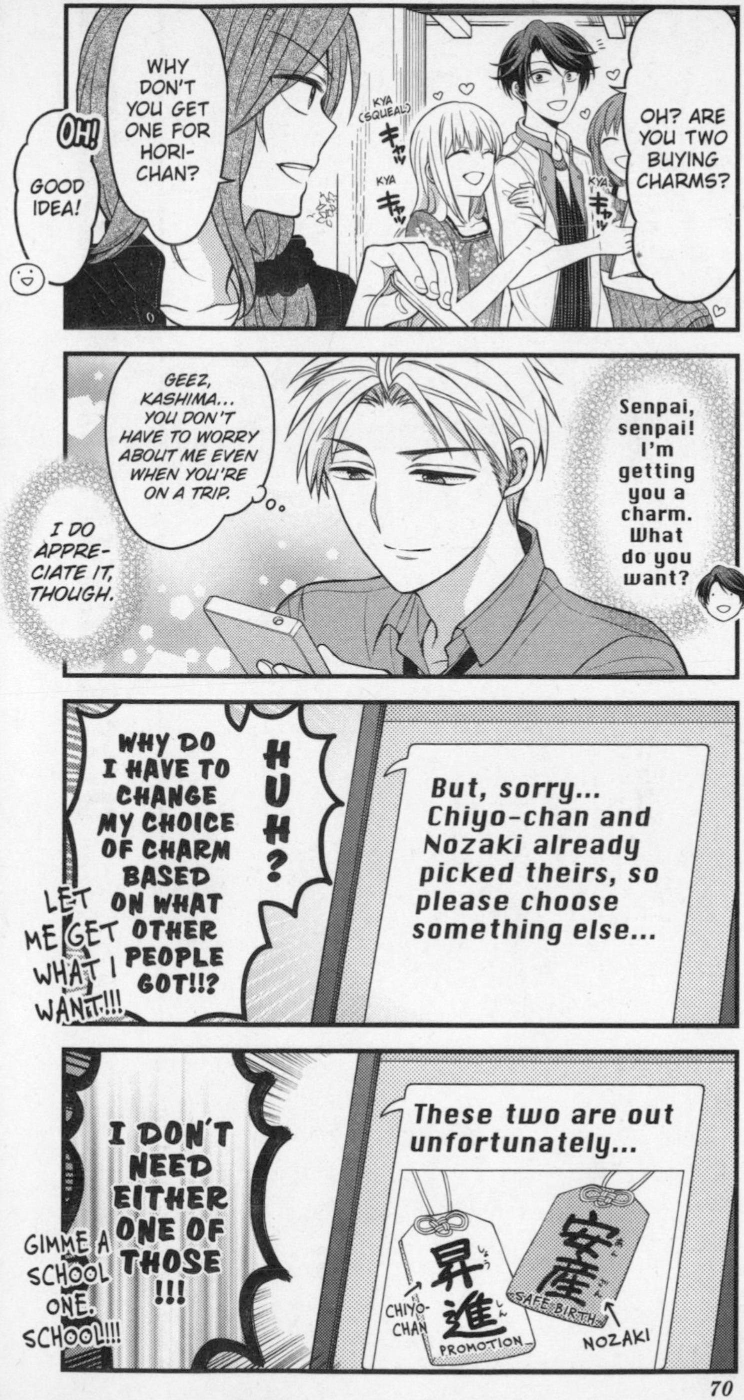
OH? ARE YOU TWO BUYING CHARMS?
KYA (SQUEAL)
KYA
KYA
WHY DON'T YOU GET ONE FOR HORI-CHAN?
OH!
GOOD IDEA!
Senpai, senpai! I'm getting you a charm. What do you want?
GEEZ, KASHIMA... YOU DON'T HAVE TO WORRY ABOUT ME EVEN WHEN YOU'RE ON A TRIP.
I DO APPRECIATE IT, THOUGH.
But, sorry... Chiyo-chan and Nozaki already picked theirs, so please choose something else...
HUH?
WHY DO I HAVE TO CHANGE MY CHOICE OF CHARM BASED ON WHAT OTHER PEOPLE GOT!!?
LET ME GET WHAT I WANT!!!
These two are out unfortunately...
安産
SAFE BIRTH
NOZAKI
昇進
PROMOTION
CHIYO-CHAN
I DON'T NEED EITHER ONE OF THOSE!!!
GIMME A SCHOOL ONE. SCHOOL!!!

BREATHTAKING AND HEART POUNDING

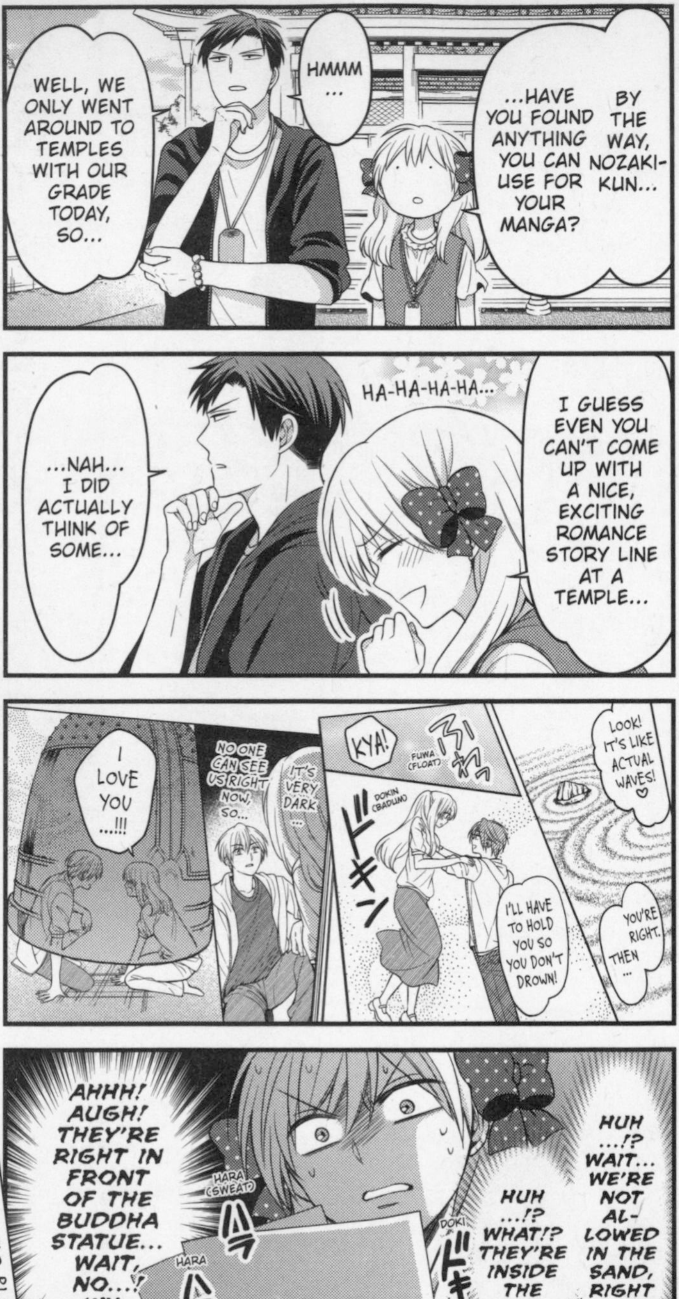
BY THE WAY, NOZAKI-KUN...
...HAVE YOU FOUND ANYTHING YOU CAN USE FOR YOUR MANGA?
HMMM...
WELL, WE ONLY WENT AROUND TO TEMPLES WITH OUR GRADE TODAY, SO...
I GUESS EVEN YOU CAN'T COME UP WITH A NICE, EXCITING ROMANCE STORY LINE AT A TEMPLE...
HA-HA-HA-HA...
...NAH... I DID ACTUALLY THINK OF SOME...
LOOK! IT'S LIKE ACTUAL WAVES! ♥
YOU'RE RIGHT. THEN...
I'LL HAVE TO HOLD YOU SO YOU DON'T DROWN!
KYA!
ふわっ
FUWA (FLOAT)
ドキン
DOKIN (BADUM)
IT'S VERY DARK...
NO ONE CAN SEE US RIGHT NOW, SO...
I LOVE YOU ...!!!
HUH ...!? WAIT... WE'RE NOT AL-LOWED IN THE SAND, RIGHT ...?
ドキ ドキ
DOKI DOKI
HUH ...!? WHAT!? THEY'RE INSIDE THE BELL ...!!?
ハラ ハラ ハラ
HARA (SWEAT) HARA HARA
AHHH! AUGH! THEY'RE RIGHT IN FRONT OF THE BUDDHA STATUE... WAIT, NO...! WH-WHOA!!!

★ THIS IS NO PLACE FOR ROMANCE...!!!

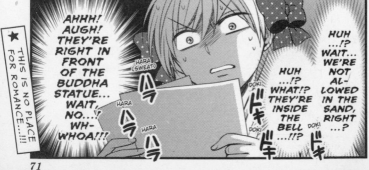

I'M DISAPPOINTED IN YOU!

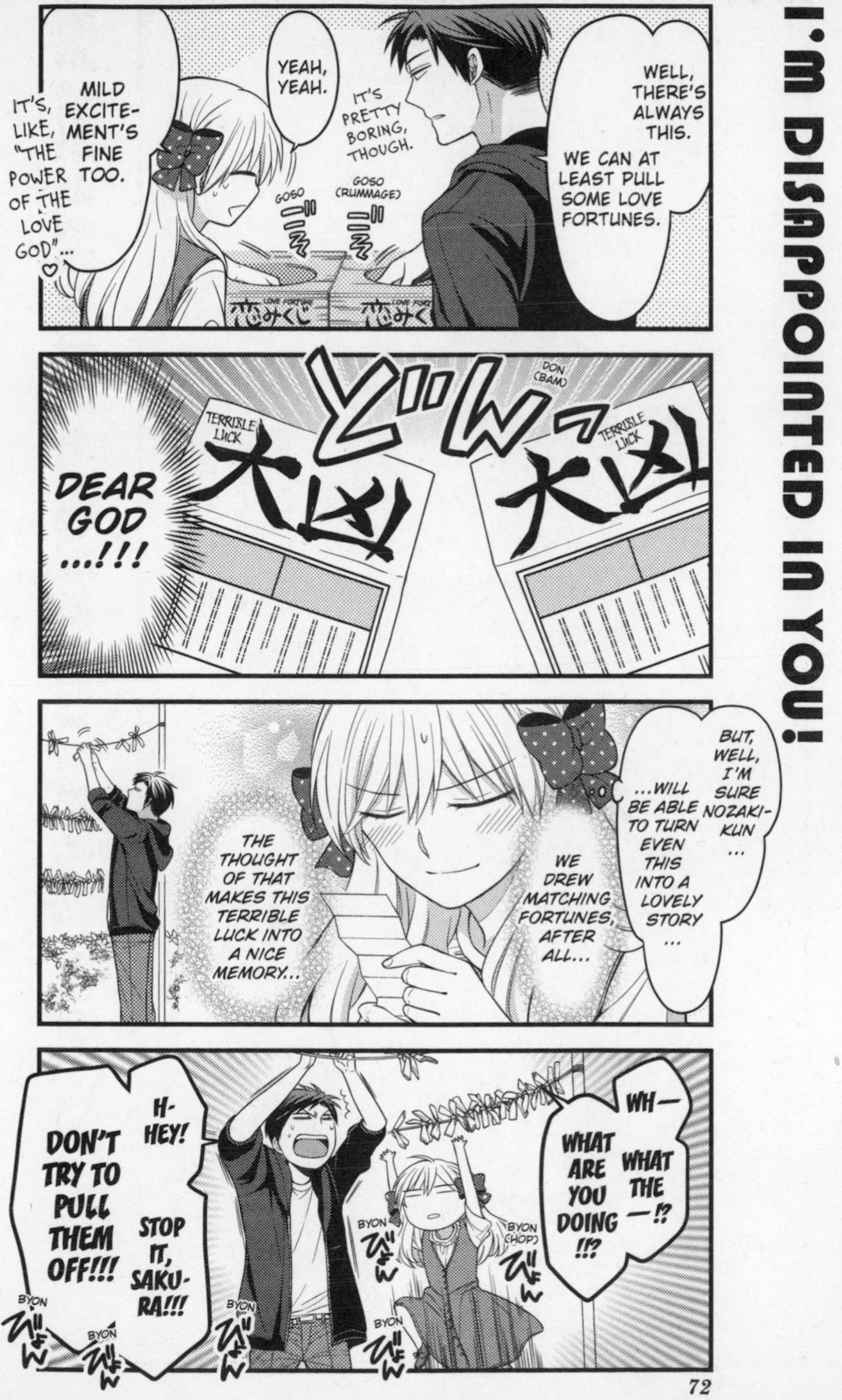
WELL, THERE'S ALWAYS THIS.
WE CAN AT LEAST PULL SOME LOVE FORTUNES.
IT'S PRETTY BORING, THOUGH.
GOSO (RUMMAGE)
YEAH, YEAH.
GOSO
MILD EXCITEMENT'S FINE TOO.
IT'S, LIKE, "THE POWER OF THE LOVE GOD"... ♡
LOVE FORTUNE 恋みくじ
LOVE FORTUNE 恋みく
DON (BAM)
TERRIBLE LUCK 大凶
TERRIBLE LUCK 大凶
DEAR GOD ...!!!
BUT, WELL, I'M SURE NOZAKI-KUN ...
...WILL BE ABLE TO TURN EVEN THIS INTO A LOVELY STORY ...
WE DREW MATCHING FORTUNES, AFTER ALL...
THE THOUGHT OF THAT MAKES THIS TERRIBLE LUCK INTO A NICE MEMORY...
WH— WHAT ARE YOU DOING!!?
WHAT THE—!?
BYON (HOP)
BYON
H-HEY!
STOP IT, SAKURA!!!
DON'T TRY TO PULL THEM OFF!!!
BYON
BYON
BYON
BYON

WE'RE TERRIBLE-LUCK BUDDIES

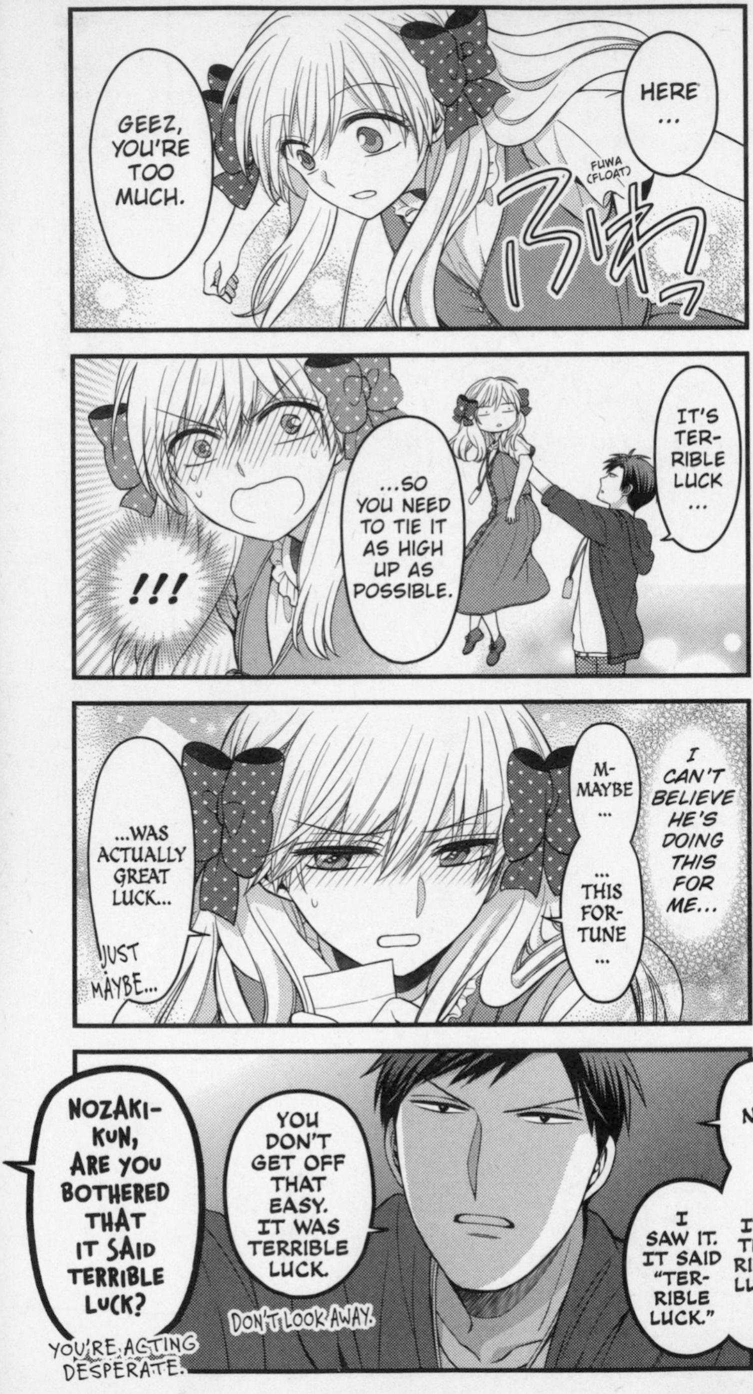
HERE ...
FUWA (FLOAT)
GEEZ, YOU'RE TOO MUCH.
IT'S TER-RIBLE LUCK ...
...SO YOU NEED TO TIE IT AS HIGH UP AS POSSIBLE.
!!!
I CAN'T BELIEVE HE'S DOING THIS FOR ME...
M-MAYBE ...
... THIS FOR-TUNE ...
...WAS ACTUALLY GREAT LUCK...
JUST MAYBE...
NO.
IT'S TER-RIBLE LUCK.
I SAW IT. IT SAID "TER-RIBLE LUCK."
DON'T LOOK AWAY.
YOU DON'T GET OFF THAT EASY. IT WAS TERRIBLE LUCK.
NOZAKI-KUN, ARE YOU BOTHERED THAT IT SAID TERRIBLE LUCK?
YOU'RE ACTING DESPERATE.

GROWING PANIC

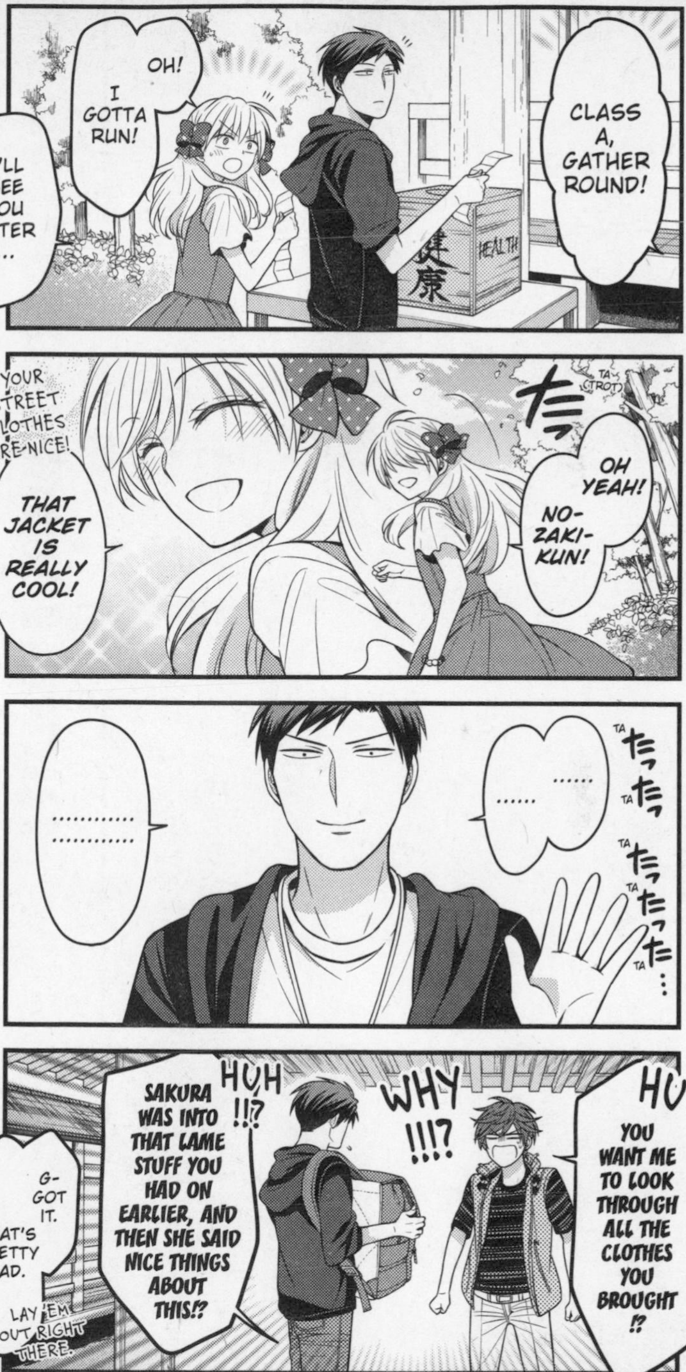
CLASS A, GATHER ROUND!
OH! I GOTTA RUN!
I'LL SEE YOU LATER ...
TA (TROT)
OH YEAH! NO-ZAKI-KUN!
THAT JACKET IS REALLY COOL!
YOUR STREET CLOTHES ARE NICE!
TA TA TA TA TA TA...
....
....
HUH!?
YOU WANT ME TO LOOK THROUGH ALL THE CLOTHES YOU BROUGHT!?
WHY!!!?
HUH!!?
SAKURA WAS INTO THAT LAME STUFF YOU HAD ON EARLIER, AND THEN SHE SAID NICE THINGS ABOUT THIS!?
G-GOT IT. THAT'S PRETTY BAD.
LAY 'EM OUT RIGHT THERE.

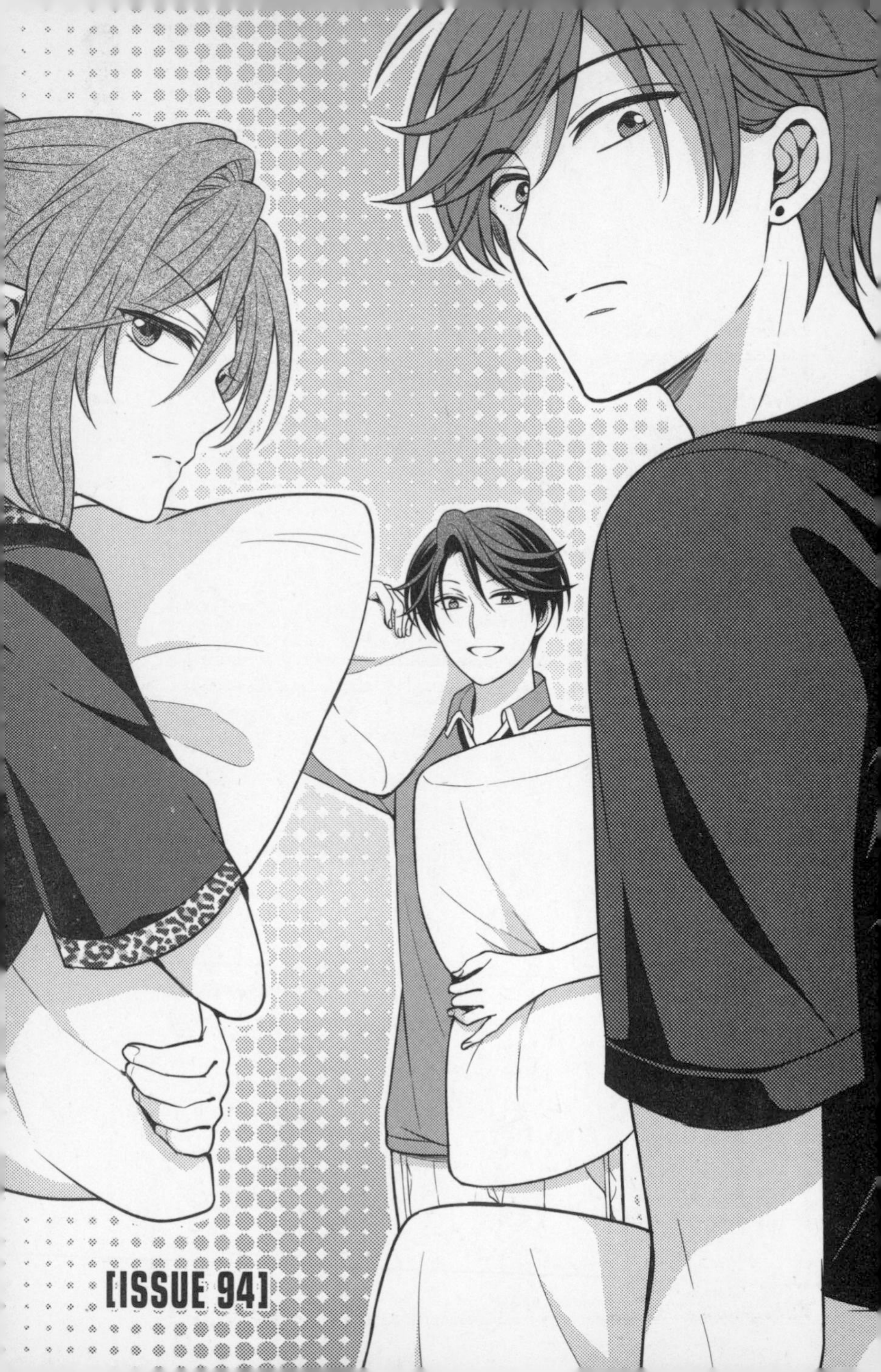
[ISSUE 94]

CASTING A LINE

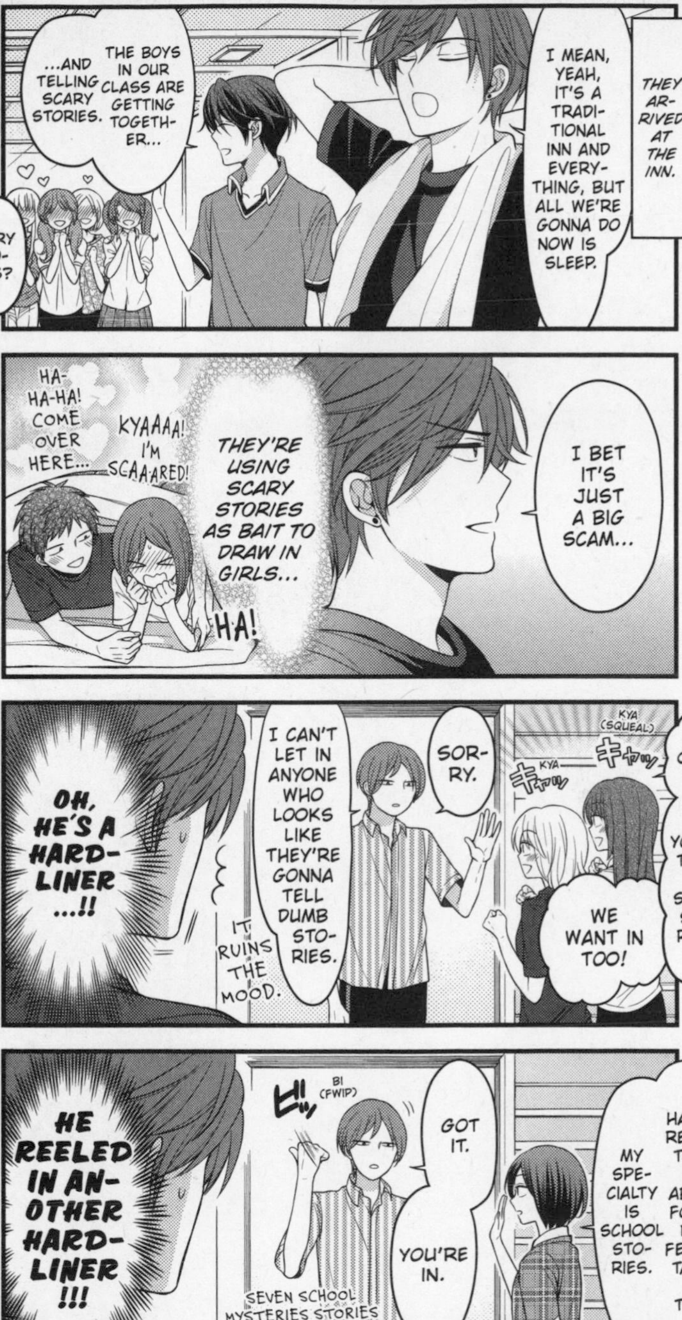

THEY ARRIVED AT THE INN.
I MEAN, YEAH, IT'S A TRADITIONAL INN AND EVERYTHING, BUT ALL WE'RE GONNA DO NOW IS SLEEP.
THE BOYS IN OUR CLASS ARE GETTING TOGETHER...
...AND TELLING SCARY STORIES.
SCARY STORIES?
I BET IT'S JUST A BIG SCAM...
THEY'RE USING SCARY STORIES AS BAIT TO DRAW IN GIRLS...
HA!
KYAAAA! I'M SCAAARED!
HA-HA-HA! COME OVER HERE...
OHH?
YOU'RE TELLING SCARY STORIES?
KYA (SQUEAL)
KYA
WE WANT IN TOO!
SORRY.
I CAN'T LET IN ANYONE WHO LOOKS LIKE THEY'RE GONNA TELL DUMB STORIES.
IT RUINS THE MOOD.
OH, HE'S A HARDLINER...!!
I HAVE A REPERTOIRE OF ABOUT FORTY DIFFERENT TALES TO TELL.
MY SPECIALTY IS SCHOOL STORIES.
BI (FWIP)
GOT IT.
YOU'RE IN.
SEVEN SCHOOL MYSTERIES STORIES ARE REALLY GOOD, AREN'T THEY?
HE REELED IN ANOTHER HARDLINER!!!

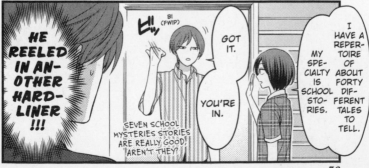

PLEASE, MY MULTITALENTED FRIEND

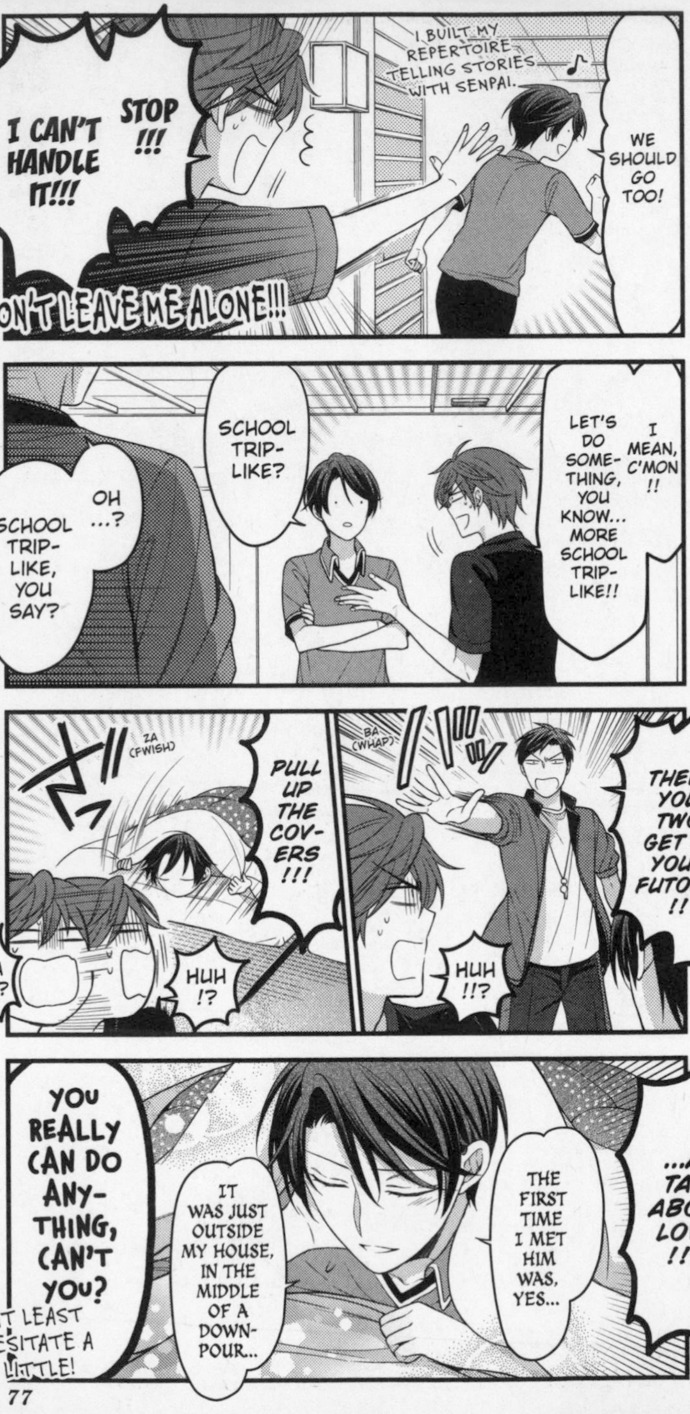
WE SHOULD GO TOO!
I BUILT MY REPERTOIRE TELLING STORIES WITH SENPAI.
STOP!!!
I CAN'T HANDLE IT!!!
DON'T LEAVE ME ALONE!!!
I MEAN, C'MON!!
LET'S DO SOMETHING, YOU KNOW... MORE SCHOOL TRIP-LIKE!!
SCHOOL TRIP-LIKE?
OH...?
SCHOOL TRIP-LIKE, YOU SAY?
THEN, YOU TWO GET IN YOUR FUTONS!!
BA (WHAP)
HUH!!?
PULL UP THE COVERS!!!
ZA (FWISH)
HUH!?
WHA—!!?
...AND TALK ABOUT LOVE!!!
THE FIRST TIME I MET HIM WAS, YES...
IT WAS JUST OUTSIDE MY HOUSE, IN THE MIDDLE OF A DOWNPOUR...
YOU REALLY CAN DO ANYTHING, CAN'T YOU?
AT LEAST HESITATE A LITTLE!

NOZAKI-SENSEI!!

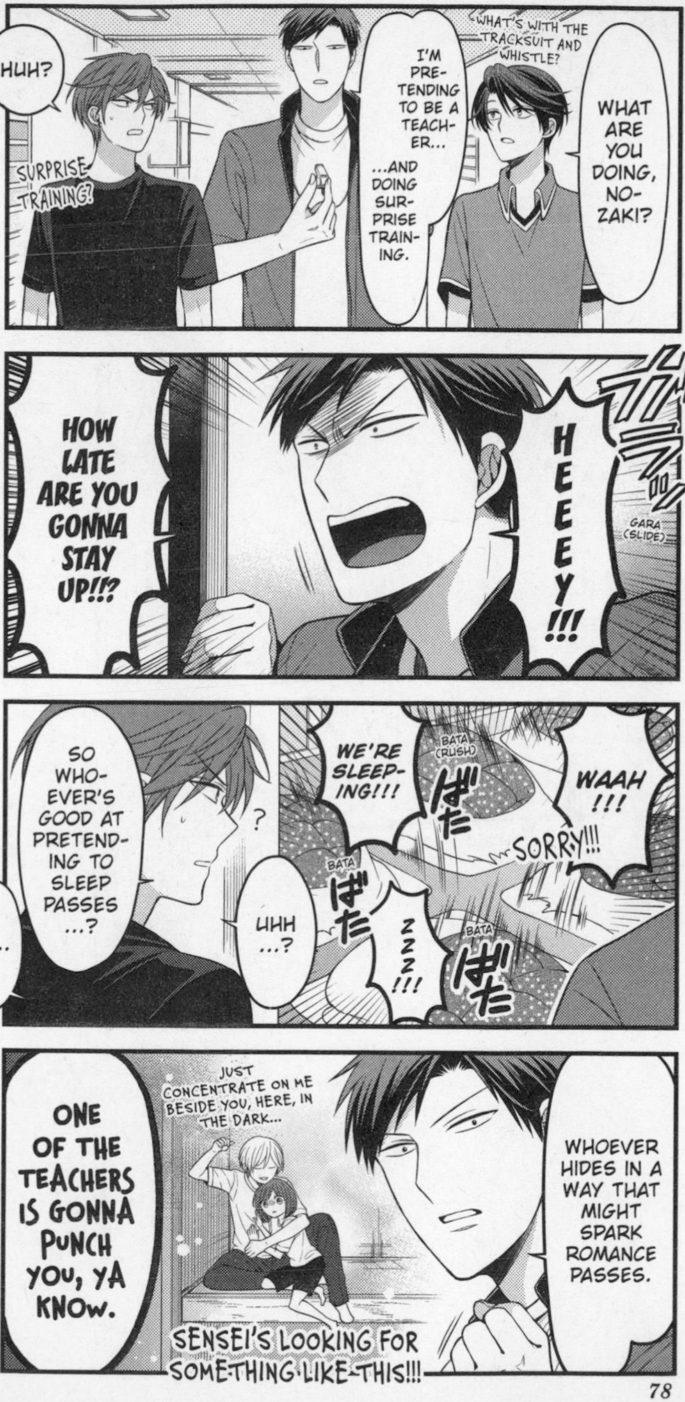
WHAT ARE YOU DOING, NO-ZAKI!?
WHAT'S WITH THE TRACKSUIT AND WHISTLE?
I'M PRE-TENDING TO BE A TEACH-ER...
...AND DOING SUR-PRISE TRAIN-ING.
HUH?
SURPRISE TRAINING!?
ガラッ
GARA (SLIDE)
HEEEEY!!!
HOW LATE ARE YOU GONNA STAY UP!!?
WAAH!!!
SORRY!!!
BATA (RUSH)
ばた
WE'RE SLEEP-ING!!!
BATA
ばた
ZZZ!!!
BATA
ばた
UHH...?
?
SO WHO-EVER'S GOOD AT PRETEND-ING TO SLEEP PASSES...?
NO...
WHOEVER HIDES IN A WAY THAT MIGHT SPARK ROMANCE PASSES.
JUST CONCENTRATE ON ME BESIDE YOU, HERE, IN THE DARK...
SENSEI'S LOOKING FOR SOMETHING LIKE THIS!!!
ONE OF THE TEACHERS IS GONNA PUNCH YOU, YA KNOW.

NOZAKI'S CHECK

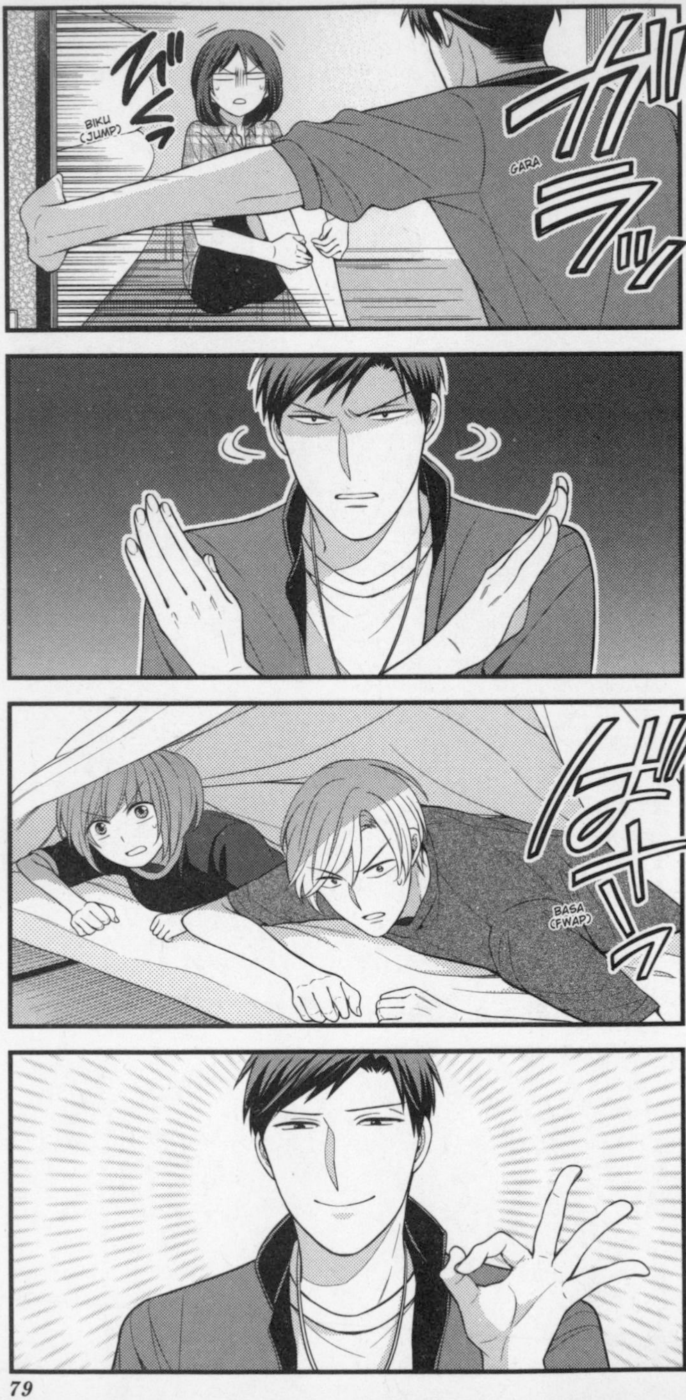
GARA
BIKU (JUMP)
BASA (FWAP)

AN UNEXPECTED SCENE

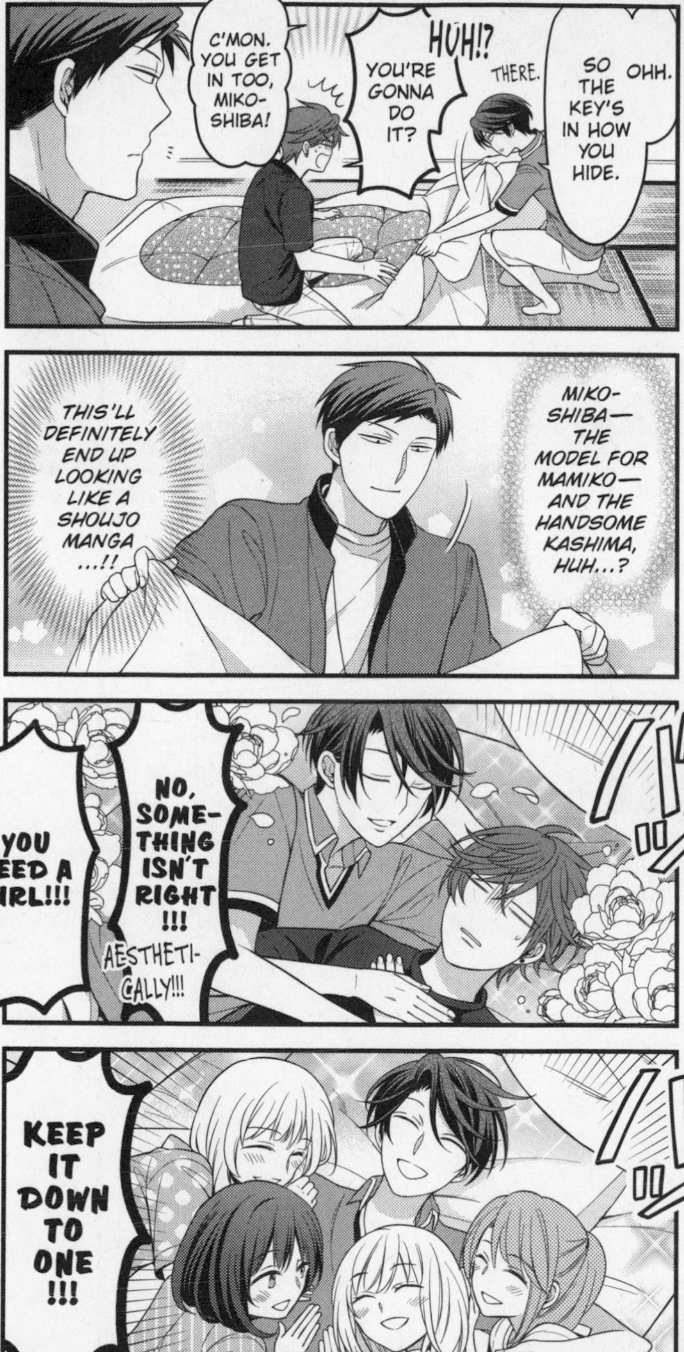

OHH.
SO THE KEY'S IN HOW YOU HIDE.
THERE.
HUH!?
YOU'RE GONNA DO IT?
C'MON. YOU GET IN TOO, MIKO-SHIBA!
MIKO-SHIBA—THE MODEL FOR MAMIKO—AND THE HANDSOME KASHIMA, HUH...?
THIS'LL DEFINITELY END UP LOOKING LIKE A SHOUJO MANGA ...!!
BA (YANK)
NO, SOME-THING ISN'T RIGHT !!!
AESTHETI-CALLY!!!
YOU NEED A GIRL!!!
BA
KEEP IT DOWN TO ONE !!!

A SHOCKING SIGHT

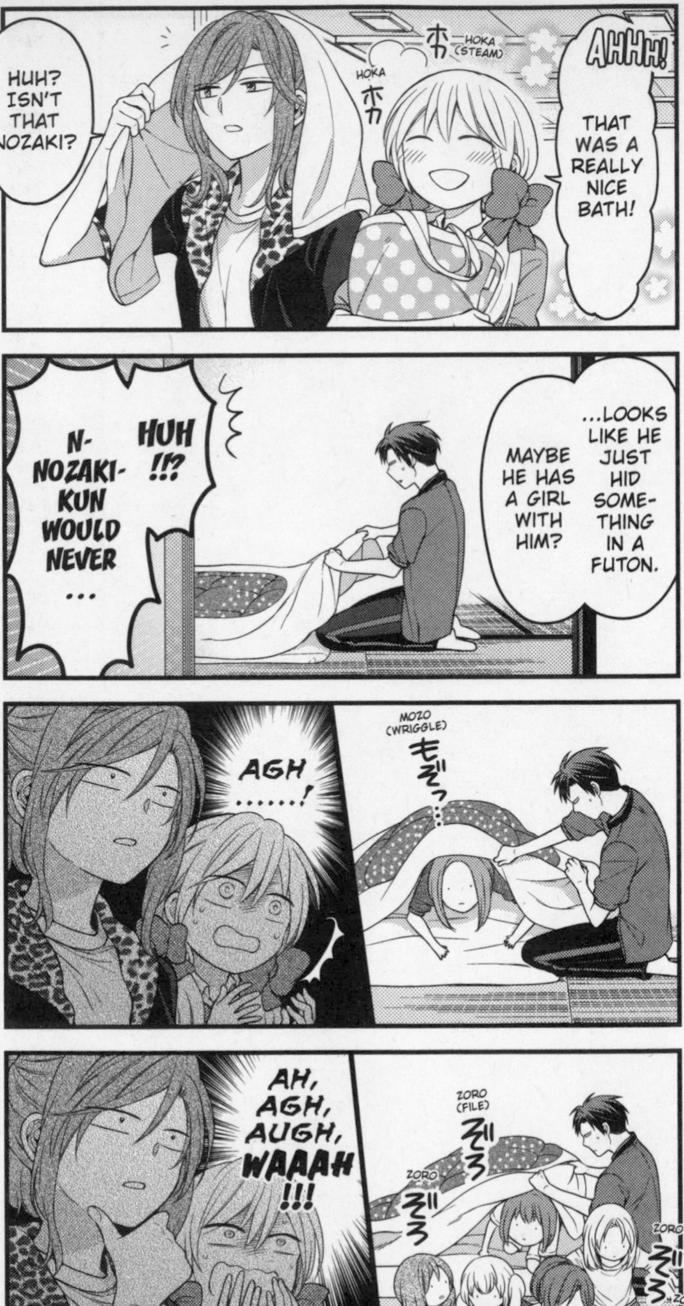
AHHH!
THAT WAS A REALLY NICE BATH!
HOKA (STEAM)
ホカ
HOKA
ホカ
HUH? ISN'T THAT NOZAKI?
...LOOKS LIKE HE JUST HID SOME-THING IN A FUTON.
MAYBE HE HAS A GIRL WITH HIM?
HUH!!?
N-NOZAKI-KUN WOULD NEVER...
MOZO (WRIGGLE)
もぞっ
AGH......!
ZORO (FILE)
ぞろ
ZORO
ぞろ
ZORO
ぞろ
ZORO
ぞろ
AH, AGH, AUGH, WAAAH!!!

A DANGEROUS MAN

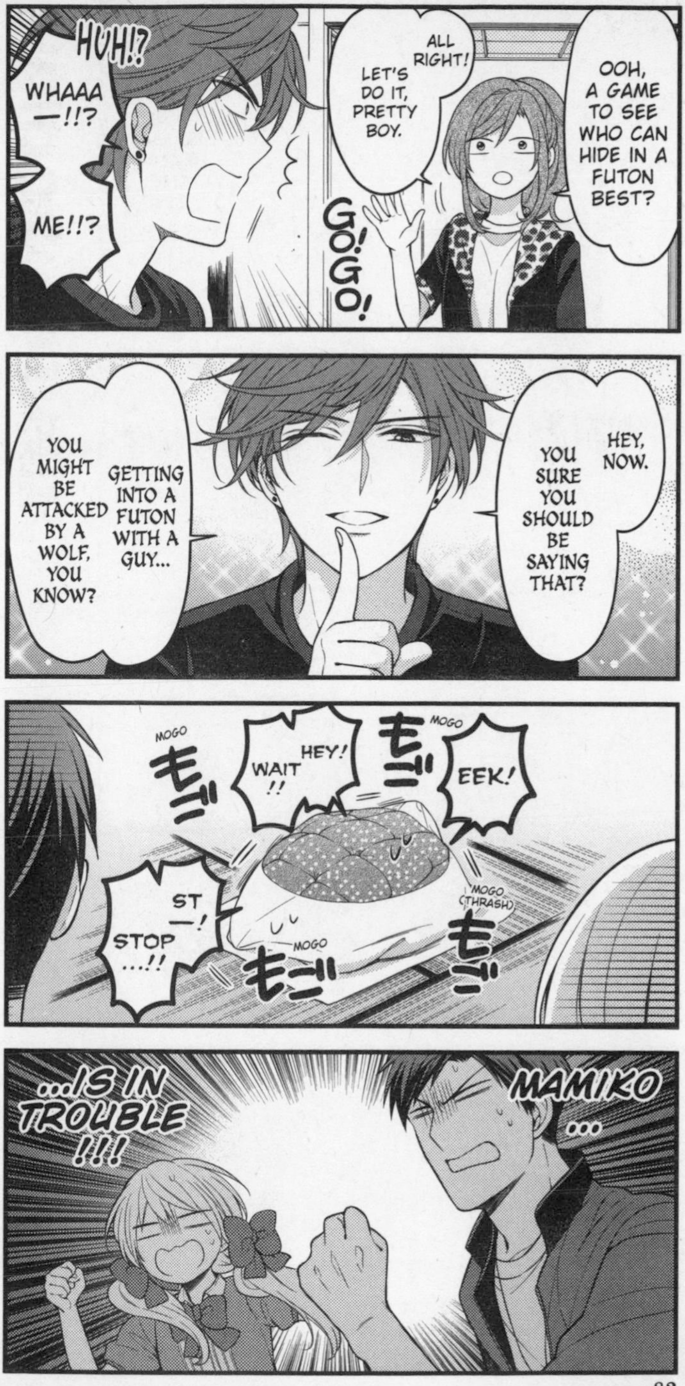
OOH, A GAME TO SEE WHO CAN HIDE IN A FUTON BEST?
ALL RIGHT! LET'S DO IT, PRETTY BOY.
GO! GO!
HUH!?
WHAAA—!!?
ME!!?
HEY, NOW.
YOU SURE YOU SHOULD BE SAYING THAT?
GETTING INTO A FUTON WITH A GUY...
YOU MIGHT BE ATTACKED BY A WOLF, YOU KNOW?
MOGO
EEK!
HEY! WAIT!!
MOGO
MOGO (THRASH)
ST—! STOP...!!
MOGO
MAMIKO...
...IS IN TROUBLE!!!

RIGHT AT THIS VERY MOMENT

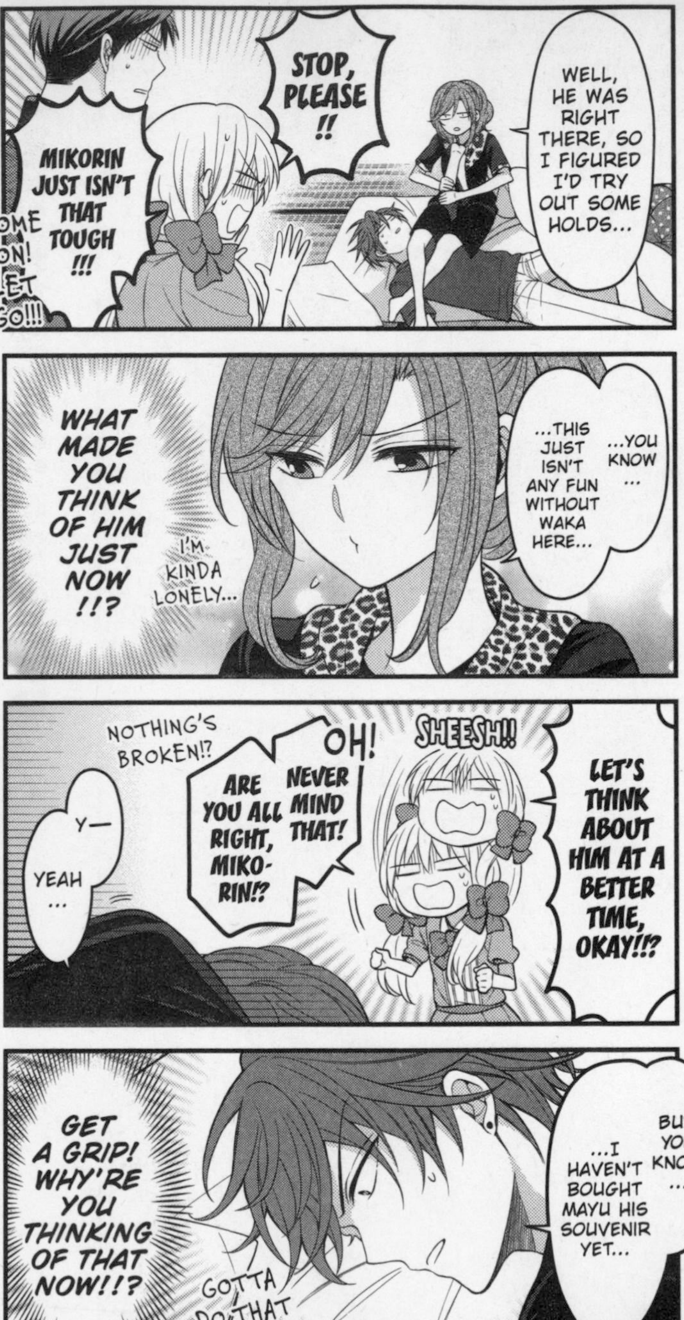

WELL, HE WAS RIGHT THERE, SO I FIGURED I'D TRY OUT SOME HOLDS...
STOP, PLEASE!!
MIKORIN JUST ISN'T THAT TOUGH!!!
COME ON! LET GO!!!
...YOU KNOW...
...THIS JUST ISN'T ANY FUN WITHOUT WAKA HERE...
I'M KINDA LONELY...
WHAT MADE YOU THINK OF HIM JUST NOW!!?
SHEESH!!
LET'S THINK ABOUT HIM AT A BETTER TIME, OKAY!!?
OH!
NEVER MIND THAT!
ARE YOU ALL RIGHT, MIKO-RIN!?
NOTHING'S BROKEN!?
Y— YEAH...
BUT, YOU KNOW...
...I HAVEN'T BOUGHT MAYU HIS SOUVENIR YET...
GOTTA DO THAT...!!
GET A GRIP! WHY'RE YOU THINKING OF THAT NOW!!?

IT IS REFRESHING, THOUGH

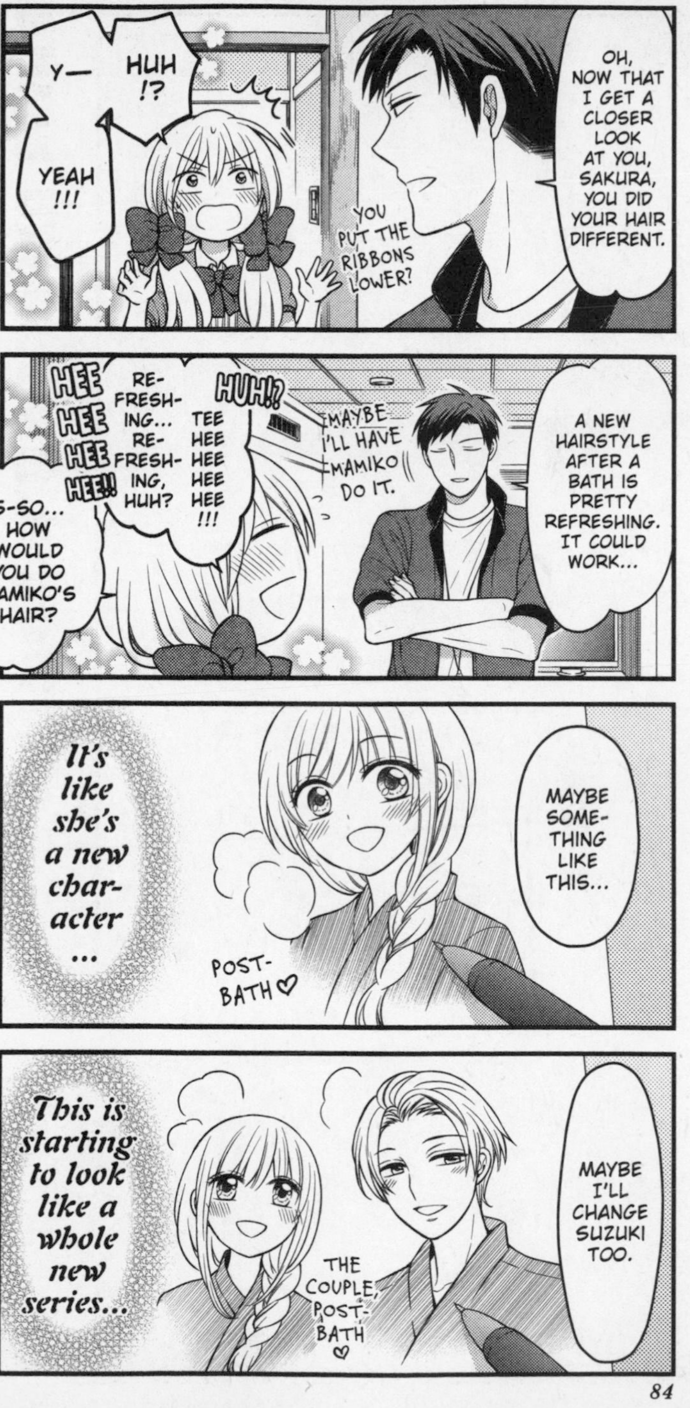
OH, NOW THAT I GET A CLOSER LOOK AT YOU, SAKURA, YOU DID YOUR HAIR DIFFERENT.
YOU PUT THE RIBBONS LOWER?
HUH!?
Y— YEAH!!!
A NEW HAIRSTYLE AFTER A BATH IS PRETTY REFRESHING. IT COULD WORK...
MAYBE I'LL HAVE MAMIKO DO IT.
HUH!?
TEE HEE HEE HEE HEE!!!
RE-FRESHING... RE-FRESHING, HUH?
HEE HEE HEE HEE!!
S-SO... HOW WOULD YOU DO MAMIKO'S HAIR?
MAYBE SOMETHING LIKE THIS...
POST-BATH♡
It's like she's a new character...
MAYBE I'LL CHANGE SUZUKI TOO.
THE COUPLE, POST-BATH♡
This is starting to look like a whole new series...

THEIR REPUTATIONS

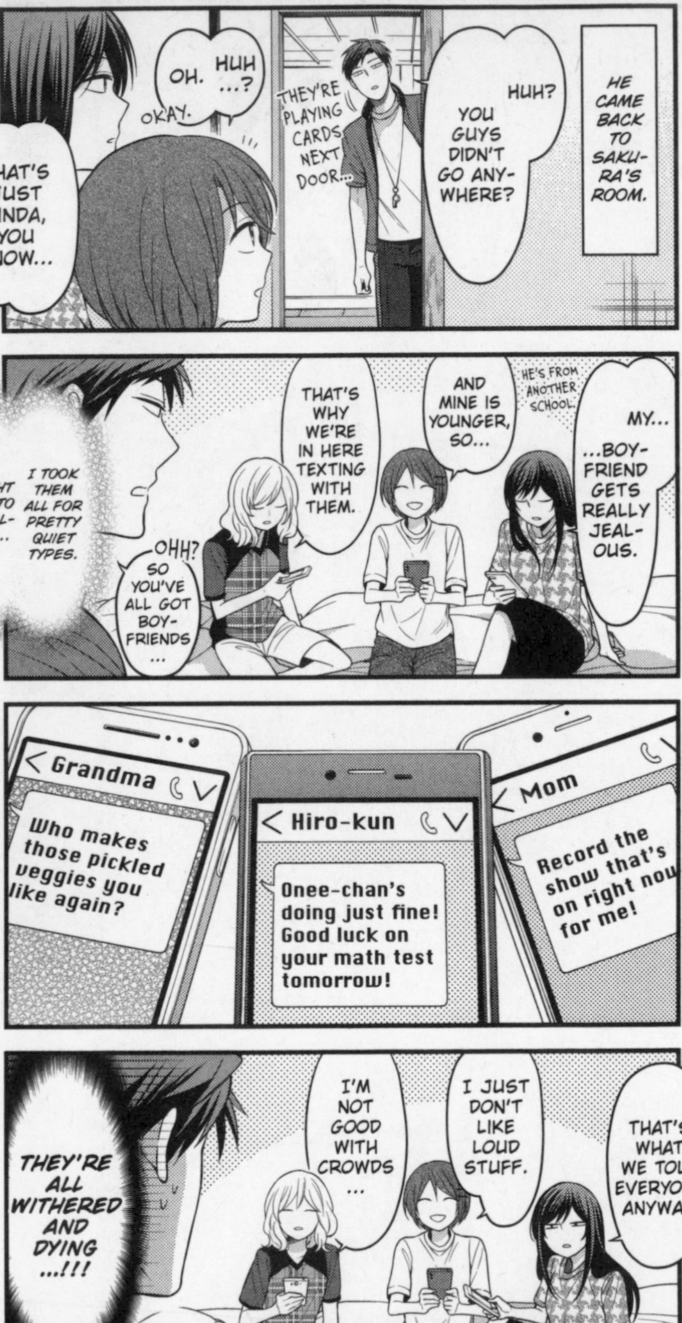
HE CAME BACK TO SAKURA'S ROOM.
HUH? YOU GUYS DIDN'T GO ANYWHERE?
THEY'RE PLAYING CARDS NEXT DOOR...
HUH...?
OH.
OKAY.
THAT'S JUST KINDA, YOU KNOW...
MY... ...BOYFRIEND GETS REALLY JEALOUS.
HE'S FROM ANOTHER SCHOOL.
AND MINE IS YOUNGER, SO...
THAT'S WHY WE'RE IN HERE TEXTING WITH THEM.
OHH? SO YOU'VE ALL GOT BOYFRIENDS...
I TOOK THEM ALL FOR PRETTY QUIET TYPES.
I MIGHT HAVE TO REEVALUATE...
Mom
Record the show that's on right now for me!
Hiro-kun
Onee-chan's doing just fine! Good luck on your math test tomorrow!
Grandma
Who makes those pickled veggies you like again?
THAT'S WHAT WE TOLD EVERYONE ANYWAY.
I JUST DON'T LIKE LOUD STUFF.
I'M NOT GOOD WITH CROWDS...
THEY'RE ALL WITHERED AND DYING...!!!

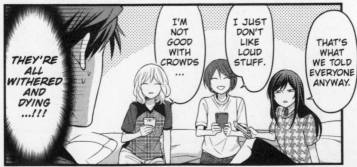

AN UNPRODUCTIVE CONVERSATION

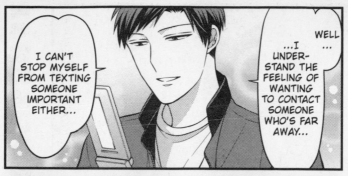

WELL... ...I UNDERSTAND THE FEELING OF WANTING TO CONTACT SOMEONE WHO'S FAR AWAY...
I CAN'T STOP MYSELF FROM TEXTING SOMEONE IMPORTANT EITHER...
DON'T TELL ME...
ZA (WHOOSH)
...YOU'RE TEXTING HORI-SENPAI...?
HUH...!!?
YOU'RE TRYING TO GET IN AHEAD OF ME, AREN'T YOU?
HUH...? WHAT IN THE WORLD ARE THEY TALKING ABOUT?
CALM DOWN. ...IT'S NOT HORI-SENPAI.
SO WHO IS IT...!?
OF COURSE IT ISN'T!!!
IT'S DEFINITELY NOT GONNA BE A GUY, RIGHT!!?
THIS IS "SOMEONE IMPORTANT"!!
IT'S KEN-SAN...
Ken-san
I'm on my school trip!♡♡♡ What would you like for a souvenir!?♪
IT IS A GUY!!?

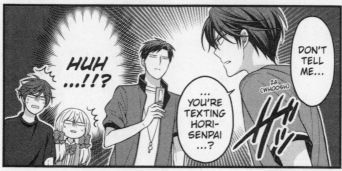

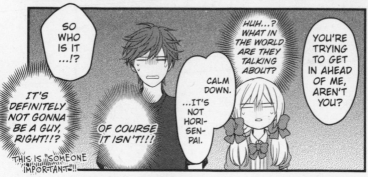

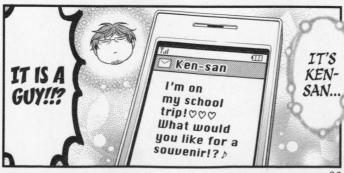

HE WANTED TO DO IT

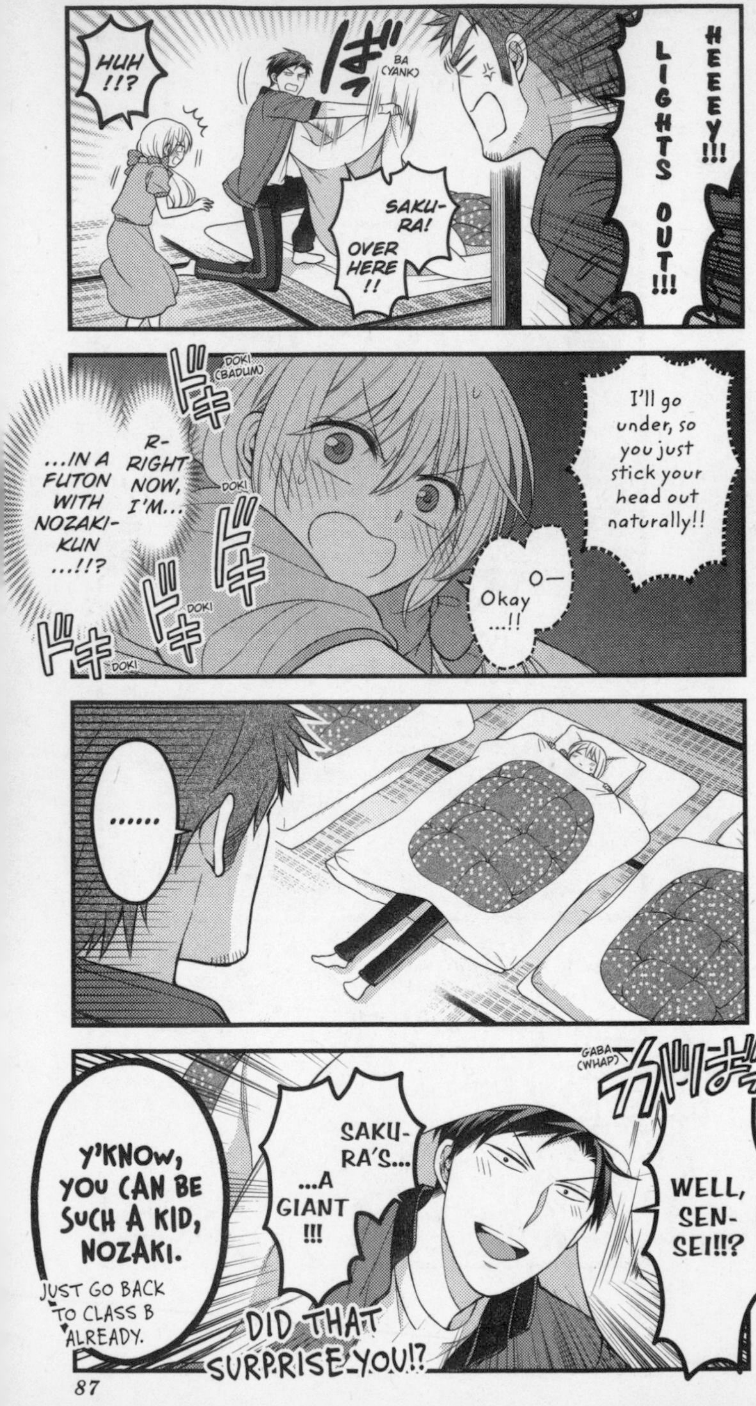

HEEEEY!!!
LIGHTS OUT!!!
BA (YANK)
SAKU-RA! OVER HERE!!
HUH!!?
DOKI (BADUM)
I'll go under, so you just stick your head out naturally!!
O— Okay...!!
R-RIGHT NOW, I'M...
...IN A FUTON WITH NOZAKI-KUN...!!?
DOKI
DOKI
DOKI
......
GABA (WHAP)
WELL, SEN-SEI!!?
SAKU-RA'S... ...A GIANT!!!
DID THAT SURPRISE YOU!?
Y'KNOW, YOU CAN BE SUCH A KID, NOZAKI.
JUST GO BACK TO CLASS B ALREADY.

MY FRIEND

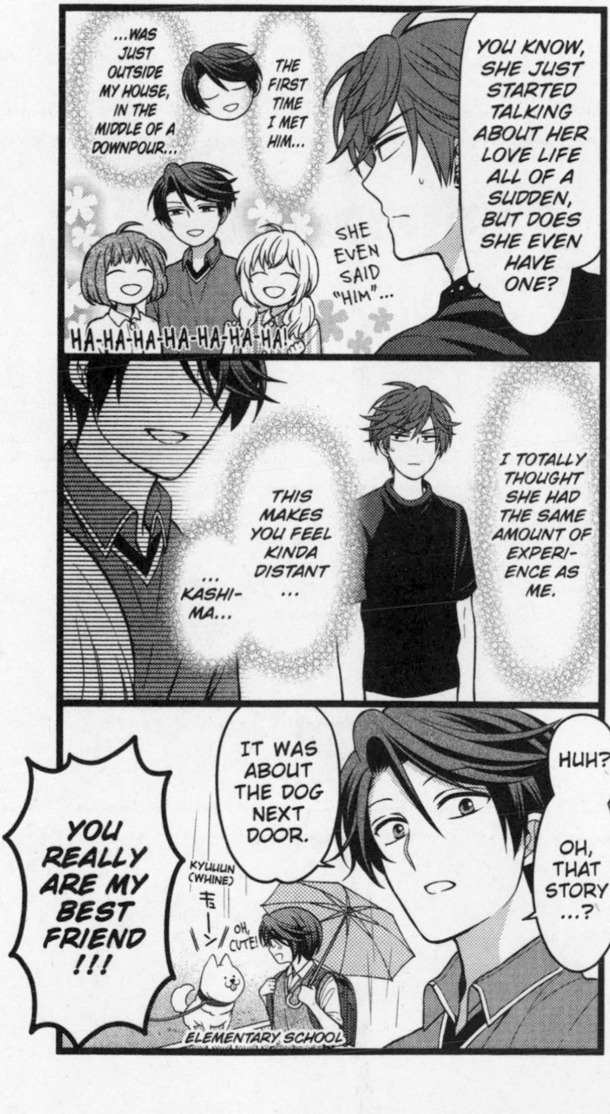
YOU KNOW, SHE JUST STARTED TALKING ABOUT HER LOVE LIFE ALL OF A SUDDEN, BUT DOES SHE EVEN HAVE ONE?
SHE EVEN SAID "HIM"...
THE FIRST TIME I MET HIM...
...WAS JUST OUTSIDE MY HOUSE, IN THE MIDDLE OF A DOWNPOUR...
HA-HA-HA-HA-HA-HA-HA!
I TOTALLY THOUGHT SHE HAD THE SAME AMOUNT OF EXPERI-ENCE AS ME.
THIS MAKES YOU FEEL KINDA DISTANT...
...KASHI-MA...
HUH?
OH, THAT STORY...?
IT WAS ABOUT THE DOG NEXT DOOR.
OH, CUTE!
KYUUUN (WHINE)
キューン
ELEMENTARY SCHOOL
YOU REALLY ARE MY BEST FRIEND!!!

[Extra]

MY YOUNG FRIEND

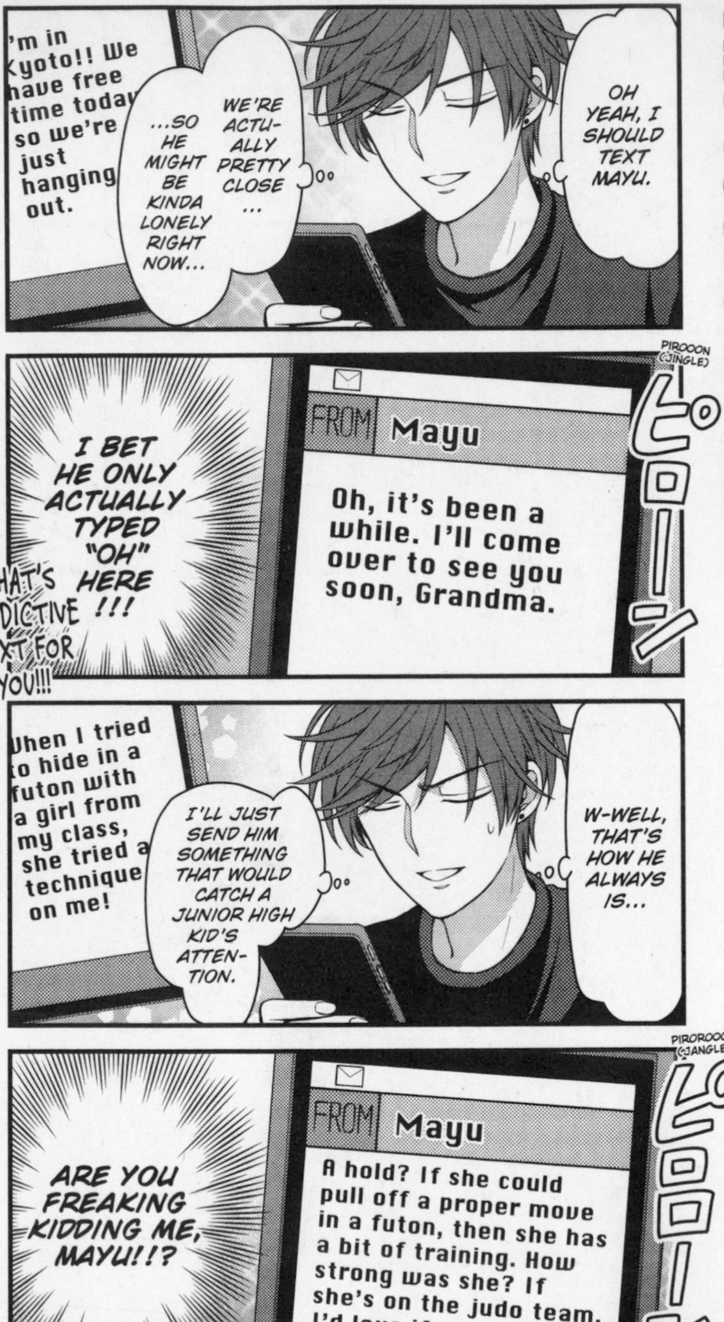
OH YEAH, I SHOULD TEXT MAYU.
WE'RE ACTUALLY PRETTY CLOSE...
...SO HE MIGHT BE KINDA LONELY RIGHT NOW...
'm in Kyoto!! We have free time today so we're just hanging out.
PIROOON (JINGLE)
ピローン
FROM Mayu
Oh, it's been a while. I'll come over to see you soon, Grandma.
I BET HE ONLY ACTUALLY TYPED "OH" HERE!!!
THAT'S PREDICTIVE TEXT FOR YOU!!!
W-WELL, THAT'S HOW HE ALWAYS IS...
I'LL JUST SEND HIM SOMETHING THAT WOULD CATCH A JUNIOR HIGH KID'S ATTENTION.
hen I tried o hide in a futon with a girl from my class, she tried a technique on me!
PIROROOON (JANGLE)
ピロローン
FROM Mayu
A hold? If she could pull off a proper move in a futon, then she has a bit of training. How strong was she? If she's on the judo team, I'd love if you could give me her number.
ARE YOU FREAKING KIDDING ME, MAYU!!?

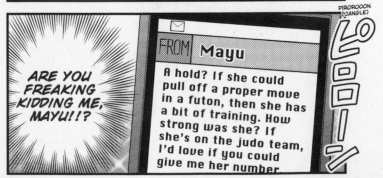

[Extra]

MY HOPELESS FRIEND

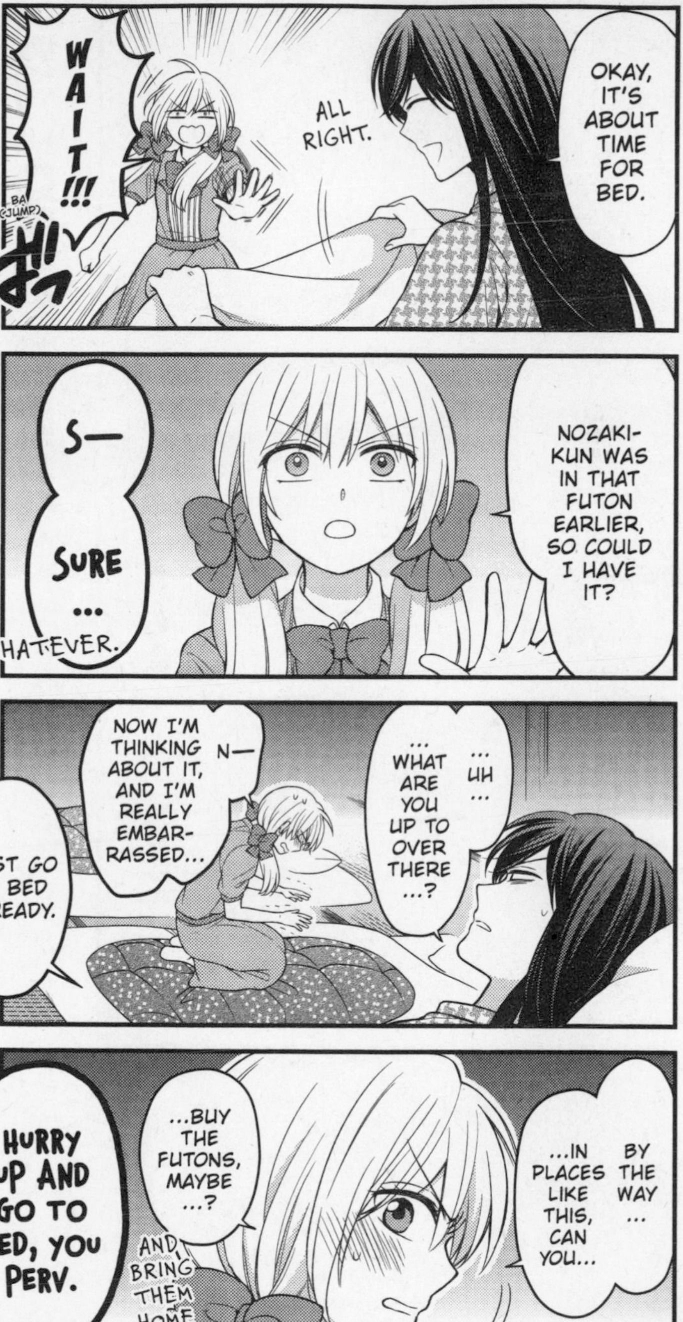

OKAY, IT'S ABOUT TIME FOR BED.
ALL RIGHT.
WAIT!!!
BA (JUMP)
ぱっ
NOZAKI-KUN WAS IN THAT FUTON EARLIER, SO COULD I HAVE IT?
S— SURE ...
WHATEVER.
... UH ...
... WHAT ARE YOU UP TO OVER THERE ...?
N—
NOW I'M THINKING ABOUT IT, AND I'M REALLY EMBARRASSED...
JUST GO TO BED ALREADY.
BY THE WAY ...
...IN PLACES LIKE THIS, CAN YOU...
...BUY THE FUTONS, MAYBE ...?
AND BRING THEM HOME ...?
HURRY UP AND GO TO BED, YOU PERV.

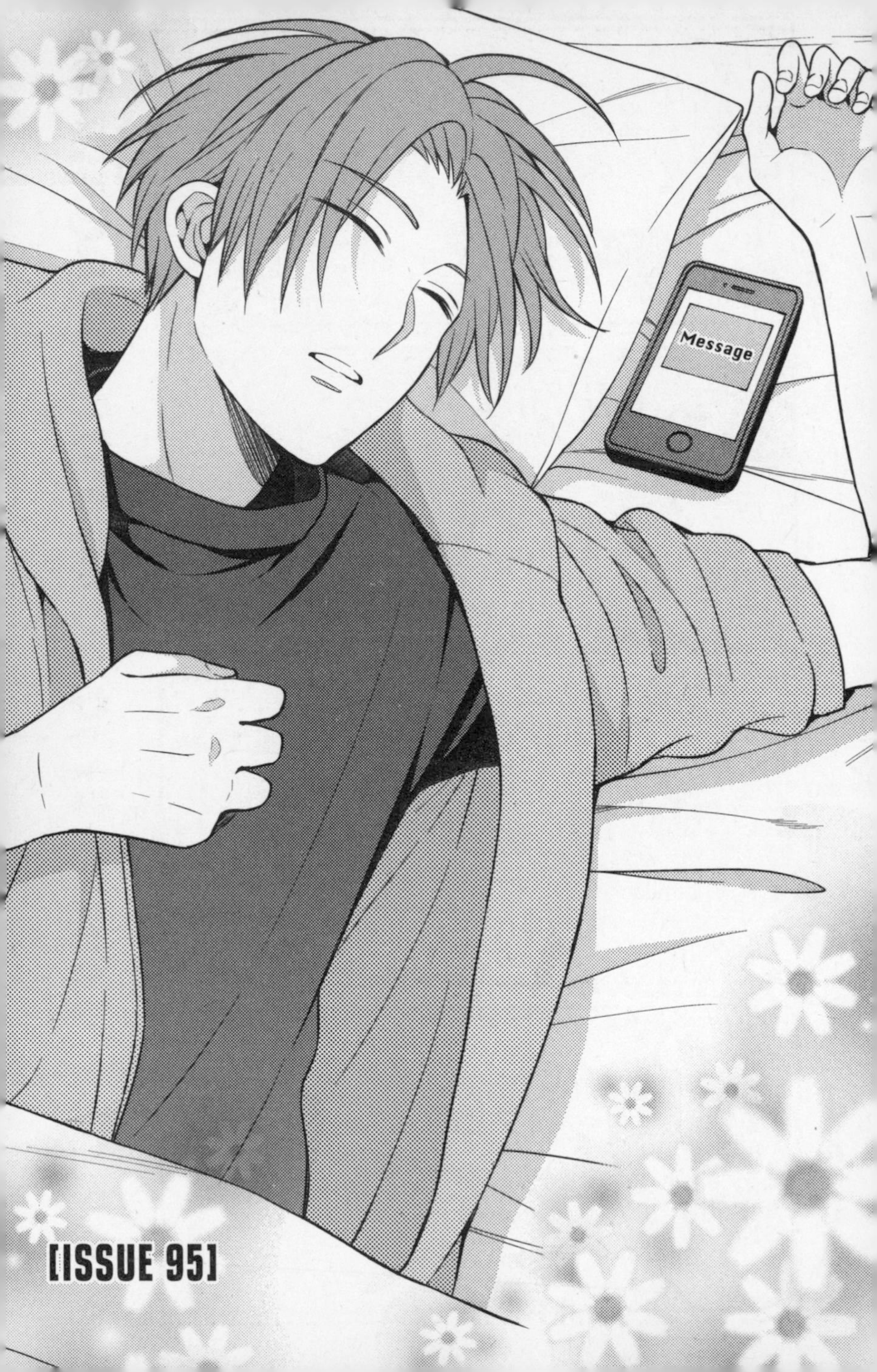
Message
[ISSUE 95]

GO ALL-OUT ON THE WIDE-OPEN COURT

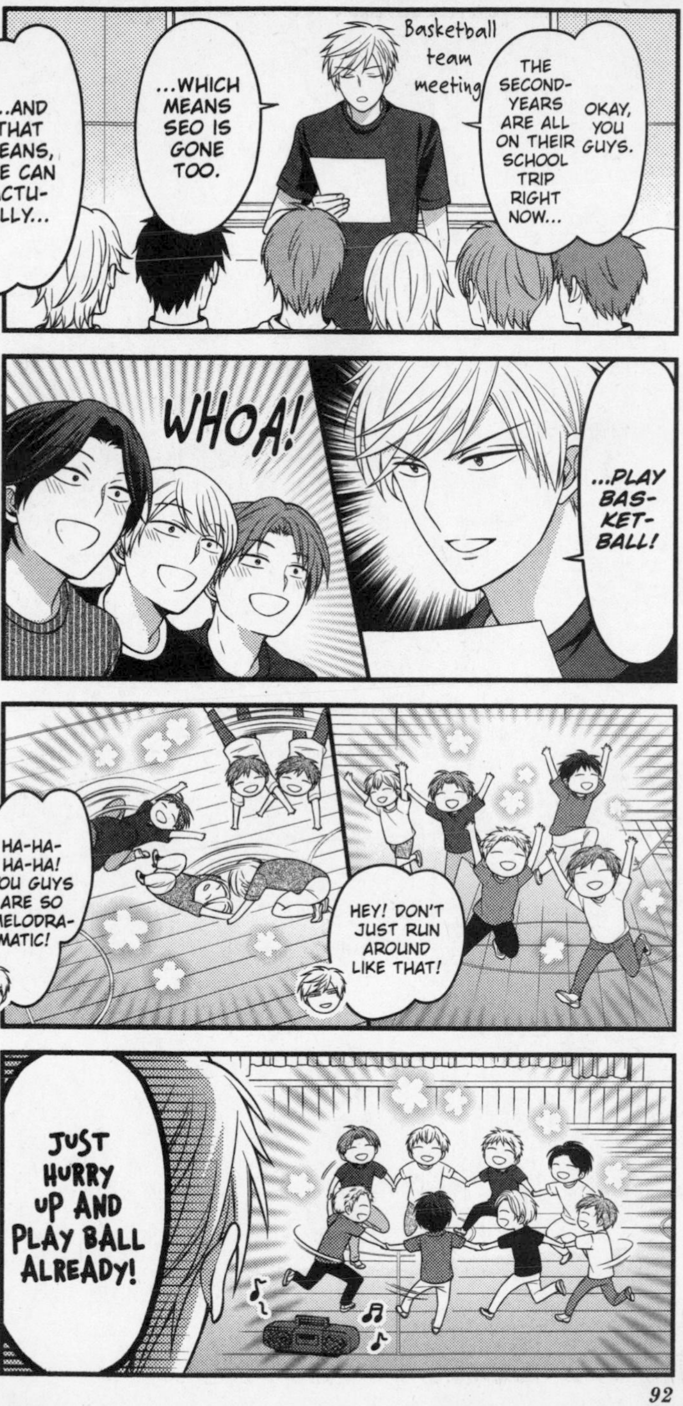
Basketball team meeting
OKAY, YOU GUYS.
THE SECOND-YEARS ARE ALL ON THEIR SCHOOL TRIP RIGHT NOW...
...WHICH MEANS SEO IS GONE TOO.
...AND THAT MEANS, WE CAN ACTUALLY...
...PLAY BASKETBALL!
WHOA!
HEY! DON'T JUST RUN AROUND LIKE THAT!
HA-HA-HA-HA! YOU GUYS ARE SO MELODRAMATIC!
JUST HURRY UP AND PLAY BALL ALREADY!

I'VE NEVER SEEN ANYTHING LIKE THIS

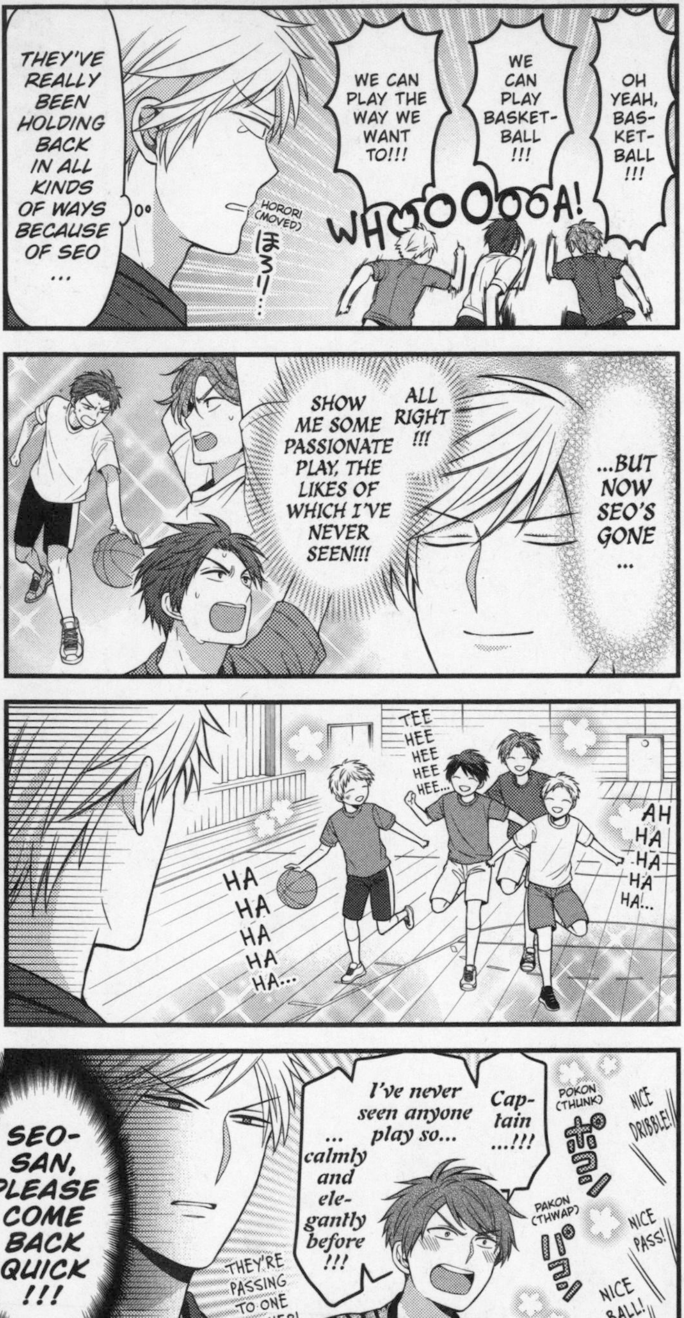
OH YEAH, BASKETBALL!!!
WE CAN PLAY BASKETBALL!!!
WE CAN PLAY THE WAY WE WANT TO!!!
WHOOOOOA!
HORORI (MOVED)
ほろリ…
THEY'VE REALLY BEEN HOLDING BACK IN ALL KINDS OF WAYS BECAUSE OF SEO…
…BUT NOW SEO'S GONE…
SHOW ME SOME PASSIONATE PLAY, THE LIKES OF WHICH I'VE NEVER SEEN!!!
ALL RIGHT!!!
AH HA HA HA HA HA!…
TEE HEE HEE HEE HEE…
HA HA HA HA HA…
NICE DRIBBLE!
POKON (THUNK)
ポン!
NICE PASS!
PAKON (THWAP)
パコッ
NICE BALL!
Captain…!!!
I've never seen anyone play so… …calmly and elegantly before!!!
THEY'RE PASSING TO ONE ANOTHER! EQUALLY!!!
SEO-SAN, PLEASE COME BACK QUICK!!!

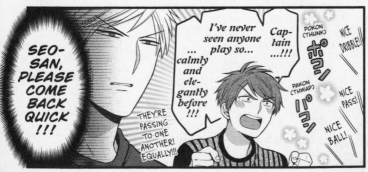

MORE ROOM IN HIS HEART

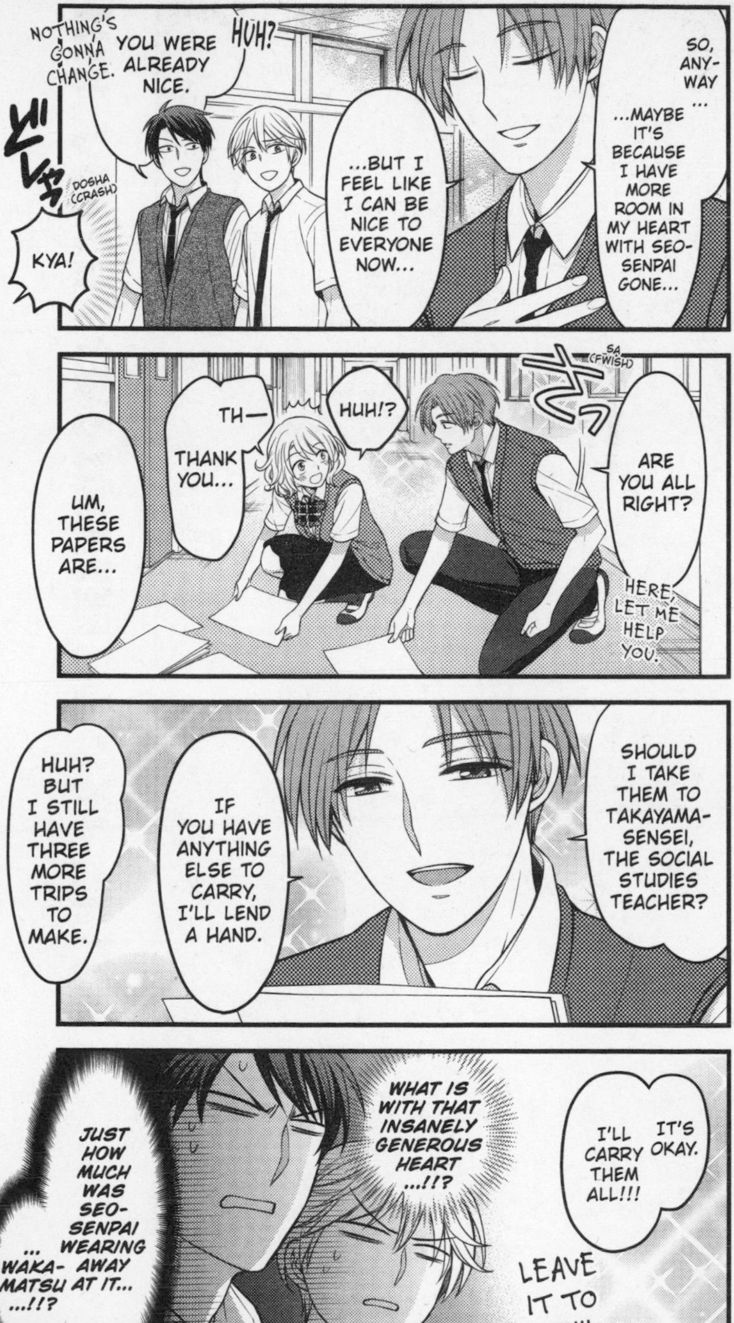
SO, ANY-WAY ...
...MAYBE IT'S BECAUSE I HAVE MORE ROOM IN MY HEART WITH SEO-SENPAI GONE...
...BUT I FEEL LIKE I CAN BE NICE TO EVERYONE NOW...
HUH?
YOU WERE ALREADY NICE.
NOTHING'S GONNA CHANGE.
どしゃ
DOSHA (CRASH)
KYA!
さっ
SA (FWISH)
ARE YOU ALL RIGHT?
HERE, LET ME HELP YOU.
HUH!?
TH— THANK YOU...
UM, THESE PAPERS ARE...
SHOULD I TAKE THEM TO TAKAYAMA-SENSEI, THE SOCIAL STUDIES TEACHER?
IF YOU HAVE ANYTHING ELSE TO CARRY, I'LL LEND A HAND.
HUH? BUT I STILL HAVE THREE MORE TRIPS TO MAKE.
IT'S OKAY.
I'LL CARRY THEM ALL!!!
LEAVE IT TO ME!!!
WHAT IS WITH THAT INSANELY GENEROUS HEART ...!!?
JUST HOW MUCH WAS SEO-SENPAI WEARING AWAY AT IT...
...WAKA-MATSU ...!!?

SHE'S FROM CLASS 3-C

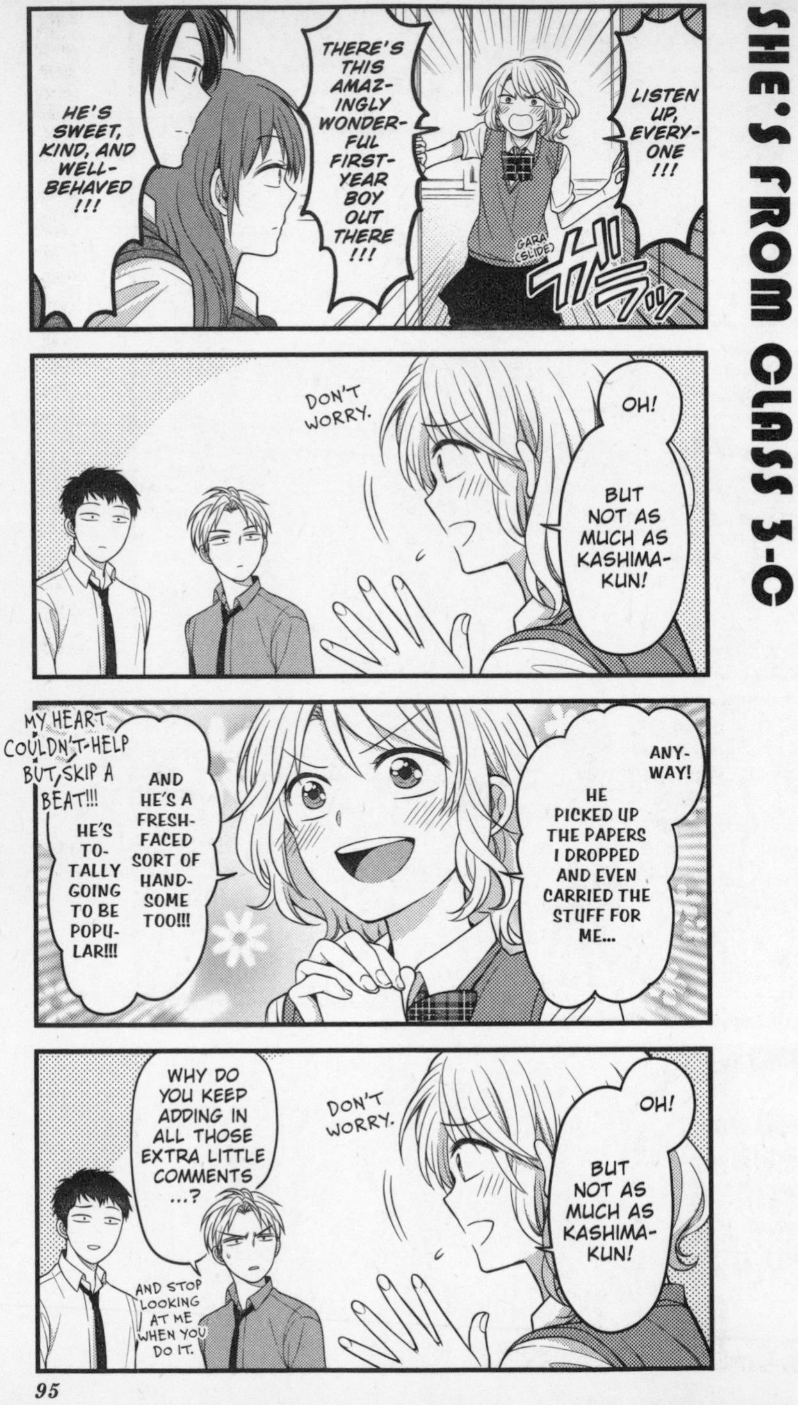
LISTEN UP, EVERYONE!!!
GARA (SLIDE)
THERE'S THIS AMAZINGLY WONDERFUL FIRST-YEAR BOY OUT THERE!!!
HE'S SWEET, KIND, AND WELL-BEHAVED!!!
OH!
BUT NOT AS MUCH AS KASHIMA-KUN!
DON'T WORRY.
ANYWAY!
HE PICKED UP THE PAPERS I DROPPED AND EVEN CARRIED THE STUFF FOR ME...
AND HE'S A FRESH-FACED SORT OF HANDSOME TOO!!!
HE'S TOTALLY GOING TO BE POPULAR!!!
MY HEART COULDN'T HELP BUT SKIP A BEAT!!!
OH!
BUT NOT AS MUCH AS KASHIMA-KUN!
DON'T WORRY.
WHY DO YOU KEEP ADDING IN ALL THOSE EXTRA LITTLE COMMENTS...?
AND STOP LOOKING AT ME WHEN YOU DO IT.

YOU TRAITOR

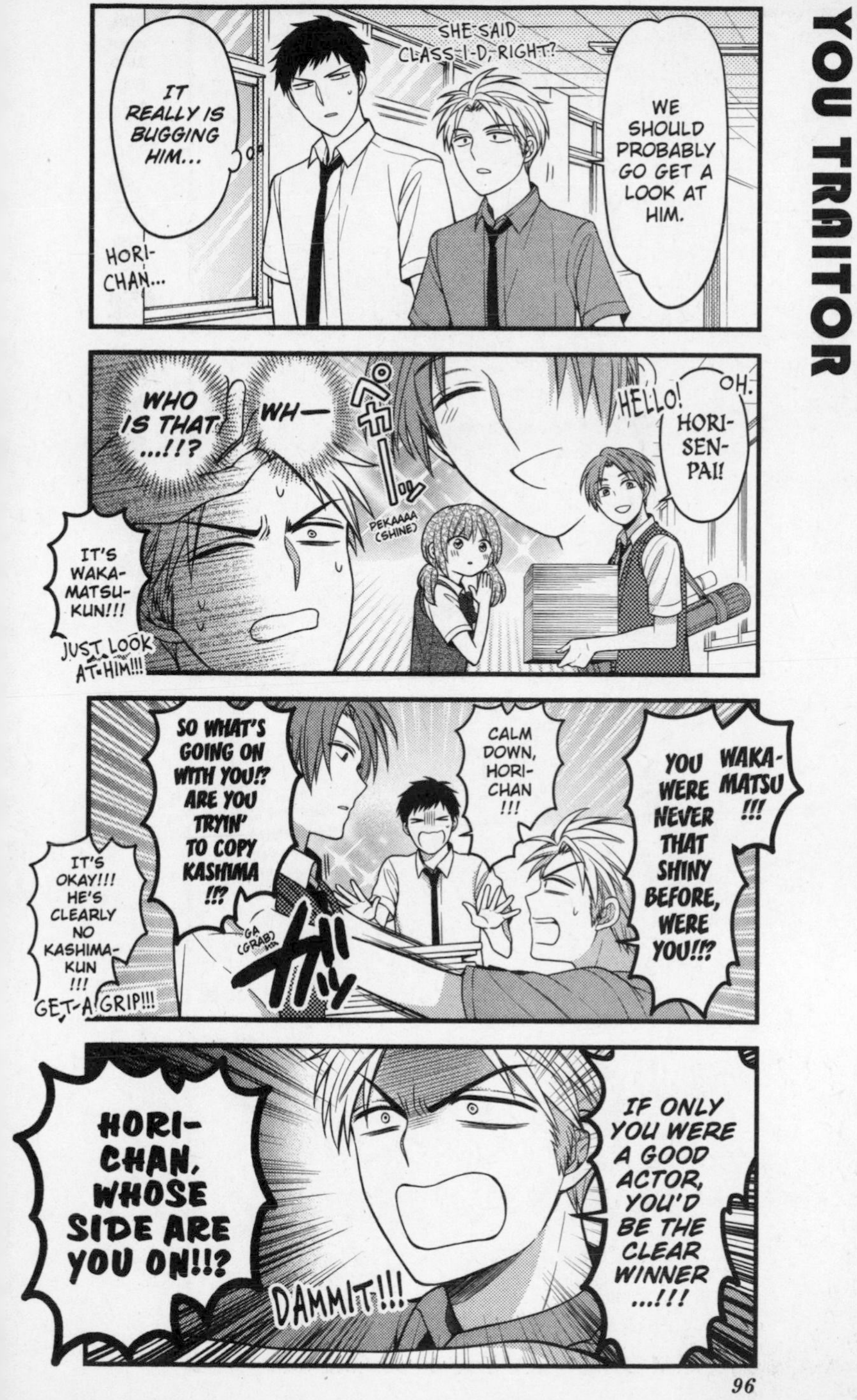

SHE SAID CLASS-1-D, RIGHT?
WE SHOULD PROBABLY GO GET A LOOK AT HIM.
IT REALLY IS BUGGING HIM...
HORI-CHAN...
OH. HORI-SENPAI!
HELLO!
ペカーッ
PEKAAAA (SHINE)
WH—
WHO IS THAT ...!!?
IT'S WAKAMATSU-KUN!!!
JUST LOOK AT HIM!!!
WAKAMATSU!!!
YOU WERE NEVER THAT SHINY BEFORE, WERE YOU!!?
CALM DOWN, HORI-CHAN!!!
SO WHAT'S GOING ON WITH YOU!? ARE YOU TRYIN' TO COPY KASHIMA!!?
ガッ
GA (GRAB)
IT'S OKAY!!! HE'S CLEARLY NO KASHIMA-KUN!!!
GET A GRIP!!!
IF ONLY YOU WERE A GOOD ACTOR, YOU'D BE THE CLEAR WINNER ...!!!
DAMMIT!!!
HORI-CHAN, WHOSE SIDE ARE YOU ON!!?

SHINY WAKAMATSU

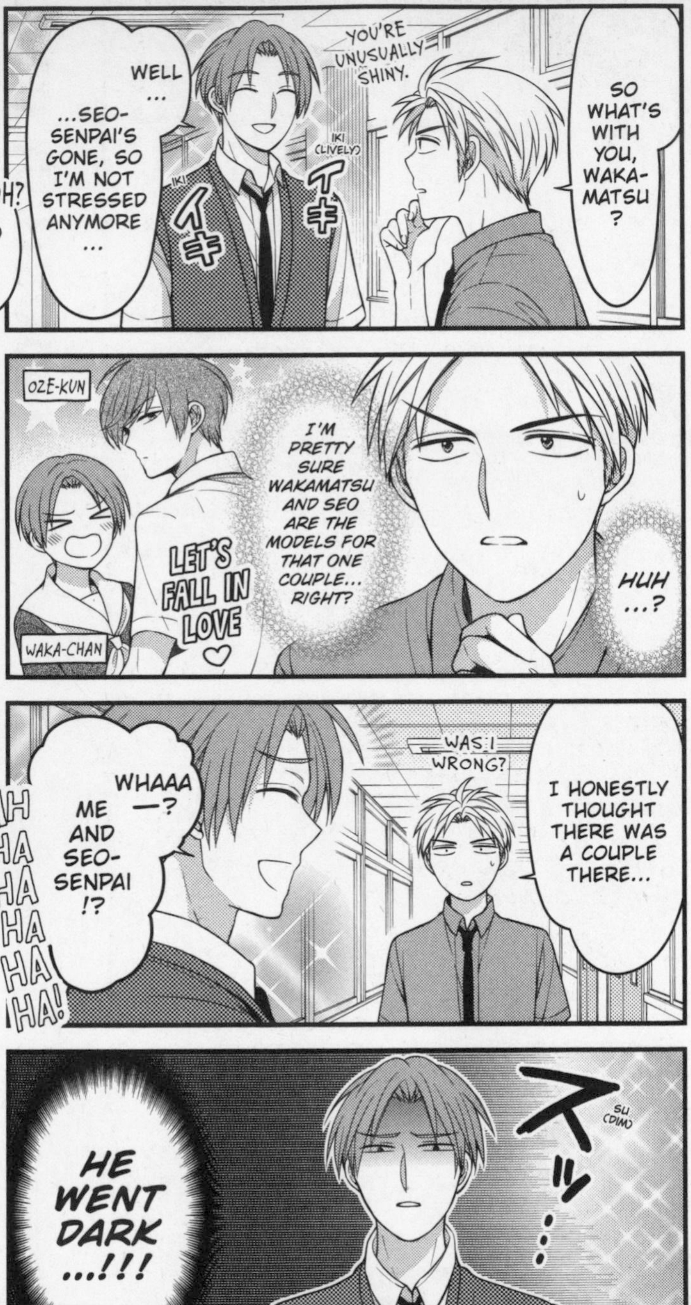

SO WHAT'S WITH YOU, WAKAMATSU?
YOU'RE UNUSUALLY SHINY.
IKI (LIVELY)
イキ
IKI
イキ
WELL ...
...SEO-SENPAI'S GONE, SO I'M NOT STRESSED ANYMORE ...
OH?
SEO ...
HUH ...?
I'M PRETTY SURE WAKAMATSU AND SEO ARE THE MODELS FOR THAT ONE COUPLE... RIGHT?
OZE-KUN
LET'S FALL IN LOVE
WAKA-CHAN
I HONESTLY THOUGHT THERE WAS A COUPLE THERE...
WAS I WRONG?
WHAAA—?
ME AND SEO-SENPAI!?
AH HA HA HA HA HA HA HA!
スッ...
SU (DIM)
HE WENT DARK ...!!!

HE'S IN DANGER

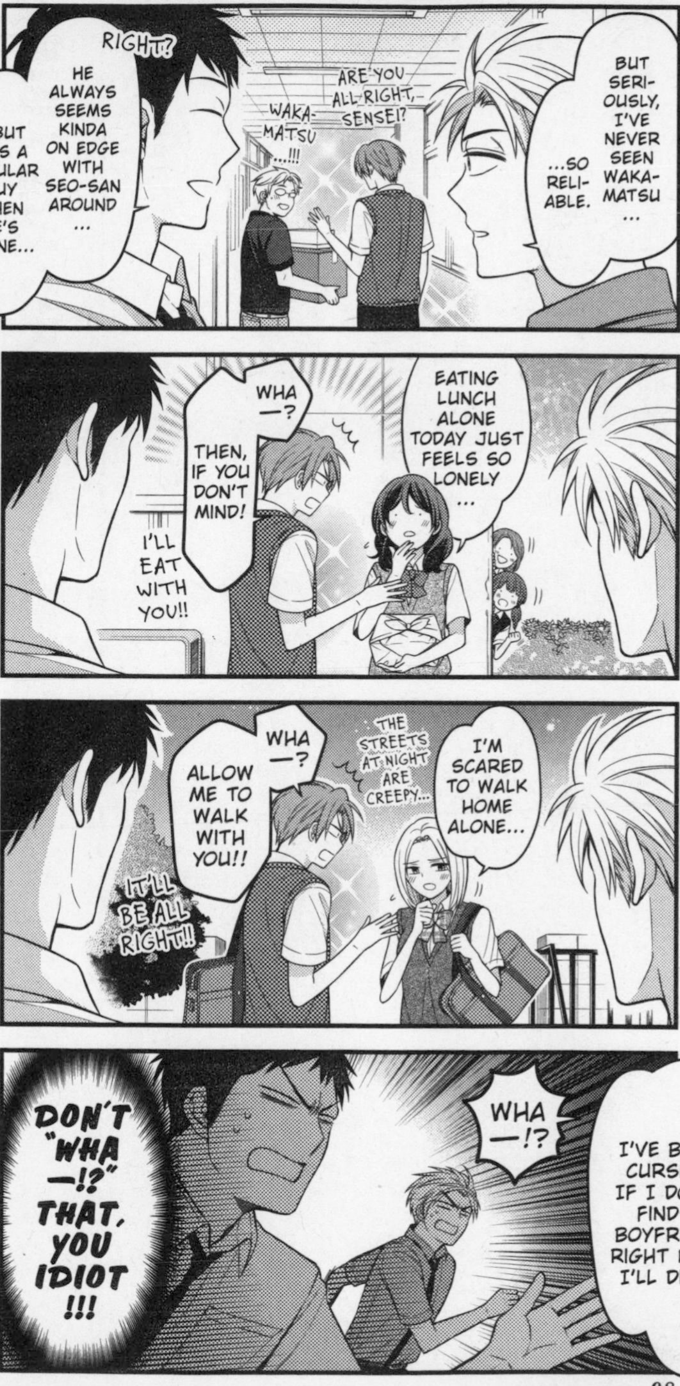
BUT SERIOUSLY, I'VE NEVER SEEN WAKAMATSU...
...SO RELIABLE.
ARE YOU ALL RIGHT, SENSEI?
WAKAMATSU...!!!
RIGHT?
HE ALWAYS SEEMS KINDA ON EDGE WITH SEO-SAN AROUND...
...BUT HE'S A REGULAR GUY WHEN HE'S ALONE...
EATING LUNCH ALONE TODAY JUST FEELS SO LONELY...
WHA—?
THEN, IF YOU DON'T MIND!
I'LL EAT WITH YOU!!
I'M SCARED TO WALK HOME ALONE...
THE STREETS AT NIGHT ARE CREEPY...
WHA—?
ALLOW ME TO WALK WITH YOU!!
IT'LL BE ALL RIGHT!!
I'VE BEEN CURSED. IF I DON'T FIND A BOYFRIEND RIGHT NOW, I'LL DIE...
WHA—!?
DON'T "WHA—!?" THAT, YOU IDIOT!!!

RUMORS ABOUT HIM

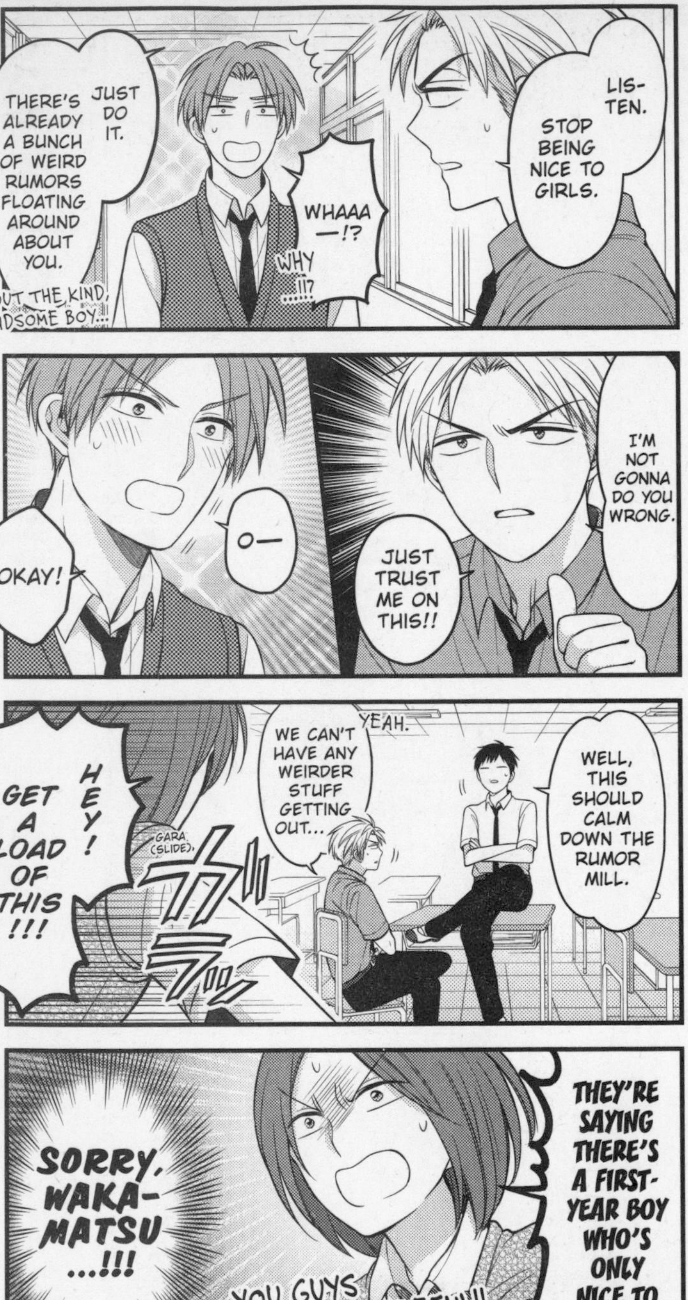
LISTEN. STOP BEING NICE TO GIRLS.
WHAAA—!?
WHY...!!?
JUST DO IT.
THERE'S ALREADY A BUNCH OF WEIRD RUMORS FLOATING AROUND ABOUT YOU.
ABOUT THE KIND, HANDSOME BOY...
I'M NOT GONNA DO YOU WRONG.
JUST TRUST ME ON THIS!!
O—
OKAY!
WELL, THIS SHOULD CALM DOWN THE RUMOR MILL.
YEAH.
WE CAN'T HAVE ANY WEIRDER STUFF GETTING OUT...
GARA (SLIDE)
HEY! GET A LOAD OF THIS!!!
THEY'RE SAYING THERE'S A FIRST-YEAR BOY WHO'S ONLY NICE TO DUDES!!!
YOU GUYS SHOULD BE CAREFUL!!
SORRY, WAKAMATSU...!!!

SENPAI'S WHEELHOUSE

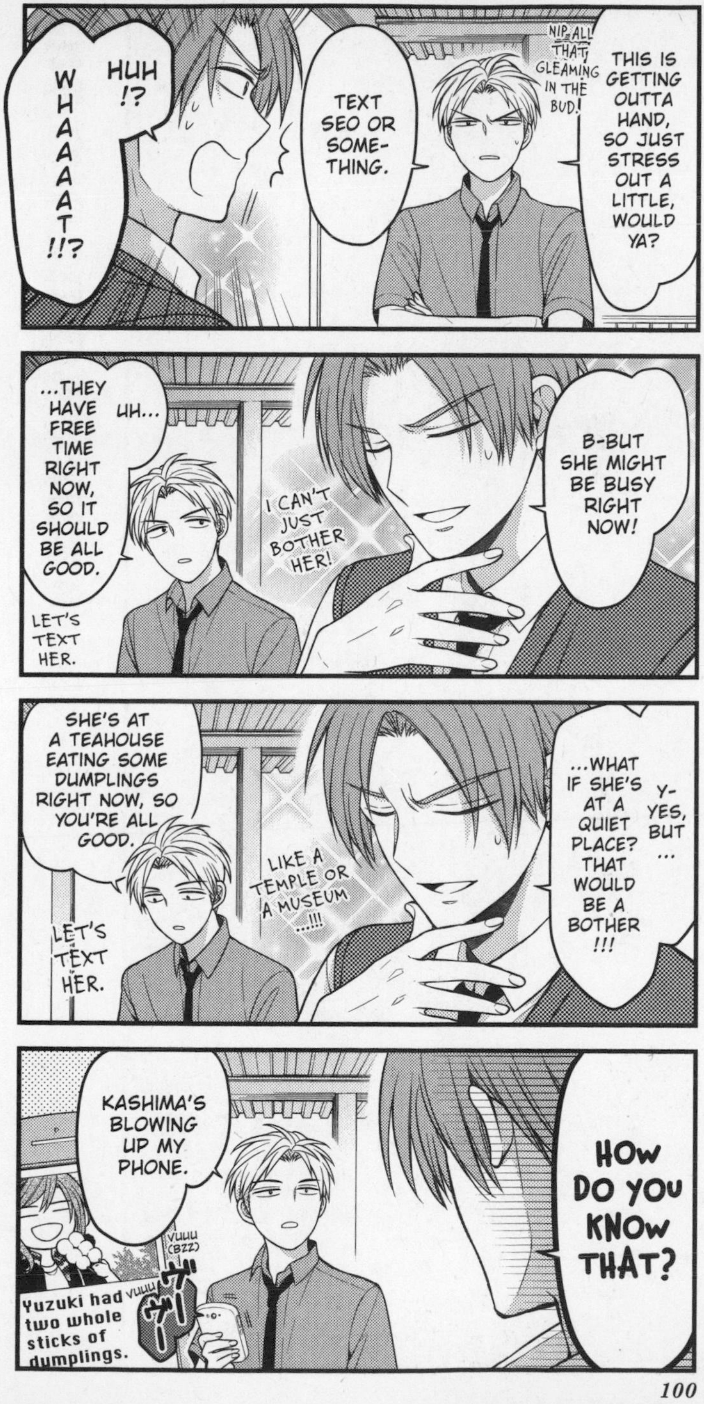
THIS IS GETTING OUTTA HAND, SO JUST STRESS OUT A LITTLE, WOULD YA?
NIP ALL THAT GLEAMING IN THE BUD!
TEXT SEO OR SOME-THING.
HUH!?
WHAAAAAT!!?
B-BUT SHE MIGHT BE BUSY RIGHT NOW!
I CAN'T JUST BOTHER HER!
UH...
...THEY HAVE FREE TIME RIGHT NOW, SO IT SHOULD BE ALL GOOD.
LET'S TEXT HER.
...WHAT IF SHE'S AT A QUIET PLACE? THAT WOULD BE A BOTHER!!!
Y-YES, BUT...
LIKE A TEMPLE OR A MUSEUM...!!!
SHE'S AT A TEAHOUSE EATING SOME DUMPLINGS RIGHT NOW, SO YOU'RE ALL GOOD.
LET'S TEXT HER.
HOW DO YOU KNOW THAT?
KASHIMA'S BLOWING UP MY PHONE.
VUUU (BZZ)
VUUU
Yuzuki had two whole sticks of dumplings.

THE SOUND OF A HEART BREAKING

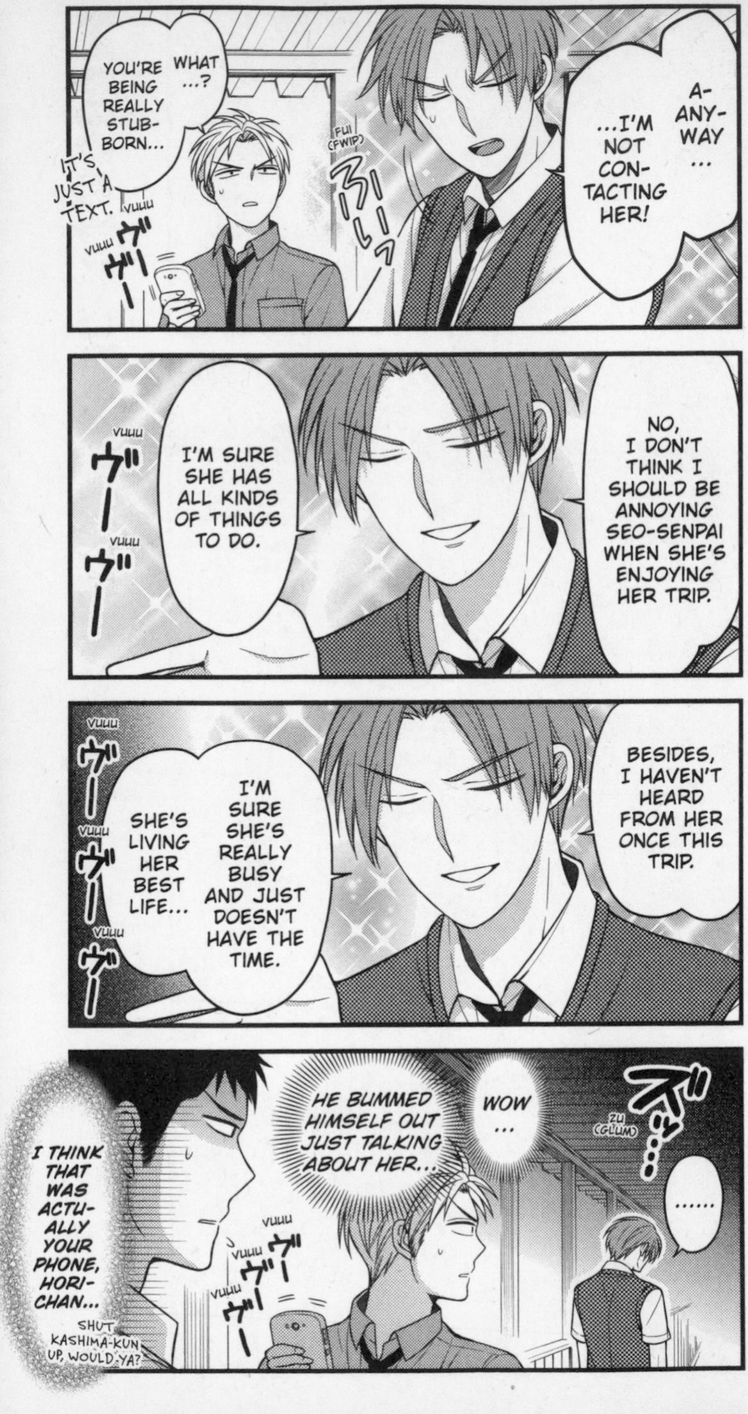
A-ANYWAY...
...I'M NOT CONTACTING HER!
FUI (FWIP)
WHAT...?
YOU'RE BEING REALLY STUBBORN...
IT'S JUST A TEXT.
VUUU
VUUU
NO, I DON'T THINK I SHOULD BE ANNOYING SEO-SENPAI WHEN SHE'S ENJOYING HER TRIP.
I'M SURE SHE HAS ALL KINDS OF THINGS TO DO.
VUUU
VUUU
BESIDES, I HAVEN'T HEARD FROM HER ONCE THIS TRIP.
I'M SURE SHE'S REALLY BUSY AND JUST DOESN'T HAVE THE TIME.
SHE'S LIVING HER BEST LIFE...
VUUU
VUUU
VUUU
ZU (GLUM)
......
WOW...
HE BUMMED HIMSELF OUT JUST TALKING ABOUT HER...
VUUU
VUUU
VUUU
I THINK THAT WAS ACTUALLY YOUR PHONE, HORI-CHAN...
SHUT KASHIMA-KUN UP, WOULD YA?

PICK ONE OF THE TWO

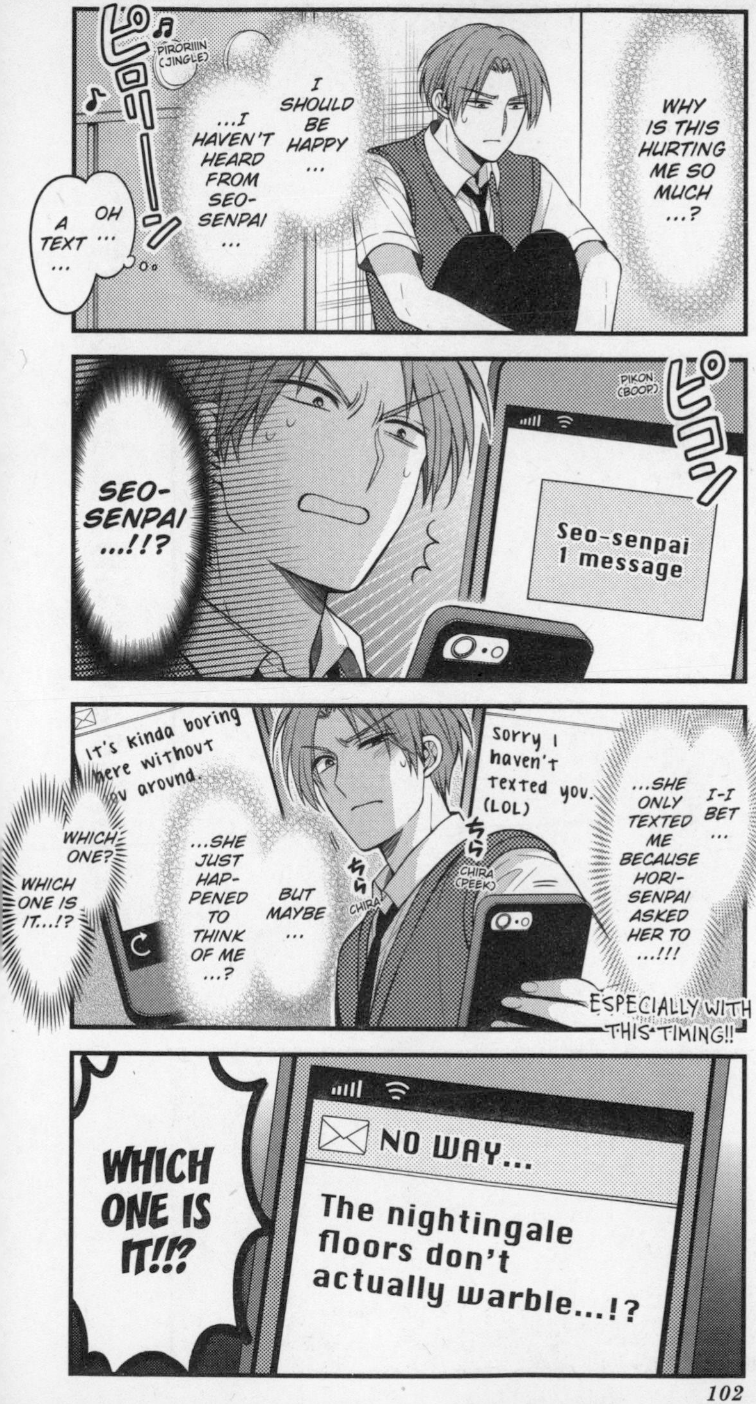
WHY IS THIS HURTING ME SO MUCH...?
I SHOULD BE HAPPY...
...I HAVEN'T HEARD FROM SEO-SENPAI...
PIRORIIN (JINGLE)
OH... A TEXT...
PIKON (BOOP)
Seo-senpai 1 message
SEO-SENPAI...!!?
I-I BET...
...SHE ONLY TEXTED ME BECAUSE HORI-SENPAI ASKED HER TO...!!!
Sorry I haven't texted you. (LOL)
CHIRA (PEEK)
CHIRA
BUT MAYBE...
...SHE JUST HAPPENED TO THINK OF ME...?
It's kinda boring here without
WHICH ONE? WHICH ONE IS IT...!?
ESPECIALLY WITH THIS TIMING!!
NO WAY...
The nightingale floors don't actually warble...!?
WHICH ONE IS IT!!?

STUPID SENPAI

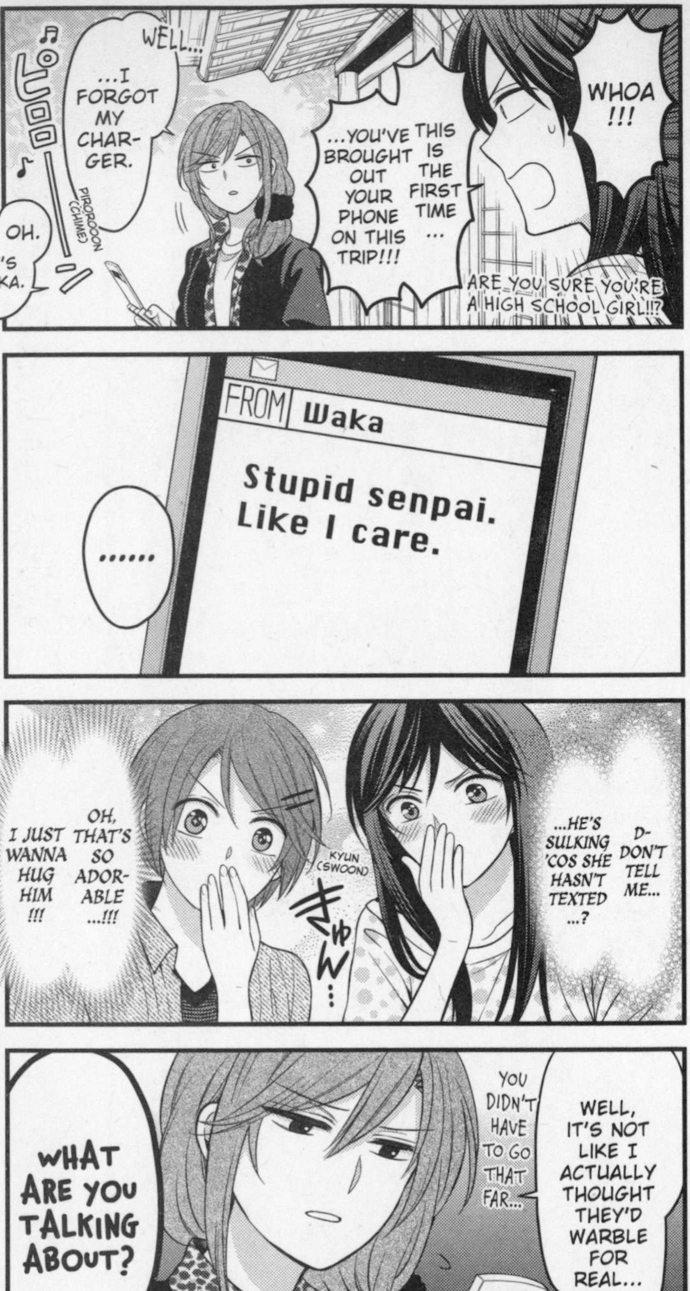

WHOA !!!
ARE YOU SURE YOU'RE A HIGH SCHOOL GIRL!!?
THIS IS THE FIRST TIME ...
...YOU'VE BROUGHT OUT YOUR PHONE ON THIS TRIP!!!
WELL...
...I FORGOT MY CHARGER.
PIROROOON (CHIME)
OH.
IT'S WAKA.
FROM Waka
Stupid senpai. Like I care.
......
D-DON'T TELL ME...
...HE'S SULKING 'COS SHE HASN'T TEXTED ...?
KYUN (SWOON)
OH, THAT'S SO ADORABLE ...!!!
I JUST WANNA HUG HIM !!!
WELL, IT'S NOT LIKE I ACTUALLY THOUGHT THEY'D WARBLE FOR REAL...
YOU DIDN'T HAVE TO GO THAT FAR...
WHAT ARE YOU TALKING ABOUT?

YOU BASTARD

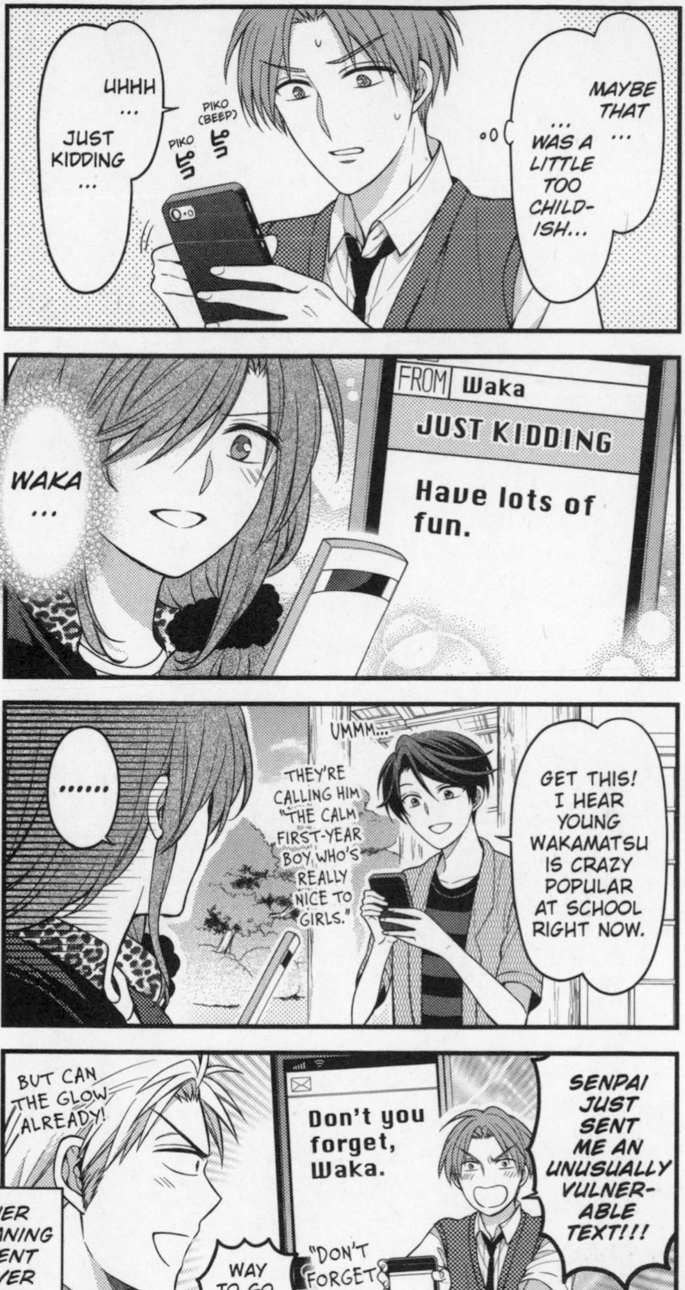
MAYBE THAT ... ... WAS A LITTLE TOO CHILD-ISH...
PIKO (BEEP)
PIKO
UHHH ... JUST KIDDING ...
FROM Waka
JUST KIDDING
Have lots of fun.
WAKA ...
GET THIS! I HEAR YOUNG WAKAMATSU IS CRAZY POPULAR AT SCHOOL RIGHT NOW.
UMMM...
THEY'RE CALLING HIM "THE CALM FIRST-YEAR BOY WHO'S REALLY NICE TO GIRLS."
......
SENPAI JUST SENT ME AN UNUSUALLY VULNER-ABLE TEXT!!!
Don't you forget, Waka.
BUT CAN THE GLOW ALREADY!
"DON'T FORGET ABOUT ME"!!!
WAY TO GO, WAKA-MATSU !!!
HER MEANING WENT OVER HIS HEAD.

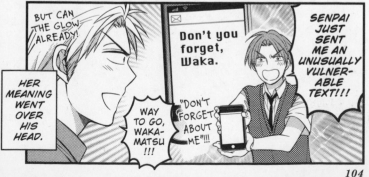

NIGHTINGALE FLOORS

A KIND OF FLOOR THAT MAKES A SOUND LIKE A NIGHTINGALE WHEN YOU WALK ON IT!

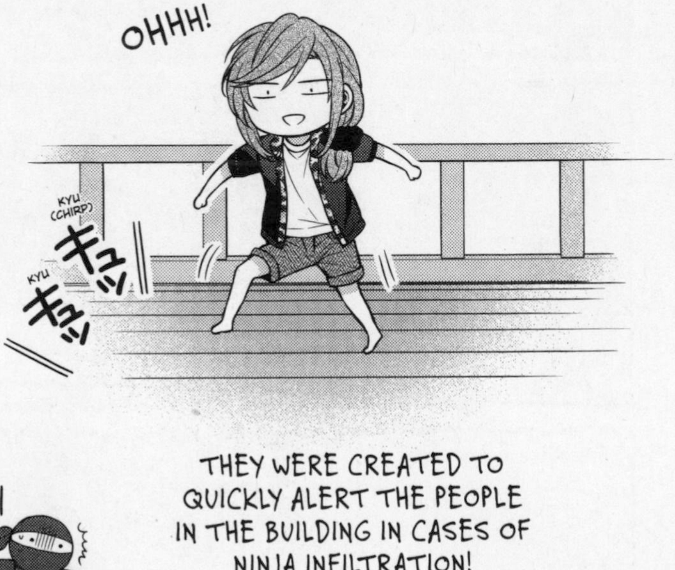
OHHH!
KYU (CHIRP)
キュッ
KYU
キュッ

THEY WERE CREATED TO QUICKLY ALERT THE PEOPLE IN THE BUILDING IN CASES OF NINJA INFILTRATION!

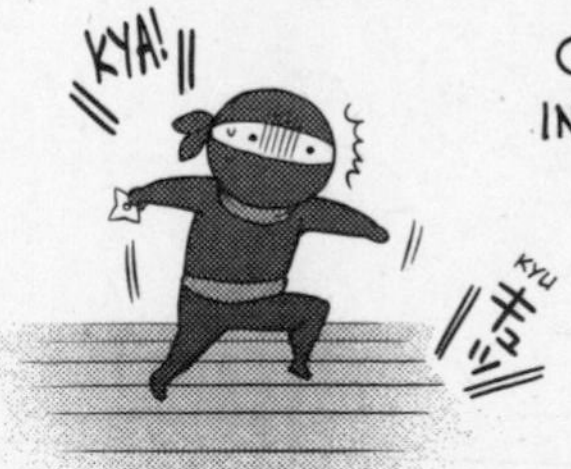
KYA!
KYU
キュッ

[Extra]

A FAMILIAR EXPRESSION

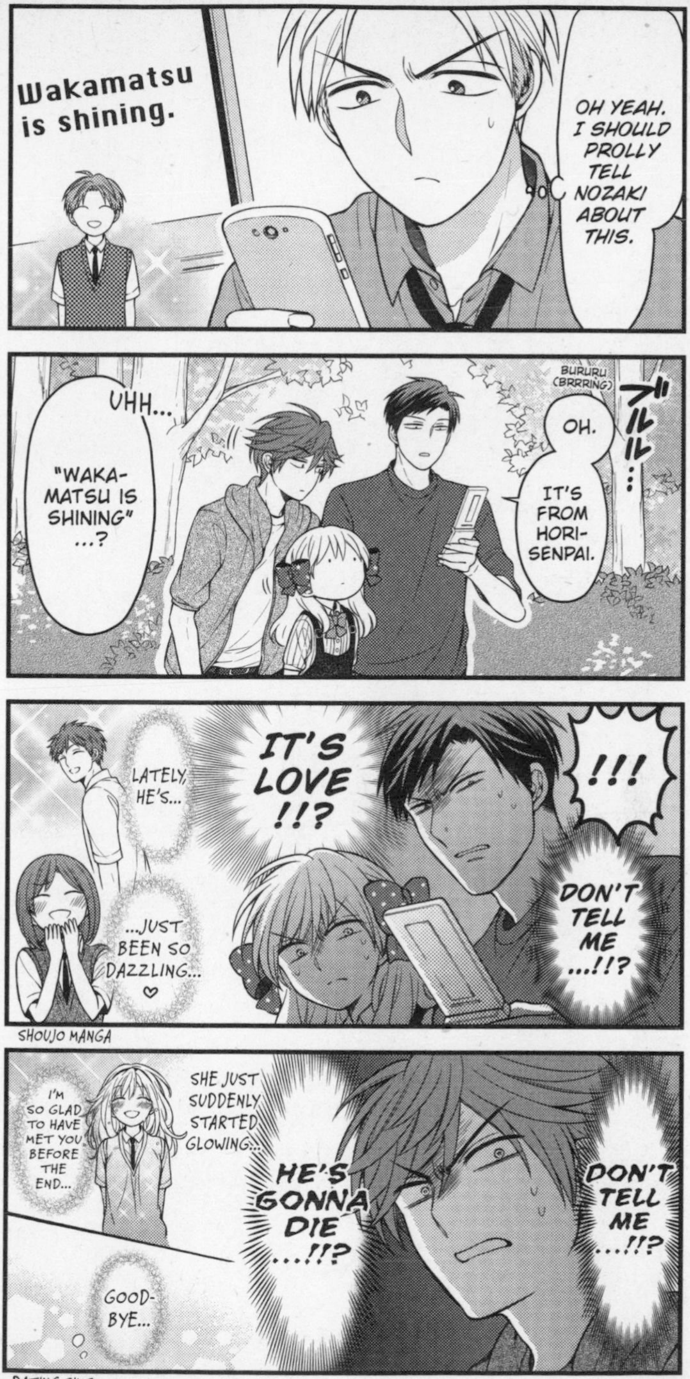
OH YEAH. I SHOULD PROLLY TELL NOZAKI ABOUT THIS.
Wakamatsu is shining.
BURURU (BRRRING)
ブルル…
OH.
IT'S FROM HORI-SENPAI.
UHH...
"WAKA-MATSU IS SHINING" ...?
!!!
DON'T TELL ME ...!!?
IT'S LOVE !!?
LATELY, HE'S...
...JUST BEEN SO DAZZLING... ♡
SHOUJO MANGA
DON'T TELL ME ...!!?
HE'S GONNA DIE ...!!?
SHE JUST SUDDENLY STARTED GLOWING...
I'M SO GLAD TO HAVE MET YOU BEFORE THE END...
GOOD-BYE...
DATING SIMS

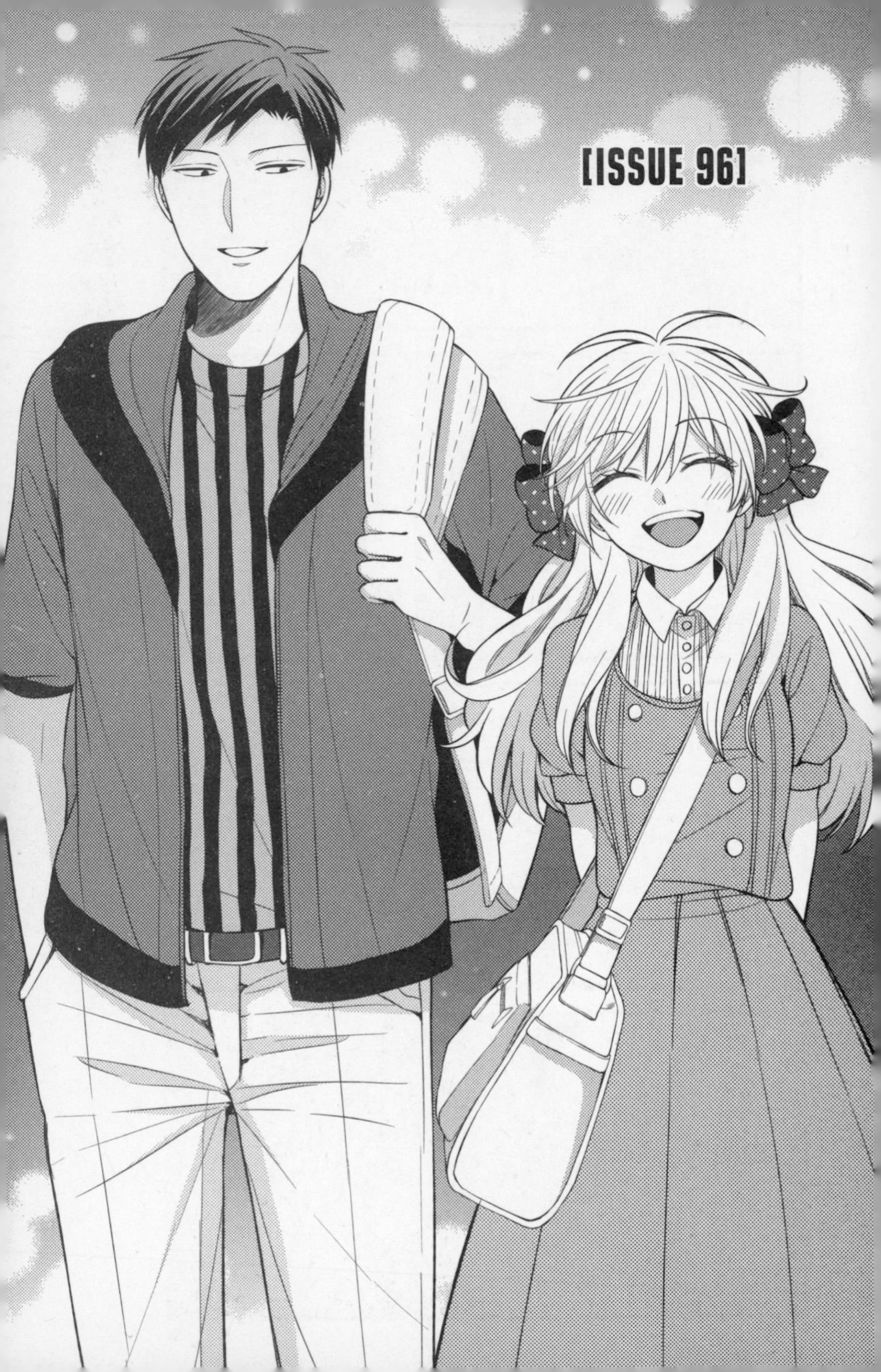
[ISSUE 96]

A PERSON'S REPUTATION

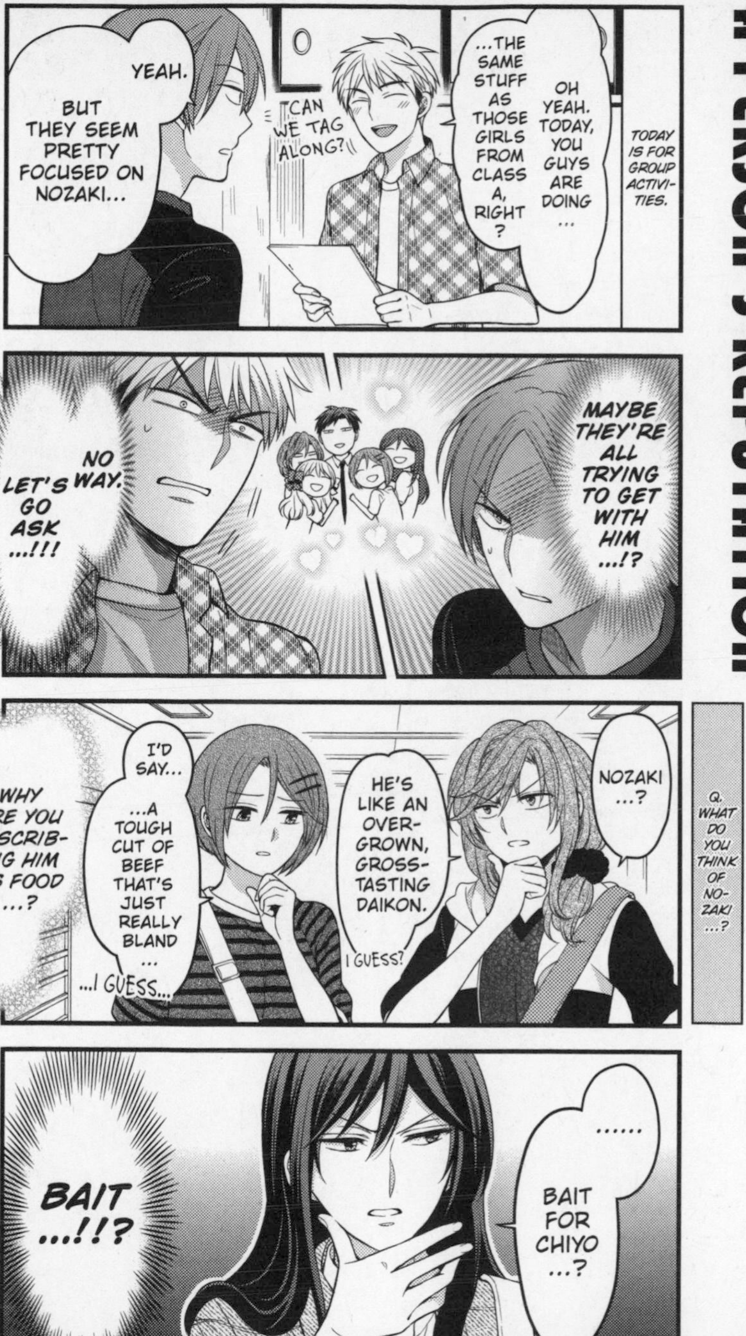
TODAY IS FOR GROUP ACTIVITIES.
OH YEAH. TODAY, YOU GUYS ARE DOING ...
...THE SAME STUFF AS THOSE GIRLS FROM CLASS A, RIGHT?
CAN WE TAG ALONG?
YEAH.
BUT THEY SEEM PRETTY FOCUSED ON NOZAKI...
MAYBE THEY'RE ALL TRYING TO GET WITH HIM ...!?
NO WAY.
LET'S GO ASK ...!!!
Q. WHAT DO YOU THINK OF NO-ZAKI ...?
NOZAKI ...?
HE'S LIKE AN OVER-GROWN, GROSS-TASTING DAIKON.
I GUESS?
I'D SAY...
...A TOUGH CUT OF BEEF THAT'S JUST REALLY BLAND ...
...I GUESS...
WHY ARE YOU DESCRIB-ING HIM AS FOOD ...?
......
BAIT FOR CHIYO ...?
BAIT ...!!?

OUR ADORABLE LEADER

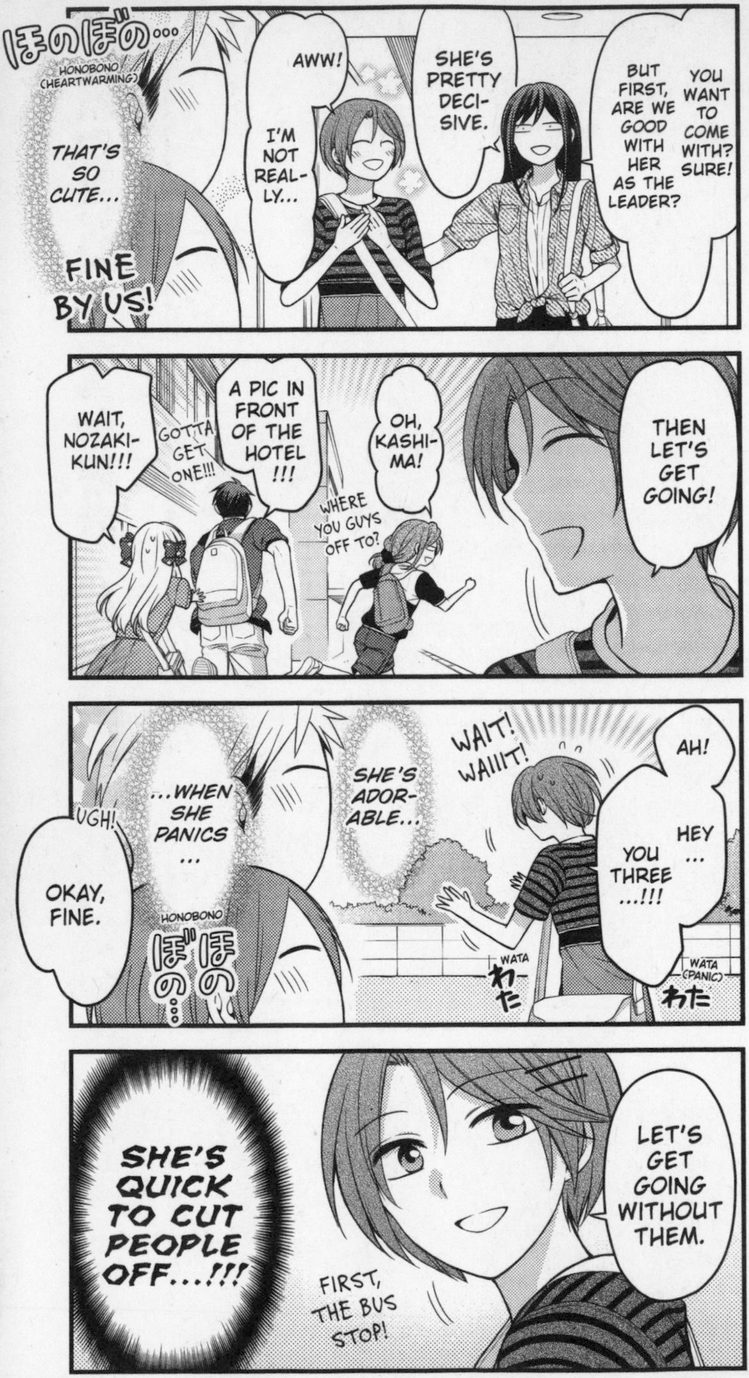
YOU WANT TO COME WITH? SURE!
BUT FIRST, ARE WE GOOD WITH HER AS THE LEADER?
SHE'S PRETTY DECISIVE.
AWW!
I'M NOT REALLY...
THAT'S SO CUTE...
FINE BY US!
ほのぼの…
HONOBONO (HEARTWARMING)
THEN LET'S GET GOING!
OH, KASHIMA!
WHERE YOU GUYS OFF TO?
A PIC IN FRONT OF THE HOTEL!!!
GOTTA GET ONE!!!
WAIT, NOZAKI-KUN!!!
AH!
HEY...
YOU THREE...!!!
わた
WATA (PANIC)
わた
WATA
WAIT! WAIIIT!
SHE'S ADORABLE...
...WHEN SHE PANICS...
ほのぼの…
HONOBONO
UGH!
OKAY, FINE.
LET'S GET GOING WITHOUT THEM.
FIRST, THE BUS STOP!
SHE'S QUICK TO CUT PEOPLE OFF...!!!

A SHOUJO MANGA-KA'S PERSPECTIVE

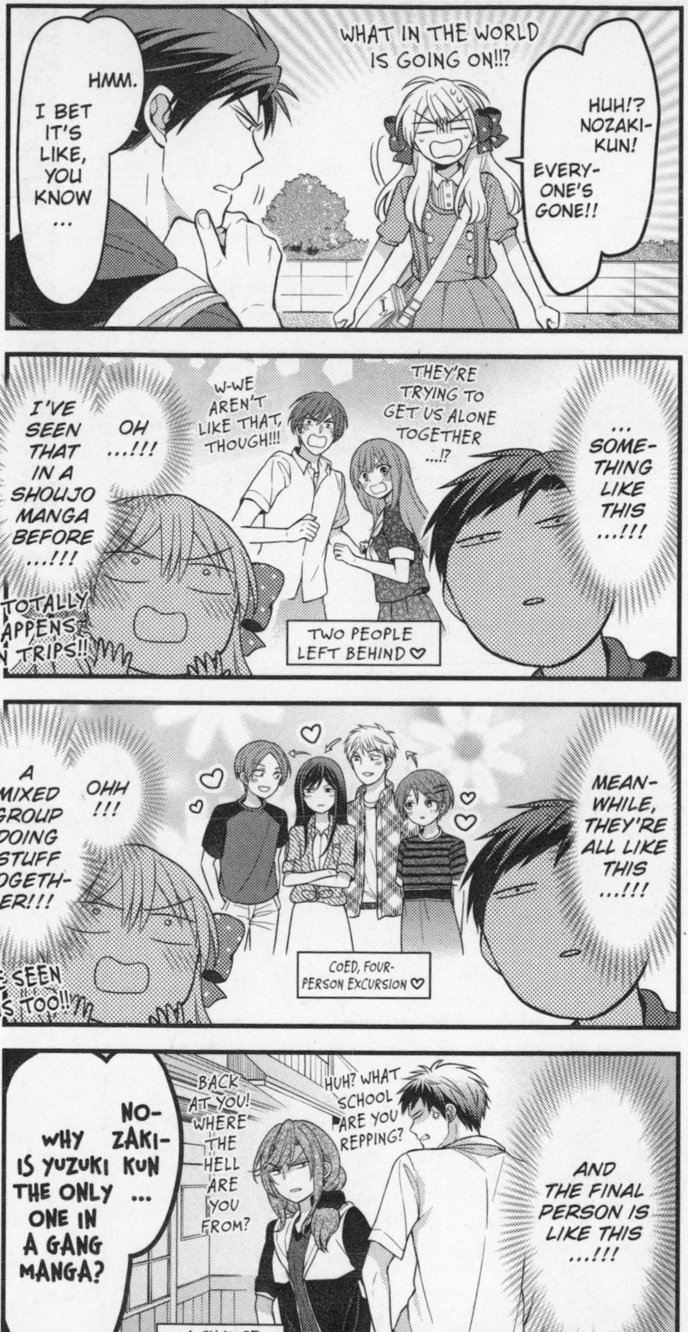
WHAT IN THE WORLD IS GOING ON!!?
HUH!? NOZAKI-KUN! EVERYONE'S GONE!!
HMM. I BET IT'S LIKE, YOU KNOW ...
... SOMETHING LIKE THIS ...!!!
THEY'RE TRYING TO GET US ALONE TOGETHER ...!?
W-WE AREN'T LIKE THAT, THOUGH!!!
TWO PEOPLE LEFT BEHIND ♡
OH ...!!!
I'VE SEEN THAT IN A SHOUJO MANGA BEFORE ...!!!
IT TOTALLY HAPPENS ON TRIPS!!
MEANWHILE, THEY'RE ALL LIKE THIS ...!!!
COED, FOUR-PERSON EXCURSION ♡
OHH !!!
A MIXED GROUP DOING STUFF TOGETHER!!!
I'VE SEEN THIS TOO!!
AND THE FINAL PERSON IS LIKE THIS ...!!!
HUH? WHAT SCHOOL ARE YOU REPPING?
BACK AT YOU! WHERE THE HELL ARE YOU FROM?
A CHANCE MEETING ON THE TRIP ♡
NOZAKI-KUN ...
WHY IS YUZUKI THE ONLY ONE IN A GANG MANGA?

STALLED CONVERSATION

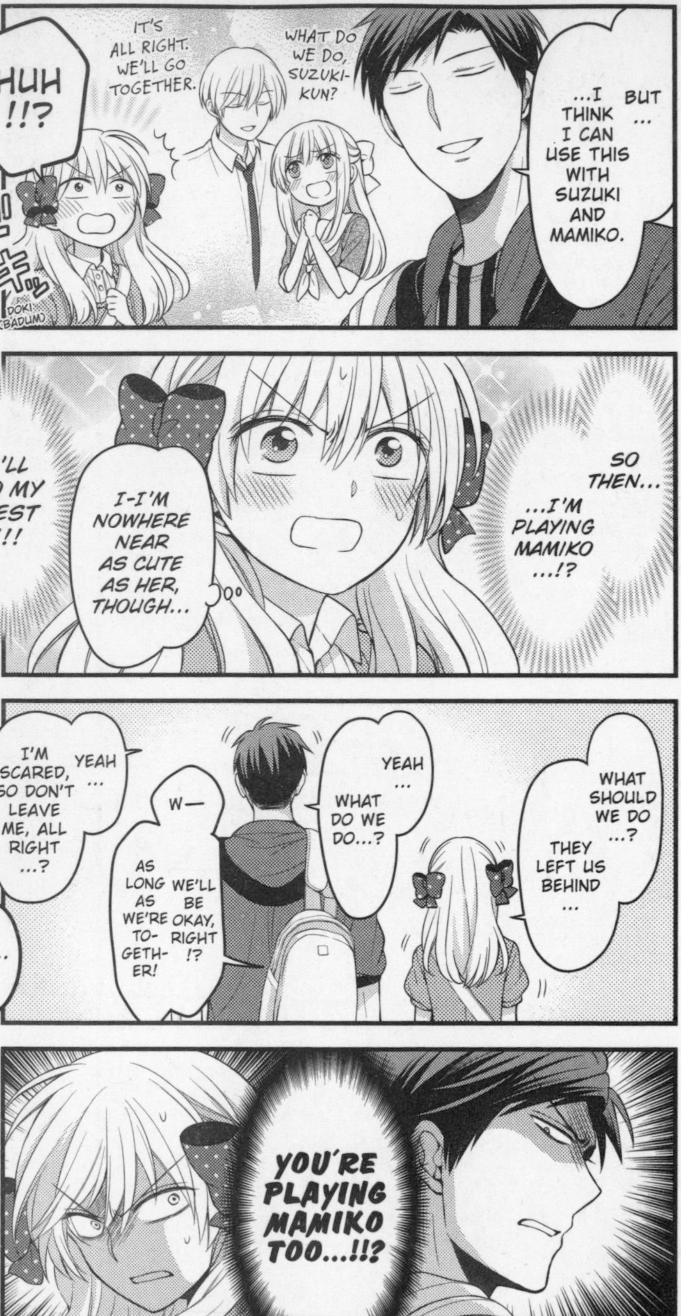
BUT... ...I THINK I CAN USE THIS WITH SUZUKI AND MAMIKO.
WHAT DO WE DO, SUZUKI-KUN?
IT'S ALL RIGHT. WE'LL GO TOGETHER.
HUH!!?
DOKI (BADUM)
SO THEN... ...I'M PLAYING MAMIKO...!?
I-I'M NOWHERE NEAR AS CUTE AS HER, THOUGH...
I'LL DO MY BEST!!!
WHAT SHOULD WE DO...? THEY LEFT US BEHIND...
YEAH... WHAT DO WE DO...?
W— WE'LL BE OKAY, RIGHT!? AS LONG AS WE'RE TOGETHER!
YEAH... I'M SCARED, SO DON'T LEAVE ME, ALL RIGHT...?
......
YOU'RE PLAYING MAMIKO TOO...!!?

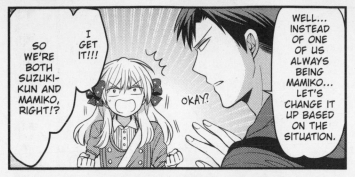

TOTALLY IN SYNC

WELL... INSTEAD OF ONE OF US ALWAYS BEING MAMIKO... LET'S CHANGE IT UP BASED ON THE SITUATION.
OKAY?
I GET IT!!!
SO WE'RE BOTH SUZUKI-KUN AND MAMIKO, RIGHT!?
Did you know ...?
Yatsuhashi only refers to the hard baked treat, Mamiko.
THE SOFT KIND IS CALLED RAW YATSUHASHI...
HA HA HA HA HA HA!
I see.
By the way, raw yatsuhashi only refers to the outer layer, Mamiko.
WHEN IT HAS A FILLING, IT'S "RED BEAN-FILLED RAW YATSUHASHI."
O-OH NOOOO ~~~!
WHAT TRAIN DO WE TAKE NEXT ~~?
AAAAAAAH!!
CHANGING TRAINS IS JUST SOOOOO HARD~!
WAAAAAH!! WE'RE GOING TO GET LOST ~~!!!
HELP MEEE, SUZUKI-KUN!!!
...WITH SUZUKI AND MAMIKO...
WE JUST CAN'T SEEM TO GET THE TIMING RIGHT...
ガタン
GATAN
I GUESS WE BOTH HAVE THE SAME STRENGTHS AND WEAKNESSES ...?
GATAN (KATHUNK)
ガタン
GOTON (KADUNK)
ゴトン
THE MAMIKO DUO IS JUST SO USELESS.

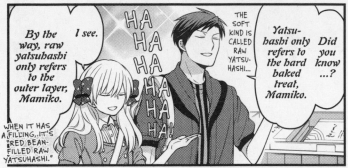

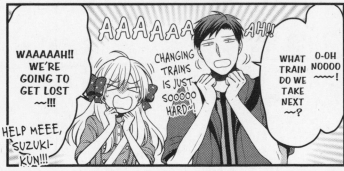

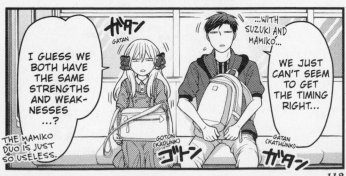

A PRO'S JUDGMENT

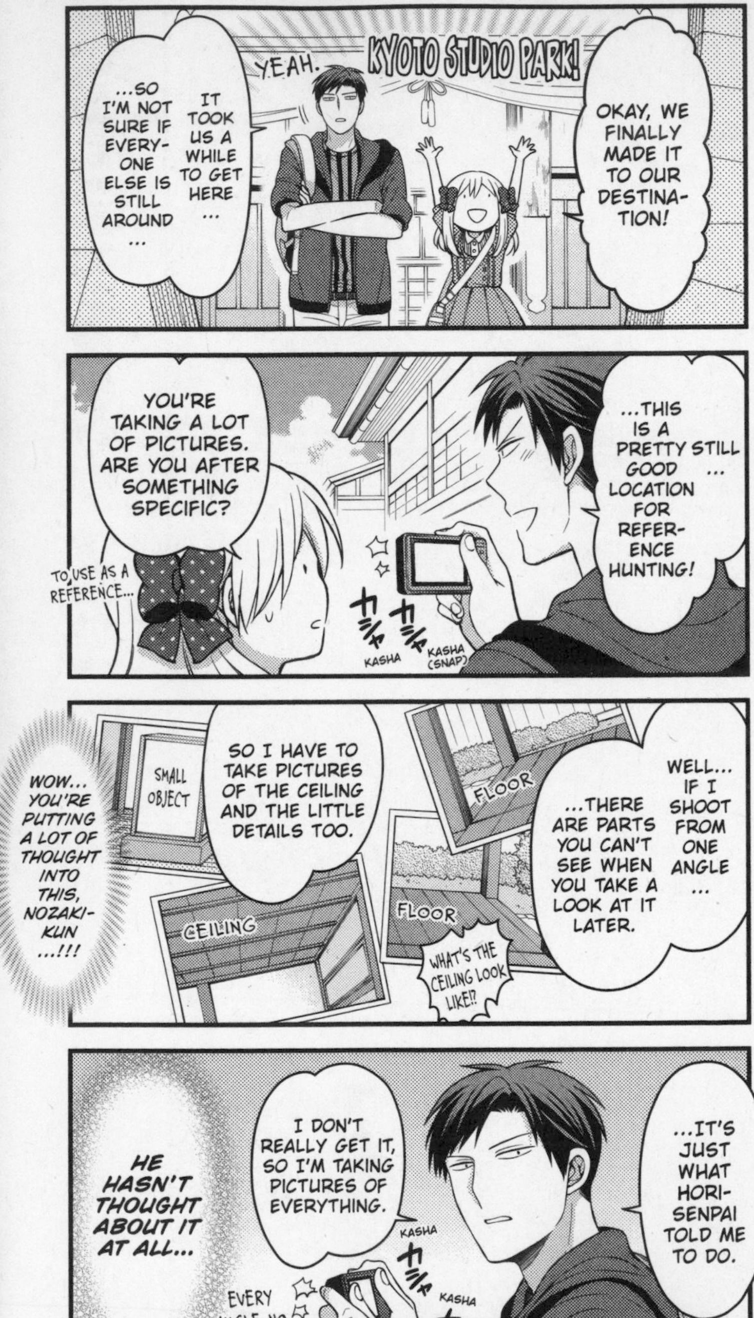
OKAY, WE FINALLY MADE IT TO OUR DESTINATION!
KYOTO STUDIO PARK!
YEAH.
IT TOOK US A WHILE TO GET HERE...
...SO I'M NOT SURE IF EVERYONE ELSE IS STILL AROUND...
...THIS IS A PRETTY GOOD LOCATION FOR REFERENCE HUNTING!
STILL...
YOU'RE TAKING A LOT OF PICTURES. ARE YOU AFTER SOMETHING SPECIFIC?
カシャ KASHA (SNAP)
カシャ KASHA
TO USE AS A REFERENCE...
WELL... IF I SHOOT FROM ONE ANGLE...
...THERE ARE PARTS YOU CAN'T SEE WHEN YOU TAKE A LOOK AT IT LATER.
FLOOR
FLOOR
WHAT'S THE CEILING LOOK LIKE!?
SO I HAVE TO TAKE PICTURES OF THE CEILING AND THE LITTLE DETAILS TOO.
SMALL OBJECT
CEILING
WOW... YOU'RE PUTTING A LOT OF THOUGHT INTO THIS, NOZAKI-KUN...!!!
...IT'S JUST WHAT HORI-SENPAI TOLD ME TO DO.
カシャ KASHA
カシャ KASHA
I DON'T REALLY GET IT, SO I'M TAKING PICTURES OF EVERYTHING.
EVERY ANGLE, NO EXCEPTIONS.
HE HASN'T THOUGHT ABOUT IT AT ALL...

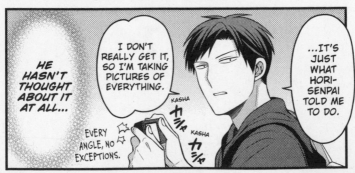

A PROPER PERIOD PIECE

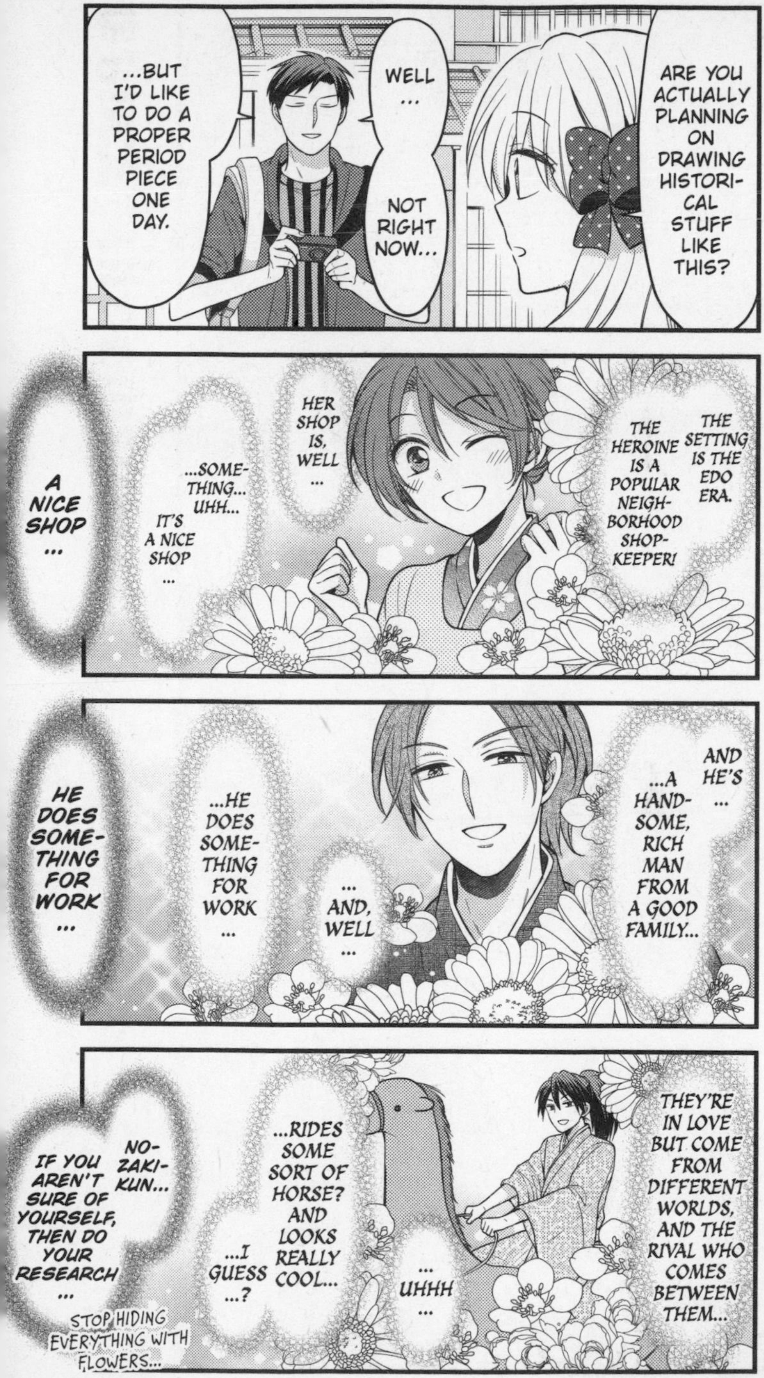
ARE YOU ACTUALLY PLANNING ON DRAWING HISTORICAL STUFF LIKE THIS?
WELL ... NOT RIGHT NOW...
...BUT I'D LIKE TO DO A PROPER PERIOD PIECE ONE DAY.
THE SETTING IS THE EDO ERA.
THE HEROINE IS A POPULAR NEIGHBORHOOD SHOPKEEPER!
HER SHOP IS, WELL ...
...SOMETHING... UHH...
IT'S A NICE SHOP ...
A NICE SHOP ...
AND HE'S ...
...A HANDSOME, RICH MAN FROM A GOOD FAMILY...
... AND, WELL ...
...HE DOES SOMETHING FOR WORK ...
HE DOES SOMETHING FOR WORK ...
THEY'RE IN LOVE BUT COME FROM DIFFERENT WORLDS, AND THE RIVAL WHO COMES BETWEEN THEM...
... UHHH ...
...RIDES SOME SORT OF HORSE? AND LOOKS REALLY COOL...
...I GUESS ...?
NOZAKI-KUN...
IF YOU AREN'T SURE OF YOURSELF, THEN DO YOUR RESEARCH ...
STOP HIDING EVERYTHING WITH FLOWERS...

CHIYO, THE TALENTED WOMAN

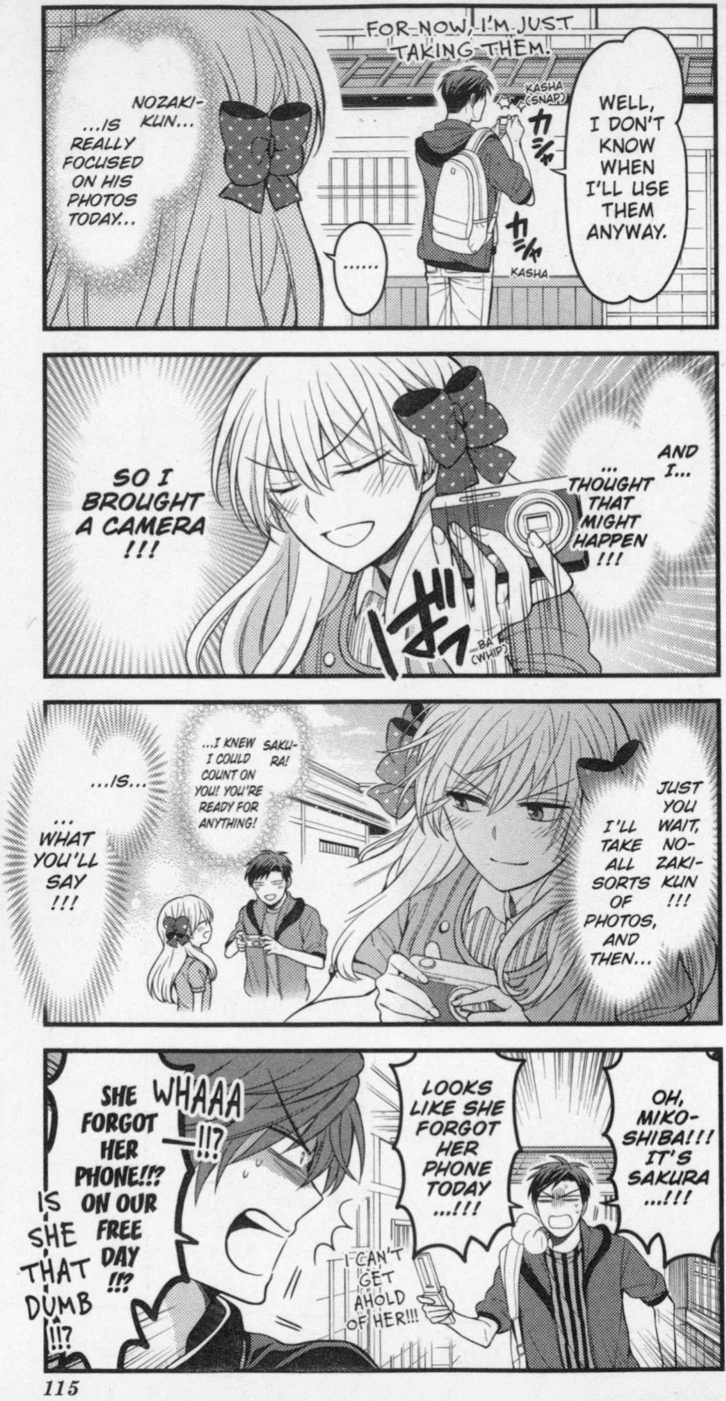
WELL, I DON'T KNOW WHEN I'LL USE THEM ANYWAY.
FOR NOW, I'M JUST TAKING THEM.
KASHA (SNAP)
KASHA
......
NOZAKI-KUN...
...IS REALLY FOCUSED ON HIS PHOTOS TODAY...
AND I...
...THOUGHT THAT MIGHT HAPPEN!!!
BA (WHIP)
SO I BROUGHT A CAMERA!!!
JUST YOU WAIT, NOZAKI-KUN!!!
I'LL TAKE ALL SORTS OF PHOTOS, AND THEN...
SAKURA!
...I KNEW I COULD COUNT ON YOU! YOU'RE READY FOR ANYTHING!
...IS...
...WHAT YOU'LL SAY!!!
OH, MIKOSHIBA!!! IT'S SAKURA...!!!
LOOKS LIKE SHE FORGOT HER PHONE TODAY...!!!
I CAN'T GET AHOLD OF HER!!!
WHAAAA—!!?
SHE FORGOT HER PHONE!!? ON OUR FREE DAY!!?
IS SHE THAT DUMB!!?

RIGHT ABOUT NOW, SHE'S...

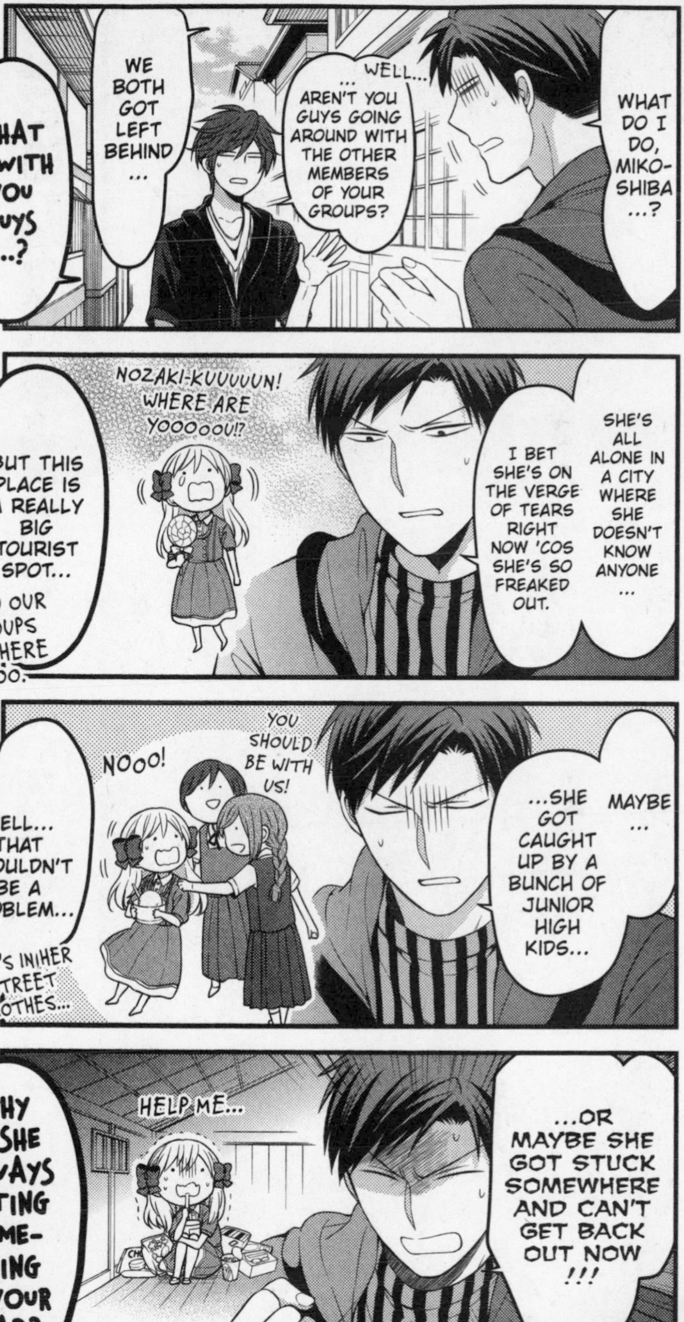

WHAT DO I DO, MIKO-SHIBA...?
WELL... ...AREN'T YOU GUYS GOING AROUND WITH THE OTHER MEMBERS OF YOUR GROUPS?
WE BOTH GOT LEFT BEHIND...
WHAT IS WITH YOU GUYS...?
SHE'S ALL ALONE IN A CITY WHERE SHE DOESN'T KNOW ANYONE...
I BET SHE'S ON THE VERGE OF TEARS RIGHT NOW 'COS SHE'S SO FREAKED OUT.
NOZAKI-KUUUUUN! WHERE ARE YOOOOOU!?
BUT THIS PLACE IS A REALLY BIG TOURIST SPOT...
...AND OUR GROUPS ARE HERE TOO.
MAYBE...
...SHE GOT CAUGHT UP BY A BUNCH OF JUNIOR HIGH KIDS...
YOU SHOULD BE WITH US!
NOOO!
WELL... THAT SHOULDN'T BE A PROBLEM...
SHE'S IN HER STREET CLOTHES...
...OR MAYBE SHE GOT STUCK SOMEWHERE AND CAN'T GET BACK OUT NOW!!!
HELP ME...
WHY IS SHE ALWAYS EATING SOME-THING IN YOUR HEAD?

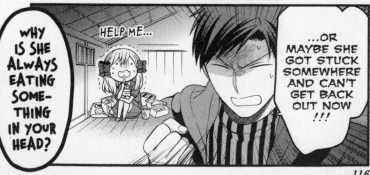

A SIMPLE EXAMPLE

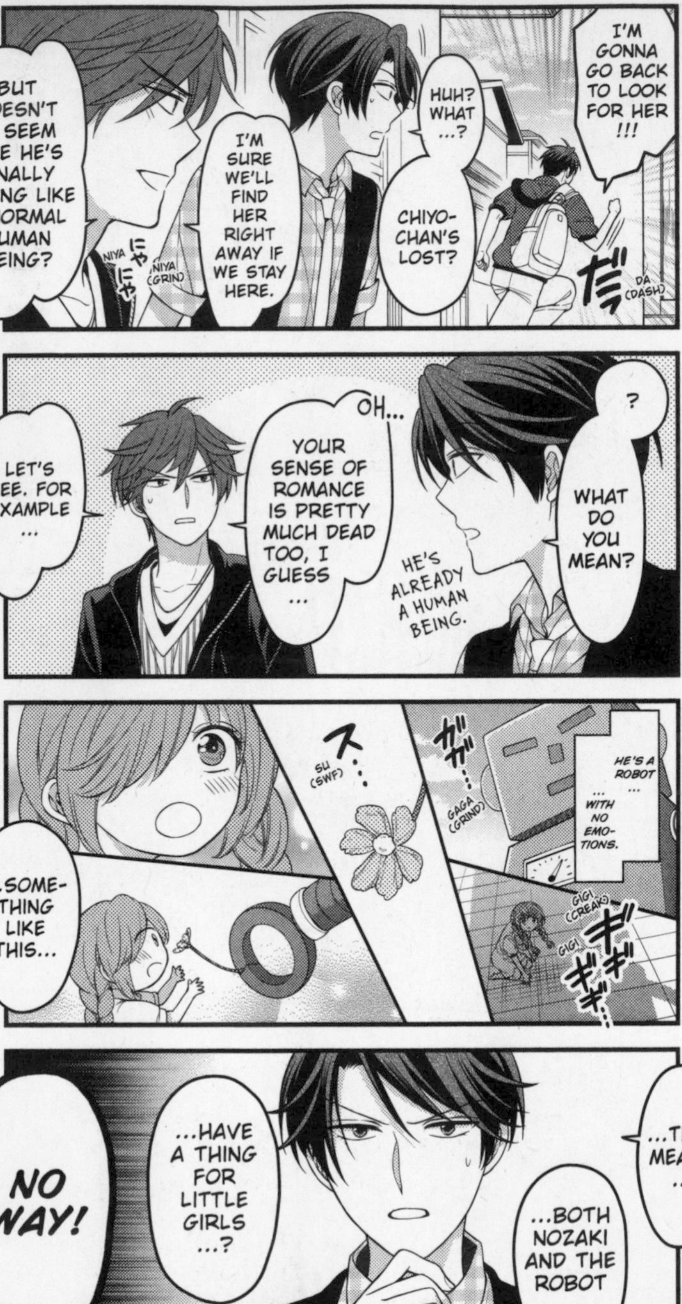

I'M GONNA GO BACK TO LOOK FOR HER!!!
ダッ DA (DASH)
HUH? WHAT ...?
CHIYO-CHAN'S LOST?
I'M SURE WE'LL FIND HER RIGHT AWAY IF WE STAY HERE.
にやにや NIYA NIYA (GRIN)
BUT DOESN'T IT SEEM LIKE HE'S FINALLY ACTING LIKE A NORMAL HUMAN BEING?
?
WHAT DO YOU MEAN?
HE'S ALREADY A HUMAN BEING.
OH...
YOUR SENSE OF ROMANCE IS PRETTY MUCH DEAD TOO, I GUESS ...
LET'S SEE. FOR EXAMPLE ...
HE'S A ROBOT ... WITH NO EMOTIONS.
ガガ GAGA (GRIND)
ギギ GIGI (CREAK)
ギギ GIGI
ス SU (SWF)
...SOME-THING LIKE THIS...
...THAT MEANS ...
...BOTH NOZAKI AND THE ROBOT ...
...HAVE A THING FOR LITTLE GIRLS ...?
NO WAY!

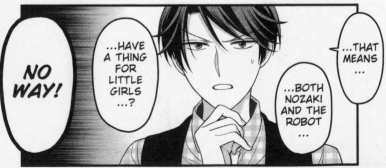

HE FOUND HER

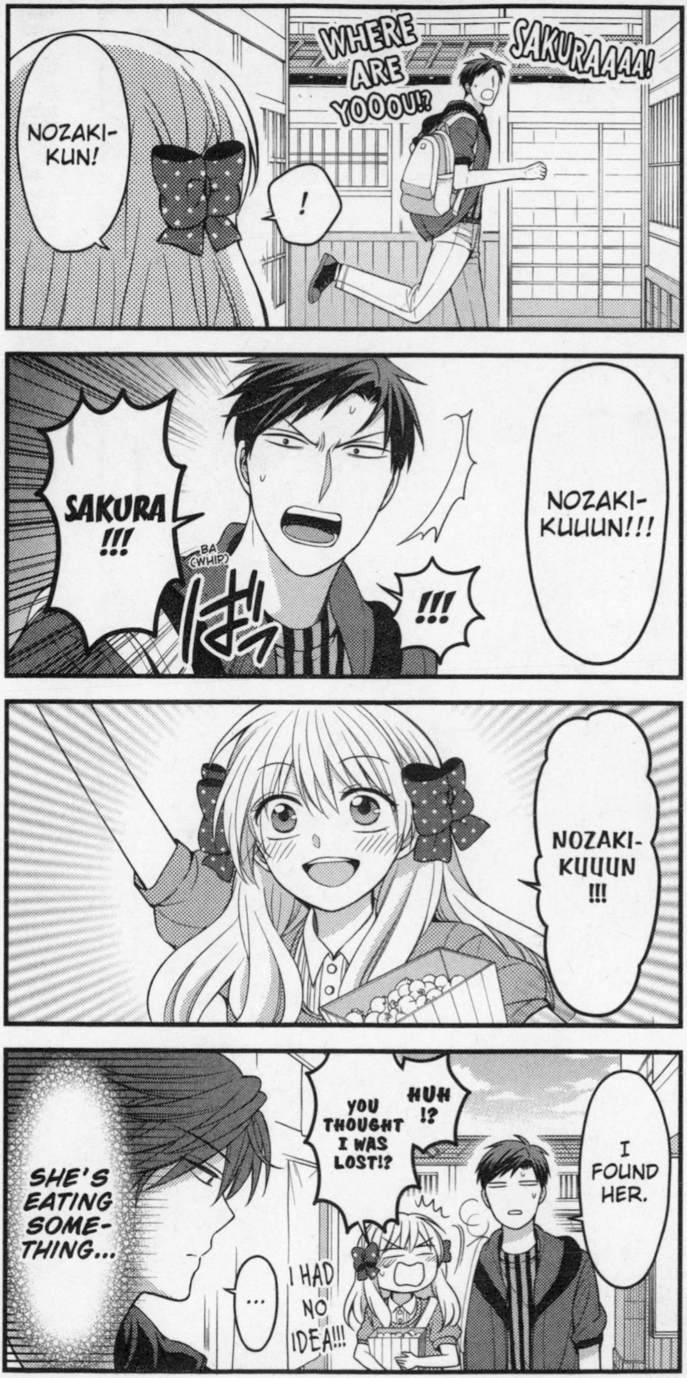
SAKURAAAA!
WHERE ARE YOOOU!?
!
NOZAKI-KUN!
NOZAKI-KUUUN!!!
!!!
BA (WHIP)
ばっ
SAKURA !!!
NOZAKI-KUUUN !!!
I FOUND HER.
HUH !?
YOU THOUGHT I WAS LOST!?
I HAD NO IDEA!!!
...
SHE'S EATING SOME-THING...

NO ULTERIOR MOTIVE

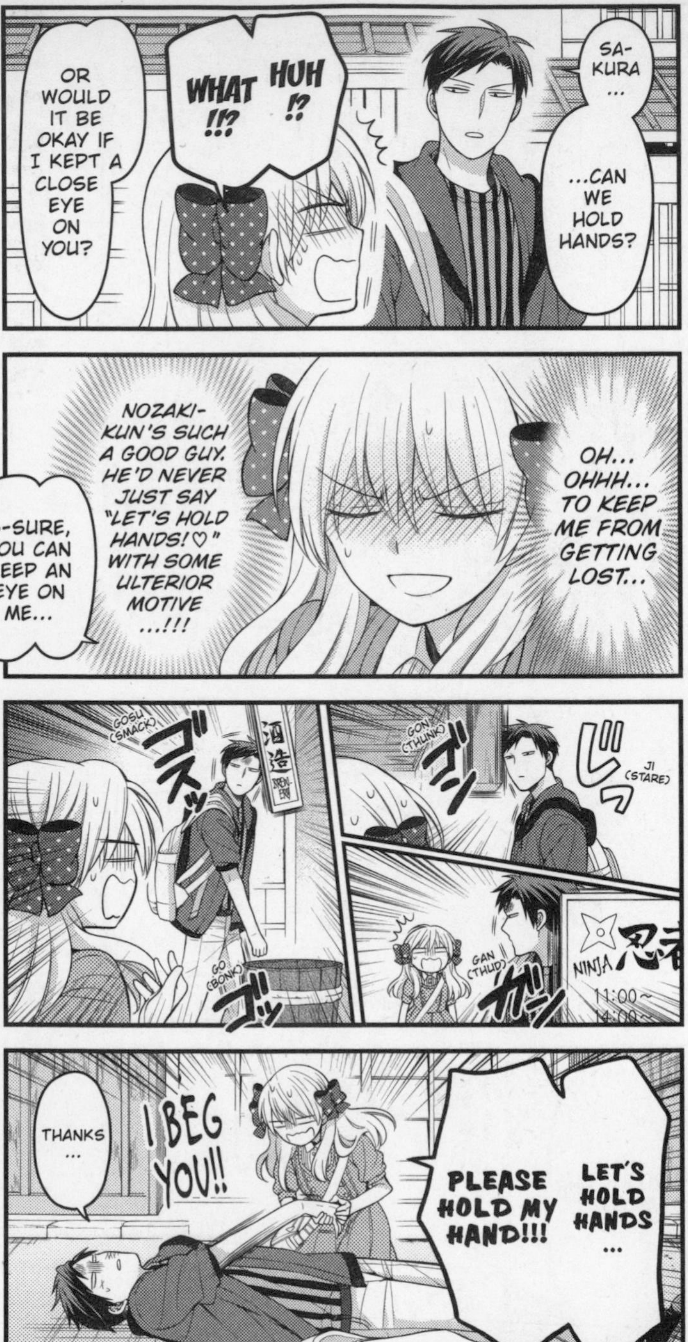
SA-KURA...
...CAN WE HOLD HANDS?
WHAT!!? HUH!?
OR WOULD IT BE OKAY IF I KEPT A CLOSE EYE ON YOU?
OH... OHHH... TO KEEP ME FROM GETTING LOST...
NOZAKI-KUN'S SUCH A GOOD GUY. HE'D NEVER JUST SAY "LET'S HOLD HANDS!♡" WITH SOME ULTERIOR MOTIVE ...!!!
S-SURE, YOU CAN KEEP AN EYE ON ME...
ジッ
JI (STARE)
ゴン
GON (THUNK)
ガン
GAN (THUD)
NINJA 忍
11:00~
ゴスッ
GOSU (SMACK)
酒造
ゴッ
GO (BONK)
LET'S HOLD HANDS...
PLEASE HOLD MY HAND!!!
I BEG YOU!!
THANKS...

A NEW FEELING

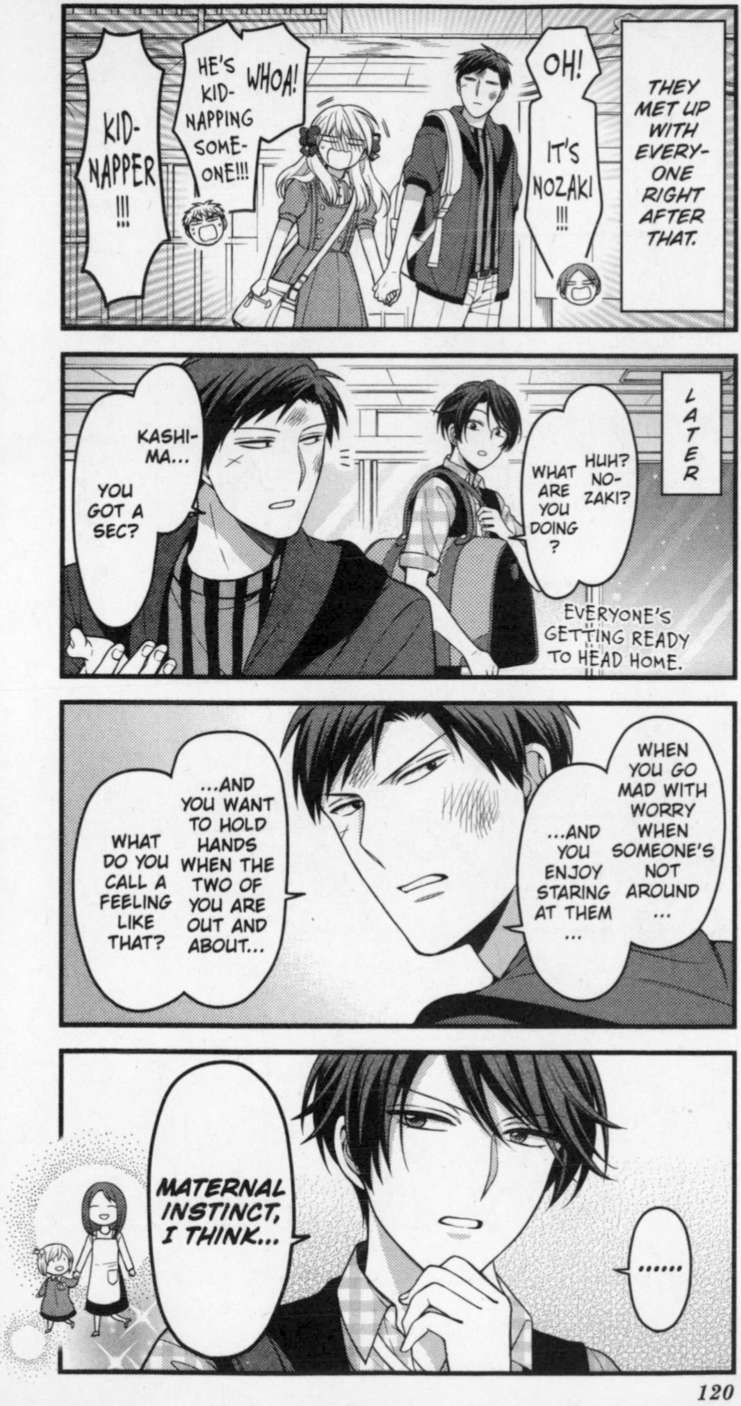
THEY MET UP WITH EVERYONE RIGHT AFTER THAT.
OH!
IT'S NOZAKI!!!
WHOA!
HE'S KIDNAPPING SOMEONE!!!
KIDNAPPER!!!
LATER
HUH? NOZAKI?
WHAT ARE YOU DOING?
EVERYONE'S GETTING READY TO HEAD HOME.
KASHIMA...
YOU GOT A SEC?
WHEN YOU GO MAD WITH WORRY WHEN SOMEONE'S NOT AROUND...
...AND YOU ENJOY STARING AT THEM...
...AND YOU WANT TO HOLD HANDS WHEN THE TWO OF YOU ARE OUT AND ABOUT...
WHAT DO YOU CALL A FEELING LIKE THAT?
......
MATERNAL INSTINCT, I THINK...

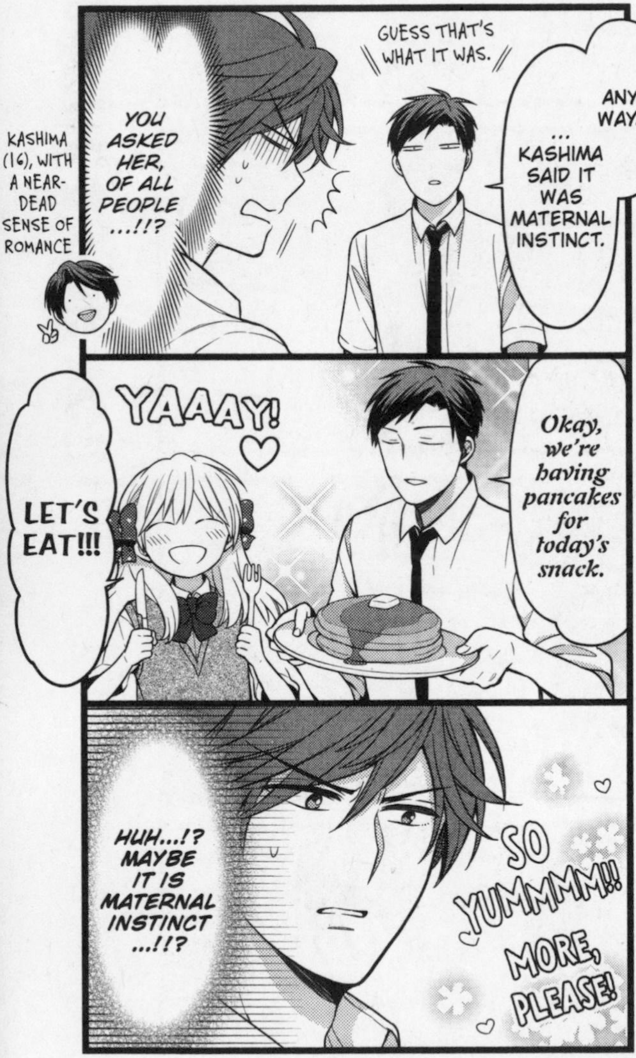
ANY-WAY... ... KASHIMA SAID IT WAS MATERNAL INSTINCT.
GUESS THAT'S WHAT IT WAS.
YOU ASKED HER, OF ALL PEOPLE ...!!?
KASHIMA (16), WITH A NEAR-DEAD SENSE OF ROMANCE
Okay, we're having pancakes for today's snack.
YAAAY!
LET'S EAT!!!
SO YUMMMM!!
MORE, PLEASE!
HUH...!? MAYBE IT IS MATERNAL INSTINCT ...!!?

[Extra]

I WAS WAITING FOR YOU!

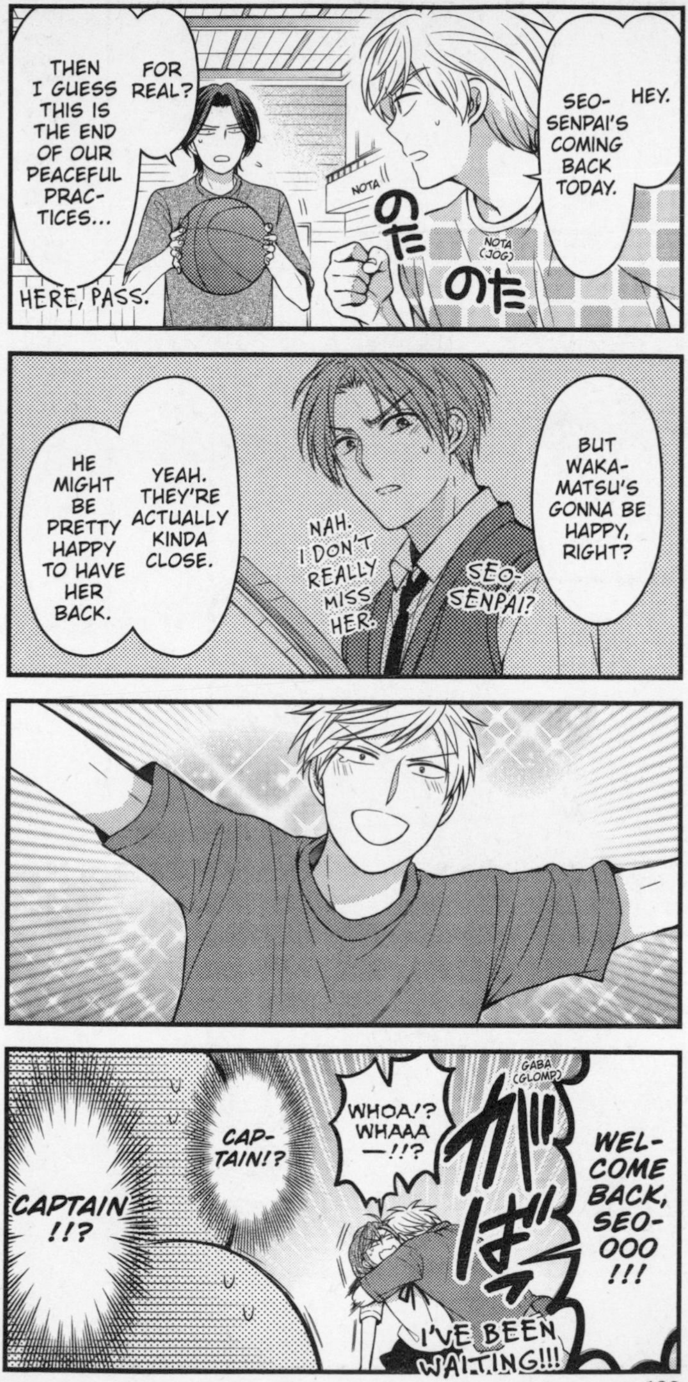
HEY.
SEO-SENPAI'S COMING BACK TODAY.
のた NOTA
のた NOTA (JOG)
FOR REAL?
THEN I GUESS THIS IS THE END OF OUR PEACEFUL PRAC-TICES...
HERE, PASS.
BUT WAKA-MATSU'S GONNA BE HAPPY, RIGHT?
SEO-SENPAI?
NAH. I DON'T REALLY MISS HER.
YEAH. THEY'RE ACTUALLY KINDA CLOSE.
HE MIGHT BE PRETTY HAPPY TO HAVE HER BACK.
WEL-COME BACK, SEO-OOO!!!
がばっ GABA (GLOMP)
I'VE BEEN WAITING!!!
WHOA!? WHAAA—!!?
CAP-TAIN!?
CAPTAIN!!?

[Extra]

In One Week

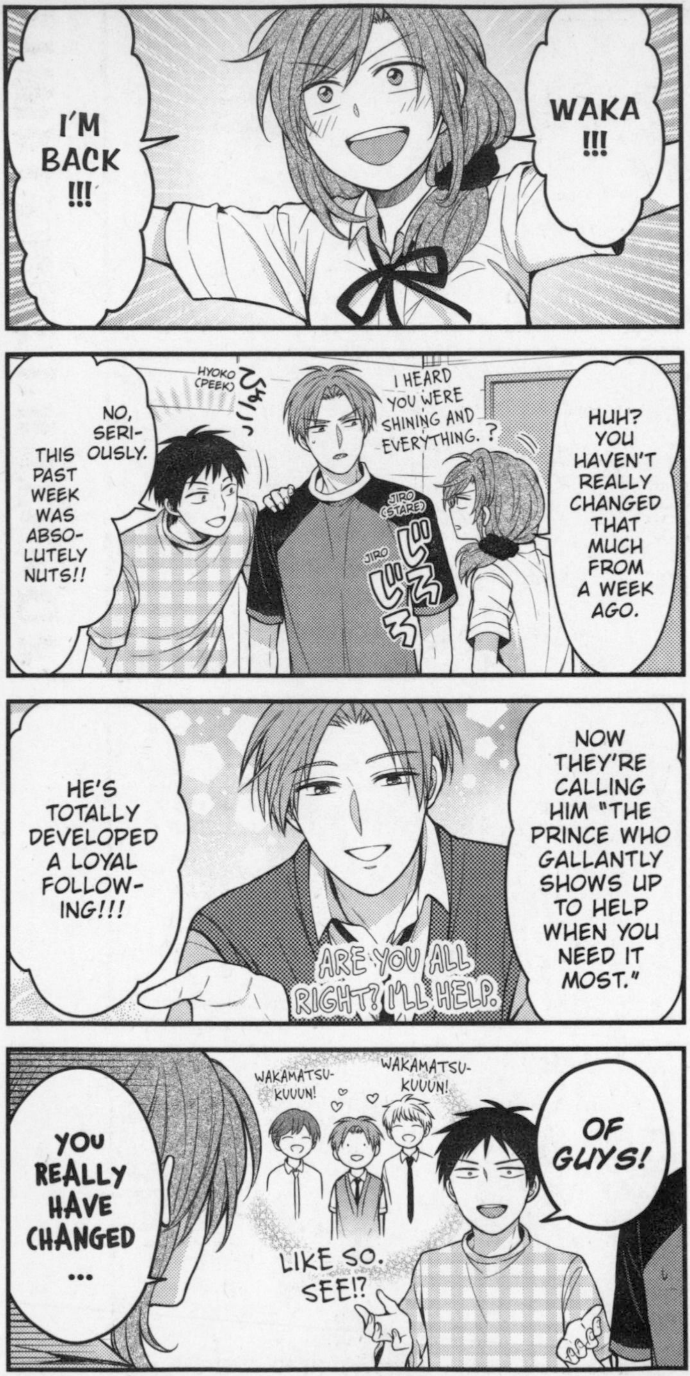
WAKA !!!
I'M BACK !!!
HUH? YOU HAVEN'T REALLY CHANGED THAT MUCH FROM A WEEK AGO.
I HEARD YOU WERE SHINING AND EVERYTHING. ?
JIRO (STARE)
JIRO
HYOKO (PEEK)
NO, SERIOUSLY. THIS PAST WEEK WAS ABSOLUTELY NUTS!!
NOW THEY'RE CALLING HIM "THE PRINCE WHO GALLANTLY SHOWS UP TO HELP WHEN YOU NEED IT MOST."
ARE YOU ALL RIGHT? I'LL HELP.
HE'S TOTALLY DEVELOPED A LOYAL FOLLOWING!!!
OF GUYS!
WAKAMATSU-KUUUN!
WAKAMATSU-KUUUN!
LIKE SO. SEE!?
YOU REALLY HAVE CHANGED ...

[Extra]

THIS IS WHY I HATE YOU

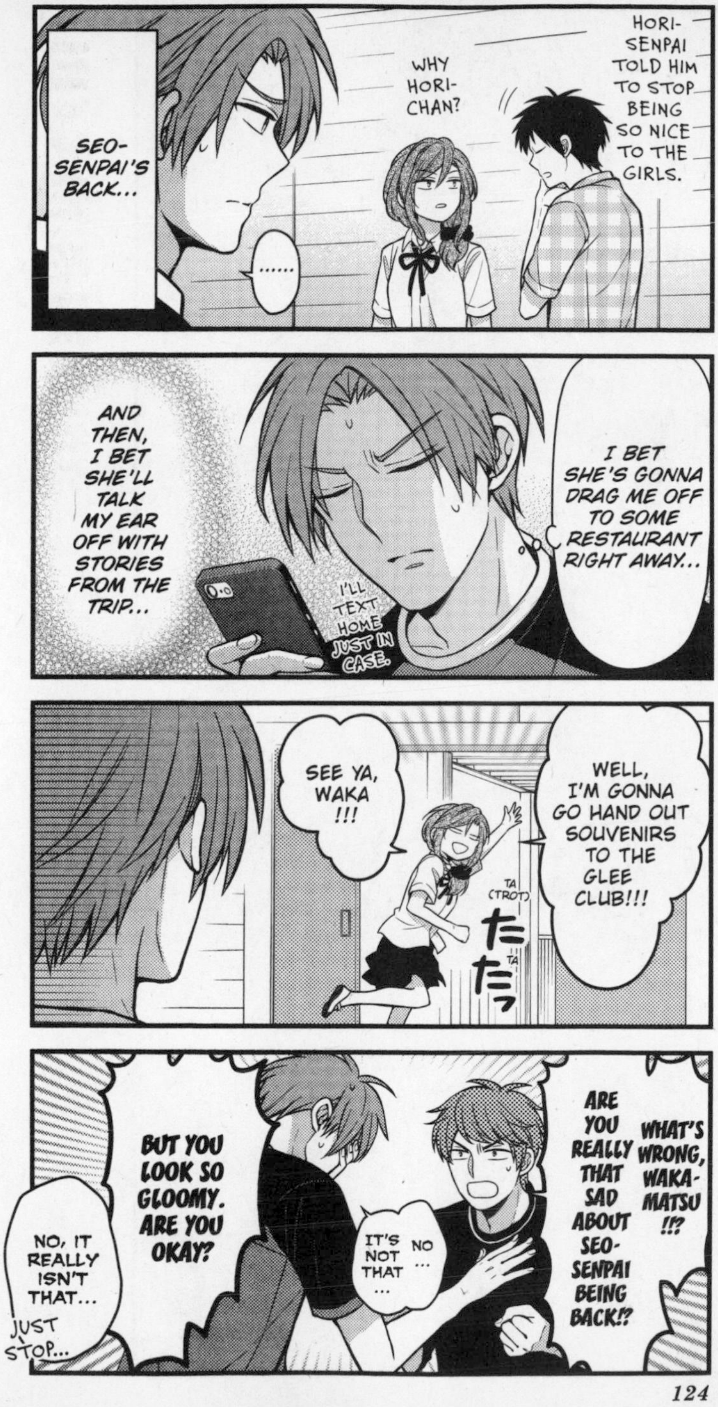
HORI-SENPAI TOLD HIM TO STOP BEING SO NICE TO THE GIRLS.
WHY HORI-CHAN?
SEO-SENPAI'S BACK...
......
I BET SHE'S GONNA DRAG ME OFF TO SOME RESTAURANT RIGHT AWAY...
I'LL TEXT HOME JUST IN CASE.
AND THEN, I BET SHE'LL TALK MY EAR OFF WITH STORIES FROM THE TRIP...
WELL, I'M GONNA GO HAND OUT SOUVENIRS TO THE GLEE CLUB!!!
SEE YA, WAKA!!!
TA (TROT)
TA
WHAT'S WRONG, WAKAMATSU!!?
ARE YOU REALLY THAT SAD ABOUT SEO-SENPAI BEING BACK!!?
NO...
IT'S NOT THAT...
BUT YOU LOOK SO GLOOMY. ARE YOU OKAY?
NO, IT REALLY ISN'T THAT...
JUST STOP...

[Extra]

HIS TRUE FEELINGS SLIPPED OUT

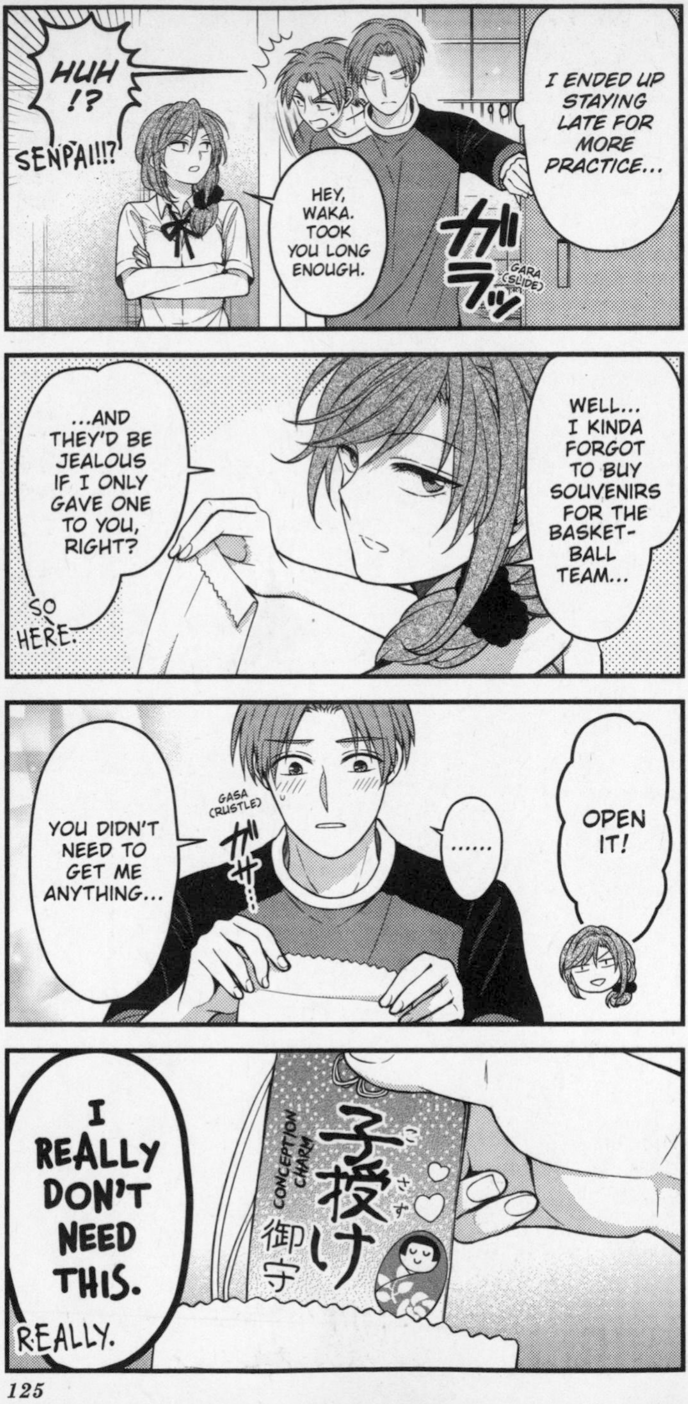
I ENDED UP STAYING LATE FOR MORE PRACTICE...
ガラッ
GARA (SLIDE)
HEY, WAKA. TOOK YOU LONG ENOUGH.
HUH !?
SENPAI!!!?
WELL... I KINDA FORGOT TO BUY SOUVENIRS FOR THE BASKET-BALL TEAM...
...AND THEY'D BE JEALOUS IF I ONLY GAVE ONE TO YOU, RIGHT?
SO HERE.
OPEN IT!
......
GASA (RUSTLE)
ガサ…
YOU DIDN'T NEED TO GET ME ANYTHING...
子授け御守
CONCEPTION CHARM
I REALLY DON'T NEED THIS.
REALLY.

MONTHLY GIRLS' NOZAKI-KUN

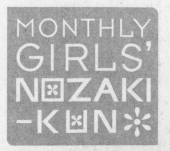

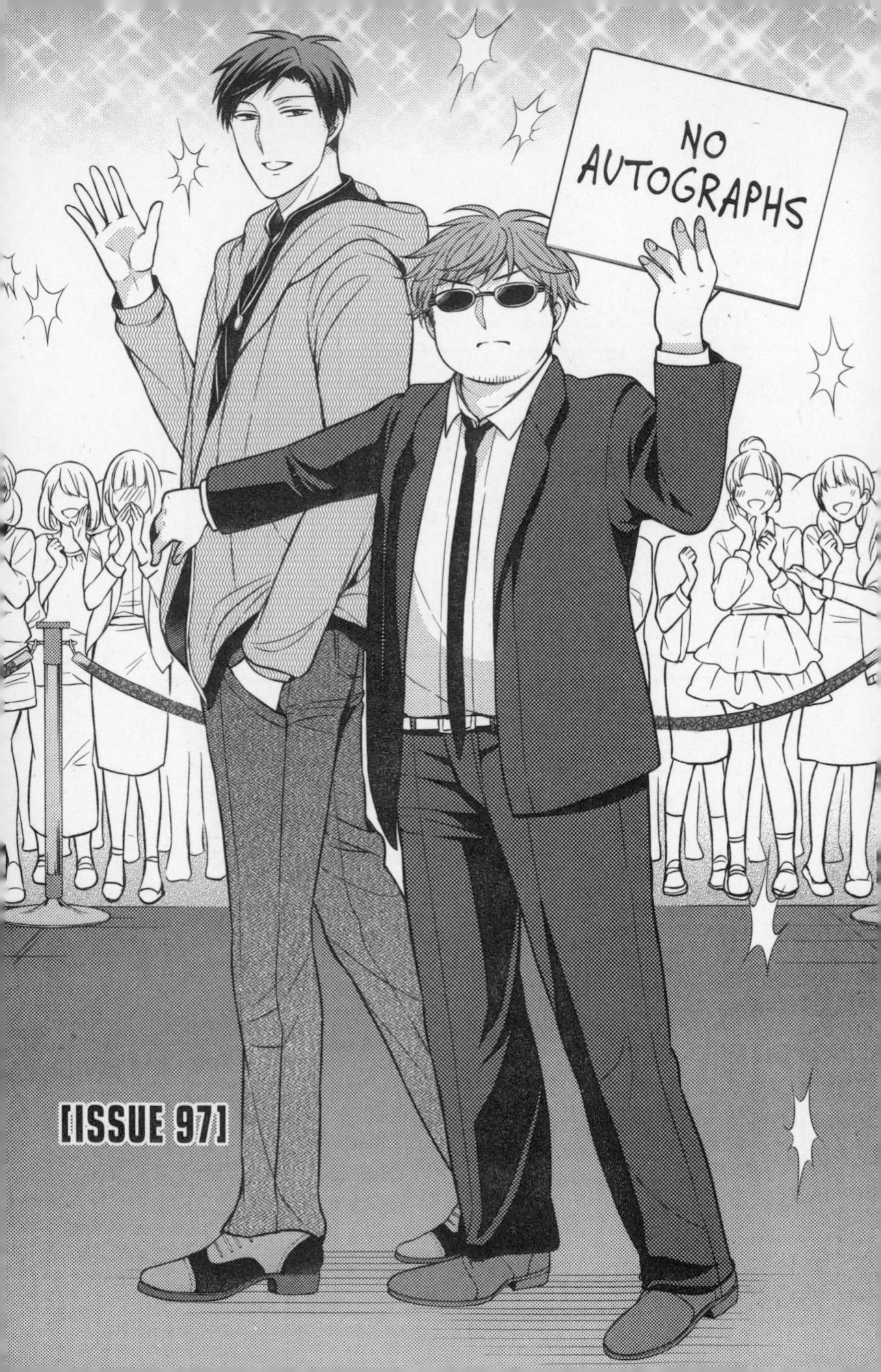
NO AUTOGRAPHS
[ISSUE 97]

PRO ADVICE

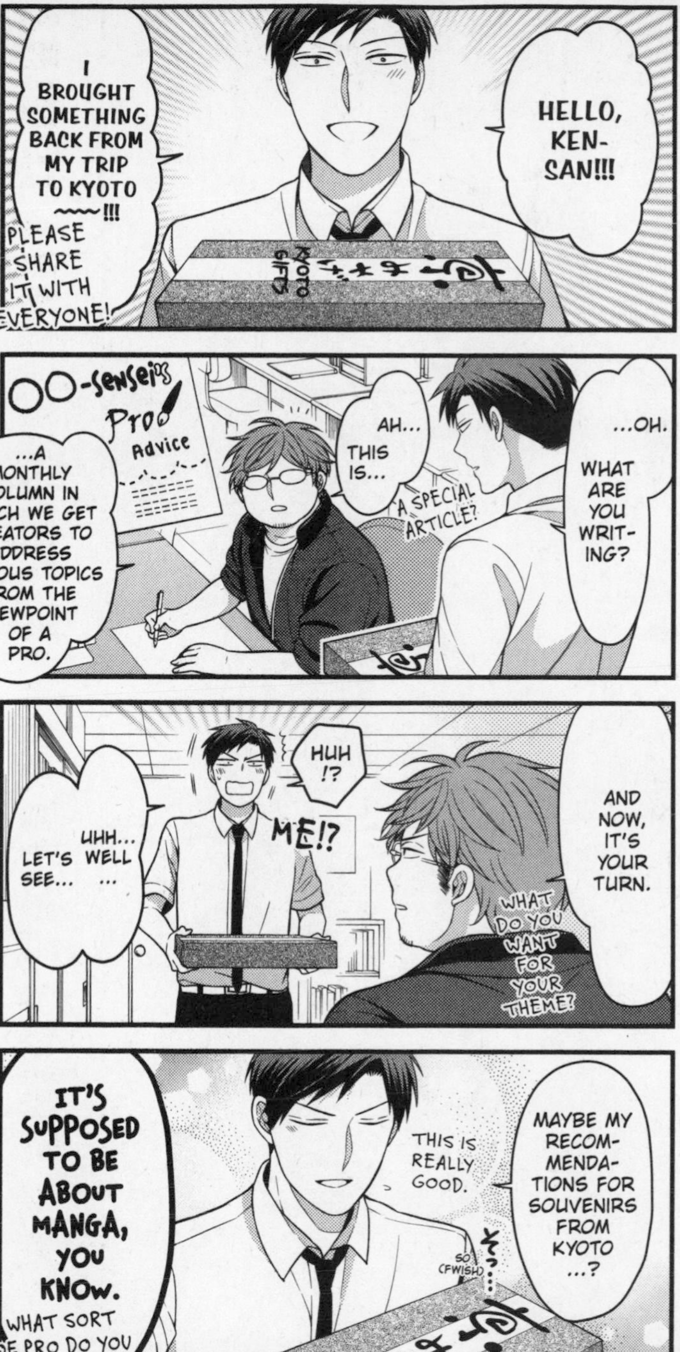
HELLO, KEN-SAN!!!
I BROUGHT SOMETHING BACK FROM MY TRIP TO KYOTO ~~~!!!
PLEASE SHARE IT WITH EVERYONE!
KYOTO GIFTS
...OH. WHAT ARE YOU WRITING?
AH... THIS IS...
A SPECIAL ARTICLE?
OO-sensei's Pro Advice
...A MONTHLY COLUMN IN WHICH WE GET CREATORS TO ADDRESS VARIOUS TOPICS FROM THE VIEWPOINT OF A PRO.
AND NOW, IT'S YOUR TURN.
WHAT DO YOU WANT FOR YOUR THEME?
HUH!?
ME!?
UHH... WELL ...
LET'S SEE...
MAYBE MY RECOMMENDATIONS FOR SOUVENIRS FROM KYOTO ...?
THIS IS REALLY GOOD.
SO (FWISH)
IT'S SUPPOSED TO BE ABOUT MANGA, YOU KNOW.
WHAT SORT OF PRO DO YOU THINK YOU ARE?

THINGS THAT SURPRISED HIM AFTER GOING PRO

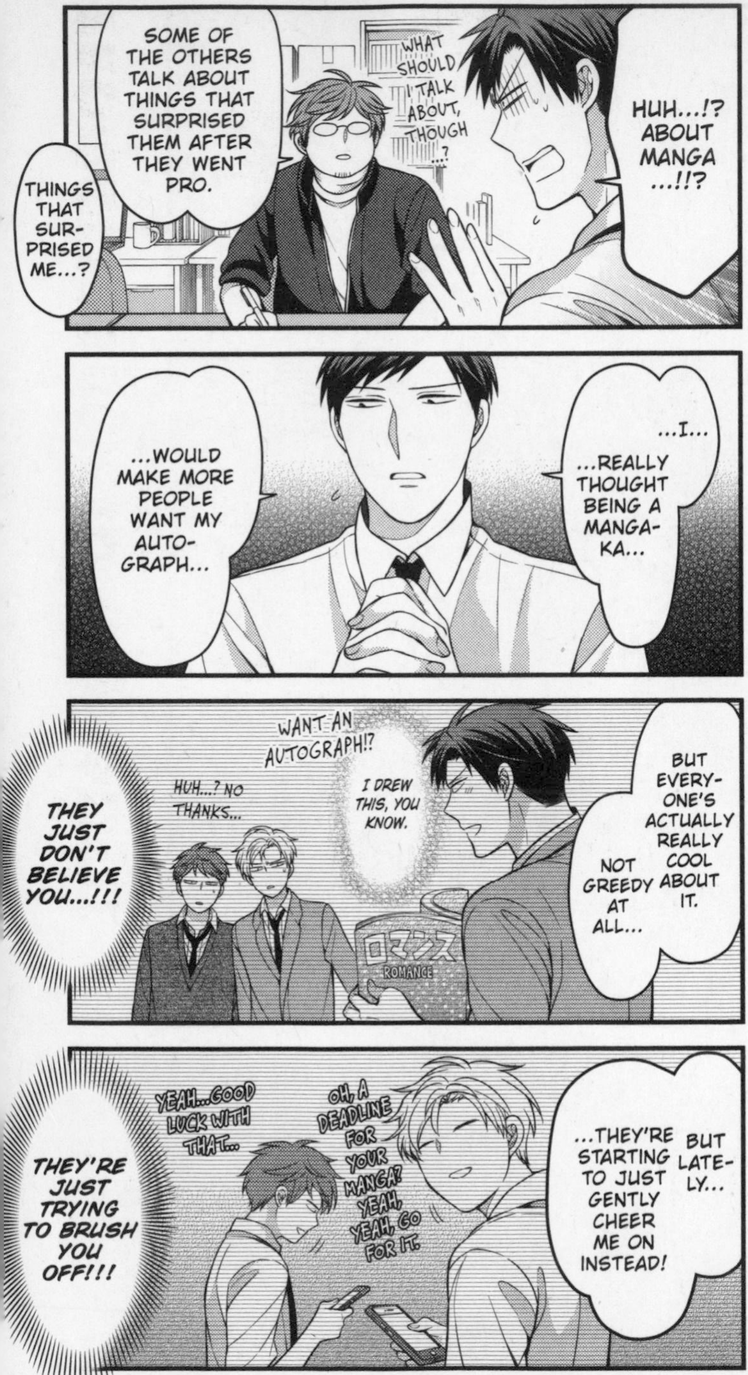

HUH...!? ABOUT MANGA ...!!?
WHAT SHOULD I TALK ABOUT, THOUGH ...?
SOME OF THE OTHERS TALK ABOUT THINGS THAT SURPRISED THEM AFTER THEY WENT PRO.
THINGS THAT SUR-PRISED ME...?
...I...
...REALLY THOUGHT BEING A MANGA-KA...
...WOULD MAKE MORE PEOPLE WANT MY AUTO-GRAPH...
BUT EVERY-ONE'S ACTUALLY REALLY COOL ABOUT IT.
NOT GREEDY AT ALL...
WANT AN AUTOGRAPH!?
I DREW THIS, YOU KNOW.
HUH...? NO THANKS...
ロマンス
ROMANCE
THEY JUST DON'T BELIEVE YOU...!!!
BUT LATE-LY...
...THEY'RE STARTING TO JUST GENTLY CHEER ME ON INSTEAD!
OH, A DEADLINE FOR YOUR MANGA? YEAH, YEAH, GO FOR IT.
YEAH...GOOD LUCK WITH THAT...
THEY'RE JUST TRYING TO BRUSH YOU OFF!!!

※THE BIG AWARDS ARE DIFFERENT.

THE WAY I IMAGINED PROS DID IT

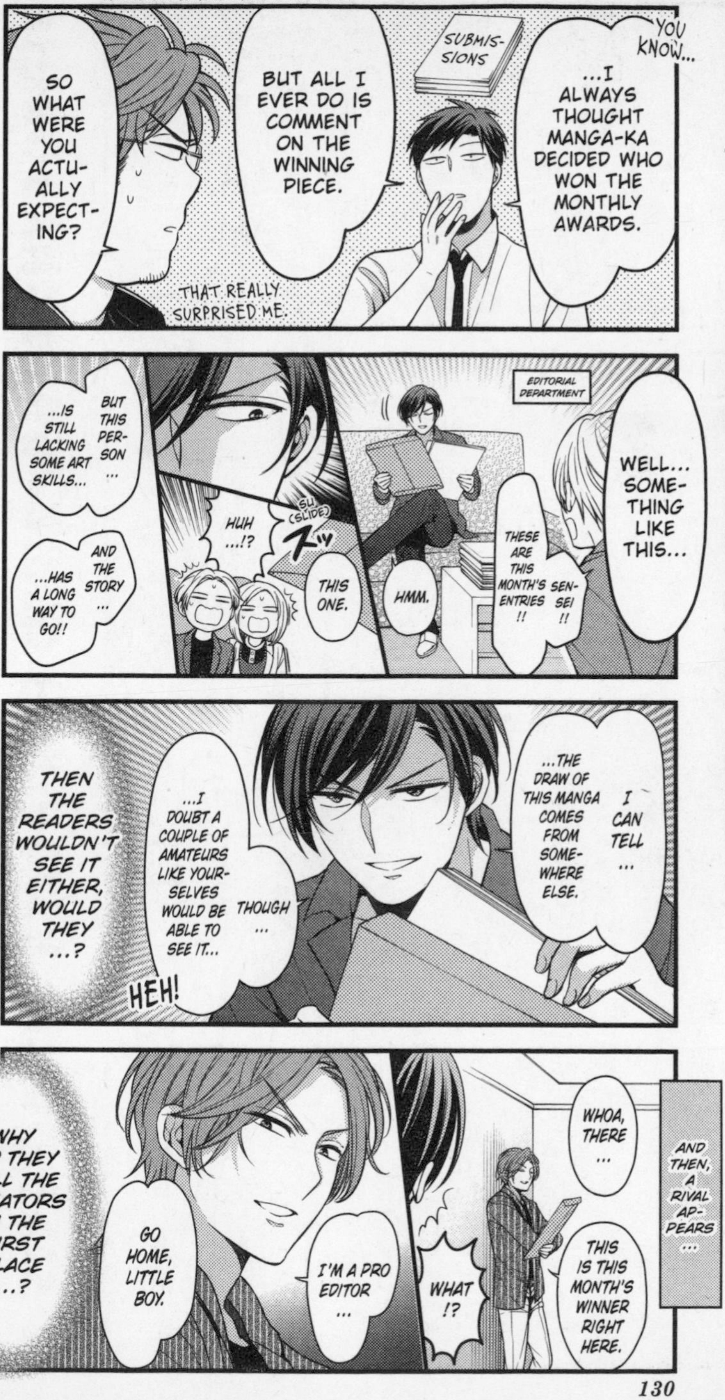
YOU KNOW...
...I ALWAYS THOUGHT MANGA-KA DECIDED WHO WON THE MONTHLY AWARDS.
SUBMISSIONS
BUT ALL I EVER DO IS COMMENT ON THE WINNING PIECE.
THAT REALLY SURPRISED ME.
SO WHAT WERE YOU ACTUALLY EXPECTING?
EDITORIAL DEPARTMENT
WELL... SOMETHING LIKE THIS...
SENSEI!!
THESE ARE THIS MONTH'S ENTRIES!!
HMM.
SU (SLIDE)
HUH...!?
THIS ONE.
BUT THIS PERSON...
...IS STILL LACKING SOME ART SKILLS...
AND THE STORY...
...HAS A LONG WAY TO GO!!
I CAN TELL...
...THE DRAW OF THIS MANGA COMES FROM SOMEWHERE ELSE.
THOUGH...
...I DOUBT A COUPLE OF AMATEURS LIKE YOURSELVES WOULD BE ABLE TO SEE IT...
HEH!
THEN THE READERS WOULDN'T SEE IT EITHER, WOULD THEY...?
AND THEN, A RIVAL APPEARS...
WHOA, THERE...
THIS IS THIS MONTH'S WINNER RIGHT HERE.
WHAT!?
I'M A PRO EDITOR...
GO HOME, LITTLE BOY.
WHY DID THEY CALL THE CREATORS IN THE FIRST PLACE...?

HOW IT ACTUALLY HAPPENS

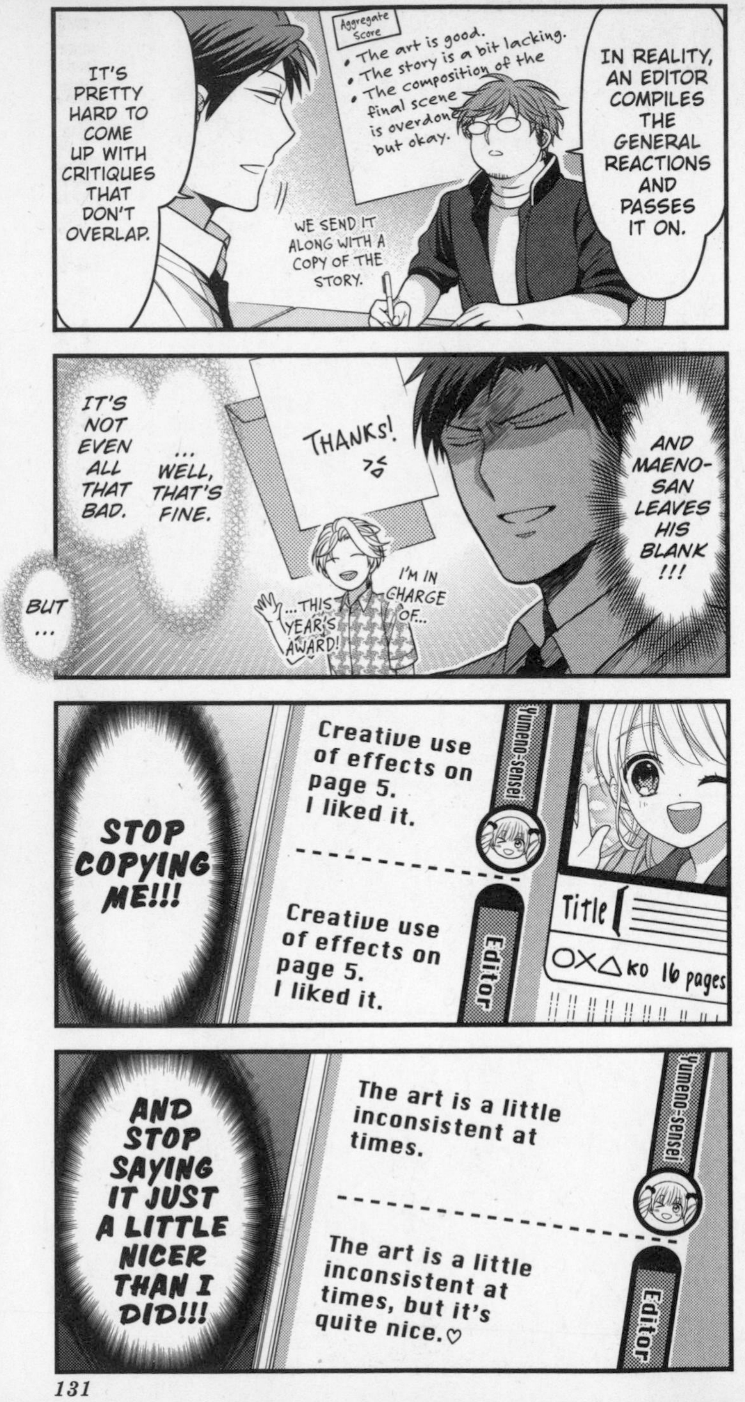
IN REALITY, AN EDITOR COMPILES THE GENERAL REACTIONS AND PASSES IT ON.
Aggregate Score
• The art is good.
• The story is a bit lacking.
• The composition of the final scene is overdone but okay.
WE SEND IT ALONG WITH A COPY OF THE STORY.
IT'S PRETTY HARD TO COME UP WITH CRITIQUES THAT DON'T OVERLAP.
AND MAENO-SAN LEAVES HIS BLANK!!!
THANKS!
I'M IN CHARGE OF...
...THIS YEAR'S AWARD!
...WELL, THAT'S FINE.
IT'S NOT EVEN ALL THAT BAD.
BUT...
Title
○×△ko 16 pages
Yumeno-sensei
Creative use of effects on page 5. I liked it.
Editor
Creative use of effects on page 5. I liked it.
STOP COPYING ME!!!
Yumeno-sensei
The art is a little inconsistent at times.
Editor
The art is a little inconsistent at times, but it's quite nice.♡
AND STOP SAYING IT JUST A LITTLE NICER THAN I DID!!!

THE FRUITS OF HIS LABOR

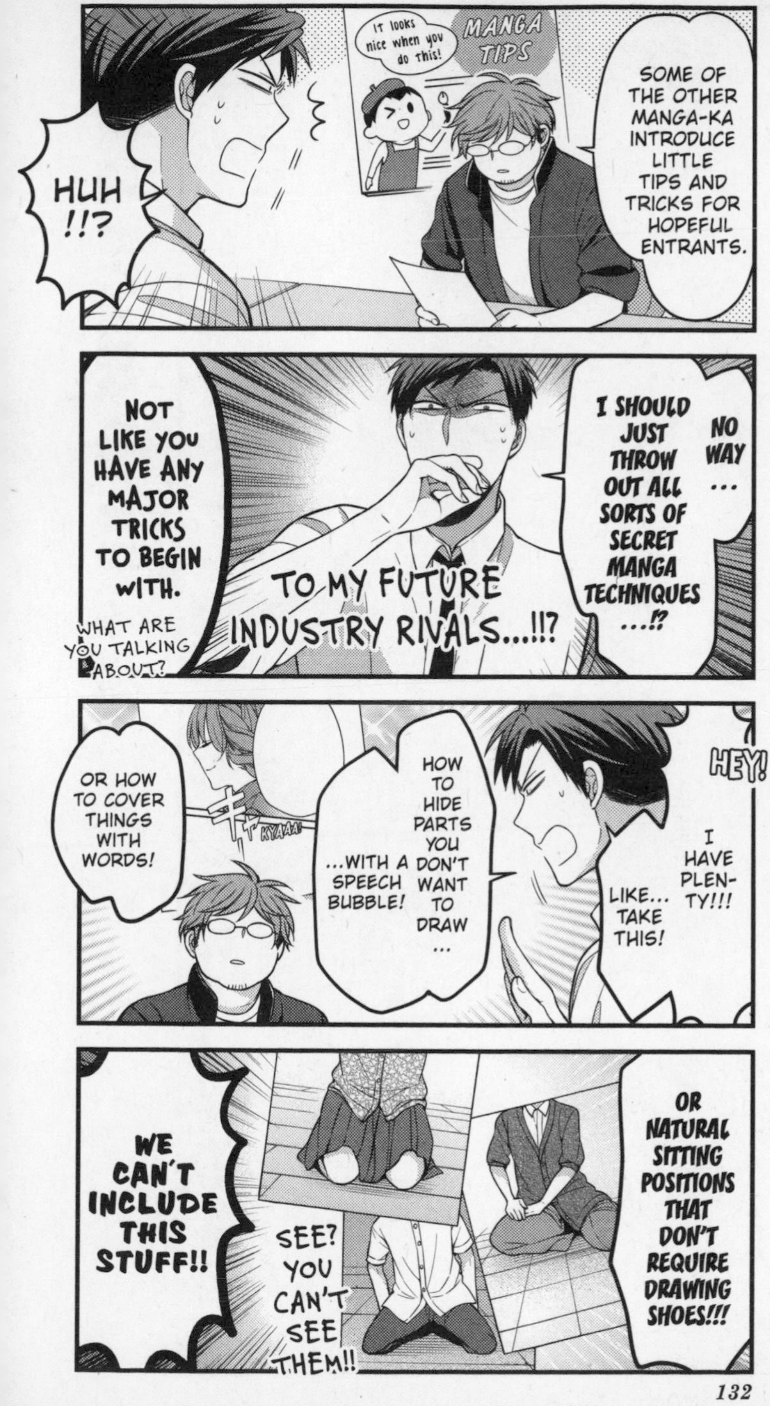
SOME OF THE OTHER MANGA-KA INTRODUCE LITTLE TIPS AND TRICKS FOR HOPEFUL ENTRANTS.
MANGA TIPS
It looks nice when you do this!
HUH !!?
NO WAY...
I SHOULD JUST THROW OUT ALL SORTS OF SECRET MANGA TECHNIQUES...!?
TO MY FUTURE INDUSTRY RIVALS...!!?
NOT LIKE YOU HAVE ANY MAJOR TRICKS TO BEGIN WITH.
WHAT ARE YOU TALKING ABOUT?
HEY!
I HAVE PLEN-TY!!!
LIKE... TAKE THIS!
HOW TO HIDE PARTS YOU DON'T WANT TO DRAW...
...WITH A SPEECH BUBBLE!
OR HOW TO COVER THINGS WITH WORDS!
KYAAA!
OR NATURAL SITTING POSITIONS THAT DON'T REQUIRE DRAWING SHOES!!!
SEE? YOU CAN'T SEE THEM!!
WE CAN'T INCLUDE THIS STUFF!!

MANGA TECHNIQUES

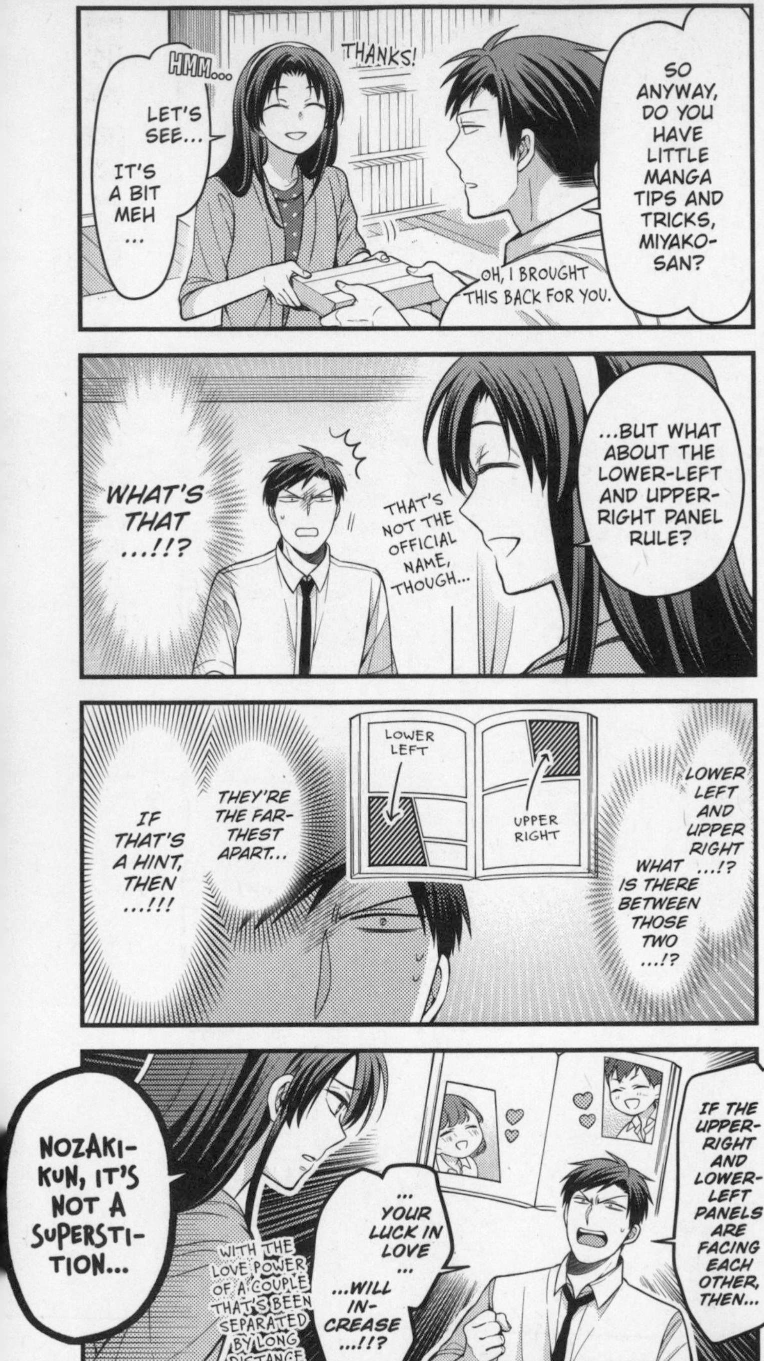
SO ANYWAY, DO YOU HAVE LITTLE MANGA TIPS AND TRICKS, MIYAKO-SAN?
OH, I BROUGHT THIS BACK FOR YOU.
THANKS!
HMM...
LET'S SEE...
IT'S A BIT MEH ...
...BUT WHAT ABOUT THE LOWER-LEFT AND UPPER-RIGHT PANEL RULE?
THAT'S NOT THE OFFICIAL NAME, THOUGH...
WHAT'S THAT ...!!?
LOWER LEFT AND UPPER RIGHT ...!?
WHAT IS THERE BETWEEN THOSE TWO ...!?
UPPER RIGHT
LOWER LEFT
THEY'RE THE FAR-THEST APART...
IF THAT'S A HINT, THEN ...!!!
I—
IF THE UPPER-RIGHT AND LOWER-LEFT PANELS ARE FACING EACH OTHER, THEN...
... YOUR LUCK IN LOVE ... ...WILL IN-CREASE ...!!?
WITH THE LOVE POWER OF A COUPLE THAT'S BEEN SEPARATED BY LONG DISTANCE ...!!!
NOZAKI-KUN, IT'S NOT A SUPERSTI-TION...

IN PRACTICE

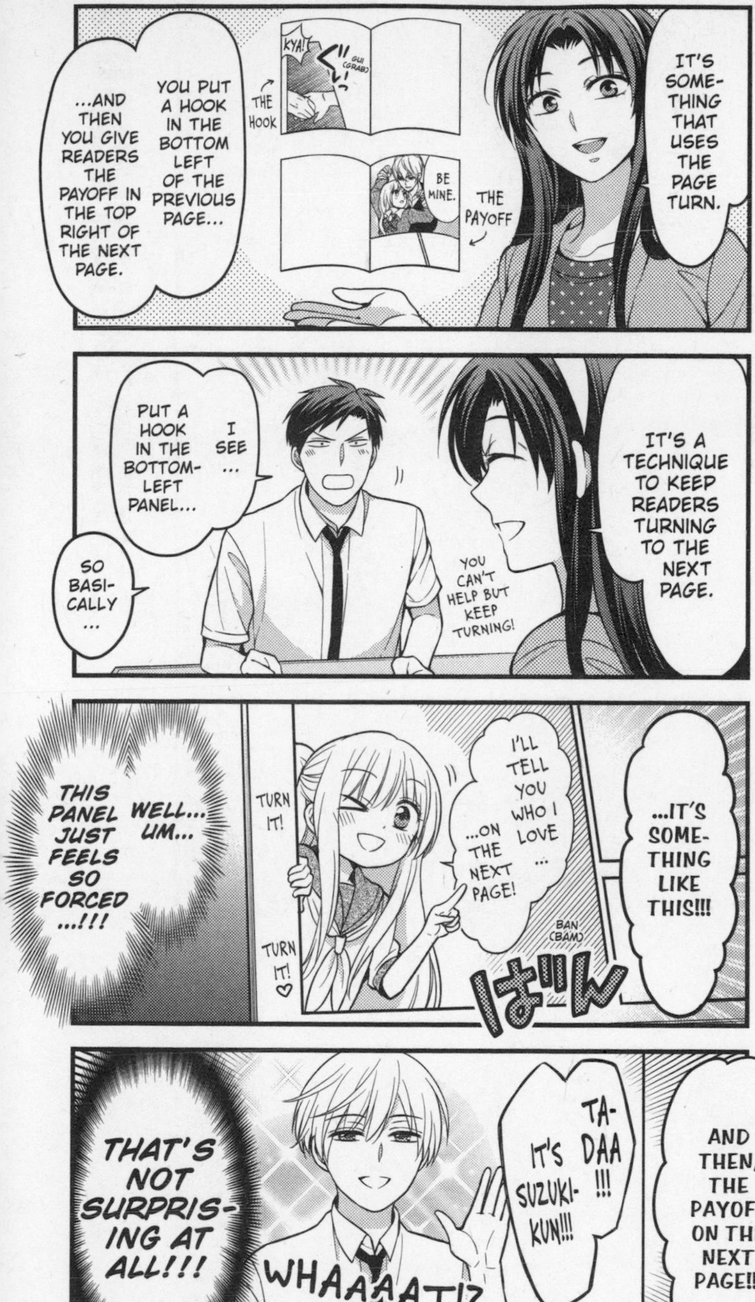
IT'S SOMETHING THAT USES THE PAGE TURN.
KYA!
GUI (GRAB)
THE HOOK
BE MINE.
THE PAYOFF
YOU PUT A HOOK IN THE BOTTOM LEFT OF THE PREVIOUS PAGE...
...AND THEN YOU GIVE READERS THE PAYOFF IN THE TOP RIGHT OF THE NEXT PAGE.
IT'S A TECHNIQUE TO KEEP READERS TURNING TO THE NEXT PAGE.
YOU CAN'T HELP BUT KEEP TURNING!
I SEE...
PUT A HOOK IN THE BOTTOM-LEFT PANEL...
SO BASICALLY...
...IT'S SOMETHING LIKE THIS!!!
BAN (BAM)
I'LL TELL YOU WHO I LOVE...
...ON THE NEXT PAGE!
TURN IT!
TURN IT! ♡
WELL... UM...
THIS PANEL JUST FEELS SO FORCED...!!!
AND THEN, THE PAYOFF ON THE NEXT PAGE!!!
TA-DAA!!!
IT'S SUZUKI-KUN!!!
WHAAAAT!? WHAAAAAT!!?
THAT'S NOT SURPRISING AT ALL!!!

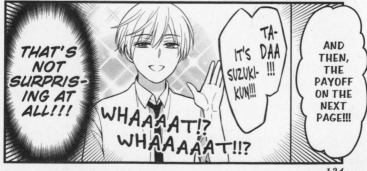

CALCULATION ERROR

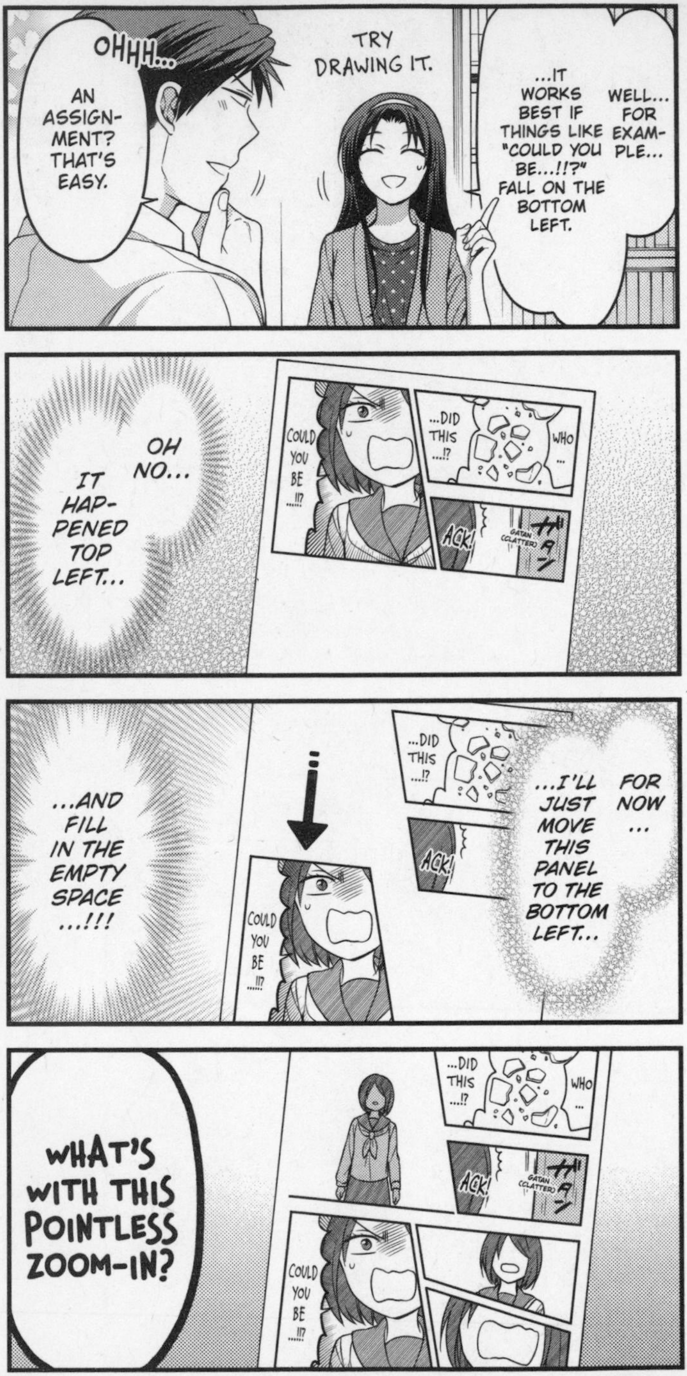

WELL... FOR EXAMPLE... ...IT WORKS BEST IF THINGS LIKE "COULD YOU BE...!!?" FALL ON THE BOTTOM LEFT.
TRY DRAWING IT.
OHHH... AN ASSIGNMENT? THAT'S EASY.
WHO ...
...DID THIS ...!?
GATAN (CLATTER)
ACK!
COULD YOU BE ...!?
OH NO... IT HAPPENED TOP LEFT...
FOR NOW... ...I'LL JUST MOVE THIS PANEL TO THE BOTTOM LEFT...
...DID THIS ...!?
ACK!
COULD YOU BE ...!?
...AND FILL IN THE EMPTY SPACE ...!!!
WHO ...
...DID THIS ...!?
GATAN (CLATTER)
ACK!
COULD YOU BE ...!?
WHAT'S WITH THIS POINTLESS ZOOM-IN?

WHAT HAPPENED?

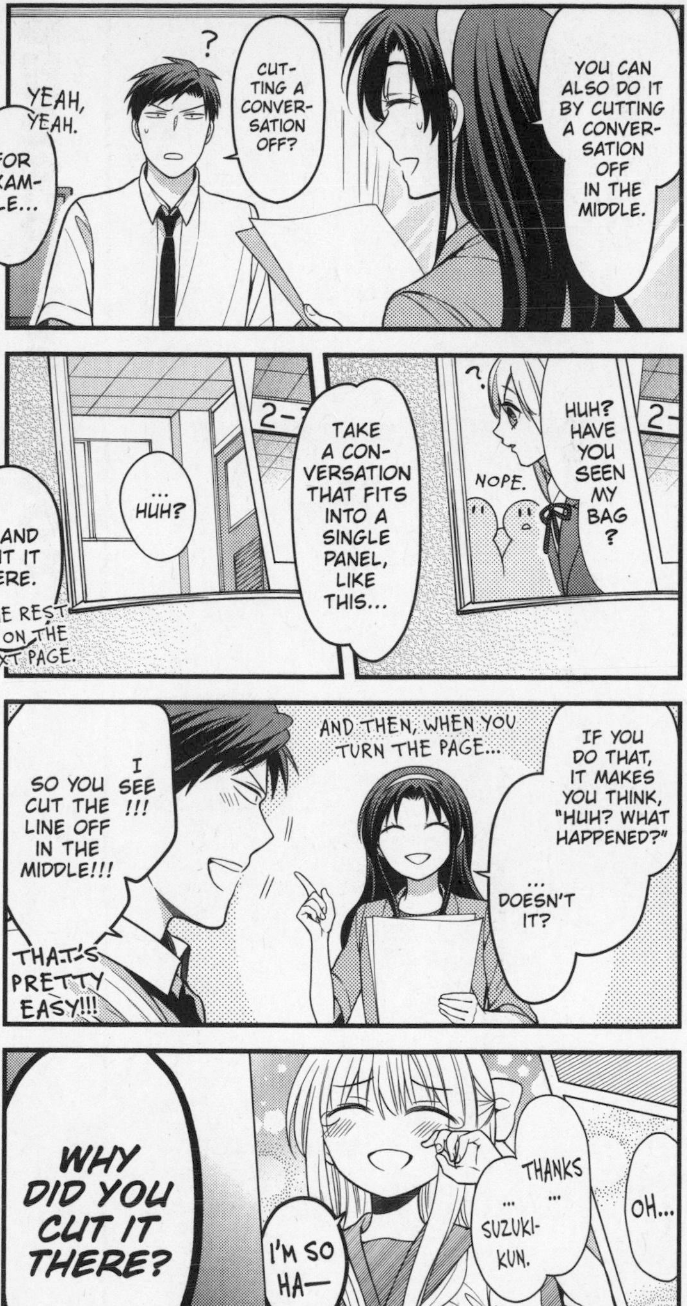

YOU CAN ALSO DO IT BY CUTTING A CONVERSATION OFF IN THE MIDDLE.
CUTTING A CONVERSATION OFF?
?
YEAH, YEAH.
FOR EXAMPLE...
HUH? HAVE YOU SEEN MY BAG?
NOPE.
TAKE A CONVERSATION THAT FITS INTO A SINGLE PANEL, LIKE THIS...
... HUH?
...AND CUT IT HERE.
THE REST IS ON THE NEXT PAGE.
IF YOU DO THAT, IT MAKES YOU THINK, "HUH? WHAT HAPPENED?"
... DOESN'T IT?
AND THEN, WHEN YOU TURN THE PAGE...
I SEE!!!
SO YOU CUT THE LINE OFF IN THE MIDDLE!!!
THAT'S PRETTY EASY!!!
OH...
THANKS ... ... SUZUKI-KUN.
I'M SO HA—
WHY DID YOU CUT IT THERE?

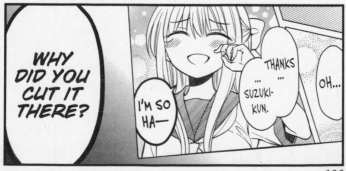

MIYAKO-SAN'S KIND WARNING

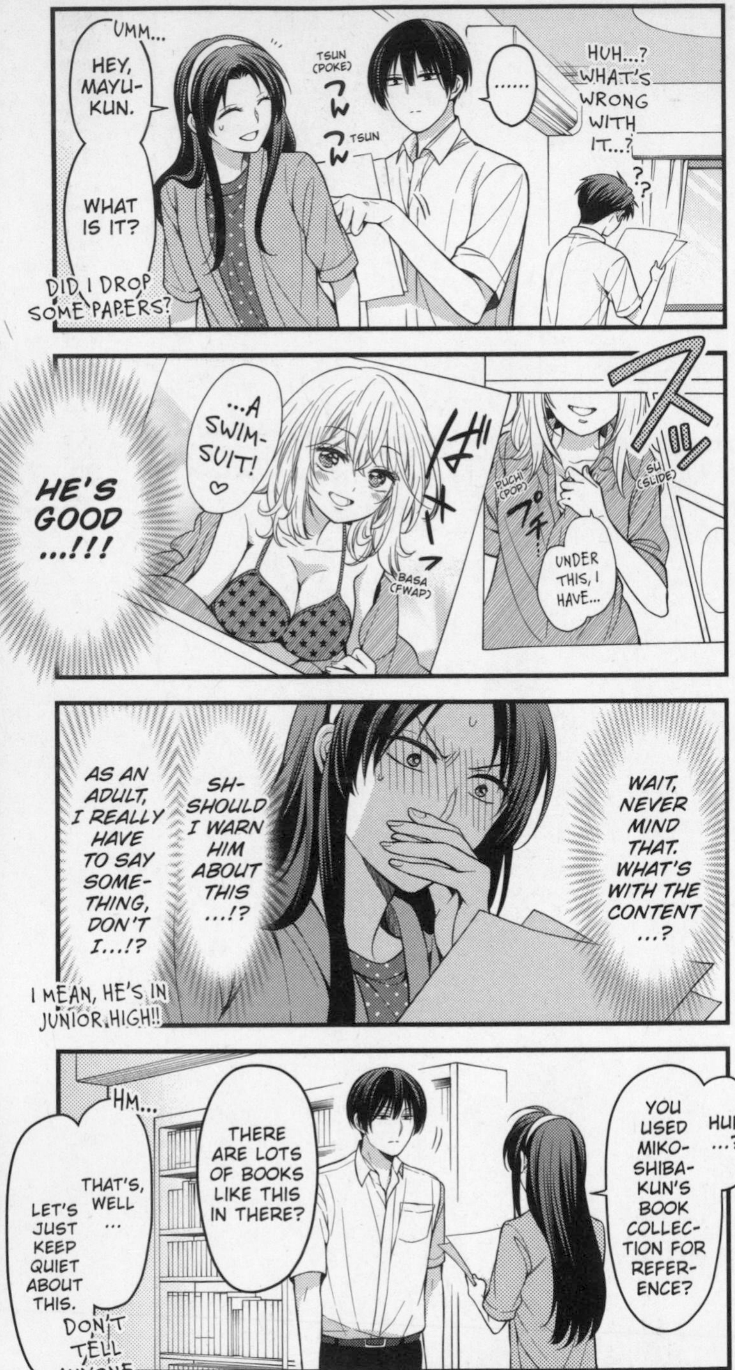
HUH...? WHAT'S WRONG WITH IT...?
??
......
TSUN (POKE)
TSUN
UMM...
HEY, MAYU-KUN.
WHAT IS IT?
DID I DROP SOME PAPERS?
SU (SLIDE)
PUCHI (POP)
UNDER THIS, I HAVE...
BASA (FWAP)
...A SWIM-SUIT! ♡
HE'S GOOD ...!!!
WAIT, NEVER MIND THAT. WHAT'S WITH THE CONTENT ...?
SH-SHOULD I WARN HIM ABOUT THIS ...!?
AS AN ADULT, I REALLY HAVE TO SAY SOMETHING, DON'T I...!?
I MEAN, HE'S IN JUNIOR HIGH!!
HUH ...?
YOU USED MIKO-SHIBA-KUN'S BOOK COLLECTION FOR REFERENCE?
THERE ARE LOTS OF BOOKS LIKE THIS IN THERE?
HM...
THAT'S, WELL ...
LET'S JUST KEEP QUIET ABOUT THIS.
DON'T TELL ANYONE.

SIMILAR BROTHERS

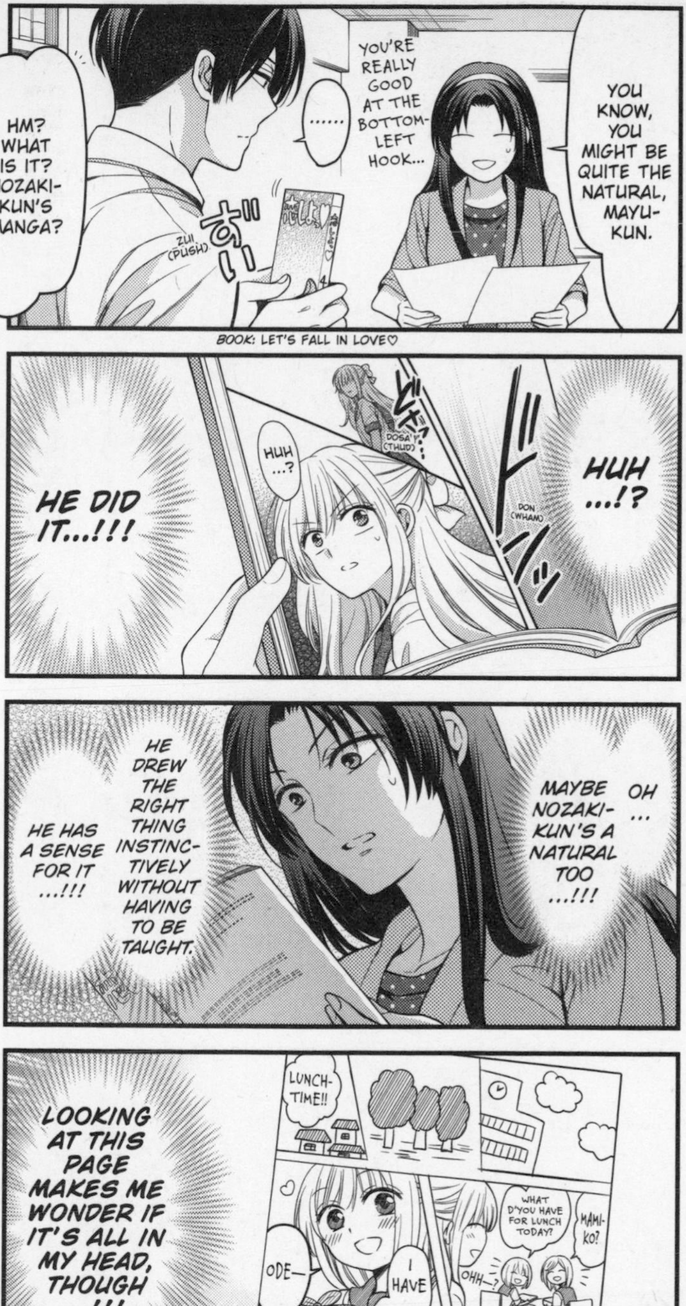
YOU KNOW, YOU MIGHT BE QUITE THE NATURAL, MAYU-KUN.
YOU'RE REALLY GOOD AT THE BOTTOM-LEFT HOOK...
......
HM? WHAT IS IT? NOZAKI-KUN'S MANGA?
ZUI (PUSH)
BOOK: LET'S FALL IN LOVE♡
HUH ...!?
DON (WHAM)
DOSA' (THUD)
HUH ...?
HE DID IT...!!!
OH ...
MAYBE NOZAKI-KUN'S A NATURAL TOO ...!!!
HE DREW THE RIGHT THING INSTINCTIVELY WITHOUT HAVING TO BE TAUGHT.
HE HAS A SENSE FOR IT ...!!!
LUNCH-TIME!!
MAMI-KO?
WHAT D'YOU HAVE FOR LUNCH TODAY?
OHH—?
I HAVE ...
TA-DAA!
ODE—
LOOKING AT THIS PAGE MAKES ME WONDER IF IT'S ALL IN MY HEAD, THOUGH ...!!!

I DID IT

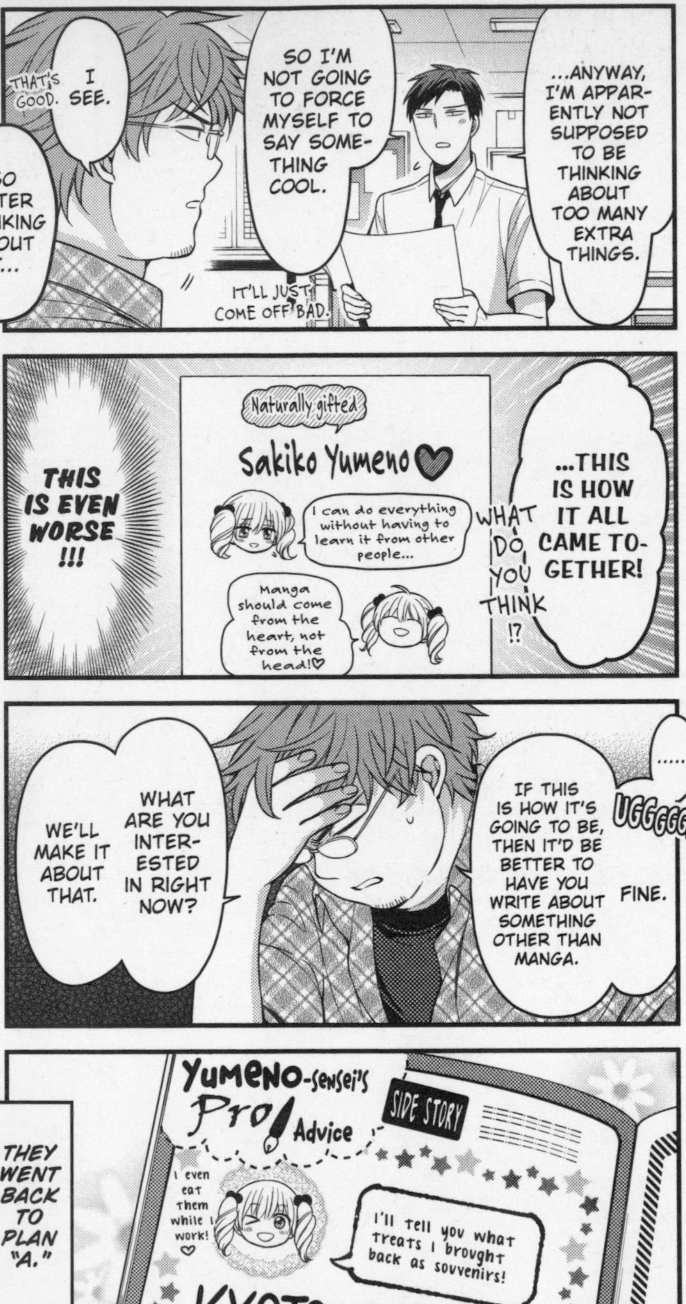
...ANYWAY, I'M APPARENTLY NOT SUPPOSED TO BE THINKING ABOUT TOO MANY EXTRA THINGS.
SO I'M NOT GOING TO FORCE MYSELF TO SAY SOMETHING COOL.
IT'LL JUST COME OFF BAD.
I SEE.
THAT'S GOOD.
SO AFTER THINKING ABOUT IT...
...THIS IS HOW IT ALL CAME TOGETHER!
WHAT DO YOU THINK!?
Naturally gifted
Sakiko Yumeno
I can do everything without having to learn it from other people...
Manga should come from the heart, not from the head!
THIS IS EVEN WORSE!!!
......
UGGGGGH...
FINE.
IF THIS IS HOW IT'S GOING TO BE, THEN IT'D BE BETTER TO HAVE YOU WRITE ABOUT SOMETHING OTHER THAN MANGA.
WHAT ARE YOU INTERESTED IN RIGHT NOW?
WE'LL MAKE IT ABOUT THAT.
YUMENO-sensei's Pro Advice
SIDE STORY
I'll tell you what treats I brought back as souvenirs!
I even eat them while I work!
KYOTO TREATS
THEY WENT BACK TO PLAN "A."

[Extra]

ALL THE CREATORS FLED AT TOP SPEED

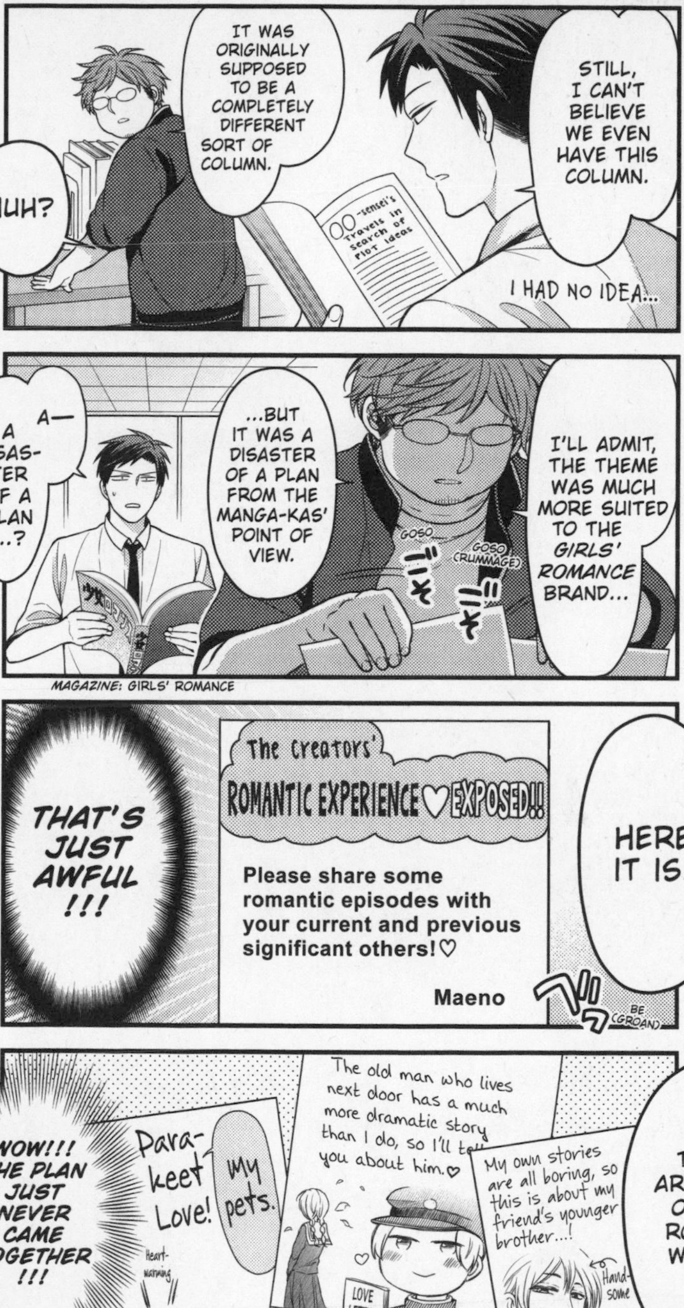
STILL, I CAN'T BELIEVE WE EVEN HAVE THIS COLUMN.
I HAD NO IDEA...
○○-sensei's Travels in search of plot ideas
IT WAS ORIGINALLY SUPPOSED TO BE A COMPLETELY DIFFERENT SORT OF COLUMN.
HUH?
I'LL ADMIT, THE THEME WAS MUCH MORE SUITED TO THE GIRLS' ROMANCE BRAND...
GOSO
GOSO (RUMMAGE)
...BUT IT WAS A DISASTER OF A PLAN FROM THE MANGA-KAS' POINT OF VIEW.
A— A DISASTER OF A PLAN...?
MAGAZINE: GIRLS' ROMANCE
HERE IT IS.
BE (GROAN)
The creators'
ROMANTIC EXPERIENCE♡EXPOSED!!
Please share some romantic episodes with your current and previous significant others!♡
Maeno
THAT'S JUST AWFUL!!!
AND THESE ARE SOME OF THE ROUGHS WE GOT IN.
My own stories are all boring, so this is about my friend's younger brother...!
Hand-some
He's a young, pretty, natural playboy who's at the heart of a bunch of legends.
The old man who lives next door has a much more dramatic story than I do, so I'll te
you about him.♡
LOVE LETTER
my pets.
Para-keet Love!
Heart-warming
WOW!!! THE PLAN JUST NEVER CAME TOGETHER!!!

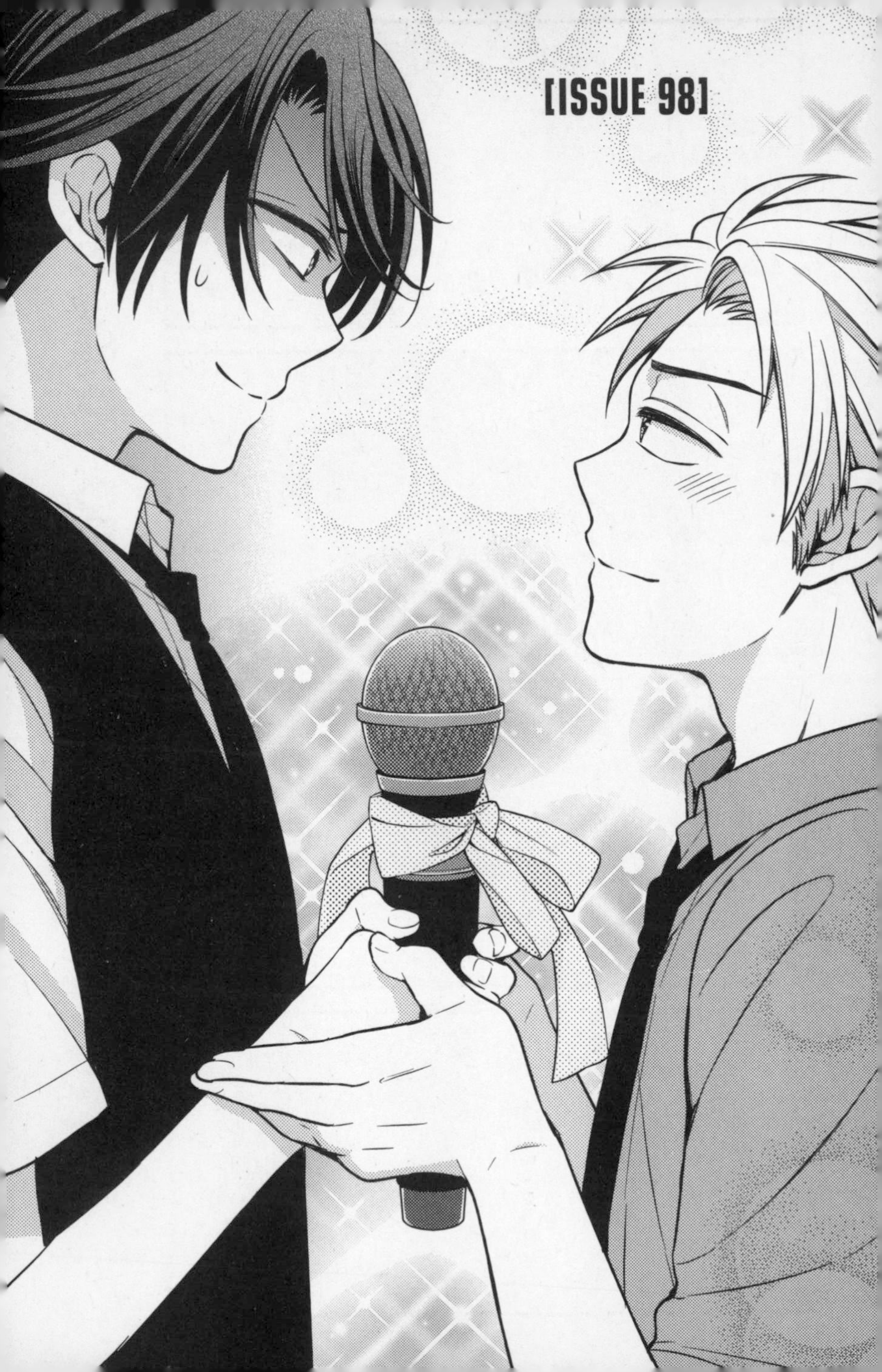
[ISSUE 98]

HIS CONVINCING EXPLANATION

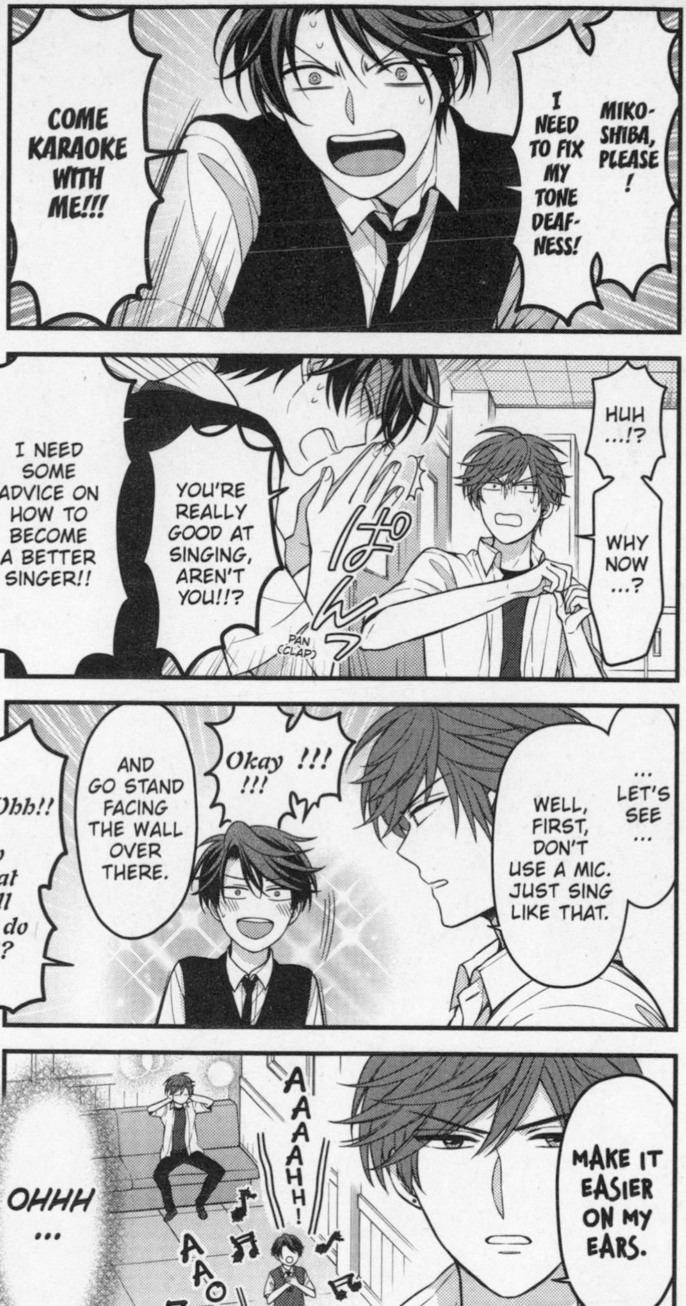
MIKO-SHIBA, PLEASE!
I NEED TO FIX MY TONE DEAF-NESS!
COME KARAOKE WITH ME!!!
HUH ...!?
WHY NOW ...?
ぱんっ
PAN (CLAP)
YOU'RE REALLY GOOD AT SINGING, AREN'T YOU!!?
I NEED SOME ADVICE ON HOW TO BECOME A BETTER SINGER!!
... LET'S SEE ...
WELL, FIRST, DON'T USE A MIC. JUST SING LIKE THAT.
Okay!!! !!!
AND GO STAND FACING THE WALL OVER THERE.
Ohh!!
So what will that do ...!?
MAKE IT EASIER ON MY EARS.
AAAAAHH!
AAOOO~!
OHHH ...

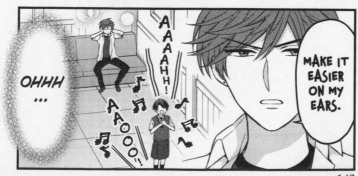

THIS IS HORI-SENPAI WE'RE TALKING ABOUT

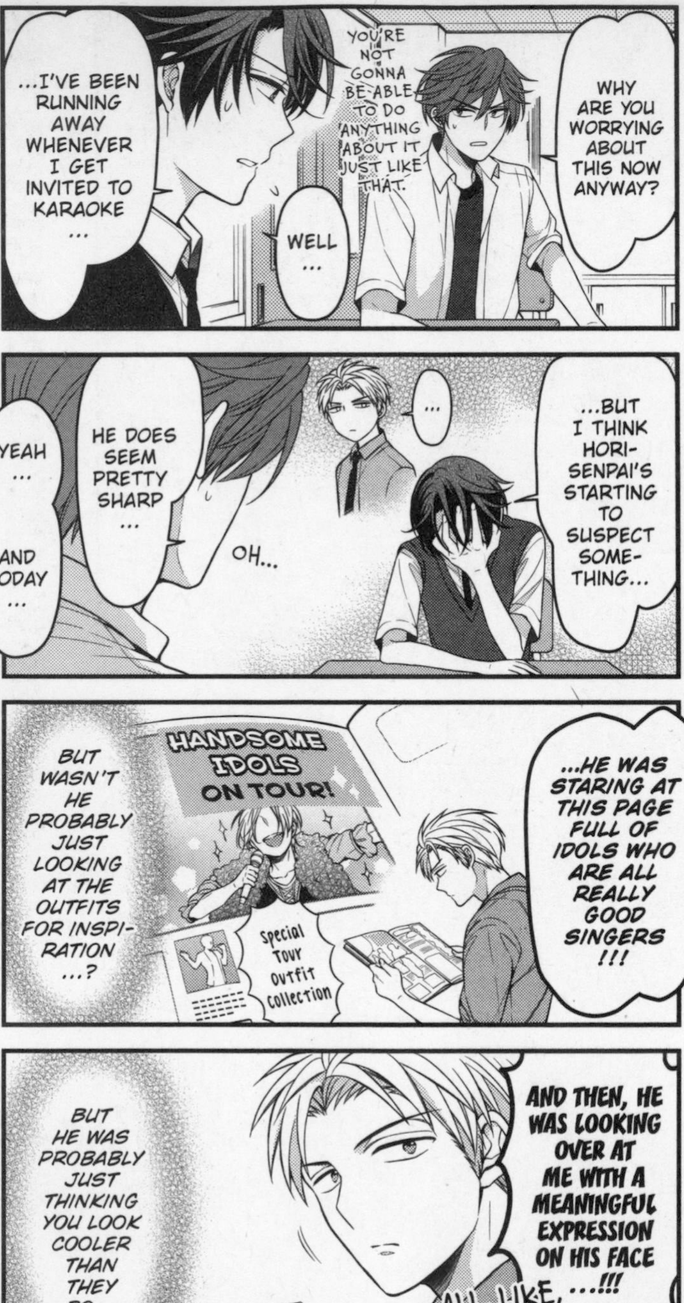
WHY ARE YOU WORRYING ABOUT THIS NOW ANYWAY?
YOU'RE NOT GONNA BE ABLE TO DO ANYTHING ABOUT IT JUST LIKE THAT.
WELL ...
...I'VE BEEN RUNNING AWAY WHENEVER I GET INVITED TO KARAOKE ...
...BUT I THINK HORI-SENPAI'S STARTING TO SUSPECT SOME-THING...
...
OH...
HE DOES SEEM PRETTY SHARP ...
YEAH ...
AND TODAY ...
...HE WAS STARING AT THIS PAGE FULL OF IDOLS WHO ARE ALL REALLY GOOD SINGERS !!!
HANDSOME IDOLS ON TOUR!
Special Tour Outfit Collection
BUT WASN'T HE PROBABLY JUST LOOKING AT THE OUTFITS FOR INSPI-RATION ...?
AND THEN, HE WAS LOOKING OVER AT ME WITH A MEANINGFUL EXPRESSION ON HIS FACE ...!!!
ALL, LIKE, "GLANCE"!!
BUT HE WAS PROBABLY JUST THINKING YOU LOOK COOLER THAN THEY DO...

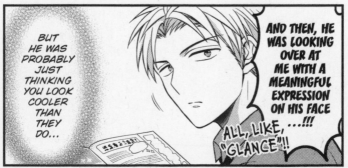

THE KARAOKE STORY

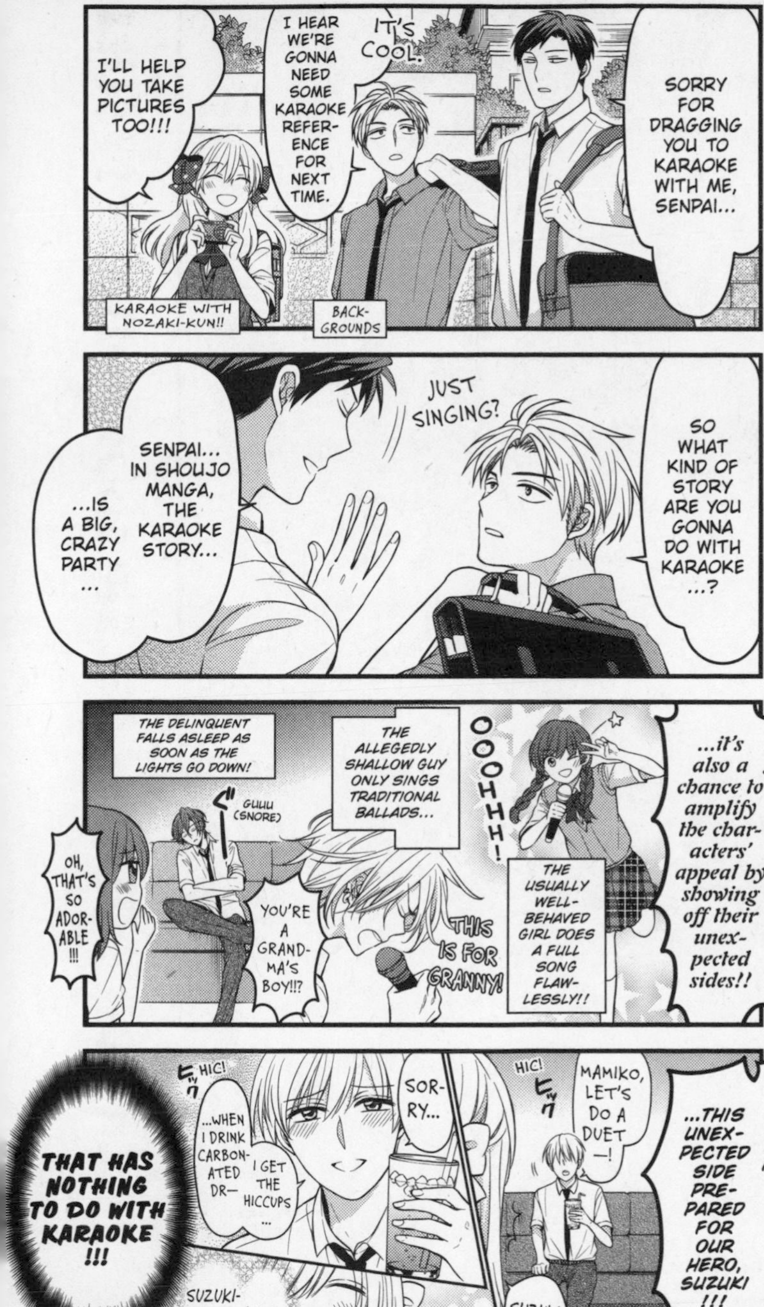
SORRY FOR DRAGGING YOU TO KARAOKE WITH ME, SENPAI...
IT'S COOL.
I HEAR WE'RE GONNA NEED SOME KARAOKE REFERENCE FOR NEXT TIME.
I'LL HELP YOU TAKE PICTURES TOO!!!
BACK-GROUNDS
KARAOKE WITH NOZAKI-KUN!!
SO WHAT KIND OF STORY ARE YOU GONNA DO WITH KARAOKE ...?
JUST SINGING?
SENPAI... IN SHOUJO MANGA, THE KARAOKE STORY...
...IS A BIG, CRAZY PARTY ...
And ...
...it's also a chance to amplify the characters' appeal by showing off their unexpected sides!!
OOOHHH!
THE USUALLY WELL-BEHAVED GIRL DOES A FULL SONG FLAWLESSLY!!
THE ALLEGEDLY SHALLOW GUY ONLY SINGS TRADITIONAL BALLADS...
THIS IS FOR GRANNY!
YOU'RE A GRANDMA'S BOY!!?
THE DELINQUENT FALLS ASLEEP AS SOON AS THE LIGHTS GO DOWN!
GUUU (SNORE)
OH, THAT'S SO ADORABLE!!!
AND IN THE MIDDLE OF IT ALL, I HAVE ...
...THIS UNEXPECTED SIDE PREPARED FOR OUR HERO, SUZUKI!!!
MAMIKO, LET'S DO A DUET—!
HIC!
SUZUKI-KUN!?
HIC!
SORRY...
...WHEN I DRINK CARBONATED DR—
I GET THE HICCUPS ...
HIC!
SUZUKI-KUN... AWW... ♡
THAT HAS NOTHING TO DO WITH KARAOKE!!!

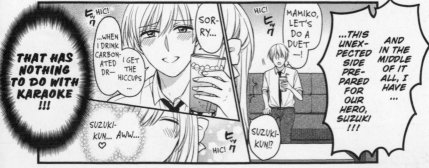

SENPAI IS SERIOUS

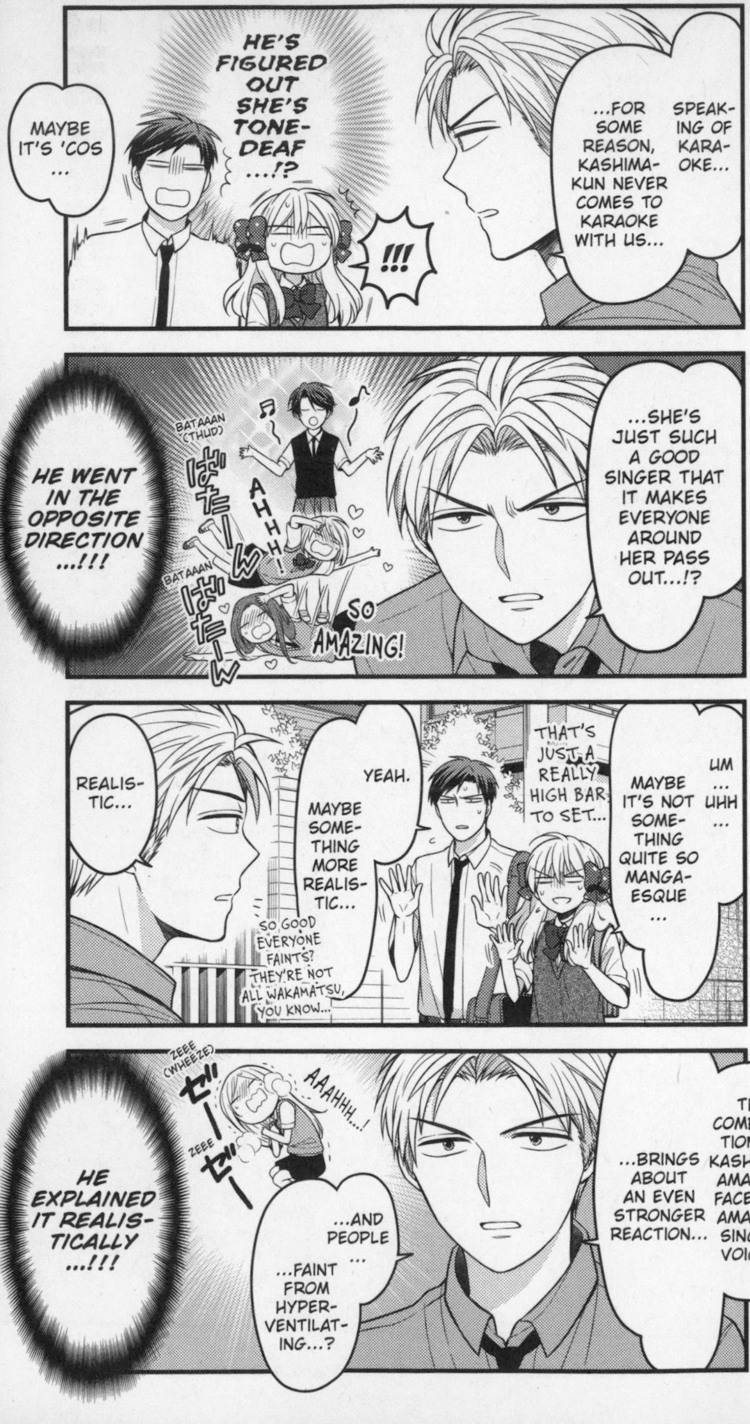
SPEAKING OF KARAOKE...
...FOR SOME REASON, KASHIMA-KUN NEVER COMES TO KARAOKE WITH US...
!!!
HE'S FIGURED OUT SHE'S TONE-DEAF ...!?
MAYBE IT'S 'COS ...
...SHE'S JUST SUCH A GOOD SINGER THAT IT MAKES EVERYONE AROUND HER PASS OUT...!?
AHHHH!
SO AMAZING!
BATAAAN (THUD)
ばたーん
BATAAAN
ばたーん
HE WENT IN THE OPPOSITE DIRECTION ...!!!
UM ... UHH ...
MAYBE IT'S NOT SOMETHING QUITE SO MANGA-ESQUE ...
THAT'S JUST A REALLY HIGH BAR TO SET...
YEAH.
MAYBE SOMETHING MORE REALISTIC...
SO GOOD EVERYONE FAINTS? THEY'RE NOT ALL WAKAMATSU, YOU KNOW...
REALISTIC...
THE COMBINATION OF KASHIMA'S AMAZING FACE AND AMAZING SINGING VOICE...
...BRINGS ABOUT AN EVEN STRONGER REACTION...
...AND PEOPLE ...
...FAINT FROM HYPERVENTILATING...?
AAAHHH...!
ZEEE (WHEEZE)
ぜーぜー
ZEEE
HE EXPLAINED IT REALISTICALLY ...!!!

THE IMMEDIATE REACTION

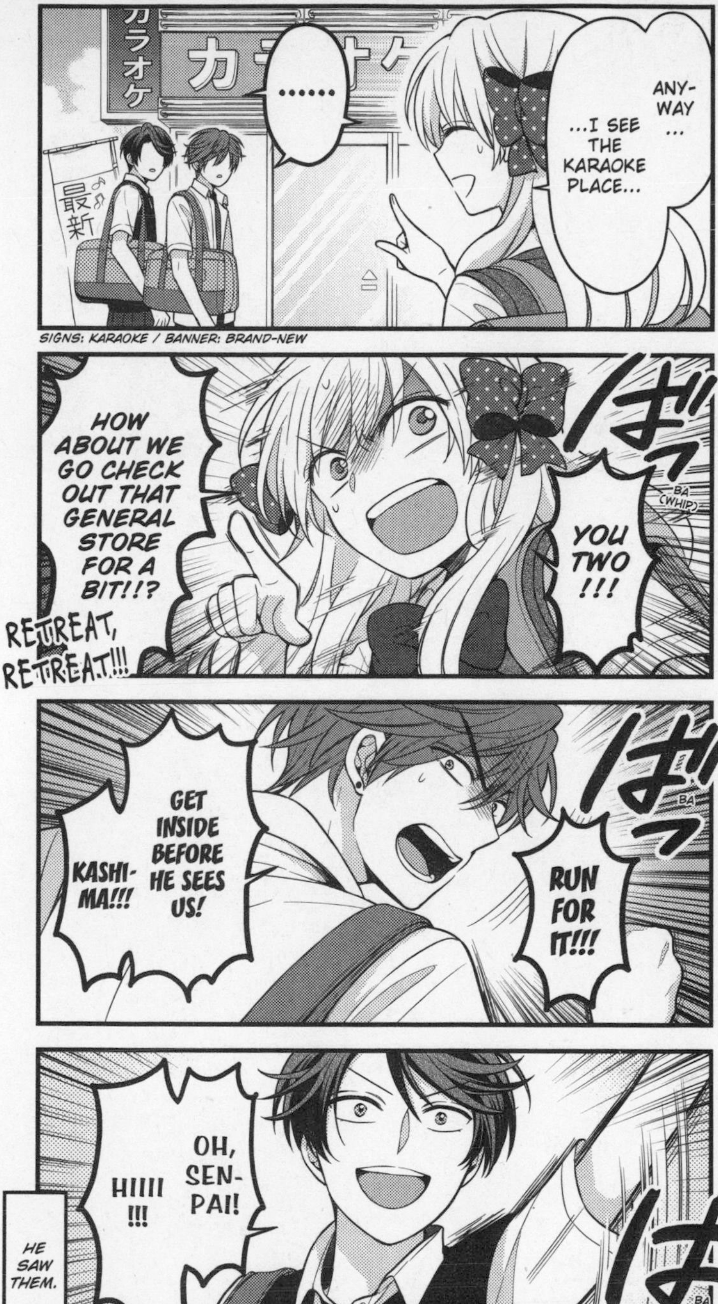
ANY-WAY... ...I SEE THE KARAOKE PLACE...
....
カラオケ
最新
SIGNS: KARAOKE / BANNER: BRAND-NEW
ばっ
BA (WHIP)
YOU TWO!!!
HOW ABOUT WE GO CHECK OUT THAT GENERAL STORE FOR A BIT!!?
RETREAT, RETREAT!!!
ばっ
BA
RUN FOR IT!!!
GET INSIDE BEFORE HE SEES US!
KASHI-MA!!!
ばっ
BA
OH, SEN-PAI!
HIIII!!!
HE SAW THEM.

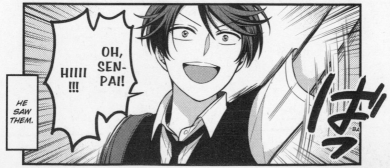

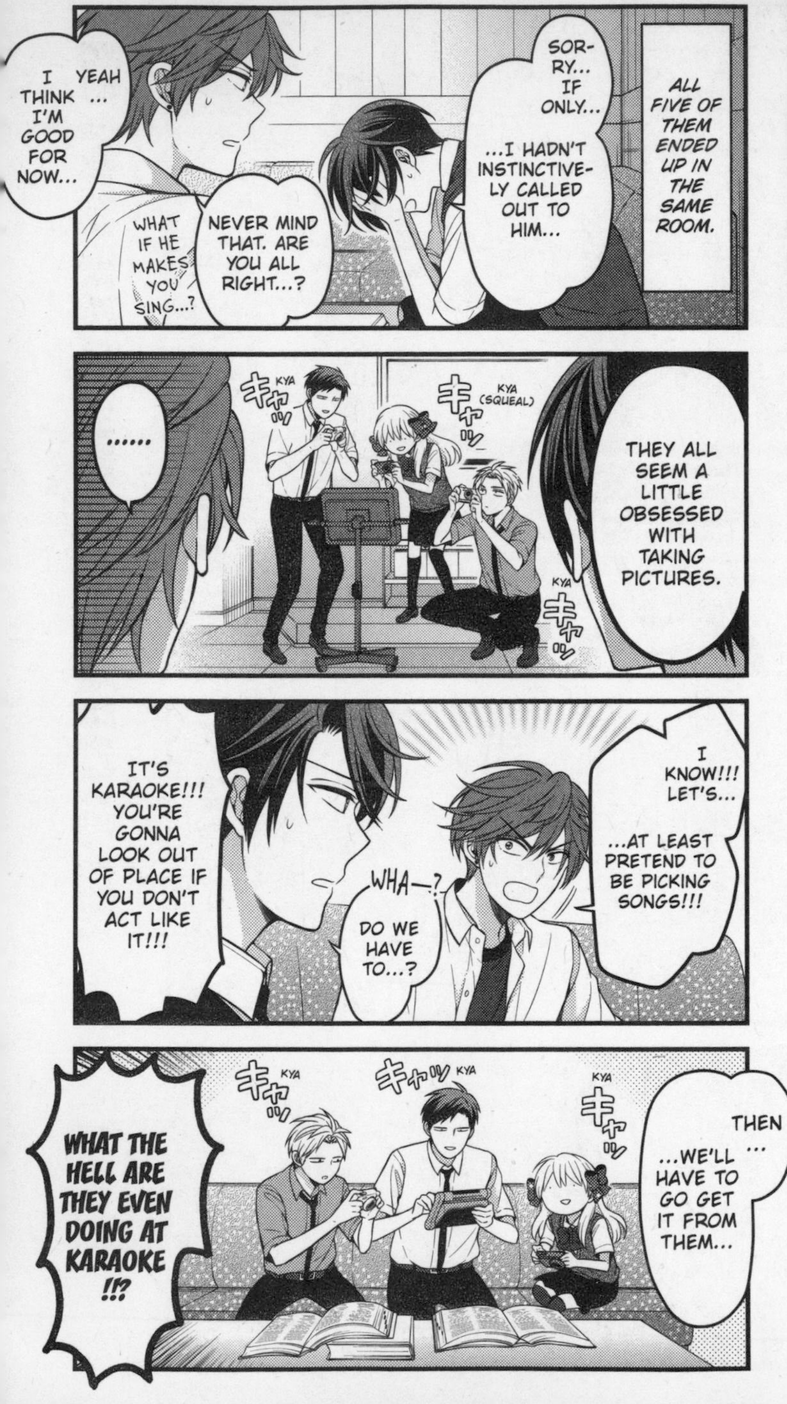
ALL FIVE OF THEM ENDED UP IN THE SAME ROOM.
SORRY... IF ONLY...
...I HADN'T INSTINCTIVELY CALLED OUT TO HIM...
NEVER MIND THAT. ARE YOU ALL RIGHT...?
WHAT IF HE MAKES YOU SING...?
YEAH...
I THINK I'M GOOD FOR NOW...
THEY ALL SEEM A LITTLE OBSESSED WITH TAKING PICTURES.
キャッ KYA
キャッ KYA (SQUEAL)
キャッ KYA
......
I KNOW!!! LET'S...
...AT LEAST PRETEND TO BE PICKING SONGS!!!
WHA—?
DO WE HAVE TO...?
IT'S KARAOKE!!! YOU'RE GONNA LOOK OUT OF PLACE IF YOU DON'T ACT LIKE IT!!!
THEN...
...WE'LL HAVE TO GO GET IT FROM THEM...
キャッ KYA
キャッ KYA
キャッ KYA
WHAT THE HELL ARE THEY EVEN DOING AT KARAOKE!!?

AT KARAOKE

BECAUSE HE'S THE CLUB PRESIDENT

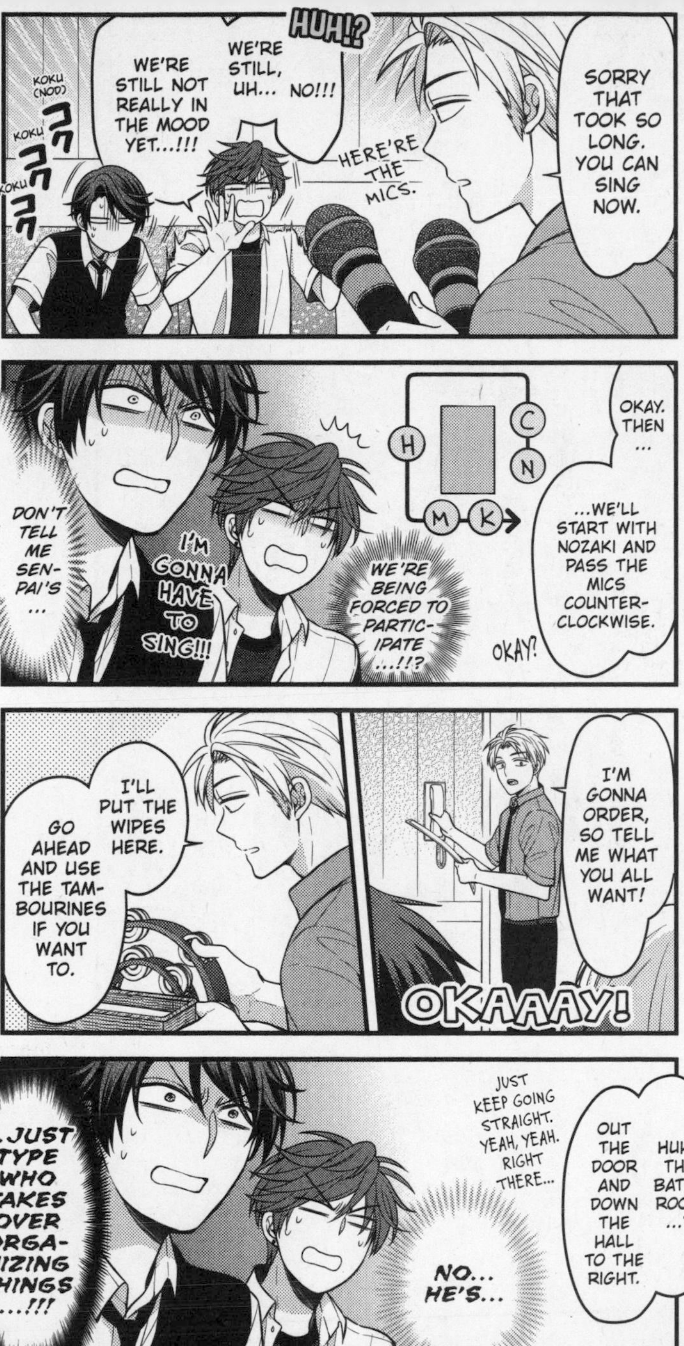
SORRY THAT TOOK SO LONG. YOU CAN SING NOW.
HERE'RE THE MICS.
HUH!?
NO!!!
WE'RE STILL, UH...
WE'RE STILL NOT REALLY IN THE MOOD YET...!!!
KOKU (NOD)
KOKU
KOKU
OKAY. THEN ...
...WE'LL START WITH NOZAKI AND PASS THE MICS COUNTER-CLOCKWISE.
OKAY?
C
N
H
M
K
WE'RE BEING FORCED TO PARTICIPATE ...!!?
I'M GONNA HAVE TO SING!!!
DON'T TELL ME SEN-PAI'S ...
...ON TO ME ...!!?
I'M GONNA ORDER, SO TELL ME WHAT YOU ALL WANT!
OKAAAY!
I'LL PUT THE WIPES HERE.
GO AHEAD AND USE THE TAMBOURINES IF YOU WANT TO.
HUH? THE BATHROOM ...?
OUT THE DOOR AND DOWN THE HALL TO THE RIGHT.
JUST KEEP GOING STRAIGHT. YEAH, YEAH. RIGHT THERE...
NO... HE'S...
...JUST TYPE WHO TAKES OVER ORGANIZING THINGS ...!!!

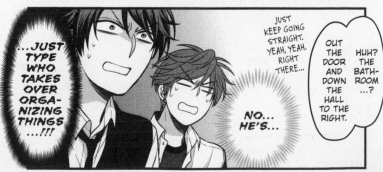

IT'S JUST REALLY WEIRD

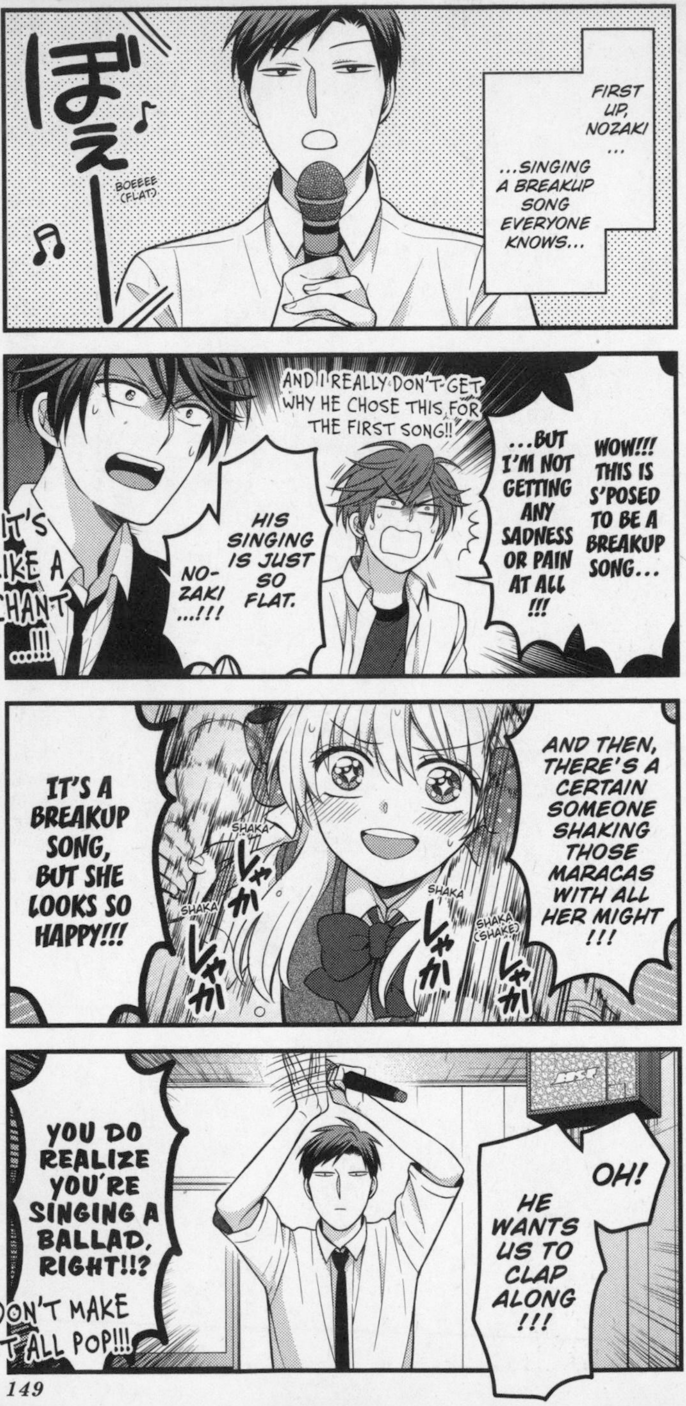
FIRST UP, NOZAKI ...
...SINGING A BREAKUP SONG EVERYONE KNOWS...
ぼえー
BOEEEE (FLAT)
WOW!!! THIS IS S'POSED TO BE A BREAKUP SONG...
...BUT I'M NOT GETTING ANY SADNESS OR PAIN AT ALL !!!
AND I REALLY DON'T GET WHY HE CHOSE THIS FOR THE FIRST SONG!!
HIS SINGING IS JUST SO FLAT.
NO-ZAKI ...!!!
IT'S LIKE A CHANT ...!!!
AND THEN, THERE'S A CERTAIN SOMEONE SHAKING THOSE MARACAS WITH ALL HER MIGHT !!!
しゃか
SHAKA (SHAKE)
しゃか
SHAKA
しゃか
SHAKA
しゃか
SHAKA
IT'S A BREAKUP SONG, BUT SHE LOOKS SO HAPPY!!!
OH!
HE WANTS US TO CLAP ALONG !!!
YOU DO REALIZE YOU'RE SINGING A BALLAD, RIGHT!!?
DON'T MAKE IT ALL POP!!!

THEIR PARTS

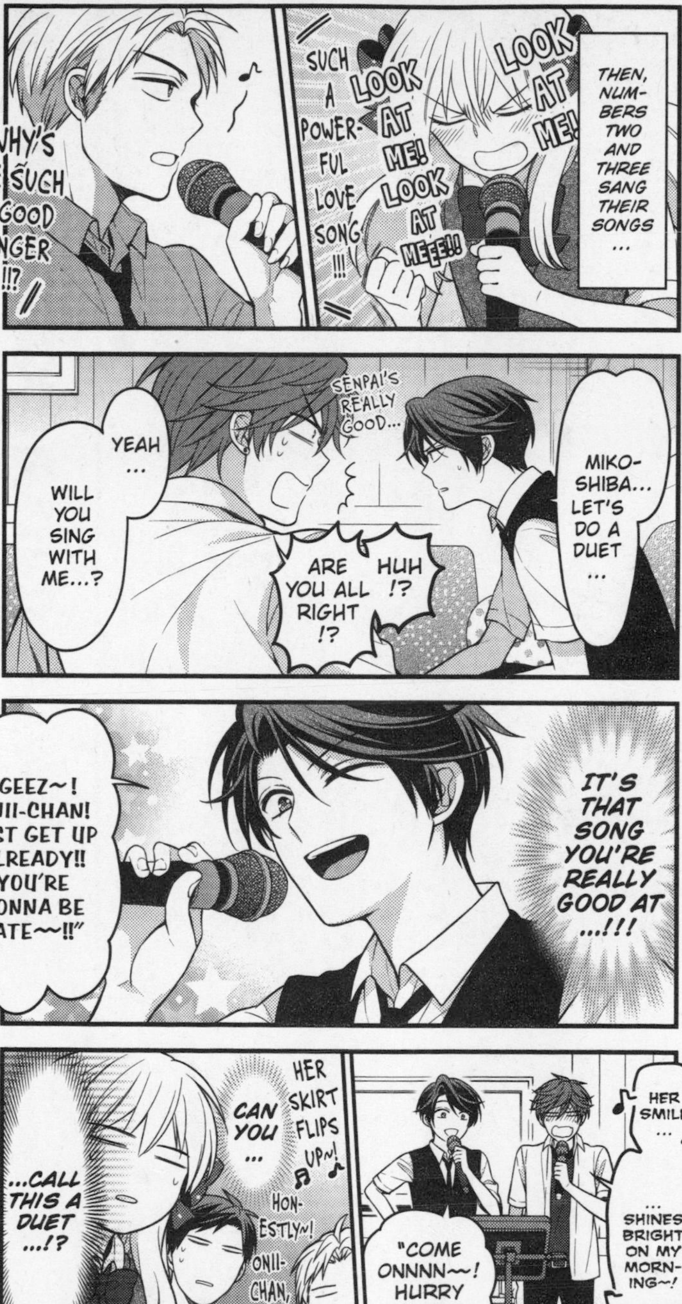
THEN, NUMBERS TWO AND THREE SANG THEIR SONGS...
LOOK AT ME!
LOOK AT ME! LOOK AT MEEE!!
SUCH A POWERFUL LOVE SONG!!!
WHY'S HE SUCH A GOOD SINGER!!?
MIKO-SHIBA... LET'S DO A DUET...
HUH!?
ARE YOU ALL RIGHT!?
SENPAI'S REALLY GOOD...
YEAH... WILL YOU SING WITH ME...?
IT'S THAT SONG YOU'RE REALLY GOOD AT...!!!
"GEEZ~! ONII-CHAN! JUST GET UP ALREADY!! YOU'RE GONNA BE LATE~~!!"
HER SMILE...
...SHINES BRIGHT ON MY MORNING~!
"COME ONNNN~~! HURRY UP, ONII-CHAN! ♡"
HER SKIRT FLIPS UP~!
HONESTLY~! ONII-CHAN, YOU PERV!
CAN YOU...
...CALL THIS A DUET...!?

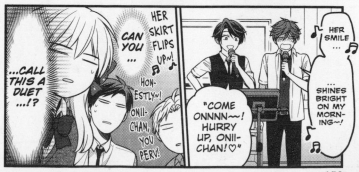

THEIR PARTS ②

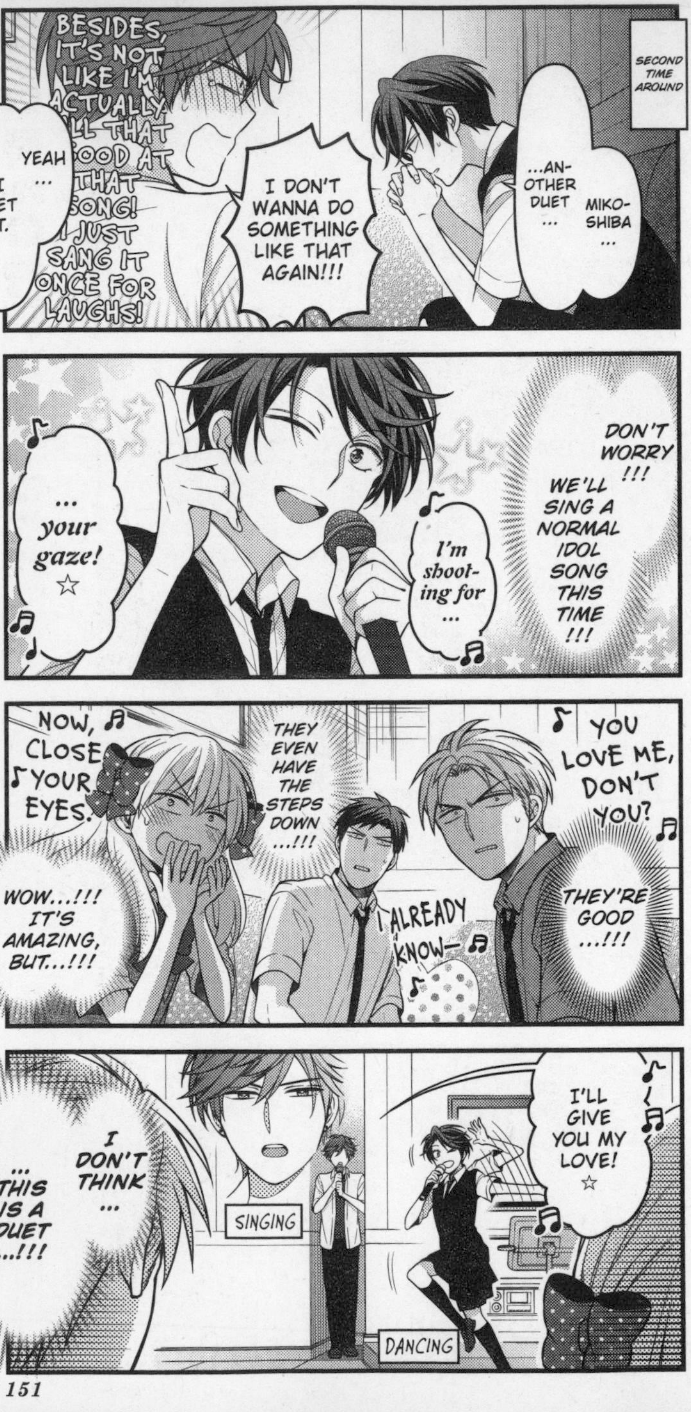
SECOND TIME AROUND
MIKO-SHIBA ... ...AN-OTHER DUET ...
I DON'T WANNA DO SOMETHING LIKE THAT AGAIN!!!
BESIDES, IT'S NOT LIKE I'M ACTUALLY ALL THAT GOOD AT THAT SONG! I JUST SANG IT ONCE FOR LAUGHS!
YEAH ... I GET IT.
DON'T WORRY!!! WE'LL SING A NORMAL IDOL SONG THIS TIME!!!
I'm shooting for ...
... your gaze! ☆
YOU LOVE ME, DON'T YOU?
THEY'RE GOOD ...!!!
THEY EVEN HAVE THE STEPS DOWN ...!!!
I ALREADY KNOW—
NOW, CLOSE YOUR EYES.
WOW...!!! IT'S AMAZING, BUT...!!!
I'LL GIVE YOU MY LOVE! ☆
DANCING
SINGING
I DON'T THINK ...
... THIS IS A DUET ...!!!

YOU KNOW, SENPAI...?

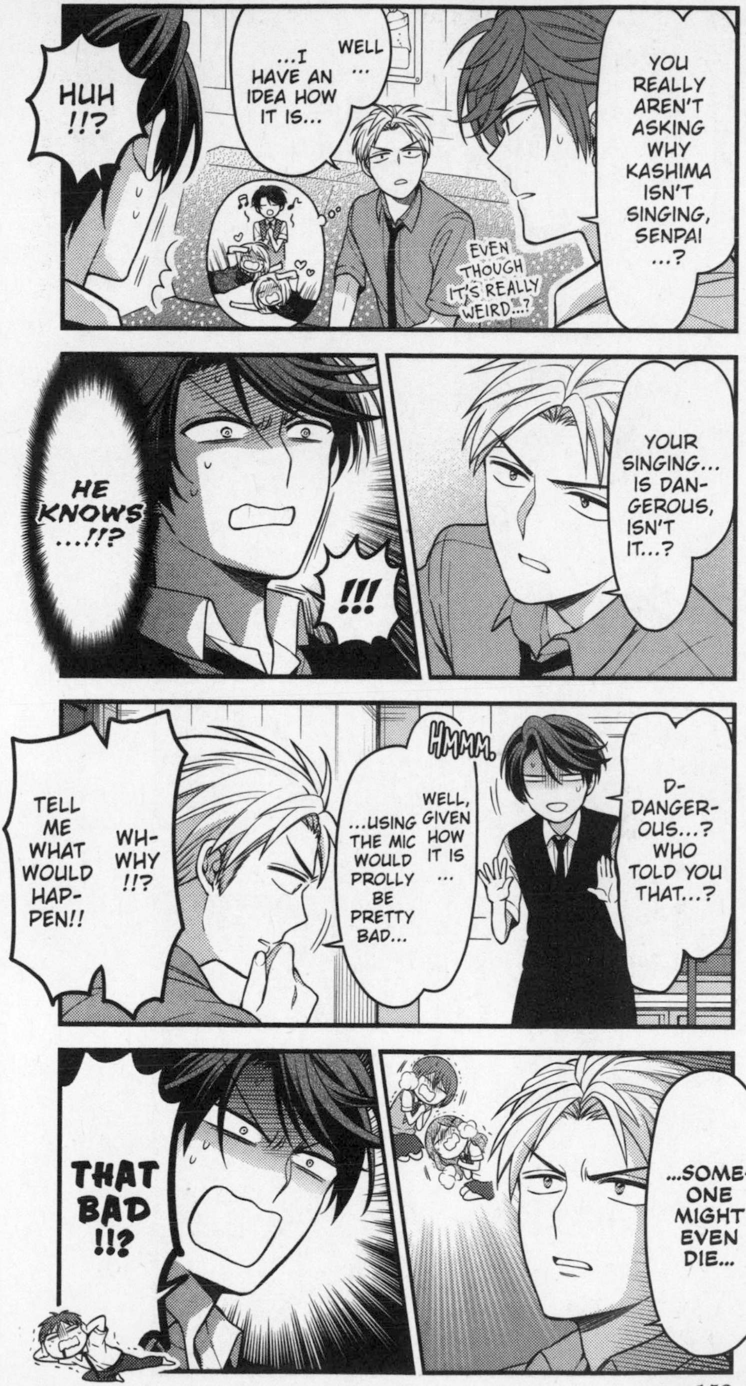

YOU REALLY AREN'T ASKING WHY KASHIMA ISN'T SINGING, SENPAI ...?
EVEN THOUGH IT'S REALLY WEIRD...?
WELL ...
...I HAVE AN IDEA HOW IT IS...
HUH !!?
YOUR SINGING... IS DANGEROUS, ISN'T IT...?
!!!
HE KNOWS ...!!?
D-DANGEROUS...? WHO TOLD YOU THAT...?
HMMM.
WELL, GIVEN HOW IT IS ...
...USING THE MIC WOULD PROLLY BE PRETTY BAD...
WH-WHY !!?
TELL ME WHAT WOULD HAPPEN!!
...SOMEONE MIGHT EVEN DIE...
THAT BAD !!?

A TERRIFYING STATEMENT

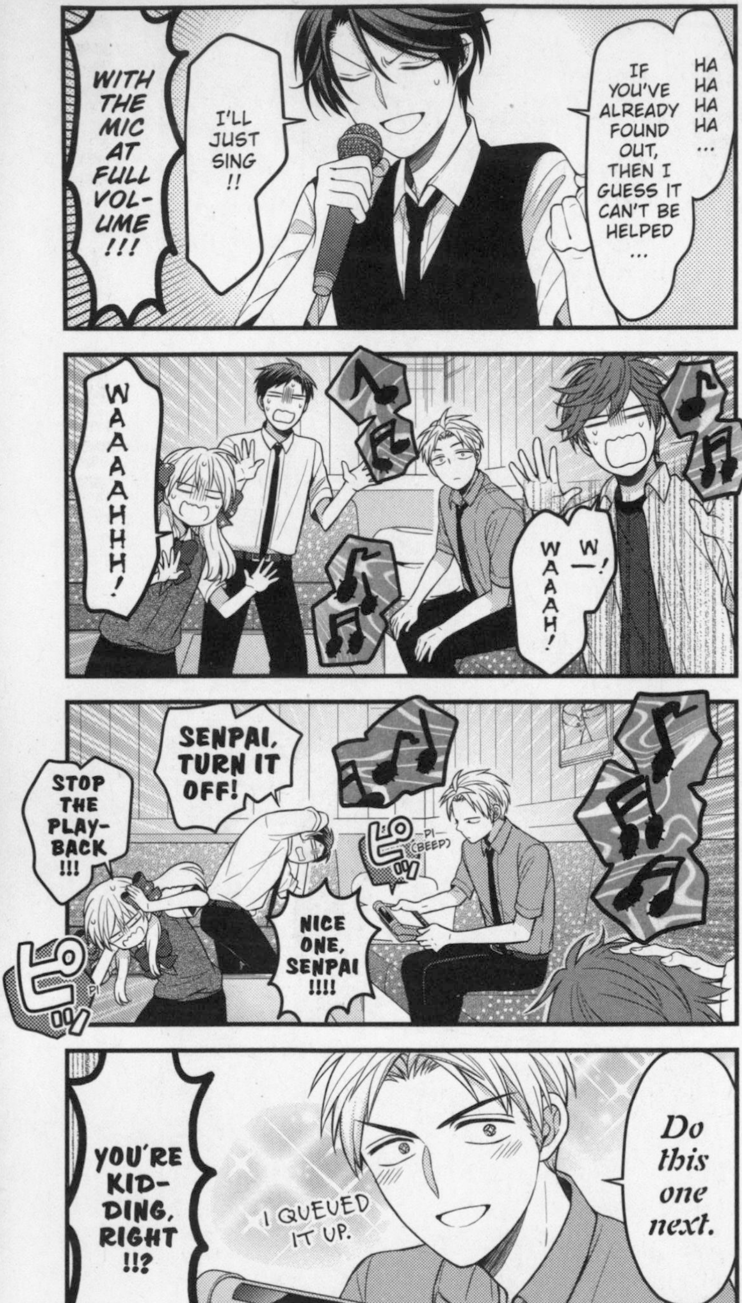

HA HA HA HA...
IF YOU'VE ALREADY FOUND OUT, THEN I GUESS IT CAN'T BE HELPED...
I'LL JUST SING!!
WITH THE MIC AT FULL VOL-UME!!!
W—! WAAAH!
WAAAAAHHH!
SENPAI, TURN IT OFF!
PI— (BEEP)
STOP THE PLAY-BACK!!!
NICE ONE, SENPAI!!!!
PI
Do this one next.
I QUEUED IT UP.
YOU'RE KID-DING, RIGHT!!?

THE CHAINS OF HELL

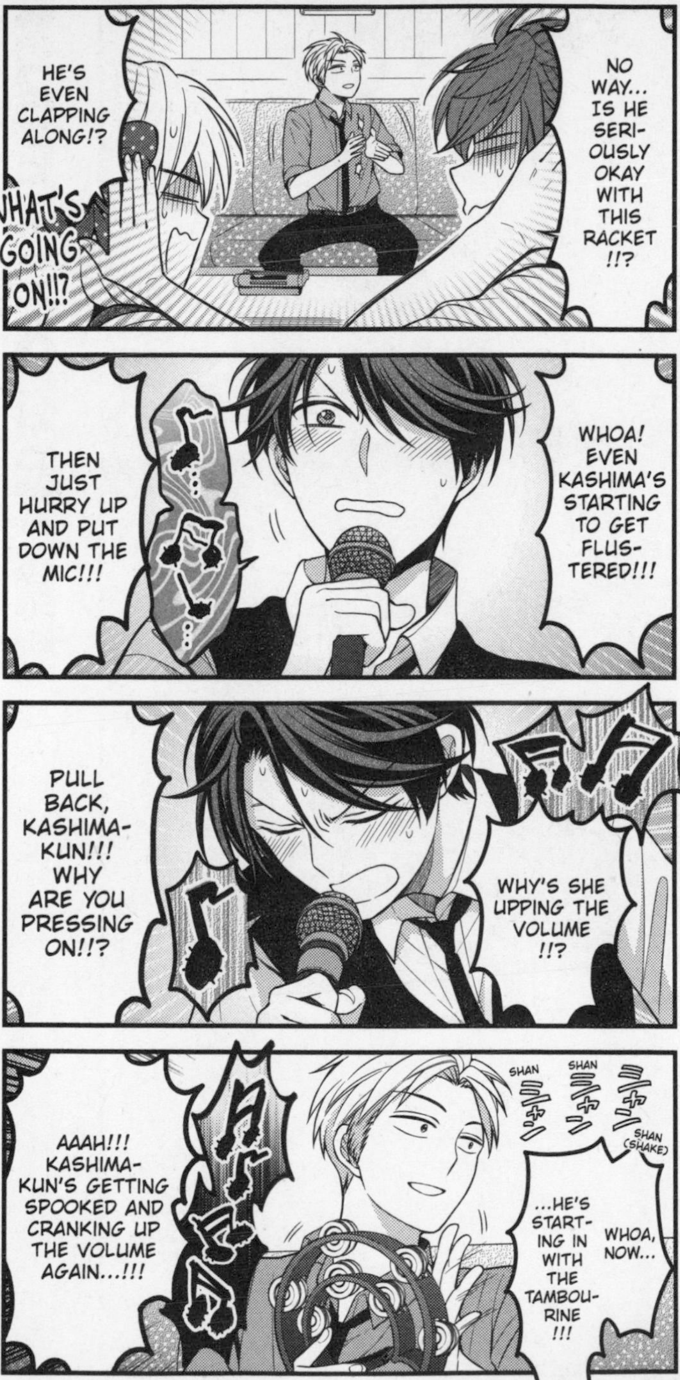
NO WAY... IS HE SERIOUSLY OKAY WITH THIS RACKET!!?
HE'S EVEN CLAPPING ALONG!?
WHAT'S GOING ON!!?
WHOA! EVEN KASHIMA'S STARTING TO GET FLUSTERED!!!
THEN JUST HURRY UP AND PUT DOWN THE MIC!!!
WHY'S SHE UPPING THE VOLUME!!?
PULL BACK, KASHIMA-KUN!!! WHY ARE YOU PRESSING ON!!?
SHAN (SHAKE)
SHAN
SHAN
WHOA, NOW...
...HE'S STARTING IN WITH THE TAMBOURINE!!!
AAAH!!! KASHIMA-KUN'S GETTING SPOOKED AND CRANKING UP THE VOLUME AGAIN...!!!

SENPAI'S LOVE RUNS DEEP

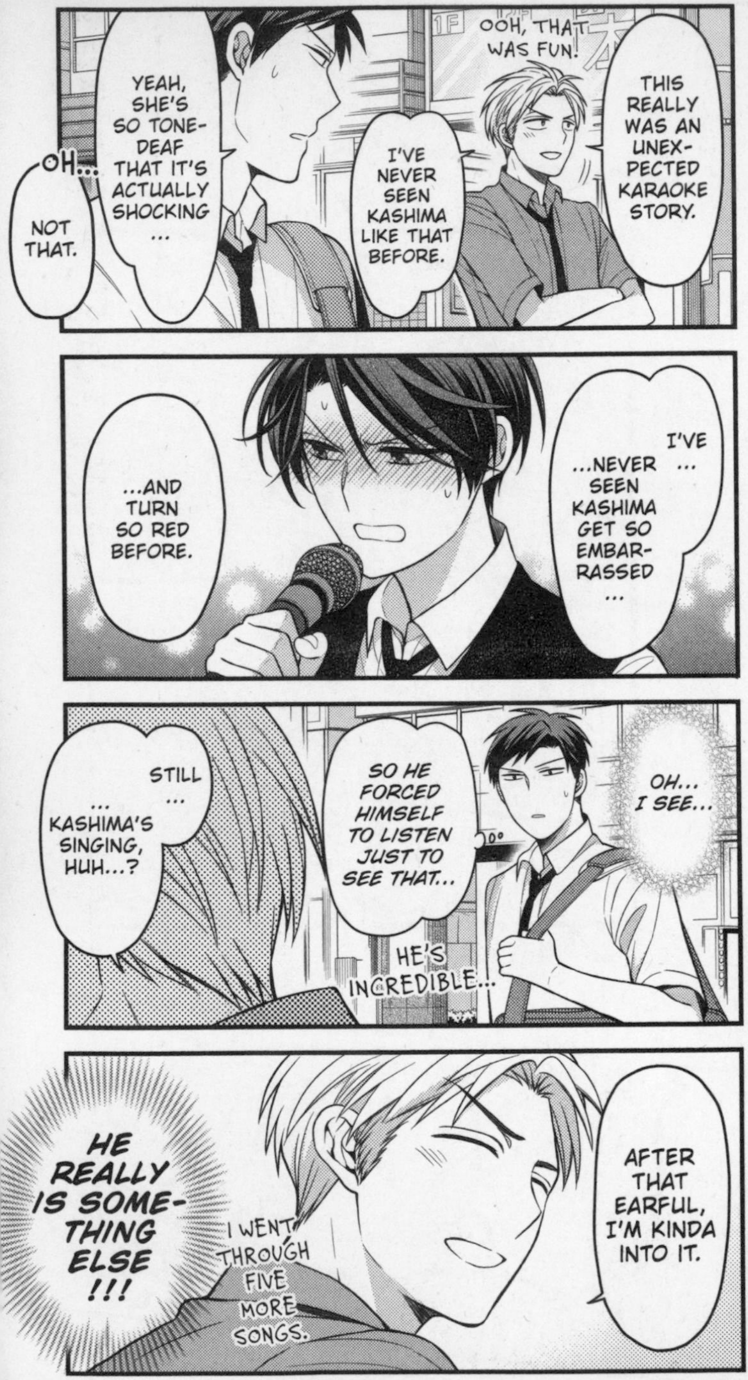
THIS REALLY WAS AN UNEXPECTED KARAOKE STORY.
OOH, THAT WAS FUN!
I'VE NEVER SEEN KASHIMA LIKE THAT BEFORE.
YEAH, SHE'S SO TONE-DEAF THAT IT'S ACTUALLY SHOCKING ...
OH... NOT THAT.
I'VE ... ...NEVER SEEN KASHIMA GET SO EMBARRASSED ...
...AND TURN SO RED BEFORE.
OH... I SEE...
SO HE FORCED HIMSELF TO LISTEN JUST TO SEE THAT...
HE'S INCREDIBLE...
STILL ... ... KASHIMA'S SINGING, HUH...?
AFTER THAT EARFUL, I'M KINDA INTO IT.
I WENT THROUGH FIVE MORE SONGS.
HE REALLY IS SOME-THING ELSE!!!

MONTHLY GIRLS' NOZAKI-KUN 10 END

SENPAI AFTER

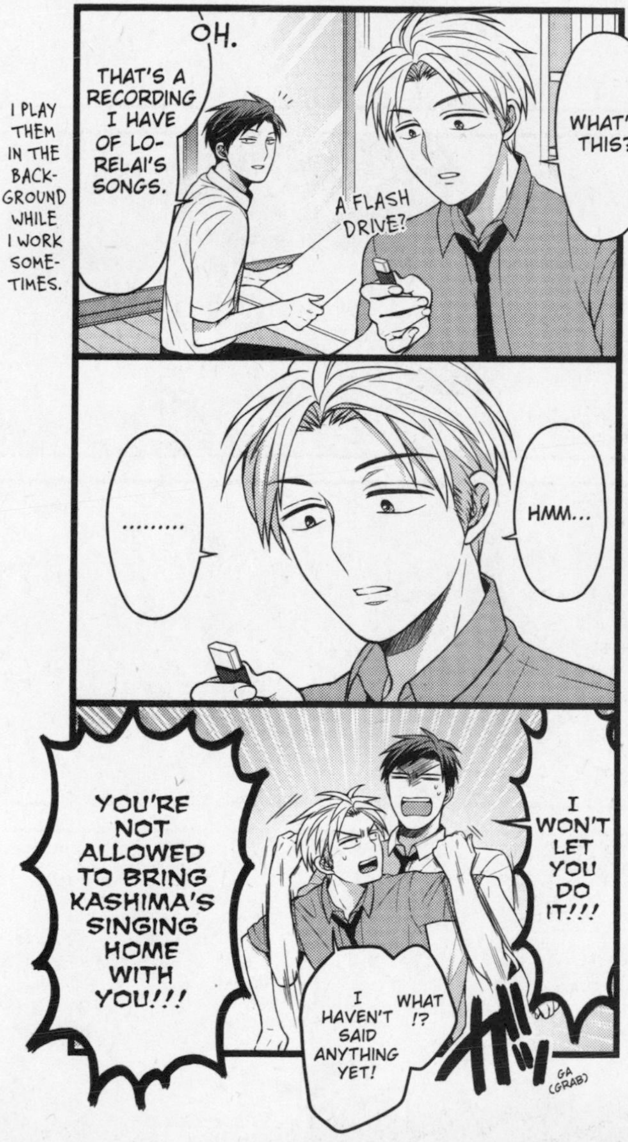
WHAT'S THIS?
A FLASH DRIVE?
OH.
THAT'S A RECORDING I HAVE OF LO-RELAI'S SONGS.
I PLAY THEM IN THE BACK-GROUND WHILE I WORK SOME-TIMES.
HMM...
....
I WON'T LET YOU DO IT!!!
YOU'RE NOT ALLOWED TO BRING KASHIMA'S SINGING HOME WITH YOU!!!
WHAT!?
I HAVEN'T SAID ANYTHING YET!
GA (GRAB)

[Extra]

MY SINGING PROGRESS

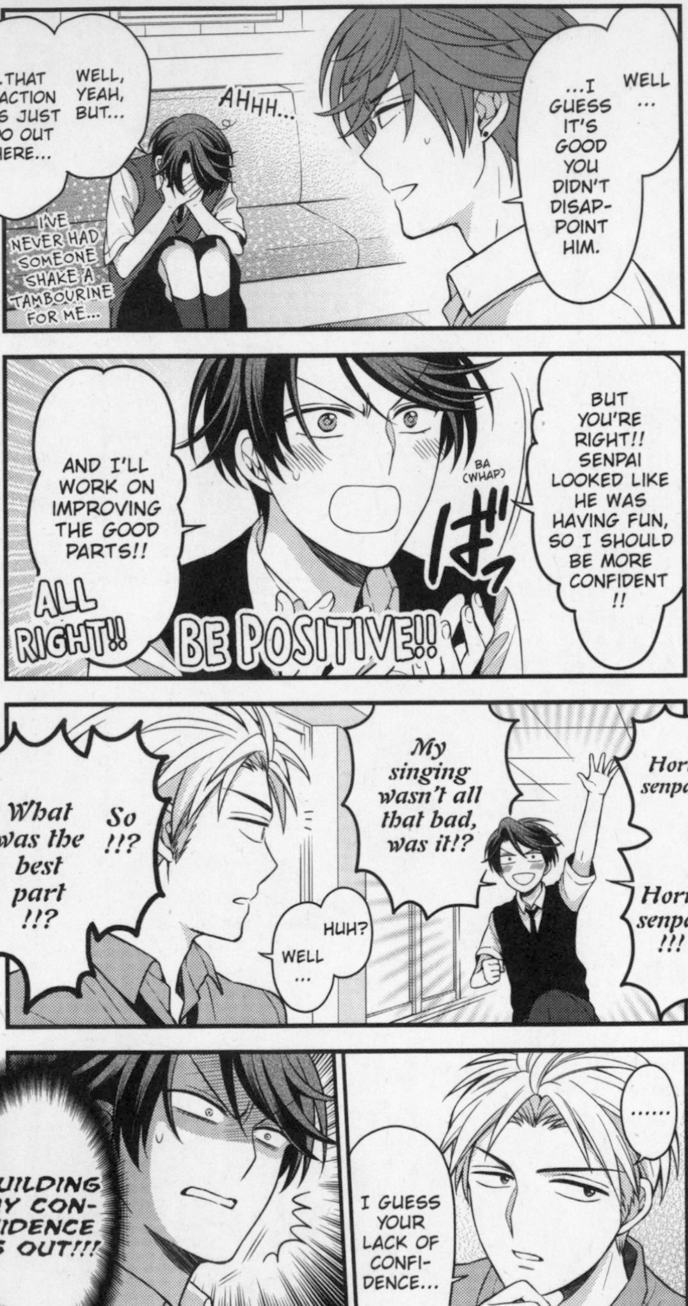
WELL ... ...I GUESS IT'S GOOD YOU DIDN'T DISAPPOINT HIM.
AHHH...
WELL, YEAH, BUT... ...THAT REACTION WAS JUST TOO OUT THERE...
I'VE NEVER HAD SOMEONE SHAKE A TAMBOURINE FOR ME...
BUT YOU'RE RIGHT!! SENPAI LOOKED LIKE HE WAS HAVING FUN, SO I SHOULD BE MORE CONFIDENT !!
BA (WHAP)
AND I'LL WORK ON IMPROVING THE GOOD PARTS!!
BE POSITIVE!!
ALL RIGHT!!
Hori-senpai!
Hori-senpai !!!
My singing wasn't all that bad, was it!?
So !!?
What was the best part !!?
HUH? WELL ...
......
I GUESS YOUR LACK OF CONFIDENCE...
BUILDING MY CONFIDENCE IS OUT!!!

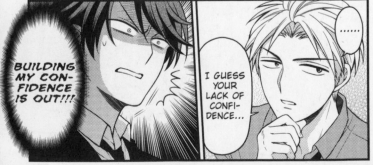

[Extra]

IF WE BOTH OPEN UP

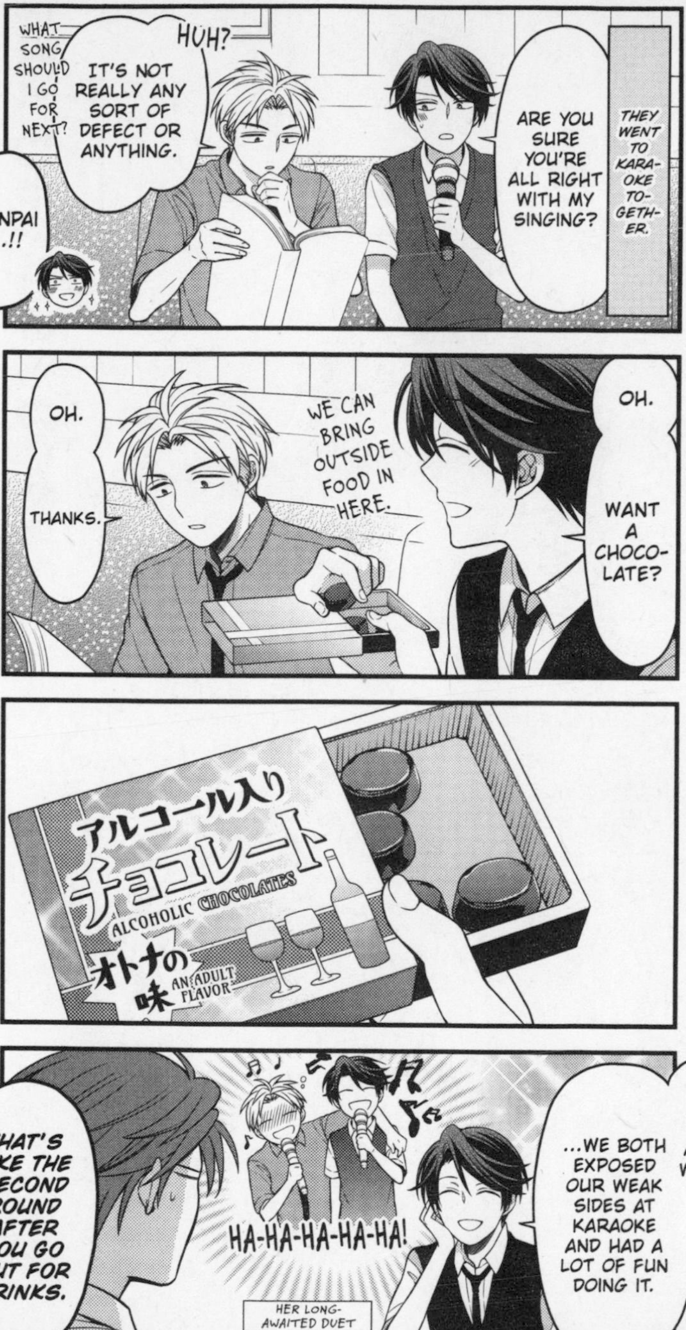
THEY WENT TO KARAOKE TOGETHER.
ARE YOU SURE YOU'RE ALL RIGHT WITH MY SINGING?
HUH?
IT'S NOT REALLY ANY SORT OF DEFECT OR ANYTHING.
WHAT SONG SHOULD I GO FOR NEXT?
SENPAI...!!
OH.
WANT A CHOCOLATE?
WE CAN BRING OUTSIDE FOOD IN HERE.
OH.
THANKS.
アルコール入り チョコレート
ALCOHOLIC CHOCOLATES
オトナの味
AN ADULT FLAVOR
ANY-WAY...
...WE BOTH EXPOSED OUR WEAK SIDES AT KARAOKE AND HAD A LOT OF FUN DOING IT.
HA-HA-HA-HA-HA!
HER LONG-AWAITED DUET
THAT'S LIKE THE SECOND ROUND AFTER YOU GO OUT FOR DRINKS.

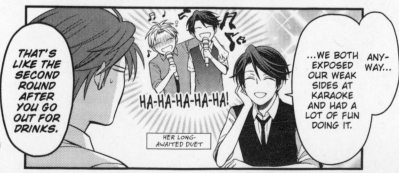

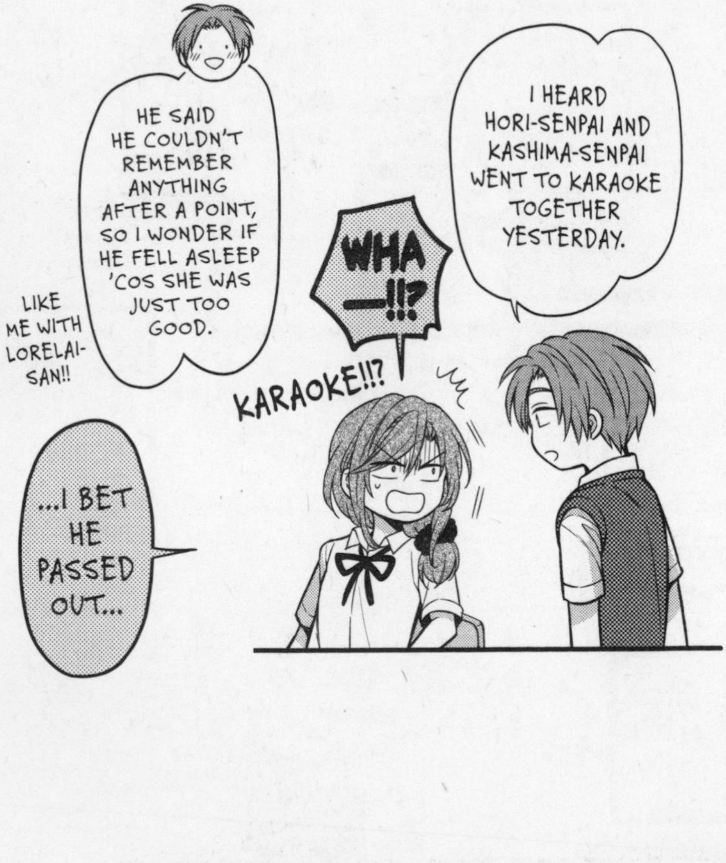
I HEARD HORI-SENPAI AND KASHIMA-SENPAI WENT TO KARAOKE TOGETHER YESTERDAY.
WHA—!!?
KARAOKE!!?
HE SAID HE COULDN'T REMEMBER ANYTHING AFTER A POINT, SO I WONDER IF HE FELL ASLEEP 'COS SHE WAS JUST TOO GOOD.
LIKE ME WITH LORELAI-SAN!!
...I BET HE PASSED OUT...

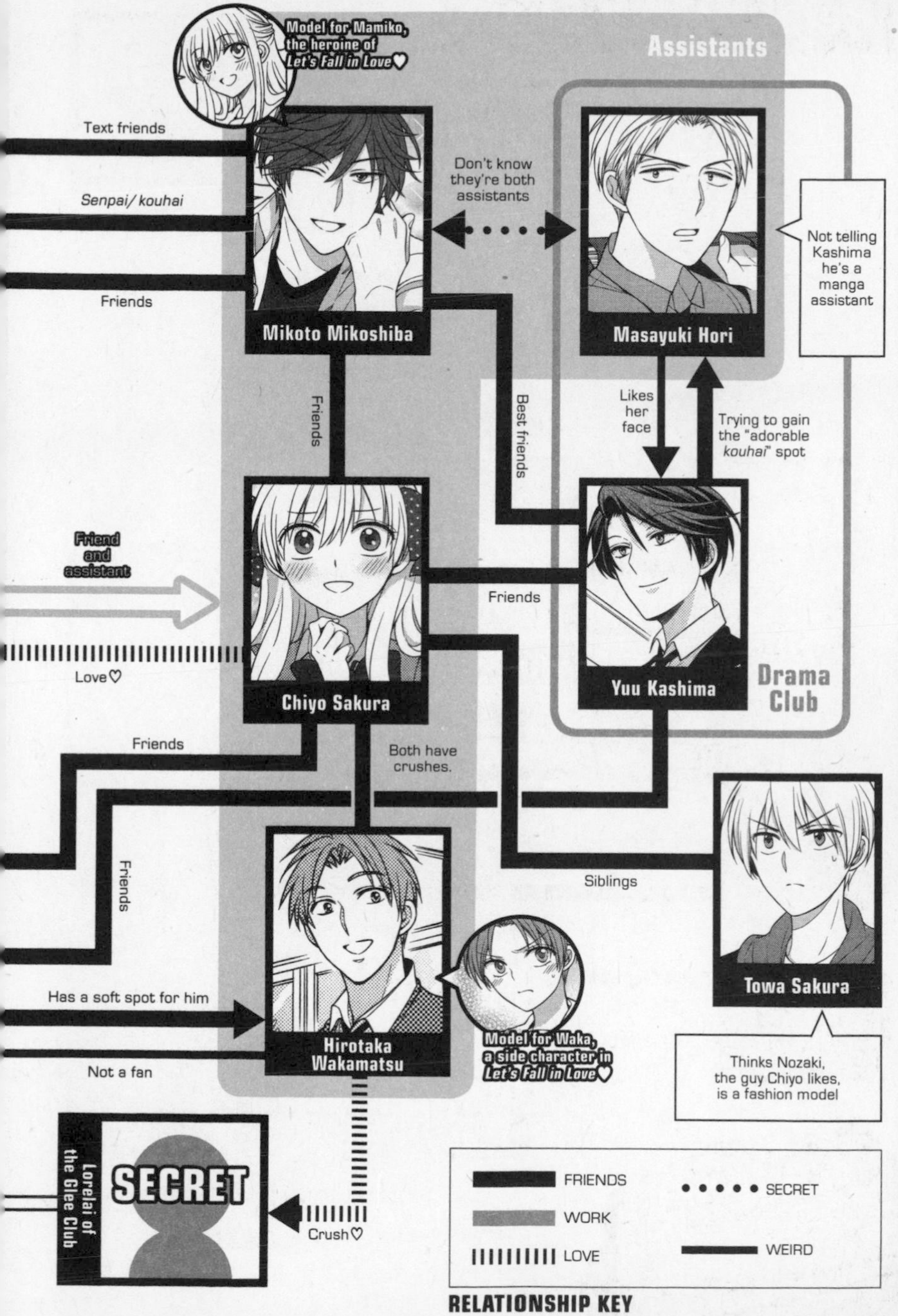

Model for Mamiko, the heroine of *Let's Fall in Love♡*
Assistants
Text friends
Senpai/ kouhai
Friends
Don't know they're both assistants
Not telling Kashima he's a manga assistant
Mikoto Mikoshiba
Masayuki Hori
Friends
Best friends
Likes her face
Trying to gain the "adorable *kouhai*" spot
Friend and assistant
Friends
Love♡
Chiyo Sakura
Yuu Kashima
Drama Club
Friends
Both have crushes.
Friends
Siblings
Has a soft spot for him
Not a fan
Hirotaka Wakamatsu
Model for Waka, a side character in *Let's Fall in Love♡*
Towa Sakura
Thinks Nozaki, the guy Chiyo likes, is a fashion model
SECRET
Lorelai of the Glee Club
Crush♡
FRIENDS
SECRET
WORK
LOVE
WEIRD
RELATIONSHIP KEY

Relationship Chart

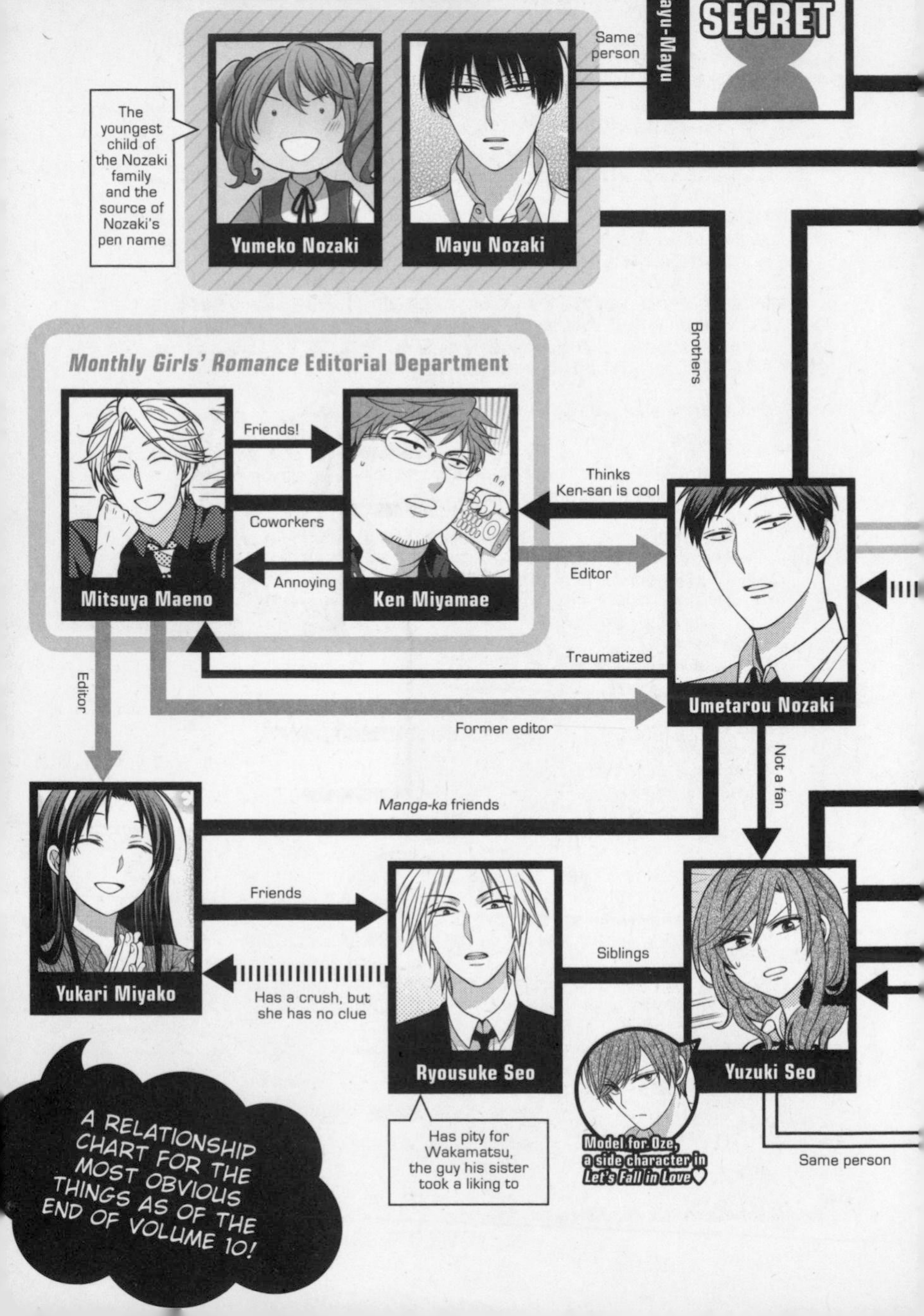

SECRET
Mayu-Mayu
Same person
The youngest child of the Nozaki family and the source of Nozaki's pen name
Yumeko Nozaki
Mayu Nozaki
Brothers
Monthly Girls' Romance Editorial Department
Friends!
Coworkers
Annoying
Mitsuya Maeno
Ken Miyamae
Thinks Ken-san is cool
Editor
Traumatized
Umetarou Nozaki
Editor
Former editor
Not a fan
Manga-ka friends
Yukari Miyako
Friends
Has a crush, but she has no clue
Siblings
Ryousuke Seo
Yuzuki Seo
Has pity for Wakamatsu, the guy his sister took a liking to
Model for Oze, a side character in Let's Fall in Love♡
Same person
A RELATIONSHIP CHART FOR THE MOST OBVIOUS THINGS AS OF THE END OF VOLUME 10!

MONTHLY GIRLS' NOZAKI-KUN 10

Izumi Tsubaki

Translation: Leighann Harvey
Lettering: Lys Blakeslee

GEKKAN SHOJO NOZAKI KUN Volume 10 © 2018 Izumi Tsubaki / SQUARE ENIX CO., LTD. First published in Japan in 2018 by SQUARE ENIX CO., LTD. English translation rights arranged with SQUARE ENIX CO., LTD. and Yen Press, LLC through Tuttle-Mori Agency, Inc.

English translation © 2019 by SQUARE ENIX CO., LTD.

Yen Press
1290 Avenue of the Americas
New York, NY 10104

Visit us!
✎ yenpress.com
✎ facebook.com/yenpress
✎ twitter.com/yenpress
✎ yenpress.tumblr.com
✎ instagram.com/yenpress

First Yen Press Print Edition: January 2019

Yen Press is an imprint of Yen Press, LLC.
The Yen Press name and logo are trademarks of Yen Press, LLC.

The publisher is not responsible for websites (or their content) that are not owned by the publisher.

Library of Congress Control Number: 2015952610

ISBN: 978-1-9753-8364-0 (paperback)

10 9 8 7 6 5 4 3 2 1

WOR

Printed in the United States of America